ROME'S WARS

ROME'S WARS
IN
PARTHIA

BLOOD IN THE SAND

ROSE MARY SHELDON

VALLENTINE MITCHELL
LONDON • PORTLAND, OR

First published in 2010 by Vallentine Mitchell

Middlesex House,	920 NE 58th Avenue, Suite 300
29/45 High Street, Edgware,	Portland, Oregon,
Middlesex HA8 7UU, UK	97213-3786, USA

www.vmbooks.com

British Library Cataloguing in Publication Data

Sheldon, Rose Mary, 1948-
  Rome's war in Parthia : blood in the sand.
  1. Rome—Foreign relations—Parthia. 2. Parthia—Foreign
  relations—Rome. 3. Rome—History, Military. 4. Parthia—
  History, Military.
  I. Title
  327.3'7035-dc22

ISBN 978 0 85303 981 5 (cloth)
ISBN 978 0 85303 931 0 (paper)

Library of Congress Cataloging in Publication Data

Printed by Good News Digital Books, Ongar, Essex

In Memoriam

MAUREEN CAVANAUGH

Ergo vivida vis animi pervicit, et extra
Processit longe flammanti moenia mundi
Atque omne immensum peragravit mente animoque

Lucretius, *De Rerum Natura* I.72

Therefore the lively power of her mind prevailed,
And forth she marched beyond the flaming walls of the heavens
And she traversed the immeasurable universe
In thought and imagination

Contents

Preface

There are many reasons why a book on Rome's wars with Parthia is timely. The most obvious reason is that no one has ever written a book solely on the military campaigns. General histories of Parthia have been written over the last century-and-a-half, starting in 1871 when George Rawlinson, Camden Professor of Ancient History at the University of Oxford, produced a now famous volume on Parthia as part of his series on oriental monarchies.[1] The need for a more updated history was recognized a half century later when in 1936 the Oriental Institute in Chicago produced George C. Cameron's *The Early History of Iran*.[2] That was supplemented in 1938 with Neilson C. Debevoise's *The Political History of Parthia*.[3] This latter book was considered a masterpiece of historical writing, and by some even superior to the later German treatments.[4]

As new evidence from archaeological, numismatic and epigraphical sources appeared, new studies benefitted from them. Later works attacked what they considered Debevoise's uncritical approach to the sources, and they tried to incorporate the new material.[5] These re-evaluations of Parthian history included W.W. Tarn's 'Parthia' in *Cambridge Ancient History*, vol. 9,[6] Michael Rostovzteff's 'Parthia: Foreign Policy' in *Cambridge Ancient History*, vol. 11,[7] and Tarn's monumental *The Greeks in Bactria and India* (1938).[8] Scholarly books and articles on Parthian history continued to appear, such as A.D.H. Bivar's 'The Political History of Iran under the Arsacids,' in *The Cambridge History of Iran*,[9] and numerous works by Jozef Wolski.[10] At the other end of the spectrum, popular works on Parthia have appeared, written for general audiences. Among them were M.A.R. College's well-illustrated *The Parthians*,[11] and Freya Stark's *Rome on the Euphrates*.[12]

Most recently, Benjamin Isaac has written a provocative book on Roman strategy in the East, in which Parthia played a small part.[13] In the absence of any major history of the Roman army in the East, David L. Kennedy edited a series of papers on different aspects of that subject as *The Roman Army in the East*.[14] And although there has been a surge of new research on the Roman East, modern political realities have limited excavation in Syria, Iraq, Iran and Turkey.[15]

The most detailed research on Rome's eastern frontier comes from those scholars involved in *limes* (frontier) studies. Their meticulous work in excavation, on occupation patterns, and their aerial photography has illuminated Rome's affect on the eastern frontier. The results have appeared in important compendia such as P. Freeman and D.L. Kennedy (eds), *The Defence of the Roman and Byzantine East*,[16] and D.L. Kennedy (ed.), *The Roman Army in the East*.[17] Large articles have appeared in *Cambridge Ancient History* or *Aufstieg und Niedergang der Römischen Welt*, discussing a specific frontier or Rome's eastern policy in general.[18] The location of the limits of the Roman frontier have been photographed and published in works very useful to those of us who do not take to the air.[19] General syntheses of Rome's frontier policies have appeared, although there is often disagreement among those who see the pattern as rational and those who see it as haphazard,[20] and no *limes* conference goes by without having at least one study on an eastern frontier.[21]

Military historians have written on Roman and Parthian tactical developments, weapons and strategy.[22] Roman diplomacy in the East has also found its devotees.[23] The subject of Rome's supposed grand strategy has produced a small literature of its own, but such works rarely go into any great detail on the wars except to explain a frontier policy, and there is disagreement among scholars as to whether such a thing as grand strategy even existed in the Roman mind.[24] Finally, many scholars have focused on the culture and social history of the region and ignored the military history entirely.[25]

One area that has been neglected is intelligence studies. Military historians rarely deal with Rome's intelligence needs on its eastern border. There have been two general studies of Roman intelligence gathering,[26] and one book about intelligence on Rome's eastern border with the Persians in late antiquity, a period outside the scope of this book.[27] The subject of Roman imperialism impinges on this discussion because opinion has been divided over whether Rome was the aggressor, or just defending itself against an aggressive Parthia. Did Rome or Parthia ever attempt to overthrow the other? Was this a bipolar world or was there a power imbalance between the two empires? Surely a detailed study of the campaigns should allow us to answer this question.

There has been no lack of books and articles on individual

Roman wars in Parthia, as one can see from the attached bibliography, but this is the first attempt to bring them together into one book.[28] This book is meant as more than just a narrative on the campaigns, however. It is an attempt to show how lack of intelligence on Parthia affected the outcome of those wars. Many books portray Rome's wars in the East as victories, but there is more to a victory than overrunning territory. I believe Roman policy was often flawed and reaped little benefit. These wars were expensive in both money and manpower for the Romans, and in the end their aggressive eastern policy only produced more wars and a much stronger and hostile enemy on their eastern frontier.

Finally, the most obvious reason why a book on Rome's wars with Parthia is timely is that America has had two of its own wars in Mesopotamia since the 1990s, and the aftermath of one of them is still in progress as this book is being written. It is tempting but dangerous to draw parallels between the ancient world and any modern situation. I have discussed each war individually and studied it in its own ancient context. I have left the drawing of any parallels to Chapter 9. I am not suggesting any greater lesson than that invading Iraq, or anywhere else, without proper intelligence is a bad idea.[29]

The most difficult part of writing this book has been, as Neilson C. Debevoise pointed out in his *Political History of Parthia*, dealing with the source material. The problem is not that it is scarce, but that it is scattered through documents, coins and inscriptions of diversified character.[30] We must always remember that we are dealing with the Parthians mostly seen through the eyes of westerners, the Greeks and Romans, who were usually waging war on them. This makes evidence from eastern sources even more important. None of the numerous histories of Parthia written in antiquity have survived, although there are cuneiform tablets that are contemporary. Documents in Pahlavi, the official languages of the Parthians, are so scarce as to be negligible.[31] Parthian coinage is extensive and well published and can at least provide us with a chronology of Parthian rulers. Authors who wrote in Armenian, Syriac and Arabic wrote much later than the Parthian period, and did not have good sources upon which to draw.

Because of this lack of written records, Parthian history must be reconstructed from elliptical sources and from Roman writings that are uniformly hostile to the Parthians. Coins are the most valuable extant Parthian documents and they may be supplemented by a few official records in Greek. Extensive passages about Parthia and

Rome can be found in Tacitus, Plutarch and Dio, supplemented by Herodian and the Augustan History. There is room, however, for speculation concerning the motivations and methods of each side in executing their foreign policies. A close examination of motives and techniques will suggest the types and relative success of intelligence gathering on both sides.

Since this book is aimed at a general audience, I have put all discussions on the reliability of the sources in the footnotes. The mere fact that a book is aimed at a general audience, however, does not mean that the author can ignore the best thinking on the subject. I have tried to present this material in a form that can be understood by intelligence laymen. In the end, I hope to show that we have come to rely upon a story told by ancient authors who are foreigners, and very often anti-Parthian and filled with value judgments about easterners. Even less excusable are modern authors who make generalizations about 'eastern character' or the 'oriental nature' in ways that can only be characterized in this post-Edward-Said world as racist and orientalist.[32] By removing such prejudices I hope this book will present a well-balanced account of the military actions between Rome and Parthia and that readers may draw some conclusions about the wisdom of following a belligerent policy in Mesopotamia without proper intelligence, both in the ancient world and the modern.

NOTES

1. G. Rawlinson, *The Seven Great Monarchies of the Ancient Eastern World: or, the history, geography, and antiquities of Chaldaea, Assyria, Babylon, Media, Persia, Parthia, and Sassanian or New Persian Empire* (New York: Publishers Plate Renting Co., 1870). This book will be cited herewith as *The Sixth Great Monarchy*. This is a standard abbreviation for it in other works. It refers to volume three of this work, Parthia being the sixth great monarchy after *Chaldaea, Assyria, Babylon, Media, and Persia*.
2. G.C. Cameron, *The History of Early Iran* (Chicago, IL: University of Chicago Press, 1936).
3. N.C. Debevoise, *The Political History of Parthia*, reprint edn (New York: Greenwood Press, 1968).
4. See the review of Debevoise, *Political*, by C. Bradford Welles of Yale University, in *CP*, 34, 4 (October 1939), pp.394–6. The German works to which he refers are Ferdinand Justi, *Geschichte des alten Persiens* (Berlin: G. Grote, 1879), pp.148–77, and A.F. von Gutschmid, *Geschichte Irans und seiner Nachbarländer von Alexander der Gross bis zum untergang der Arsaciden* (Tübingen: H. Laupp, 1888), which contributed the perspective derived from Chinese sources.
5. See, for example, J. Wolski, 'Quellen zur frühen Geschichte Parthiens', *Eos*, 38 (1937), pp.492ff.
6. W.W. Tarn, 'Parthia', in *CAH*, 9 (1963), chapter 14, pp.574–612.
7. M. Rostovtzeff, 'Parthia: Foreign Policy', in *CAH*, 11 (1936), chapter 3, pp.104–24.
8. W.W. Tarn, *The Greeks in Bactria and India* (Cambridge: Cambridge University Press, 1938).
9. A.D.H. Bivar, 'The Political History of Iran under the Arsacids', in *CHI*, vol. 3, 1: *The Seleucids, Parthian and Sasanian Period*, ed. E. Yarshater (Cambridge: Cambridge University Press, 1983), chapter 2, pp.21–99.

10. For example, J. Wolski, *L'Empire des Arsacides* (Louvain: Peeters, 1993), and J. Wolski, 'Iran und Rom: Versuch einer historischen Wertung der gegenseitigen Beziehungen', in *ANRW*, 2, 9.1, pp.195–214.

11. M.A.R. College, *The Parthians* (New York: Praeger, 1967).

12. F. Stark, *Rome on the Euphrates: The Story of the Frontier* (New York: Harcourt, Brace & World, 1967).

13. B. Isaac, *The Limits of Empire: The Roman Army in the East* (Oxford: Clarendon Press, 1992).

14. See the comments of D.L. Kennedy, 'The Roman Army in the East', in D.L. Kennedy (ed.), *The Roman Army in the East* (Ann Arbor, MI: *Journal of Roman Archaeology*, Supplementary Series, 18, 1996), p.9.

15. See the comments of Kennedy (ed.), *Roman Army in the East*, pp.12, 19. Histories of individual provinces have begun to appear. See K. Butcher, *Roman Syria and the Near East* (Los Angeles, CA: Getty Publications, 2003).

16. P. Freeman and D.L. Kennedy (eds), *The Defence of the Roman and Byzantine East: Proceedings of a Colloquium held at the University of Sheffield in April 1986*, British Institute of Archaeology at Ankara Monograph no. 8 (Oxford: British Archaeological Reports, International Series, 297, 1 & 2, 1986).

17. Kennedy (ed.), *Roman Army in the East*, pp.229–76.

18. J.G.C. Anderson, 'The Eastern Frontier under Augustus', in *CAH*, 10 (1934), pp.239–83, and 'The Eastern Frontier from Tiberius to Nero', in *CAH*, 10 (1934), pp.743–80; M.L. Chaumont, 'L'Arménie entre Rome et l'Iran I: De l'avènement d'Auguste à l'avènement de Dioclétian', in *ANRW*, II, 9.1 (1979), pp.71–194.

19. D.L. Kennedy and D. Riley, *Rome's Desert Frontier from the Air* (London: Batsford; Austin, TX: University of Texas Press, 1990).

20. J.C. Mann, 'The Frontiers of the Principate', in *ANRW*, 2, 1 (1974), pp.508–33.

21. Beginning with M. Wheeler, 'The Roman Frontier in Mesopotamia', in Eric Birley (ed.), *Congress of Roman Frontier Studies* (1949) (Durham, NC: University of North Carolina Press, 1952), p.118, to T.B. Mitford, 'The Euphrates Frontier in Cappadocia', in *SMR 2*, pp.501ff. See also E. Dabrowa, 'The Frontier in Syria in the First Century AD', in Freeman and Kennedy (eds), *Defence of the Roman and Byzantine East*, pp.93–108. Earlier surveys included D. Oates, 'The Roman Frontier in Northern Iraq', *Geographical Journal*, 122, 2 (June 1956), pp.188ff., and A. Stein, 'Surveys on the Roman Frontier in Iraq and Transjordan', *Geographical Journal*, 95, 6 (June 1940), pp.428ff.

22. J. C. Coulston, 'Roman, Parthian and Sassanid Tactical Developments', in Freeman and Kennedy (eds), *Defence of the Roman and Byzantine East*, vol. 1, pp.59–75; A.D.H. Bivar, 'A Recently Discovered Compound Bow', *Seminarium Kondrakovianum*, 9 (1937), pp.1–10; J.W. Eadie, 'The Development of Roman Mailed Cavalry', *JRS*, 57 (1967), pp.161–73.

23. B. Campbell, 'War and Diplomacy: Rome and Parthia, 31 BC – AD 235', in J. Rich and G. Shipley (eds), *War and Society in the Roman World* (New York and London: Routledge, 1993), pp.213–40; K.H. Ziegler, *Die Beziehungen zwischen Rom und dem Partherreich* (Wiesbaden: F. Steiner, 1964).

24. E. Luttwak, *The Grand Strategy of the Roman Empire* (Baltimore, MD: Johns Hopkins University Press, 1976), reviewed by J.C. Mann, 'Power, Force and the Frontiers of the Empire', *JRS*, 69 (1979), pp.175–83; Isaac, *Limits of Empire*; Butcher, *Roman Syria*, pp.405–6.

25. F. Millar, *The Roman Near East 31 BC – AD 337* (Cambridge, MA: Harvard University Press, 1993).

26. R.M. Sheldon, *Intelligence Activities in Ancient Rome: Trust in the Gods, but Verify* (London and New York: Routledge, 2005); and N.J.E. Austin and B. Rankov, *Exploratio: Military and Political Intelligence in the Roman World from the Second Punic War to the Battle of Adrianople* (London and New York: Routledge, 1995).

27. A.D. Lee, *Information and Frontiers: Roman Foreign Relations in late Antiquity* (Cambridge: Cambridge University Press, 1993). On the Persian wars in general, see M.H. Dodgeon and S.N.C. Lieu, *The Roman Eastern Frontier and the Persian Wars AD 226–363: A Documentary History* (London and New York: Routledge, 1991).

28. See especially F.A. Lepper, *Trajan's Parthian War* (London: Oxford University Press, 1948).

29. This should no longer even be a debatable point since George W. Bush, in his first exit interview on television, said about the Iraq War that the biggest regret of his presidency was the 'intelligence failure'. Intelligence professionals seem to concur; see E. Bancroft, 'The Price of Toadyism and the Madness of Groupthink', *The Intelligencer: Journal of US*

Intelligence Studies, 16, 2 (Fall 2008), p.5. See, however, in B. Grob-Fitzgibbon's review of my article in *Intelligence, Statecraft and International Power: Irish Conferences of Historians*, edited by E. O'Halpin, R. Armstrong, and J. Ohlmeyer, *JMH*, 72, 4 (October 2008), pp.1273–4; he seems to think my criticisms of this very mistake inappropriate.
30. Debevoise, *Political*, p.xxv.
31. Ibid., p.xxvi.
32. See Rawlinson's comments in *Sixth Great Monarchy*, vol. 3: passivity of the East, p.197. Luxury debilitating them, p.188; 'oriental cruelty'. Neither Romans nor Parthians having their families sullied by 'blood mixture', p.202; p.203 about 'Orientals being wont to regard any infringement of the sanctity of the grave' as serious (as if other people enjoyed it). On page 85 the Parthians are accused of acting 'with the fickleness common among Orientals'.

Acknowledgements

A project of this size could not have been completed without the help of many other people. First and foremost because I started the project with one set of knees and ended it with another. So I thank the staff at Augusta Medical Center for pulling me through that process. Next come the librarians who got the materials on which this book is based. I believe I've kept several of them busy full time. Megan Newman, our inter-library loan officer, never ceases to amaze me with her ability to track down obscure nineteenth-century periodicals and, indeed, anything else I need. No book or article can stay out of her grasp for long. Janet Holly, our research librarian, was equally helpful, as was Nilya Carrato who has the rare skill of finding what I need to see even before I know I need it. Our IT office took care of the hardware which inevitably broke down in the middle of the manuscript process. And a thank you goes to the staffs of the libraries at Washington & Lee University, the University of Virginia and the Library of Congress for being efficient and courteous to a scholar who greatly enjoys working at their facilities. The great tragedy of this year was the loss of Major David Hess of our Media Center who was always generous with his time when I needed maps drawn or found myself in a software snafu. This is the last project we will have done together and he will be greatly missed.

No matter how many languages one knows, it is always good to have a second pair of eyes to go over translations. I thank Kathleen Bulger-Barnett with helping to translate the Spanish articles on Trajan's campaigns, Patricia Hardin with her help on the Italian, and Liane Houghtalin for a reference to the *Fasti Ostienses*.

At VMI I thank the Dean's Office for supplying the travel funds and BG Charles F. Brower IV for his support generally throughout the project. I thank Deneise Shafer for keeping the office running while I was having the usual nervous breakdown towards the end of the writing process. She also proof-read parts of the manuscript.

On the subject of proof-reading, a great deal of gratitude goes to Barbara Grancell-Frank who took me to task on spelling, grammar and syntax and made this book eminently more readable. Birgitta Hoffman provided critical comments – as only she can – and saved me from many a false generalization. John MacIsaac also generously donated a great deal of his time to pointing out other interpretations. While our world views may be different, there is no room for shoddy scholarship. Any faults or errors that remain are entirely mine.

There were many organizations before which I presented parts of this book as lectures. The Classical Association of Virginia helped in the discussion of the Trajan chapter, as did the Hadrianic Society at their Roman Army School, Carlos III University, Leganes, Madrid. I thank the College of New Jersey for their invitation to lecture at the conference honouring John P. Karras, as well as the twenty-seventh Irish Conference of Historians in Dublin, the International Spy Museum, and the Virginia Governor's Latin Academy.

I thank my editor, Heather Marchant at Vallentine Mitchell. It has been a pleasure working with her again. And I thank the copy-editor whose eye for consistency always makes the final copy a pleasure to read. I thank Christopher Plum who donated Furneaux's Commentary on Tacitus to me from his late wife's collection. It is to her memory that I dedicate this book. And grateful thanks go to my husband Jeffrey for keeping the most important place in the world always open to me – the space next to him.

Maps

Abbreviations

AAASH	*Acta Antiqua Academiae Scientiarum Hungaricae*
AE	*L'Année épigraphique* ... (see Bibliography for full reference).
Aelius Aristides, *Or. Sac.*	*Sacred Discourses* in Aelius Aristides, *The Complete Works*, trans. Charles Behr
AJA	*American Journal of Archaeology*
AJAH	*American Journal of Ancient History*
AJPh	*American Journal of Philology*
AMI	*Archäologische Mitteilungen aus Iran*
Ampelius, *Lib. Mem.*	Lucius Ampelius, *Liber Memorialis*, ed. Edwin Assmann
ANRW	*Aufstieg und Niedergang der römischen Welt: Geschichte und Kultur Roms im Spiegel der neueren Forschung*, ed. Hildegard Temporini
Appian, *BC*	Appianus, *Bella Civilia*
Appian, *Mith.*	Appianus, *Mithridatica*
Appian, *Praef.*	Appian, Preface (to his Histories)
Appian, *Syr.*	Appianus, *Syriaca*
Aurelius Victor, *de vir. ill.*	Sextus Aurelius Victor, *Liber de viris illustribus urbis Romae*
BASOR	*Bulletin of the American Schools of Oriental Research*
BMC	H. Mattingly *et al.*, *Coins of the Roman Empire in the British Museum*
Byz. Zeit.	*Byzantinische Zeitschrift*
CAH	*Cambridge Ancient History*
CHI	*Cambridge History of Iran*
CHJ	*Cambridge History of Judaism*
Cicero, *Ad Att.*	Cicero, *Marcus Tullius: Letters to Atticus*, trans. E.O. Windstedt
Cicero, *Ad Fam.*	Cicero, *Marcus Tullius: Letters to His Friends*, trans. W. Glynn Williams

Cicero, *de Div*	Cicero, *de Divinatione* (Concerning Divination)
Cicero, *Pis.*	Cicero, *In Pisonem*
Cicero, *Planc.*	Cicero, *Pro Plancio*
Cicero, *Rab. Post.*	Cicero, *Pro Rabirio Postumo*
CIG	*Corpus Inscriptionum Graecarum*
CIL	*Corpus Inscriptionum Latinarum*
CJ	*Classical Journal*
CP	*Classical Philology*
CR	*Classical Review*
CRAI	*Comptes rendus de l'Academie des Inscriptions et Belle-Lettres*
Dio	Cassius Dio Cocceianus
DOP	*Dumbarton Oaks Papers*
Eusebius, *HE*	Eusebius, *Historia Ecclesiastica* (History of the Church)
Eutropius, *Brev.*	Eutropius, *Breviarum historiae Romanae*
Frontinus, *Strat.*	Sextus Julius Frontinus, *Stratagematicon*
Fronto, *De. bell.*	M. Cornelius Fronto, *De bello Parthico*
Fronto, *Epist. ad Verum*	M. Cornelius Fronto, *Letters to the Emperor Lucius Verus*
Fronto, *Princ. Hist.*	M. Cornelius Fronto, *Principia Historiae*
G&R	*Greece and Rome*
GRBS	*Greek, Roman and Byzantine Studies*
HM	L. Dillemann, *Haute Mésopatamie orientale* ... (see Bibliography for full reference)
HSCP	*Harvard Studies in Classical Philology*
IGRR	*Inscriptiones graecae ad res Romanas pertinentes avctoritate et impensis*, Academiae inscriptionum et litterarum humaniorum collectae et editae, Académie des Inscriptions et Belles-lettres
IHR	*International History Review*
ILS	*Inscriptiones Latinae Selectae*, ed. H. Dessau (see Bibliography for full reference)
JAOS	*Journal of the American Oriental Society*
JJS	*Journal of Jewish Studies*
JMH	*Journal of Military History*

JNES	*Journal of Near Eastern Studies*
Josephus, *AJ*	Josephus, *Antiquitates Judaicae* (Jewish Antiquities)
Josephus, *BJ*	Josephus, *Bellum Judaicum* (The Jewish War)
JPOS	*Journal of the Palestine Oriental Society*
JQR	*Jewish Quarterly Review*
JRA	*Journal of Roman Archaeology*
JRS	*Journal of Roman Studies*
JSJ	*Journal for the Study of Judaism*
JSS	*Journal of Semitic Studies*
Justin	Marcus Junianus Justinus, *Epitome historiarum Philicarum Pompei Trogi* (see Bibliography for full reference).
Juvenal, *Sat.*	Juvenal, *Satires*
Livy, *Epit.*	Livy, *Epitomes = Periochae* (fourth century summaries).
Lucan, *de Bell. Civ.*	Lucan, *de Bello Civili*
Lucian, *Hist. conscr.*	Lucian of Samosata, *Quomodo Historia conscribenda sit*
Lucian, *Quomodo hist.*	Lucian of Samosata, *Quomodo historia* (How history is written)
MAAR	*Memoirs of the American Academy in Rome*
NEA	*Near Eastern Archaeology*
OCD	*Oxford Classical Dictionary*, ed. S. Hornblower and A. Spawforth
Ovid, *Ars Ama.*	Ovid, *Ars Amatoria* (The Art of Love)
PBSR	*Papers of the British School at Rome*
PCPhS	*Proceedings of the Cambridge Philological Society*
Philostratus, *Vita Apoll.*	Philostratus, *Vita Apollonii* (Life of Apollonius of Tyana)
Pliny, *Ep.*	*Epistles*: Pliny the Younger, *Letters and Panygyricus*, trans. Betty Radice
Pliny, *HN*	Pliny the Elder, *Historia Naturalis* (Natural History)
Pliny, *Pan.*	Pliny the Younger, *Panegyricus*
Polyaenus, *Strat.*	Polyaenus, *Stratagemata* (Stratagems of War)
PP	*Past and Present*
RAS	*Revue Archéologique Syrienne*

RE	August Pauly and Georg Wissowa *et al.* (eds), *Pauly's Real-Encyclopädie der classischen Altertumswissenschaft*
RFPE	*Roman Foreign Policy in the East*, A.N. Sherwin-White (see Bibliography for full reference)
RGDA	*Res Gestae Divi Augusti*
RIC	*Roman Imperial Coinage*, H. Mattingly and E.A. Sydenham (see Bibliography for full reference)
RIN	*Rivista Italiana di Numismatica e Scienze Affini* (Societa Numismatica Italiana in Milano)
Sallust, *Hist. Rom.*	Sallust, *Historiae Romanae* (Roman Histories)
Schol. Bob.	*Scholia Bobiensia* in Thomas Stangl, *Ciceronis Orationem Scholiastae*
SEG	*Supplementum Epigraphicum Graecum*
Seneca, *Quaes. Nat.*	Seneca, *Quaestiones Naturales*
SHA	*Scriptores Historiae Augustae* (The Augustan History)
SHA, Alex	*Scriptores Historiae Augustae*, Life of Severus Alexander
SHANE	*Studies in the History of the Ancient Near East*
SMR 2	*Studien zu den Militargrenzen Roms 2: Vorträge des 10 International Limes Kongresses in der Germania Inferior*
SMR 3	*Studien zu den Militargrenzen Roms* (Köln, Graz: Böhlau Verlag, 1967–86)
Suetonius, *Div. Jul.*	Suetonius, *Divus Julius* (Life of the Divine Julius)
TAPA	*Transactions and Proceedings of the American Philological Association*
YCS	*Yale Classical Studies*
ZPE	*Zeitschrift für Papyrologie und Epigraphik*

Parthian Rulers

Arsaces I c. 247–211 BCE
Phraates III c. 70–57 BCE
Mithridates III c. 57–54 BCE
Orodes II c. 57–38 BCE
Pacorus I c. 39–38 BCE (*co-ruler with his father Orodes II*)
Phraates IV c. 38–2 BCE
Tiridates II c. 30–26 BCE
Phraates V (Phraataces) c. 2 BCE–4 CE
Musa c. 2 BC–4 CE (*co-ruler with her son Phraates V*)
Orodes III c. 6 CE
Vonones I c. 8–12 CE
Artabanus II c. 10–38 CE
Tiridates III c. 35–36 CE
Vardanes I c. 40–47 CE
Gotarzes II c. 40–51 CE
Sanabares c. 50–65 CE
Vonones II 51 CE
Vologases I c. 51–78 CE
Vardanes II c. 55–58 CE
Vologases II c. 77–80 CE
Pacorus II c. 78–105 CE
Artabanus III c. 80–90 CE
Vologases III c. 105–147 CE
Osroes I c. 109–129 CE
Parthamaspates c. 116 CE
Mithridates IV c. 129–140 CE
Unknown king c. 140 CE
Vologases IV c. 148–191 CE
Osroes II c. 190 CE (*rival claimant*)
Vologases V c. 191–208 CE
Vologases VI c. 208–228 CE
Artabanus IV c. 216–224 CE

Chronological Table

as King of Parthia in exchange for his son as a hostage.
41–54   **Claudius**
Claudius supports a pretender, Meherdates, in an unsuccessful bid for the Parthian throne.
54–68   **Nero**
54   The new Parthian king Vologases I invades Armenia and installs his brother Tiridates on the Armenian throne.
58–63   Parthian War.
58   Corbulo invades Armenia and drives out Tiridates.
64/65   Kingdom of Pontus in northern Asia Minor annexed by Rome.
68–69   **Galba, Otho, Vitellius, Vespasian**
72   The province of Commagene was permanently added to the province of Syria.
81–96   **Domitian**
96–98   **Nerva**
98–117 **Trajan**
106   Nabataean Kingdom annexed by Rome.
114–117 Parthian War.
114   Occupation of Armenia and Upper Mesopotamia.
115/116 Earthquake strikes Antioch.
116   Parthian usurper Osroes driven from his capital at Ctesiphon.
116   Trajan reaches the Persian Gulf.
116   Annexation of Assyria and Lower Mesopotamia. Revolt in Mesopotamia.
116   Roman armies burn Seleucia on the Tigris, Sack Edessa and besiege Edessa.
117   Trajan besieges Hatra.
117   Trajan dies in Cilicia.
117–138 **Hadrian**
117   Abandonment of Assyria and Mesopotamia. Armenia a client kingdom.
132–135 Bar Kokhba War.
138–161 **Antoninus Pius**
148   Parthian King Vologases IV succeeds to the throne.
150/151 Characene, the former Parthian vassal state that had supported Rome, reconquered by Vologases IV.
155   Vologases IV invades Armenia but is convinced to withdraw by Roman diplomacy.
161–180 **Marcus Aurelius**

161–169 **Lucius Verus**
162   Vologases IV returns to Armenia, defeats a Roman army and installs his own nominee as king.

Vologases IV moves on northern Mesopotamia where he overthrows pro-Roman ruler of Edessa and installs Parthian nominee. Vologases invades the Roman province of Syria.

163   M. Sediatius Severianus, legate of Cappadocia takes the field against Vologases III. He is defeated and commits suicide.

165   Avidius Cassius leads a three-pronged attack into Mesopotamia.

164–66 Parthians are defeated on the Euphrates at Sura.

165   Romans march down the Euphrates, reach Seleucia on the Tigris and Ctesiphon and burn them. A new frontier is established on the Khabur River. Roman control now extends down the Euphrates as far as Dura Europus.

166   Avidius Cassius is governor of Syria.

175   False reports of the emperor's death circulate. Avidius Cassius is proclaimed emperor by the armies. Avidius Cassius is murdered by his own officers.

177–192 **Commodus**
193   **Pertinax**
193   **Didius Julianus**

During the civil war, Osrhoene and Adiabene revolt and lay siege to the Roman stronghold of Nisibis.

193–211 **Septimius Severus**
195–196 Invasion of Parthia.

Severus directs his armies against Osrhoene and Adiabene. He takes the titles *Parthicus Arabicus* and *Parthicus Adiabenicus*. Osrhoene is restricted to Edessa and its territory. North-west Mesopotamia becomes a province known as Osrhoene.

197–199 Parthian War renewed. Conquest of Upper Mesopotamia.

197   Parthians retaliate by invading Mesopotamia and besieging Nisibis. Severus returns to Syria with three newly raised legions the I, II and III Parthica. War follows pattern established by Trajan and Lucius Verus. Severus marches his armies down the Euphrates and sacks Ctesiphon.

197/98 Severus retreats up the Tigris, with a detour to besiege (unsuccessfully) Hatra.

199   Severus launches a second attack on Hatra.
199   A province called Mesopotamia is established alongside
         of Osrhoene. Severus claims to have created a 'bulwark of
         Syria'.

211–217 Caracalla

c. 212   Civil war between two brothers, Vologases VI and Arta-
         banus IV.
214   Caracalla takes advantage of the situation by deposing the
         kings of Osrhoene and Armenia and annexes them. A
         rebellion in Armenia prevents the Romans from estab-
         lishing their authority there. Caracalla offers to marry the
         daughter of Artabanus. At an agreed meeting Caracalla
         falls upon the Parthian. Artabanus escapes.
216   Caracalla begins a campaign against the Parthians.
         He marches through Adiabene and Media and returns in
         the winter to Edessa, where he expected to conduct an at-
         tack on Ctesiphon in 217.
217   Between Edessa and Carrhae, Caracalla is assassinated.

217–218 Macrinus

         Carcalla's praetorian prefect becomes emperor. He has to
         contend with Artabanus's retaliatory invasion of
         Mesopotamia. The Romans are defeated at Nisibis and
         agree to pay an indemnity for the damage of Caracalla's
         campaign. This is the last major confrontation with a
         Parthian king. Macrinus offers the Armenians reparations
         for the actions of Caracalla.

218–222 Elagabalus

222–235 Severus Alexander

224   The vassal ruler Ardashir of Fars (Persis) brough Arsacid
         supremacy to an end. Allied with other Parthian vassals
         who were dissatisfied with Artabanus IV, Ardashir over-
         throws the Parthian king.
227/228 Parthian rival Vologases VI tries to re-establish Parthian
         hegemony. Establishment of Persian Sassanid Kingdom.

230–233 War with Persia.

230   Ardashir lays siege to Nisibis.
231/32   Severus Alexander tries negotiation, but when this fails he
         launches a three-pronged attack on Sassanian Persia.
         Results are inconclusive. Rome is successful in Media but
         is defeated on the Euphrates. Hatra is brought in fuller
         alliance with Rome.

1

INTRODUCTION

A leader of an empire decides to invade Iraq. He has inadequate intelligence and underestimates the resistance of the locals, but he believes his overwhelming military might will bring him a swift victory. His mighty army overruns the area between the Tigris and the Euphrates, but no sooner does he occupy the area than a massive insurgency arises, made up of various ethnic and religious groups. What began as a simple conquest for glory and dominance now becomes bogged down in deadly fighting as the once-victorious commander-in-chief desperately searches for an exit strategy.

This scenario could just as easily be any number of Roman campaigns, not to mention America in 2003 CE. Both ancient and modern attempts to invade Iraq have been plagued with the same problems. These problems have been caused by lack of adequate intelligence gathering, both strategic and tactical, and have resulted in long-drawn-out wars that have been costly in both money and manpower. Ultimately they led to no real gain, either political or military. I suggest here that many more gains can be made by diplomacy than are ever gained by these types of pre-emptive wars.

Many have written about the motives for individual Roman campaigns against Parthia (and later Persia) but there is little agreement, especially about how big a threat the Parthians posed.[1] The modern literature is divided between those who think Parthia was the only real 'systematic threat' to Rome, and those who believe that the Parthians were not a threat at all, but were unnecessarily provoked by Roman aggression. The Romans attacked the Parthians, not in self-defence, but because they simply would not tolerate the coexistence of an equal power on their border.[2] The fact is that, except in the 150s CE, Parthia never took the initiative in attacking first. Whatever their motives, the relationship between the Romans and Parthians soon became a continuous struggle for control of the left bank of the Euphrates.[3]

I am not suggesting that the Parthians were helpless victims or sitting ducks waiting for the big, bad Roman wolf to attack. An argument can certainly be made that the Parthian Empire had both the means and the intent to be a threat to Rome. They were more than just 'the people at the edge of the sand', as Horace called them.[4] Its size alone made the Parthian Empire formidable. Parthia at one time occupied areas now in Iran, Iraq, Turkey, Armenia, Georgia, Azerbaijan, Turkmenistan, Afghanistan, Tajikistan, Pakistan, Syria, Lebanon, Jordan and Israel. The Parthians had conquered most of the Middle East and south-west Asia; they controlled the Silk Road; and they built Parthia into an eastern empire that revived the greatness of the Achaemenid Empire. This certainly counterbalanced Rome's hegemony in the West. This does not necessarily mean, however, that they were a constant threat to Rome.[5]

Were Rome and Parthia destined to come to blows? They were both aggressive empires trying to muscle each other away from the Euphrates border. This has caused many recent writers to portray the three centuries during which the two powers battled each other as a 'bipolar world', no doubt making parallels to our own Cold War.[6] I believe this is a flawed view. It is quite true that in the wake of Alexander's invasions, and the fratricidal warfare that plagued his successors, the Parthians created an empire stretching from the Mediterranean to the Indus. It is also true they were the only major power on Rome's borders. But this is not the same as saying they were a power equal to Rome, or that they immediately perceived Rome as an enemy. Quite the contrary; they tried hard to maintain good diplomatic relations with the Romans. Instead the Parthians became the target of a succession of Roman commanders and emperors seeking power, glory and loot. It was not Parthian aggression that created these wars. It was their sheer proximity to Rome that made them a problem. Rome could not tolerate an equal so close to its borders. The aggressive Romans did not wish to absorb Parthia so much as to make it subject. Roman desire for universal rule and dominion envisioned a world in which everybody was subject to the Romans.[7] This process would continue until obedience to Rome was universal.

In comparing Rome to Parthia, one of the biggest mistakes a historian can make is to define Parthia as a centrally controlled 'superpower' with a centralized government similar to Rome's. The Parthians built a feudal empire loosely ruled over by the King of

Kings. Beneath him were nobles with their private armies who controlled the land and lived in the larger cities. In the many Parthian dependencies, the form of government varied widely. In some cases governors were appointed, in others the local dynasty was retained or some other ruler acceptable to the Parthians was installed. Armenia was ruled by a member of the Arsacid family, as was Media Atropatene at times. There were vassal kings appointed in Adiabene, Characene, Elymais and Persis and in some city kingdoms such as Hatra and Osrhoene. When the Parthian feudal system was at its height, its military power was immense. But it would be wrong to assume that all these parts acted in concert with each other. Sometimes Parthia came to the defence of its client states, sometimes it did not. Sometimes Parthian allies defected and sometimes they stayed loyal. Rome often tried to drive a wedge between Parthia and its client states in order to weaken and isolate Parthia and to annex its client states.[8]

The Parthians could not even rely on the loyalty of their own nobililty. Parthian nobles became wealthy from fighting wars and acquiring more lands, but their power was often expressed *in defiance* of the king, and this brought about frequent periods of disruption. If these feudal lords no longer responded to the call to arms, or no longer paid their annual tribute, disorganization within the empire resulted. The nobles would defy the king by force of arms if he interfered with their rights, and they often engaged in plots against the king's life. The royal family, the Arsacidae, was also weakened by intrigue, murder and quarrels between members of the dynasty. Such disorganization opened the way for Roman legions to insert themselves into Mesopotamia.[9] The Romans were attracted by the wealth that could be gained by plundering the great commercial centres and looting the royal treasures. The constant succession of invasions by Rome eventually weakened Parthian rule and in the end caused a takeover by the Sassanid Persians who were a much more formidable enemy.

Militarily the two sides were probably evenly matched. Both sides could field large armies, were well equipped and tactically well matched.[10] Neither side had a secret weapon. The Parthian feudal structure, however, meant that when feudal lords revolted against the central authority of the king, he took his retainers with him, while the Romans, at least during the empire, had a standing army they could rely on.[11] The Romans could maintain long-service or professional armies on a scale and over periods of time that the Parthians could not match.[12] Even the Roman sources such as Justin and Cassius Dio believed that the Parthian reputation was greater than their achievements.[13] Were the Parthians really militarily threatening or was it just convenient for the Romans to portray them that way in order to glorify their constant victories over them? If the Parthian military was so formidable, why did the Romans keep winning the battles and the wars?[14]

The Romans may have been able to defeat Parthia in a war, but they were never able to absorb more than 20 per cent of its territory or make it a Roman dependency. The Parthian Empire was too large, and its native cultures too strong for long-term integration into the Roman cultural and political spheres. Even with the feudal structure of the Parthian government and their constant internal squabbling, they were still resilient and strong enough to prevent their successful annexation as new Roman provinces.[15] Did the Romans have enough strategic intelligence to understand this? If annexation was not the goal, then why the constant invasions and declaring 'provinces' of territories they hardly controlled? Were they just massive raids? It was not enough to overrun a capital and declare the war over. Occupation required much more than Rome could afford to invest. As one scholar remarked to me: 'The Romans helped themselves to a very rich piece of a large cake, but only one piece.'[16] For all the Roman effort, Parthia remained an independent kingdom whose rulers never became totally dependent on Rome.

Among the questions I wish to answer about Rome's relationship to Parthia are:

1. Were Rome and Parthia military equals, and was Parthia really that much of a threat?
2. What made Rome invade Parthia so many times? Could the wars between them have been prevented?
3. What were the Romans' goals, and what were their chances of achieving them?[17]
4. What did the Romans know about the Parthians and when did they know it?[18] What were the intelligence needs of each side and did lack of intelligence planning on either or both sides place them in untenable positions?

I believe I can demonstrate that Rome's wars with Parthia were often plagued by a lack of accurate intelligence. This lack of hard intelligence affected Rome's foreign policy on the strategic level and hampered Rome's military effectiveness on the tactical level. Each one of these campaigns demonstrates that point in a different way, and it does not seem to matter if the commander were a superb soldier like Trajan or an arrogant fool like Crassus; the ending was always the same.

Studying the Parthians wars individually allows us to examine not only the use of tactical intelligence but also strategic intelligence, and this impinges on one of the thorniest problems in current writing on Roman history. Scholars have debated over the last three decades whether the Romans had a unified 'Grand Strategy' for their frontiers, or whether their approach was ad hoc and consisted of a fairly simple form of strategic planning. A corollary to this debate is the question of whether Roman Grand Strategy developed into a system of defensive frontiers.[19]

Ever since the idea of a Roman Grand Strategy was put forward over thirty years ago there have been supporters[20] and detractors.[21] C.R. Whittaker went to the heart of the matter when he pointed out that the Romans were certainly capable of military planning, and of logistical supply for the Roman army, but all these examples of Roman planning do not add up to Grand Strategy in the modern sense of the word.[22] Strategy with a small 's' existed, of course. If a Roman army was attacked, generals had to decide how to retaliate. Generals and emperors in search of battle glory and booty had to make decisions about how to realize their aims. Whittaker goes on to point out that Grand Strategy is not just the art of controlling and utilizing the resources of a nation, but must also include 'the successful integration of policy and arms to achieve political ends'.[23] The political ends should not just be winning wars, but using wars to achieve a better peace. This means that a single ideological objective repeated over and over by the Roman sources – to win victory and glory[24] – was not a Grand Strategy, since it was not a balanced decision taking into account the effects of such wars. And even when the central government made plans to achieve a political objective, often priorities got reversed when generals and officers in the field made unilateral decisions that were only later turned to policy by the home government.[25]

The Romans did not have the tools or the information to formulate a geopolitical strategy in the modern sense. Frontiers were not chosen for strategic reasons but solidified as a result of failure or non-military factors.[26] The Roman view of the geopolitical world was too simplistic a framework for a complex geopolitical strategy.

Their intelligence on peoples outside the empire was also simplistic and stereotypical. They had no specific understanding of foreign social or political institutions. Rome's basic policy stayed consistent throughout the empire. They had a deeply-entrenched desire to extend Roman power to the ends of the earth. They did not recognize boundaries if they wanted to possess something on the other side of it. When Pompey declared the Euphrates 'a boundary of Roman hegemony' it was rightly recognized that he had the intention to do just the opposite.[27]

The Romans understood very well what they wanted from the Parthians – symbolic deference. This was their only policy goal. In this sense Roman strategy was more psychological, and cannot be traced on a map. Arrogance and insult on the part of the Parthians was enough of a cause for a just and necessary war, as far as the Romans were concerned. Terror and vengeance were their instruments for maintaining the empire's image. They had certain tried and true methods of controlling enemies on their frontier, but this did not amount to a Grand Strategy. Their aggressive attitude dictated different responses to specific situations which remained consistent over a long period of time. The drive to expand the empire was the impetus, and money in the form of plunder and personal glory were the result. The cause-and-effect pattern we see throughout these eastern wars is that insult brings revenge, and revolt brings retaliation. Neither the status of the Roman state nor the image of the individual emperor must be besmirched. This system may seem too simplistic for modern geopolitical thinkers, but the Romans believed in their system and as long as they had twenty-eight legions to back it up, it worked. In my book, *Intelligence Activities in Ancient Rome*, I concluded that Roman policy was aggressive, but that Rome's intelligence apparatus was too minimal for them to conceive of a Grand Strategy. I am still in agreement with those scholars who see a consistent pattern of Roman expansionism.[28] I do not believe, however, that the expansion on the Parthian border was justified by aggression from either the Parthians or later the Persians (although the latter fall outside the scope of this book).[29]

The last issue brought up by Luttwak was his assertion that the Roman Empire changed from a hegemonic power to a territorial structure. In other words, Rome stopped expanding and shifted to a defensive frontier strategy.[30] This theory has been branded unsustainable by C.R. Whittaker, who discusses the matter in great detail.[31] Since the shift would involve a discussion of the late empire, it is beyond the scope of this book. Suffice it to say, there is nothing in this discussion that would suggest that Rome was anything but expansive.[32] There will no doubt always be those who believe that the Roman frontier was a carefully planned and rationally constructed system of defence,[33] and those who believe that the frontier structures reflected local circumstances rather than a coherent empire-wide plan.[34] I am among those who do not believe there is any defensive 'frontier system' on the eastern border to be detected in the first three centuries of the Roman Empire.[35]

We know that the Romans were perfectly aware of the diplomatic advantages to be gained from their long-standing custom of employing client kings.[36] Looking over their relations with the Parthians, we may ask whether the Roman policy added up to consistent and long-term political gains. Did its wars lead to a better peace? If one argues that the Romans had a Grand Strategy, then we must ask, did the Romans make a genuine economic accounting of their resource expenditure against estimated gains? Did they indulge in a constant intelligent reassessment of their political objectives?[37] If not, then there was no Grand Strategy.

How can we know what policies were considered by Roman leaders, if all their discussions were held behind closed doors and did not appear in any written texts? We can assume that security, and how to pay for it, was high on their list. Certainly they discussed ad hoc solutions: Shall we take the offer of a truce? Shall we move troops from here to there? The same question can be asked of modern policy decisions.[38] All we can do is observe Roman behaviour and ask whether their actions against Parthia demonstrated a good use of the available intelligence, both tactical and strategic, and see whether the huge output of money and manpower brought in the estimated gains.

A brief sketch of their foreign relations will illustrate the structure of this book. Chapter 1 discusses the first contacts with Sulla, Lucullus, Pompey and Gabinius. Gabinius made preparations for an invasion in 65 BCE, but was deflected. Chapter 2 discusses the first major invasion by Crassus, that ended in disaster for the Romans. The Parthian incursions into Syria that occurred in 51 BCE are discussed in Chapter 3. They were easily repelled, and the campaign of Ventidius shows that the Parthians could be easily handled by a commander, with accurate intelligence, who was willing to use surprise attack and who gave a little thought to what weapons would be most effective against the Parthians. Caesar prepared for a grand Parthian campaign, but he died before carrying it out.[39]

During the civil war, both sides called to Parthia for aid. In 45 BCE, for example, Q. Caecilius Bassus (a Pompeian), shut up at Apamea by Caesarian forces, appealed to the Parthians for aid. Pacorus forced the abandonment of the siege.[40] In 40 BCE, Labienus persuaded the Parthian king to invade Roman territory. This resulted in the only large-scale Parthian invasion of Roman territory (41–38 BCE). This brought on Antony's unsuccessful campaign into Media Atropatene (Azerbaijan) and beyond in 36 BCE, ending in another Roman disaster which is the subject of Chapter 4. Later, in 35/4, Sextus Pompeius offered the Parthians his services.[41]

Chapter 5 discusses the Augustan solution that made many gains by means of diplomacy. The standards lost by Crassus were returned, and although a great deal of clandestine manoeuvring was going on, open warfare was avoided. Rome and Parthia remained at peace until Nero turned a diplomatic conflict over Armenia into a military one.

By 52–63 CE, Nero's general, Corbulo, had to resolve the problem caused by his emperor. Chapter 6 discusses the invasion of Armenia in 57–58 CE which turned that state into a client kingdom with a garrison of Roman troops. In 61–62 CE, Tigranes of Armenia, supported by Corbulo, invaded Adiabene. Corbulo threatened the Parthian King Vologases with an invasion of Mesopotamia and made actual preparations by throwing bridgeheads across the Euphrates.[42] When Caesennius Paetus invaded Armenia, he made a mess of things and had to surrender there. The end result was the withdrawal of Roman troops to Syria and Cappadocia and an agreement on Armenia. This did not bring Rome's activist policy to an end. Chapter 7 discusses Trajan's invasion of Mespotamia and his annexation of Armenia in 112–114 CE. By a campaign in 115–116 CE, he captured Seleucia and Ctesiphon and new provinces were organized. Yet this too ended in failure and withdrawal.

In 112–114 CE the Parthians invaded Armenia but subsequently withdrew. Chapter 8 discusses how in the reign of Marcus Aurelius and Lucius Verus in 161, the Parthians invaded Armenia a second time and an Arsacid was placed on the Armenian throne. Having defeated the Cappadocian and Syrian troops, they then razed Syrian cities. Avidius Cassius led a Parthian campaign deep into Mesopotamia. Seleucia and Ctesiphon were plundered again.[43] This resulted in the plague being carried back by the army when it withdrew. Roman garrisons may have been left in northern Mesopotamia, and Dura Europos was permanently occupied by Roman troops. Chapter 8 also includes the two campaigns in 194–198 CE led by Septimius Severus, in which Seleucia and Ctesiphon were once more captured and plundered. Northern Mesopotamia was annexed as a province.[44] In 215–217 CE, Caracalla marched against Adiabene. According to Dio and Herodian, the pretext for the campaign had been that Artabanus had refused Caracalla the hand of his daughter in marriage. More than likely, he simply wanted to invade and occupy Parthia.[45] Caracalla died at Carrhae, Macrinus met with a reverse near Nisibis and a negotiated peace followed. Chapter 9 summarizes the intelligence assets Rome had at its disposal, and Chapter 10 weighs the costs of all the Parthian campaigns to the Roman economy and society.

While many of the ancient sources describe the campaigns, they do not explicitly discuss the reasons for all these wars between Rome and Parthia. I believe the known facts show a consistent pattern of Roman expansionism in Mesopotamia. The defence of Syria does not work as an explanation for Roman policy.[46] The Roman invasions invariably led to the annexation of Parthian territory when they were successful, but there is no evidence that the Parthians seriously ever tried to occupy Roman territory, although they occasionally raided Syria. This behaviour can be explained easily by the fact that whenever the Roman army operated in Armenia, a successful Parthian raid into Syria was the most effective move to bring Roman troops back to Syria. No part of Syria or Cappadocia was ever occupied by the Parthians for any length of time.[47] When the Parthians attacked, it was to prevent a Roman takeover of Armenia or Roman expansion east of the Euphrates. Some scholars have argued that the Persian policy in the fourth century was no different; others disagree.[48]

In sum, a survey of the contacts between Rome and Parthia shows that Rome was usually the attacker, and the distributions of troops, especially after the Flavian period, was set up for large-scale warfare and advance, not defence.[49] Because of this, major campaigns took place roughly every fifty years. Scholars have come to recognize that there is surprisingly little evidence for believing that Parthia ever sought open conflict with Rome.[50] On the contrary, the Parthian kings were most often distracted by their own dynastic struggles, and appear to have preferred peaceful coexistence with Rome. More often than not, they initiated the various treaties

between the two empires, in the knowledge that the Parthian people lacked both the cohesion and determination for expansion beyond the territories already ruled. Instead, it was the megalomania
of successive Roman military leaders prompting expeditions across
the Euphrates, abrogating existing agreements in the process,
which usually brought about confrontation between Parthia and
her imperious neighbour.

NOTES

1. B. Isaac, *The Limits of Empire: The Roman Army in the East* (Oxford: Clarendon Press, 1992),
    p.19; J. Mann, 'The Frontiers of the Principate', in *ANRW*, 2, 1 (1974), pp.508–33, esp.
    509ff; D.L. Kennedy and D. Riley, *Rome's Desert Frontier from the Air* (London: Batsford;
    Austin, TX: University of Texas Press, 1990), p.29: 'the most potent threat to Rome on
    her eastern frontier'. C. Lerouge, *L'image des Parthes dans le monde gréco-romain* (Stuttgart:
    Franz Steiner Verlag, 2007), pp.75–81 on Rome's ignorance of Parthia.
2. Theodor Mommsen early on detected that the Romans begrudged the weaker Parthian
    state its position and power, because the only thing they could tolerate on their borders
    was sea or undefended land. T. Mommsen, *The Provinces of the Roman Empire: From Cae-
    sar to Diocletian* (New York: Barnes & Noble, 1996), pp.20–1.
3. Isaac, *Limits of Empire*, pp.27–8.
4. Horace, *Epistles* 1.11.6: *'populam extrema totiens exoret harena'*.
5. On Parthian political ideology and foreign policy, see J. Neusner, 'Parthian Political Ide-
    ology', *Iranica Antiqua*, 3, 1 (1963), pp.40–59.
6. V.L. Bullough, 'The Roman Empire vs Persia, 363–502: A Study of Successful Deterrence',
    Journal of Conflict Resolution, 7, 1 (March 1963), pp.55–68. On the perceptions of Parthian
    equality, see Lerouge, *L'image des Parthes*, pp.317–21.
7. Polybius 3.3.9. See P.S. Derow, 'Polybius, Rome and the East', *JRS*, 69 (1979), pp.1–15.
8. On the alleged Parthian instability, see Lerouge, *L'image des Parthes*, pp.267–70.
9. D.L. Kennedy, 'Parthia and Rome', in D.L. Kennedy (ed.), *The Roman Army in the East*
    (Ann Arbor, MI: *Journal of Roman Archaeology*, Supplementary Series, 18, 1996), p.88.
10. On the Parthian army, see M. Mielczarek, *Cataphracts and Clibanarii: Studies in the Heavy
    Armoured Cavalry on the Ancient World* (Lodz: Oficyna Naukowa MS, 1993).
11. On the Parthian military, see A.D.H. Bivar, 'Cavalry Equipment and Tactics on the Eu-
    phrates Frontier', *DOP*, 26 (1972), pp.271–91; J.C. Coulston, 'Roman, Parthian and Sas-
    sanid Tactical Developments', in P. Freeman and D.L. Kennedy (eds), *The Defence of the
    Roman and Byzantine East: Proceedings of A Colloquium held at the University of Sheffield in
    April 1986*, British Institute of Archaeology at Ankara Monograph no. 8 (Oxford: British
    Archaeological Reports, International Series, 297, 1986), part 2, pp.59–75; M. Mielczarek,
    Cataphracti and Clibanarii: Studies in the Heavy Armoured Cavalry in the Ancient World (Lodz:
    Oficyna Naukowa MS, 1993); E. Gabba, 'Sulle influenze reciproche degli ordinamenti
    militari dei Parti e dei Romani', in *La Persia e il mondo greco-romano (Per la storia dell'escercito
    Romana in età imperiale* (Bologna: Patron, 1974); on the administration of Parthia, see F.
    Cumont, 'The Frontier Provinces of the East', *CAH*, 11 (1963), pp.606–13. On perceived
    Parthian weaknesses, see Lerouge, *L'image des Parthes*, pp.308–13.
12. A.N. Sherwin-White, *Roman Foreign Policy in the East, 168 BC to AD1* (Norman, OK: Uni-
    versity of Oklahoma Press, 1984), p.331.
13. Dio 40.14.3; Justin 41.17; Dio 40.15.6. Lucan, *The Civil War (Pharsalia)*, with an English
    translation by J.D. Duff (Cambridge, MA: Harvard University Press, 1928), 8.368–90;
    Justin Trogus 41.2; Tacitus, *Annals* 11.10. Julius Africanus, *Kestoi* 1.1.6–9, on the other
    hand, believed the Romans never conquered the Parthians completely because of infe-
    rior Roman equipment. See E.L. Wheeler, 'Why the Romans Can't Defeat the Parthians:
    Julius Africanus and the Strategy of Magic', in W. Groenman-van Waateringe, B.L. van
    Beek, W.J.H. Willems, and S.L. Wynia (eds), *Roman Frontier Studies, 1995* (Oxford: Oxbow
    Monograph 91, 1997), p.576.

14. K. Butcher, *Roman Syria and the Near East* (Los Angeles, CA: Getty Publications, 2003), p.407, points out that we do not know if Parthian attacks on Rome have been left unrecorded because of poor historical records in the first and second centuries.
15. See the remarks of B. Campbell, 'War and Diplomacy: Rome and Parthia, 31 BC – AD 235', in J. Rich and G. Shipley (eds), *War and Society in the Roman World* (New York and London: Routledge, 1993), p.213.
16. Dr. Birgitta Hoffman, private communication, 6 October 2008.
17. On Rome's perceptions of Parthia as a threat, see Isaac, *Limits of Empire*, pp.22–3.
18. See Lerouge, *L'image des Parthes*, pp.76–81, who rightfully points out that the Greco-Roman sources of the Parthians do not pre-date the Augustan period, so it is difficult to evaluate what Republican Romans knew of the Parthians.
19. See Isaac, *Limits of Empire*; C.R. Whittaker, *Frontiers of the Roman Empire: A Social and Economic Study* (Baltimore, MD: Johns Hopkins University Press, 1994); S. Mattern, *Rome and the Enemy* (Berkeley, CA: University of California Press, 1999); C.R. Whittaker, 'Where are the Frontiers Now?' in Kennedy (ed.), *Roman Army in the East*, pp.25–41.
20. Among his supporters see E. Wheeler, 'Methodological Limits and the Mirage of Roman Strategy', *JMH*, 57 (January 1993), 2 parts, pp.7–41 and 215–40, and A. Ferrill, *Roman Imperial Grand Strategy* (Lanham, MD: University Press of America, 1991). See a critique of their work in Whittaker, 'Where are the Frontiers Now?', pp.25–41.
21. For detractors, see Whittaker, 'Where are the Frontiers Now?', pp.25–41; Isaac, *Limits of Empire*; J. Mann, 'Power, Force, and the Frontiers of the Roman Empire', *JRS*, 69 (1979), pp.175–83; F. Millar, 'Emperors, Frontiers and Roman Foreign Relations', *Britannia*, 13 (1982), pp.1–23.
22. Whittaker, 'Where are the Frontiers Now?', p.29.
23. Ibid., p.29; P. Kennedy (ed.), *Grand Strategies in War and Peace* (New Haven, CT: Yale University Press, 1991); E.M. Earle (ed.), *The Makers of Modern Strategy* (Princeton, NJ: Princeton University Press, 1943), p.viii.
24. On the theme of wars for glory, see Mattern, *Rome and the Enemy*.
25. See Mattern, *Rome and the Enemy*; A. Eckstein, *Senate and General* (Berkeley, CA: University of California Press, 1987); Whittaker, *Frontiers of the Roman Empire*, pp.8–10.
26. Mann, 'Frontiers of the Principate', pp.508–33; Mann, 'Power, Force, and the Frontiers of the Roman Empire', pp.175–83; Millar, 'Emperors, Frontiers and Roman Foreign Relations', pp.1–23; Isaac, *Limits of Empire*; Whittaker, *Frontiers of the Roman Empire*.
27. Plutarch, *Pompey* 33; Whittaker, 'Where are the Frontiers Now?' p.32; T. Mommsen, *The History of Rome*, trans. W.P. Dickson (London: Dent; New York: E.P. Dutton, 1929–31) book 5, chapter 4, p.141.
28. Isaac, *Limits of Empire*, p.31.
29. Butcher, *Roman Syria*, pp. 407–9, would seem to agree with this assessment.
30. E. Luttwak, *The Grand Strategy of the Roman Empire* (Baltimore, MD: Johns Hopkins University Press, 1976), p.30.
31. Whittaker, 'Where are the Frontiers Now?', p.37.
32. A recent study has shown that the legionary dispositions on the Euphrates are not evidence of static frontiers, nor of the political and military boundaries beyond the river. E.L. Wheeler, 'Rethinking the Upper Euphrates Frontier: Where was the Western Border of Armenia?' in V.A. Maxfield and M.J. Dobson (eds), *Roman Frontier Studies* (Exeter, England: University of Exeter Press, 1991), pp.505–11; J.G. Crow, 'A Review of the Physical Remains of the Frontiers of Cappadocia', in Freeman and Kennedy (eds), *Defence of the Roman and Byzantine East*, pp.724–9.
33. Luttwak, *Grand Strategy of the Roman Empire*; A. Ferrill, 'The Grand Strategy of the Roman Empire', in Kennedy, *Grand Strategies in War and Peace*, pp.71–85; Wheeler, 'Methodological Limits', pp.7–41; D.S. Potter, 'Emperors, their Borders and their Neighbors: The Scope of Imperial Mandata', in Kennedy (ed.), *Roman Army in the East*, pp. 49–68.
34. Isaac, *Limits of Empire*; Mattern, *Rome and the Enemy*; Mann, 'Frontiers of the Principate', pp.508–33; Millar, 'Emperors, Frontiers and Roman Foreign Relations', pp.1–23; Whittaker, *Frontiers of the Roman Empire*; Butcher, *Roman Syria*, p 407.
35. Whittaker, 'Where are the Frontiers Now?', p.26.
36. Ibid., p.30; D. Braund, *Rome and the Friendly King* (London: Croom Helm, 1984); Butcher, *Roman Syria*, p.407; Tacitus, *Agricola* 14.
37. Whittaker, 'Where are the Frontiers Now?', p.30.

38. Ibid., p.30; J.B. Hattendorf, 'Alliance, Encirclement and Attrition: British Grand Strategy in the Wars of the Spanish Succession', in Kennedy (ed.), *Grand Strategies in War and Peace*, pp.11–13. What we know about imperial councils suggests that the strategy they discussed was simple and dealt with crisis management. See Whittaker, 'Where are the Frontiers Now?', p.31, and J.A. Crook, *Consilium Principis* (Cambridge: Cambridge University Press, 1955), p.116, who conveys the impression that the emperor's *consilium* was more concerned with regulating internal administrative and organizational matters.

39. Appian, *BC* 2.110. It was scheduled to last three years and was no small undertaking. Caesar planned to take sixteen legions: 90,000 infantry and 10,000 cavalry.

40. Cicero, *Ad Att.* 14.9; Dio 47.27; Appian *BC*, 4.59.

41. Appian, *BC* 5.133; Dio 49.18; Livy, *Epit.* 131.

42. Tacitus, *Annals*, 15.3.5.

43. Dio 61.2; Ammianus Marcellinus 23.6, 23–4; SHA, *Verus* 8.3–4; Orosius 7.15.2; Fronto, *Princ. Hist.* 2.209; M.G. Angeli-Bertinelli, 'I Romani oltre l'Euphrate nell II secolo dC', in *ANRW*, 2, 9.1 (1976), pp.23–31; N.C. Debevoise, *The Political History of Parthia*, reprint edn (New York: Greenwood Press, 1968), pp.246–53; A. Birley, *Marcus Aurelius: A Biography*, revised edn (New Haven, CT: Yale University Press, 1966), p.161.

44. Dio 76.9.3–4; SHA, *Severus* 16.1; Herodian 3.9.9–12. For the expedition, see Angeli-Bertinelli, 'I Romani oltre l'Euphrate', pp.32–45; Debevoise, *Political*, pp. 259–62. For the chronology of the campaign see F. Millar, *The Roman Near East 31 BC – AD 337* (Cambridge, MA: Harvard University Press, 1993), p.143; J. Hasebroek, *Untersuchungen zur Geschichte des Kaisers Septimius Severus* (Heidelberg: C. Winter, 1921), pp.119ff; Isaacs, *Limits of Empire*, p.30. Whether the province was formed in 195 or 198 is unclear. The first prefect of the province is now known from an inscription discussed by D.L. Kennedy, 'Ti. Claudius Subatianus Aquila, "First Prefect of Mesopotamia" ', *ZPE*, 36 (1979), pp.255–62.

45. Dio 79.1; Herodian 4.10.1.

46. As argued by Butcher, *Roman Syria*, pp.406–7.

47. Isaac, *Limits of Empire*, p.32.

48. Ibid., p.32. This is in opposition to Luttwak, *Grand Strategy of the Roman Empire*, pp.150–2.

49. Isaac, *Limits of Empire*, p.53.

50. See especially ibid., pp.22–3.

2

FIRST CONTACT

Parthia and Rome first came into contact with one another as each laid claim to parts of the crumbling Seleucid Empire.[1] The Romans perceived themselves as the legitimate successors of the Seleucids, and began to play a more aggressive role in the affairs of the Hellenistic world of Asia Minor. Unfortunately, so did the Parthians, and the Roman move East impinged on the Parthian sphere of influence. The regions of dispute between the two powers were Armenia and the headwaters of the Tigris and Euphrates rivers, rich areas crossed by east–west trade routes and lacking natural barriers to invasions.[2] The Parthians had a deep distrust of the Romans, a people who were pushing their power east – a power that might turn out to be more permanently formidable than the Macedonians.[3] The Romans had been acquiring the kingdoms of Asia Minor, and setting up puppet kings on their borders to do their bidding.[4] Now they were heading for the Euphrates (see Map 1).

Before Rome and Parthia went to war, there were three agreements concluded between the empires, one each by Sulla, Lucullus and Pompey (in 66 BCE).[5] Each time the initiative came from the Parthians, who obviously wanted to keep their belligerent neighbours at a distance. Rome responded to these peace-feelers by bullying and insulting Parthia without actually attacking it.[6] No sooner were Syria and Pontus made part of the Roman Empire than Rome stopped recognizing the Euphrates as the boundary delimiting the influence of the two states.[7] If we look at the thirty years between c. 95 and 64 BCE, we see that the attitudes and policies of Rome and Parthia toward one another changed but little.[8]

SULLA'S RELATIONS WITH THE PARTHIANS

In 96 BCE during his propraetorship, Sulla was engaged in restoring Ariobarzanes to the throne of Cappadocia.[9] Sulla's operations

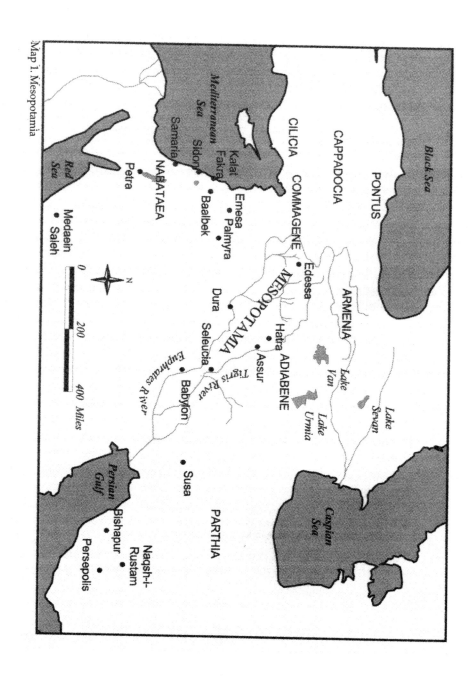

Map 1. Mesopotamia

brought him to the banks of the Euphrates, where he became the first Roman to meet a Parthian embassy. The reason for the Parthian mission is clear from its content. Sulla was involved in conflict with Armenian forces supporting the rival of Ariobarzanes in the name of Tigranes, at this time a vassal of Mithridates the Great who had recently installed him as king of Armenia. To this he rapidly annexed the principality of Sophene, adjacent to Cappadocia. The Parthian envoy came to investigate the situation, and discovered that a new power had appeared on the borders of the Parthian Empire. We are told it came '*ut amicitiam populi Romani peterent* – so that they would seek the friendship of the Roman people.'[10] There may have been talk of friendly relations, but nothing was referred to Rome.

In the description of their first meeting Sulla arranged three chairs, with ambassador Orobazus on one side and Ariobarzanes on the other side of him. By this action Sulla made it clear that Rome was to be the dominant party at the talks.[11] At the time some people commended Sulla for the airs which he assumed with the 'barbarians', while others accused him of vulgarity and ill-timed arrogance.[12] He was even prosecuted for collecting large sums of money from a friendly and allied kingdom.[13] As one scholar has pointed out the Parthians probably did not gauge Rome or its intentions correctly, but the converse is equally true. They would certainly have been offended by Rome's world view which placed even the most powerful neighbours on an inferior level.[14] There seems to be no doubt in the Parthian king's mind about what happened. The king put his ambassador to death for suffering Sulla to take the seat of honour between himself and Ariobarzanes.[15]

The view at the time was that Sulla gratuitously insulted the representative of a great power unnecessarily.[16] Some have argued that Sulla did not even know to whom he was talking and mistook the Parthian ambassador as the representative of 'some tin-pot principality' whose offer of friendship was to be interpreted as what was fast becoming the 'normal approach': a wish to become a Roman client.[17] This seems highly unlikely since all the kings Sulla dealt with in the East knew who the Parthians were. Others have suggested that Sulla did not understand the Hellenistic mode of diplomacy in which Orobazus worked, but again this seems unlikely, considering Sulla was an accomplished Hellenist.[18] His behaviour seems to be normal for Roman generals in the East driving hard bargains from a position of power. Sulla knew perfectly well what he was doing. He was trying to gain an initial advantage in negotiations with the ambassador of a great kingdom. He was trying to bully the Parthians in order to extract concessions from them.[19]

It is still not clear what the outcome of this meeting was. Our sources use terms such as the Greek *symmachia* or the Latin *amicitia*. This latter term is particularly ambiguous since it could refer to either a treaty or simply to a state of friendship between Rome and another nation without a formal agreement.[20] It suggests an envoy was sent to make contact, but instead committed Parthia to terms he was not empowered to discuss. All Sulla could do on his part was communicate the terms back to Rome. The correct diplomatic move, after contact was established, would surely have been for Orobazus to have been escorted to Rome or, if he were authorized to negotiate terms, to have returned to his king and for a suitably-empowered embassy to have been sent to Rome. Orobasus may have been executed, not because he allowed himself to be insulted by the Romans, or for being outmanoeuvred in the discussion, but for engaging in discussions beyond the competence of both himself and Sulla.[21] The Romans were still willing at this point to make an equitable treaty with those whom they regarded as their equals, but it is unclear if Parthia yet held this status.[22] We can only guess about the contents of the agreement. They probably pledged to observe strict neutrality towards each other, and promised not to aid each other's enemies.[23] The parties no doubt defined their spheres of influence, and perhaps the Euphrates was agreed on as the common frontier.[24] Thus any Roman force that crossed the river unprovoked, as Crassus later would, was in violation of the treaty.[25]

Parthia's policy throughout this period seems pacific. Whatever agreements they made with the Romans, they also tried to maintain peaceful alliances with Tigranes of Armenia and Mithridates of Pontus. Parthia generally wanted to be friends with all of its neighbours and they showed a marked reluctance to get involved in quarrels between their allies.[26] Quite simply, Parthia wished to be independent. The Parthians were governed, quite naturally, by self interest. To protect themselves and their territory, they felt it was best to be on good terms with their powerful and boisterous neighbours. They were just as likely to turn to other powers as they were to Rome. Again and again we shall see the Parthians attempting to hold the middle ground between the powers around them. Their policy seems consistent, and they did not try to embrace one power over another.

LUCULLUS AND THE PARTHIANS

After the agreement with Sulla, we hear of no further contact between the two empires until some thirty-odd years later.[27] In the interval between Mithridates II who ruled in Sulla's time and Phraates III Theos with whom Lucullus had dealings, there were several Parthian kings, all of whom were preoccupied with their own troubles. The Parthians made no effort to renew the treaty and so Sulla's treaty was allowed to lapse. Sulla's agreement had lasted thirty years, but now it was time to renew his successor's *foedus amicitiae*, otherwise it would no longer be valid.[28] Lucullus negotiated a new one. The terms seem to have been the same. Some scholars believe the Euphrates was set as the boundary between the two powers.[29]

The agreement between Rome and Parthia was especially important while Lucullus was campaigning against Mithridates of Pontus and his ally, Tigranes of Armenia. In the winter of 69/68 BCE Mithridates and Tigranes approached Phraates with a view to an alliance. When Lucullus heard of this he, too, sent ambassadors to the Parthian king, asking that he should either help the Romans or remain strictly neutral. Lucullus made all sorts of promises if they should take the Roman side, but he also backed this up with threats as to what he would do to them if they aided the enemy. The Parthian king replied by sending envoys to Lucullus and another treaty/agreement was concluded. Lucullus found out through one of his agents who had gone to the Parthian court, however, that the Parthian king had also made alliances with Tigranes and Mithridates. What was this officer, named Sextilius, doing at the Parthian court? There is a suggestion in the sources that he was a spy. He had to have a respectable cover story to explain his presence. Perhaps he was there to help the Parthian war effort on Rome's behalf?[30] Dio 36.45.3 remarks about what the king did once he discovered what Sextilius was up to. The Romans were going to attack Armenia to settle a score with Tigranes. This would do both the Parthians and the Romans a favour.

Lucullus advanced across the highlands of Anatolia, crossing both the Euphrates and the Tigris, and invaded Armenia. Unfortunately for Rome, this invasion did not produce the expected result (Tigranes's betrayal of his father-in-law). Instead, despite heavy defeats inflicted by the Roman army, and Lucullus's capture of Tigranes's own capital, Tigranocerta, in 69 and Nisibis in 68, the Armenian king hung on doggedly, while Mithridates was able to

slip back into his kingdom in 68 with a new army provided by
Tigranes. This was a major coup for Mithridates and an inexcus-
able error on the part of Lucullus. Now, the resourceful Mithridates
was once again in Pontus, able to disrupt the Roman rear, and
where he inflicted a devastating defeat upon Lucullus's legate, Tri-
arius, at Zela in 67.[31] Whether Lucullus's ultimate intention was to
go after the Parthians remains a hotly debated issue.[32]

POMPEY AND THE PARTHIANS

In 66 BCE, under the Lex Manilia, Pompey was appointed to replace
Lucullus and he renewed the agreement with Phraates, the king
of Parthia, to insure Parthian neutrality on the same terms as the
last treaty.[33] If, as some have argued, this established the Euphrates
as the frontier between the Roman and Parthian spheres of influence, the agreement did not last long.[34] As time passed, Roman policy became increasingly heavy-handed. First, Pompey extracted
from Phraates a guarantee that he would not only refrain from
attacking Rome, but would move against Armenia.[35] Then Pompey
violated his own treaty, seized the western provinces of Parthia and
intrigued with local vassal princes. When Phraates inquired about
the Euphrates frontier, Pompey responded arrogantly and omi-
nously that he would observe whatever frontier seemed just
to him.[36] The Romans were not yet contemplating a full-scale
invasion of Parthia, but once Mithridates had been eliminated as a
serious threat, Pompey had no motive to make concessions to the
Parthians since their help was no longer needed. Thus, the period
of direct confrontation between the two powers was ushered in.
By 64 BCE Pompey met the local king, Antiochus XIII Asiaticus, at
the city of Antioch and put him out of a job. Pompey claimed Syria
by right of conquest.[37]

Many historians have also ignored Pompey's aggressive actions
in Transcaucasia. It was Sherwin-White who first proposed that
Pompey's actions against the rulers of Albania and Iberia was a premeditated step aimed at the incorporation of Transcaucasia into the
sphere of Roman influence.[38]

GABINIUS AND THE PARTHIANS

Aulus Gabinius, proconsul of Syria from 57–55 BCE, contributed to
these worsening relations by supporting a rebel claimant to the

Parthian throne.[39] In 58/57 BCE, King Phraates III was murdered by his sons Orodes and Mithridates. Mithridates began his rule by resuming the struggle with Armenia that his father had begun. The object of the war was probably the recovery of the lost province of Gordyene (see Map 2), which had been given to the elder Tigranes by Pompey. Whatever support he had during the Armenian war, however, was lost soon afterwards by the severity of his rule at home. There is reason to believe that he drove his brother Orodes into banishment.[40] He ruled so harshly that after a few years the Parthian nobles deposed him and recalled Orodes from his place of exile. At first Mithridates was allowed to govern Media as a subject monarch, but his brother still did not trust him and he was deprived of this position. Mithridates fled to the Romans and was favourably received by Gabinius – then proconsul of Syria – and requested aid to recover his throne.[41] Gabinius, who was both weak and ambitious, lent a ready ear to this plan. Since he was already on the verge of a Parthian campaign himself anyway, he was ready to accept the offer, but then a more tempting invitation came from another quarter. Ptolemy XII Auletes, expelled from Egypt by his rebellious subjects, asked for his aid.[42]

The news of Gabinius's planned expedition to Parthia had caused quite a stir in Rome, and made it necessary for Pompey to send him a letter explaining the arrangements at Luca. If Pompey expected Gabinius to abandon a lucrative Parthian campaign and a possible triumph, he would need to give him an adequate reason and compensation. Thus Ptolemy arrived with a letter from Pompey accompanied by Rabirius Postumus who was to be the king's *dioiketes* (chief royal treasurer).[43] Ptolemy had recommendations from Pompey and a large amount of money to disburse, which should have persuaded Gabinius to help him instead of invading Parthia.[44] Gabinius was still reluctant, however, to be diverted to the Egyptian mission even at the high price of 10,000 talents, but he was finally persuaded by Mark Antony, his cavalry commander.[45] And although we do not know the contents of the letter, we can guess that Gabinius appealed to his ally to consider the necessity of securing Egypt and promised the support of the triumvirs. Gabinius would have been assured financing for the operation and considerable rewards to make up for the loot he would not be robbing from Parthia.[46]

Mithridates, meanwhile, stayed with the Romans but, when he realized that in the end they would offer little help, he returned to

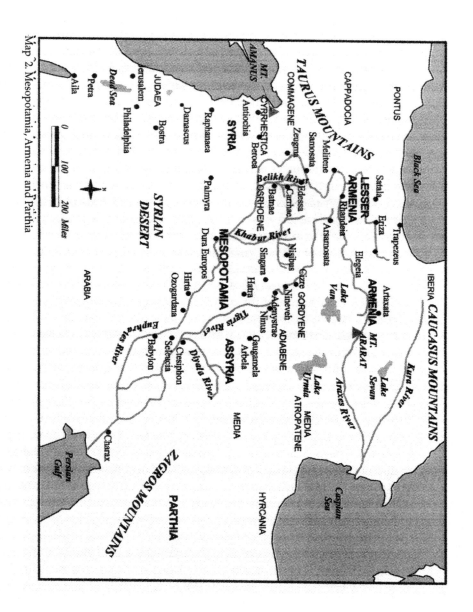

Map 2. Mesopotamia, Armenia and Parthia

Parthia to raise a rebellion with the help of local allies.[47] In the end he did not succeed and had to cast himself on the mercy of his brother who had him instantly executed. Orodes II thus became sole ruler of Parthia by 55 BCE. Relations between Parthia and Rome remained at a stand-off.[48]

ROMAN MOTIVES

Even the ancient sources do not agree on the motives of these commanders. Cassius Dio believed Gabinius was a thoroughly worthless, greedy, grasping and oppressive governor who had plundered a province and was now after the riches of Parthia.[49] Certainly an argument can be made that all the Roman generals we have discussed in this chapter were motivated by personal ambition. They were aggressive in their attitudes towards Parthia, even when peace existed.[50] Josephus reports that Gabinius was already across the Euphrates and ready to attack Parthia when he turned back to assist Ptolemy to his throne.[51] Since this action occurred in late 56 or early 55, Gabinius had obviously begun the campaign on his own initiative.[52] This is a pattern that would continue. One scholar of Parthian history writes that the Parthian king Phraates was 'always correct in his attitude toward the Romans, but they in their pride and ignorance continued to show little regard for the people who had kept their pledges so scrupulously'.[53]

Pompey violated Rome's agreements with Parthia, seized the western provinces from them, intrigued with its vassal princes and insulted Phraates when he protested. Following the assassination of Phraates, Gabinius too would have made a move on the Parthian throne had he not been bribed by a pretender to the Egyptian throne. Josephus claimed Gabinius had performed glorious deeds in Syria, and Caesar praised his military efficiency and success. Cicero, however, accused him of leaving a plundered and exhausted province behind for Crassus. After his three years as proconsul, Gabinius was prosecuted on his return to Rome under the *Lex Julia de maiestate* in two ways.[54] He had made war on his own initiative and had left his province without the Senate's permission. The former governor denied that he had profited from the Parthian campaign and justified his actions as necessary to protect the province of Syria.[55] Yet there is no doubt that Gabinius acquired a fortune in his province as Roman governors in the East regularly did, and he had exceeded his *imperium*.[56] How interesting that the wealth of

Syria was considered a mere trifle compared to what he hoped to gain from the Parthian campaign which he planned without authorization from the Senate. The fiction of senatorial control of foreign affairs was thus maintained.[57]

The greed of the Roman leaders would reach its apogee when Crassus was made governor of Syria. What Gabinius did would be nothing compared to Crassus's deed which became a byword for avarice even in the eastern lands where Rome became synonymous with *auri sacra fames* (the sacred lust for gold – Virgil, *Aeneid* 3.56–7). Indeed, Crassus would become famous for using Syria simply as a base for his fatal Parthian campaign.

The attitude toward Parthia in the late republic was a dream of fabulous wealth to be wrested from a people easy to conquer. Any convenient Parthian dynastic crisis would provide a specious excuse for intervention beyond the Euphrates.[58] History is replete with examples, both ancient and modern, of wars initiated by major powers and they are always able to produce rational arguments for why they are defending their own basic security. From the point of view of the invaded country, these arguments are a thin disguise for imperialist expansion at their expense.

We are not suggesting that all of Rome's wars were arbitrary or initiated for territorial aggrandizement, but these motives certainly played a part in Roman thinking. Neither are we suggesting that Parthia was the innocent victim of Roman aggression. Its own expansive qualities certainly had to be taken into consideration by Rome.[59] Still, Rome's aggressive attitude did not make coexistence easy. What did the Romans really 'win'? Was Rome foolish to waste so much money and manpower on eastern campaigns that produced no results either in security or good will? It may seem like an act of monumental hypocrisy for an American in 2007 to be criticizing another world power for getting bogged down in a land war in Mesopotamia. Even ancient authors writing about Rome's wars in the East emphasized caution versus unprofitable adventures.[60] Yet there were always those authors too, such as Herodian, who admired expansionist policies, and encouraged emperors 'to return in triumph, leading home barbarian kings and governors as prisoners in chains', because this is what made their predecessors great and famous.[61] Expansionist policy was both praised and criticized, although the argument was never made that one should refrain from it for moral reasons; that is a more modern stance.[62]

THE PEACEFUL PARTHIANS

There was no particular reason for Gabinius or Crassus to invade Parthia at all. Parthia's foreign policy toward Rome, although not towards others, was essentially pacific.[63] Rome began the hostilities with the acts and arrangements of Pompey the Great. Even though the Romans were not yet contemplating a full-scale invasion of Parthia, once Mithridates had been eliminated as a serious threat, Pompey had no motive to make concessions to the Parthians since their help was no longer needed. Thus, the period of direct confrontation between the two powers was ushered in.[64]

A number of studies have shown how the actions of successive Roman commanders on the spot and the later rulings of the Roman Senate created foreign policy.[65] There was no preconceived 'plot' to take over Parthia, but the aggressive actions of successive Roman commanders and ambitious emperors created a pattern of hostile relations between the two empires.[66] The mere fact that the *Lex Iulia de Repetundis* was passed in 59 BCE, which forbade a governor to start an unauthorized war, shows that this was not an uncommon practice.[67] Unlike the provinces in Greece and Asia Minor that Rome absorbed, Rome never annexed Parthia, but the unwillingness or the inability to annex does not mean there is any reluctance to control.[68] And this drive to make Parthia subservient to Roman demands would set up three centuries of expensive and possibly needless warfare.

NOTES

1. On the origin of the Parthians, see J. Wolski, 'The Deacy of the Iranian Empire of the Seleucids and the Chronology of the Parthian Beginnings', *Berytus*, 12 (1956/57), pp.35–552. See also the comments of C. Lerouge, *L'image des Parthes dans le monde gréco-romain* (Stuttgart: Franz Steiner Verlag, 2007), pp.43–4, on this historiographical question and the image each power had of the other.
2. On rivers not acting as barriers, see D. Braund, 'River Frontiers in the Environmental Psychology of the Roman World', in D.L. Kennedy (ed.), *The Roman Army in the East* (Ann Arbor, MI: *Journal of Roman Archaeology*, Supplementary Series, 18, 1996), pp.43–7. Cf. Appian, *Celtic Wars* 13 on the Roman disregard for the defensive value of natural obstacles in general. Cf. B. Isaac, *The Limits of Empire: The Roman Army in the East* (Oxford: Clarendon Press, 1992), p.379; E.L. Wheeler, 'Methodological Limits and the Mirage of Roman Strategy', *JMH*, 57, 1 (January 1993), pp.24–5. For rivers as frontiers, see C.R. Whittaker, *Frontiers of the Roman Empire* (Baltimore, MD: Johns Hopkins University Press, 1994), pp.8, 19–20, 26–7, 61, 69, 78, 82, 84–6, 89, 99, 156, 167, 187, 201, 253.
3. G. Rawlinson, *The Sixth Great Monarchy* (New York: Publishers Plate Renting Co., 1870), chapter 10, p.79, who bases this on the speech which Trogus puts in the mouth of Mithridates, Justin, 38.4–7, and to the alleged letter of Mithridates to the Parthian king, Sallust, *Hist. Rom.* 9, fr.12.
4. Rawlinson, *Sixth Great Monarchy*, chapter 10, p.80.

5. Plutarch, *Sulla* 5.4; Velleius Paterculus 2.24.3. A. Keaveney, 'Roman Treaties with Parthia c. 95 – c. 64 BC', *AJPh*, 102 (1981), pp.197–8, bases his belief that Sulla arranged a formal treaty with Parthia on Florus 1.46.4 – a passage that hardly inspires confidence. According to R. Morstein Kallet-Marx, *Hegemony to Empire: The Development of Roman Imperium in the East from 148 to 62 BC* (Berkeley, CA: University of California Press, 1995), p.249, the later pacts with Lucullus and Pompey that Keaveney regards as formal treaties (pp.199–204) may well have been only agreements for wartime cooperation. There is no suggestion in Dio 36.3.2 and 36.45.3 of referral to the Roman Senate or people and, according to Appian, *Mith.* 87, at least the pact with Lucullus was secret.

6. Isaac, *Limits of Empire*, p.28; Keaveney, 'Roman Treaties', pp.195–212; A. Keaveney, 'The Kings and Warlords: Romano-Parthian Relations circa 64–53', *AJPh*, 103 (1982), pp.412–28.

7. Isaac, *Limits of Empire*, pp.28–9; P.A. Brunt, 'Laus imperii', in P.D.A. Garnsey and C.R. Whittaker, *Imperialism in the Ancient World* (Cambridge: Cambridge University Press, 1978), pp.159–91, esp. 170ff. On Rome not recognizing and formal delimitation of its power, see B. Campbell, 'War and Diplomacy: Rome and Parthia, 31 BC – AD 235', in R. Rich and G. Shipley, *War and Society in the Roman World* (New York and London: Routledge, 1993), p.225. Older scholars like T. Mommsen, *The Provinces of the Roman Empire: From Caesar to Diocletian* (New York: Barnes & Noble, 1996), vol. 2, p.21, argued for the Euphrates as a boundary. More recently, Whittaker, *Frontiers of the Roman Empire*, p.142, argued that the Euphrates had never, even in the early empire, been a political or military boundary. See also A.N. Sherwin-White, *Roman Foreign Policy in the East, 168 BC to AD1* (London: Duckworth, 1984), pp.222–3.

8. Keaveney, 'Roman Treaties', p.195, argues that the attitudes of the generals between Sulla and Pompey remained constant.

9. It was E. Badian, 'Sulla's Cilician Command', *Athenaeum*, 37 (1959), pp.279ff. = *Studies in Greek and Roman History* (Oxford: Blackwell, 1964), pp.157–78, who first proposed a date of 96 BCE for Sulla meddling in eastern affairs by restoring Ariobarzanes to the throne of Cappadocia. T. Liebmann-Frankfort, *La frontière orientale dans la politique extérieure de la République romaine depuis le traité d'Apamée jusqu'à la fin des conquêtes asiatiques de Pompée (189/199/63)* (Bruxelles: Palais des Académies, 1969), pp.167–9. This date was challenged by A. Keaveney, 'Deux Dates Contestées de la carrière de Sylla', *Les Etudes Classiques*, 48 (1980), pp.149–59; A.N. Sherwin-White, 'Ariobarzanes, Mithridates, and Sulla', *Classical Quarterly*, 27, 1 (1977), pp.173–83; and G.V. Sumner, 'Sulla's Career in the Nineties', *Athenaeum*, 56 (1978), pp. 395–6, whose arguments were refuted by T.R.S. Broughton in *The Magistrates of the Roman Republic*, with the collaboration of M.L. Paterson (New York: American Philological Association, 1951–52), vol. 3, p.74. See, more recently and in greater detail, T. Corey Brennan, 'Sulla's Career in the Nineties', *Chiron*, 22 (1992), pp.103–58. On Sulla's settlement in the East, see Morstein Kallet-Marx, *Hegemony to Empire*, pp.261–90.

10. Livy, *Epit.* 70.7; see also Plutarch, *Sulla* 5.4–6; Festus 15.2; Lucius Ampelius 31; Velleius Paterculus 2.24.3, who erroneously places it during the First Mithridatic War. For a discussion of the sources, see J. Dobrias, 'Les premiers rapports des Romains avec les Parthes', *Archiv Orientalni*, 3 (1931), pp. 218–21, and Lerouge, *L'image des Parthes*, p.45.

11. Plutarch, *Sulla* 5.4–6. On Roman dominance, see Lerouge, *L'image des Parthes*, pp.46–7. For another occasion when this tactic was used, see Plutarch, *Cato Minor* 57.1–2. Campbell, 'War and Diplomacy', p.215, believes it was out of ignorance. See J. Wolski, 'Les Parthes et la Syrie', *Acta Iranica*, 12 (1976), pp.404–5.

12. Plutarch, *Sulla* 5.5. Sherwin-White, *RFPE*, p.219, believes people have made too much of this incident and that there was no formal treaty.

13. Plutarch, *Sulla* 5.6.

14. Mithridates vented his anger on Orobazus, who lowered the dignity of the Arsacid king by treating the Romans as equals. Sherwin-White, *RFPE*, p.220. Neilson C. Debevoise, *The Political History of Parthia*, reprint edn (New York: Greenwood Books, 1968), p.46; D.L. Kennedy, 'Parthia and Rome: Eastern Perspectives', in Kennedy (ed.), *Roman Army in the East*, p.75; P.M. Sykes, *History of Persia* (London: Macmillan, 1951), vol. 1, p.338.

15. Plutarch, *Sulla* 5.

16. Debevoise, *Political*, pp.47–8, believed that Sulla's insult to the ambassador had serious consequences for Rome's relations with Parthia. The theory is also propounded by K.W.

Dobbins, 'Mithridates II and his Successors: A Study of the Parthian Crisis', *Antichthon*, 8 (1974), p.70. They believe Sulla's behaviour drove the king to seek closer ties with Mithridates and Tigranes. Keaveney, 'Roman Treaties', p.198, points out that this interpretation perhaps overestimates the value the Parthian king placed on his ambassador. See also J. Dobrias, 'Les premiers rapports', p.219.

17. Keaveney, 'Roman Treaties', p.196. See the conflicting views of Dobrias, 'Les premières rapports', pp.220–1, and Debevoise, *Political*, p.46. On the arrogance of Roman aristocrats overseas, see the famous story of C. Popilius Laenas's treatment of Antiochus III Epiphanes in 168 BCE: Polybius 29.27.

18. Keaveney, 'Roman Treaties', p.197; Debevoise, *Political*, p.41.

19. Keaveney, 'Roman Treaties', p.197. It has been suggested that Sulla treated the Parthians this way because he knew their empire was weakened and troubled by usurpers: Debevoise, *Political*, pp.48–9; Keaveney, 'Roman Treaties', p.197, n.13. The argument depends on the dating of Sulla's propraetorship and the troubles. Kennedy, 'Parthia and Rome', p.75, finds it unusual that the Parthians would send a negotiator to a low-level governor, but see V.L. Bullough, 'The Roman Empire vs. Persia, 363–502: A Study of Successful Deterrence', *Journal of Conflict Resolution*, 7, 1 (March 1963), p.60, who points out that in a crisis situation, the loss of national face is somewhat less if the negotiators are of low rank than if they are high.

20. See M. Holleaux, *Rome, Grèce et les monarchies Hellénistiques au IIIe siècle avant JC (273–205)*, reprint of 1935 edn (Paris: Boccard, 1969), p.40, n.2; p.54, n.3; pp.69–70; Keaveney, 'Roman Treaties', p.197. Florus 1.46.4 says that when Crassus was planning to attack Parthia, the king sent a message to remind him of the treaties (*foederum*) with Pompey and Sulla. On the nature of Roman treaties in the East, see also Morstein Kallet-Marx, *Hegemony to Empire*, pp.190–7.

21. Debevoise, *Political*, pp.46–7, believed it was the insult; A. Keaveney, 'Roman Treaties with Parthia circa 95–circa 64 BC', *AJPh*, 102 (1981), p. 197, believed it was because he allowed himself to be outmanoeuvred. See Kennedy, 'Parthia and Rome', who points out that it is unlikely that Sulla returned to Rome with a treaty to be ratified. See Sherwin-White, *RPFE*, pp. 219–20, contra Keaveney, 'Roman Treaties', p.198; Keaveney, 'Kings and Warlords', p.42.

22. See, for example, Polybius 3.22 on the treaty with Carthage.

23. Keaveney, 'Roman Treaties', p.198, citing Holleaux, *Rome, La Grèce et les Monarchies Hellénistiques*, p.40, n.2; p.54, n.3; pp. 69–70; Daremberg-Saglio, 'Amicitia', in C.V. Daremberg and E. Saglio, *Dictionnaire des antiquités grecques et romaines* (Paris: Librairie Hachette et Cie., 1877–1919), p.229; and L.E. Mattaei, 'The Classification of Roman Allies', *Classical Quarterly*, 1 (1900), pp.182–204.

24. Many scholars doubt there was ever an agreement on the Euphrates as a boundary, and even if there were, it would refer to the Upper Euphrates, not to the part south of the Taurus. See Kennedy, 'Parthia and Rome', p.76.

25. On the agreements, see K.-H. Ziegler, *Die Beziehungen zwischen Rom und dem Partherreich* (Wiesbaden: F. Steiner, 1964), 20ff; Liebmann-Frankfort, *La frontière orientale*, pp.171ff., 239ff., 263ff., 276ff., 296ff., 308ff., for evidence and discussion. Of course there was never any formal treaty ratified at Rome, and perhaps no more than a vague understanding. P.A. Brunt, 'Laus imperii', in C.B. Champion, *Roman Imperialism: Readings and Sources* (Oxford: Blackwell, 2004), p.182.

26. Keaveney, 'Roman Treaties', p.199; Dobrias, 'Les premiers rapports', pp.221–8; Appian, *Mith.* 13.87.

27. Keaveney, 'Roman Treaties', pp.199–200, on Plutarch's compression of the story. See also Appian, *Mith.* 87; Dio 36.1–3; 'Sextilius' in *RE*, no. 2, col. 2034; Plutarch, *Lucullus* 30.1.

28. M. Holleaux, *Rome, Grèce et les monarchies Hellénistiques*, p.49, n.2; p.69, n.1; Keaveney, 'Roman Treaties', pp.199–200; 'Amicitia', in *Brill's New Pauly: Encyclopedia of the Ancient World: Antiquity*, ed. H. Cancik and H. Schneider (Leiden; Boston, MA: Brill, 2002), pp.590–1.

29. R. Seager, *Pompey the Great: A Political Biography* (Oxford: Blackwell, 2002), p.54, writes that it is unclear whether Pompey or Phraates took the initiative in renewing the treaty. Orosius, 6.13.2, tells us that when Crassus invaded Parthia, the king demanded to know why he was crossing the Euphrates contrary to the treaties of Lucullus and Pompey. Debevoise, *Political*, p.47, n.68, thinks there is a mention of Sulla's treaty in this passage.

Keaveney, 'Roman Treaties', p.201, argues there is not. Florus 1.46.4 talks about treaties with Sulla and Pompey. Both these authors could be correct and all the treaties used the Euphrates as the boundary. Keaveney, 'Roman Treaties', p.201, n.28.

30. Keaveney, 'Roman Treaties', p.201; Lerouge, *L'image des Parthes*, p.53.
31. On the relations between Lucullus and the Parthians, see Lerouge, *L'image des Parthes*, pp.50–8; Morstein Kallet-Marx, *Hegemony to Empire*, p.312. On these campaigns see Sherwin-White, *RFPE*, pp.176–85; BC. McGing, *The Foreign Policy of Mithridates VI Eupator, King of Pontus* (Leiden: Brill, 1986), pp.154–63.
32. Lerouge, *L'image des Parthes*, pp.52–8.
33. Dio 36.45.3; Keaveney, 'Roman Treaties' p.202. J. van Ooteghem, *Pompée le grand*, (Brussels: Académie royale de Belgique, 1954), p.205, n.7, believed it was Sulla's treaty that Pompey renewed. Keaveney argues that the Dio passage is proof that Lucullus intended the Parthians to attack Armenia. Holleaux, *Rome, Grèce et les monarchies Hellénistiques*, p.49, n.2; p.69, n.1; Keaveney, 'Roman Treaties', p.203; 'Amicitia', in *Brill's New Pauly*, pp.590–1.
34. The agreement, sealed by a *foedus* or grant of *amicitia*, was reached with the Parthians in 66BC. Florus 1.40.31, foedus; Ampelius 31.1; amicitia in Justin 42.4.6; Livy, *Periochae* 100. Cf. Dio 36.45.3 and 51.1. Agreement on the Euphrates frontier is suggested by Orosius 6.13.2, but denied by implication in Florus 1.46.4. Dio 36.3.1ff. Appian, *Mith.* 13.87. See Whittaker, *Frontiers of the Roman Empire*, p.53. Sykes, *History of Persia*, vol. 1, p.345, claims Phraates made the demand, but it was never acknowledged or observed by Pompey. Those accepting the Euphrates frontier: Dobrias,' Les premieres rapports'; Ziegler, *Die Beziehungen*, pp.28–30; doubted by Liebmann-Frankfort, *La frontière orientale*, pp.263–5.
35. Seager, *Pompey the Great*, p.54; Dio 36.45.3; Livy, *Periochae* 100.
36. A.D.H. Bivar, 'The Political History of Iran under the Arsacids', in *CHI*, vol. 3, 1: *The Seleucid, Parthian and Sasanian Period*, ed. E. Yarshater (Cambridge: Cambridge University Press, 1983), p.47.
37. For the full story of the annexation of Syria and its ramifications, see K. Butcher, *Roman Syria and the Near East* (Los Angeles, CA: Getty Publications, 2003), pp.17–31.
38. Sherwin-White, *RFPE*, pp.195–203, and E. Dabrowa, 'Roman Policy in Transcaucasia from Pompey to Domitian', in D.H. French and C.S. Lightfoot (eds), *The Eastern Frontier of the Roman Empire: Proceedings of a Colloquium held at Ankara in September 1988*, British Institute of Archaeology at Ankara Monograph no. 11 (London: British Archaeological Reports, International Series, 553, 1 & 2, 1989), pp.67–75.
39. On the sources for campaign of Gabinius and the political milieu, see Lerouge, *L'image des Parthes*, pp.63–7.
40. Plutarch tells us that the Parthian general who defeated Crassus had previously brought back Orodes from exile. Plutarch, *Crassus* 21.7; Appian, *Parthia* 5.
41. The numismatic evidence seems to support the claim that the elder brother, Mithridates III, succeeded to the throne after the murder of his father. But he made himself so objectionable that he was expelled by the nobles who installed Orodes as ruler. Debevoise, *Political*, p.76, n.23.
42. Under the law of Clodius, Gabinius was given a large force of legions and a substantial grant of money, although neither is further specified by the sources. His command was for three years, during which he was to deal with the troublesome Arabs outside his territorial province. See Sherwin-White, *RFPE*, p.272 and n.2 for the sources.
43. Rabirius was appointed to secure this and other loans (Cicero, *Rab. Post.* 4–5, 22, 25, 28). Rabirius would have been a good choice to carry Pompey's letter to Gabinius. See E. Fantham, 'Trials of Gabinius', *Historia*, 24 (1975), p.430, n.13; E.M. Sanford, 'The Career of Aulus Gabinius', *TAPA*, 70 (1939), pp.85–7. Cicero, *Rab. Post.* 19 indicates that Rabirius helped persuade Gabinius to restore the king.
44. Most ancient writers asserted that the principal inducement for Gabinius to abandon the Parthian campaign was Ptolemy's offer of a massive bribe of 10,000 talents. Cicero, *Pis.* 48, 49; Cicero, *Pro Planc.* 86; *Schol. Bob.* on *Pro Planc.* 86; Plutarch, *Antony* 3.2; Appian, *Syr.* 51; Dio 39.55.3. The actual sum is from Cicero, *Rab. Post.* 21, 30. Dio 39.55.2–3; 56.3, however, claims that Ptolemy bore a letter from Pompey ordering Gabinius to undertake this mission. He does not give details on the circumstances of Pompey's decision. The modern literature is divided between those who believe Gabinius was the agent of the triumvirs. See Sanford, 'Career of Aulus Gabinius', p.86; R.S. Williams, 'The Role of Amicitia

in the Career of A. Gabinius (COS 58)', *Phoenix*, 32, 3 (Autumn 1978), p.205 and n.48.

45. Plutarch, *Antony* 2. Gabinius had persuaded Mark Antony to leave his studies in Greece and join his staff.
46. Williams, 'Role of Amicitia', p.207; According to Cicero, *Rab. Post.* 21, Ptolemy is reputed to have offered Gabinius the princely sum of 10,000 talents, an amount equal to five-sixths of a year's income from Egypt. At Gabinius's trial, ambassadors from Ptolemy denied that any money had been given to Gabinius and a letter was read from the king stating that money had been given only for military purposes (*Rab. Post.* 34). Some doubt that these stories are true, but there is no reason to doubt that a king who had doled out such large sums to other Romans would hesitate to offer Gabinius money. The amount does not seem to have been paid (*Rab. Post.* 8).
47. Justin 42.4. He is thought to have numerous partisans around the area of Babylon. Seleucia, the second largest city in the Empire, went over to him. Plutarch, *Crassus* 21 relates that Seleucia had been in rebellion against Orodes before 54 BCE and had been recovered for him by the general whom he had employed against Crassus. See T. Mommsen, *The History of Rome*, trans. W.P. Dickson (London: Dent; New York: E.P. Dutton, 1929–31), vol. 4, p.309.
48. Dio 37.5.1–7.5. Mithridates resumed the struggle with Armenia that his father had begun. The object of the war was probably the recovery of the lost province of Gordyene which had been given to the elder Tigranes by Pompey. He seems to have succeeded.
49. Dio 39.55.5, 56.1; Debevoise, *Political*, pp.75–7.
50. Williams, 'Role of Amicitia', pp.195–210.
51. Josephus, *AJ* 14.98; Josephus, *BJ* 1.175.
52. Williams, 'Role of Amicitia', p.206, points out that Gabinius must have been unaware of the agreements made at Luca in April 56 in which Crassus was assured a major Syrian command. Cicero, *Ad Att.* 4.9, indicates that the provincial commands were arranged and been public knowledge in Rome by the spring of 55. On the limits of Gabinius's command, see Sanford, 'Career of Aulus Gabinius', p.79.
53. R. Ghirshman, *Iran from the Earliest Times to the Islamic Conquest* (London: Penguin Books, 1954), p.251.
54. Three indictments were levelled against him: *maiesta* (exceeding the power conferred on him by his *imperium* for restoring Ptolemy without senatorial authorization); *repetundae* (giving the tax collectors full opportunity to display their animosity); *ambitus* (bribery or buying votes). On the charges see Fantham, 'Trials of Gabinius', pp.432–43.
55. Cicero, *Rab. Post.* 20.
56. Sanford, 'Career of Aulus Gabinius', p.82. Sulla was tried for extortion after his return from Cilicia. See M.C. Alexander, *Trials in the Late Roman Republic 149 BC to 50 BC*, (Toronto: University of Toronto Press, 1990), no. 92, and Brennan, 'Sulla's Career in the Nineties', pp.154–8; Keaveney, 'Kings and Warlords', p.413, and B.A. Marshall, *Crassus* (Amsterdam: A.M. Hakkert, 1976), p.140, who points out that this invalidates any claim Gabinius has *imperium infinitum*.
57. Sanford, 'Career of Aulus Gabinius', p.87.
58. Ibid., p.84; Dio 39.56; 40.12; Debevoise, *Political*, pp.75–7.
59. Although on Parthia as an innocent victim, see P. Arnaud, 'Les guerres parthiques de Gabinius et de Crassus et la politique occidentale des Parthes arsacides entre 70 et 53 av. J-C', in E. Dabrowa (ed.), *Ancient Iran and the Mediterranean World* (Cracow: Jagiellonian University Press, 1998), pp.13–35, esp. p.14.
60. See Aelius Aristides, *Roman Oration* 70ff. on such wars being a thing of the past. Herodian 6.6; cf. Strabo 6.4.2 (288); 17.3.24 (839) which describes Rome's dominions.
61. Isaac, *Limits of Empire*, pp.27–8.
62. Ibid.
63. Kennedy, 'Parthia and Rome', p.76, who accepts Parthia's non-aggression at least in this in this period; Isaac, *Limits of Empire*, p.28; S. Mattern, *Rome and the Enemy* (Berkeley, CA: University of California Press, 1999), p.21.
64. Pompey's march into Syria opened a new epoch in the history of Rome's Eastern expansion. His activities in Syria and Palestine in 64–63 BCE, and especially his refusal to restore the Seleucid Antiochus XIII to the kingdom from which he had been expelled by Tigranes, in effect abolished the moribund Seleucid monarchy. On his embroilment in the dispute between Parthia and Armenia over Gordyene, see Sherwin-White, *RFPE*,

pp.206–26; Seager, *Pompey the Great*, pp.57–8; M. Gelzer, *Pompeius* (Munich: F. Bruckmann, 1949), pp.76–99; Ooteghem, *Pompée le grand*, pp.204–38; Debevoise, *Political*, pp.72–5.

65. A. Eckstein, *Senate and General* (Berkeley, CA: University of California Press, 1987), pp.xi–xiii; Mattern, *Rome and the Enemy*, pp.8–10. For earlier works suggesting that Rome had no formal foreign policy in this period, see E. Badian, *Roman Imperialism in the Late Republic* (Ithaca, NY: Cornell University Press, 1971).

66. Morstein Kallet-Marx, *From Hegemony to Empire*, p.1, whose work deals with the question of what exactly went into the making of a province, and Eckstein, *Senate and General*, pp.319–24.

67. Isaac, *Limits of Empire*, p.379.

68. See the comments of J. Gallagher and J. Robinson, 'The Imperialism of Free Trade', *Economic History Review*, 6, 1 (1953), pp.1–15, in their seminal article on nineteenth-century British expansion; Morstein Kallet-Marx, *From Hegemony to Empire*, p.1; Eckstein, *Senate and General*, pp.xi–xxii and *passim*.

3

THE HIGH PRICE OF FAILURE: CRASSUS AND THE PARTHIANS

CRASSUS IN SYRIA

While the struggle between Mithridates and Orodes was still in progress, M. Licinius Crassus was appointed governor of Syria in 55 BCE.[1] It seems to have been well known that he was planning a Parthian war.[2] Crassus was now over 60 years of age, and a military triumph was the one prize that had escaped him. In spite of the fact that the Parthians had done nothing to provoke the Romans, their expansion may have been seen as a threat to Roman interests. Although there was popular opposition to the war in Rome itself, Crassus, like so many Roman commanders, let this opportunity, his ambition and the encouragement of his colleagues urge him on to glory in the East. At least one scholar has called it 'the first instance of Roman aggression in the eastern regions for which no ancient writer could find any vestige of justification'.[3] Other scholars, however, believe he was intervening in the Parthian civil war on the side of the Mithridates with the hope of installing a pro-Roman client prince on the throne.[4] Caesar wrote to Crassus from Gaul urging him to pursue a Parthian campaign, and Cicero defended this position.[5]

The appointment of Crassus to the Syrian command continued this trend of deliberate Roman aggression toward Parthia, and it set the stage for one of the worst, and least understood, military disasters in Roman history. Envying the prestige earned by Pompey in the East and by Caesar in Gaul, Crassus shattered the policy of cautious non-belligerency against the Parthians and simply invaded their territory.[6] This adventure was typical of Roman commanders in the late Republic, for whom greed or martial glory were sufficient motives to undertake a foreign campaign.[7] Despite the popular opposition for this unjustified attack, Italy was scoured for troops, 40,000 soldiers were mustered and Crassus left Rome on the ides of November, 55 BCE. Plutarch describes how the curses of the tribune Aetius Capito, leader of the anti-war party, followed him as he departed from Brundisium. He burned incense and cursed Crassus 'with dreadful imprecations, naming several strange and horrible deities'.[8] Other terrible omens would be reported before and during the campaign.[9] In Lucania it was said to have rained iron in the shape of sponges and the augurs prophesied wounds from above (Parthian arrows?). Little intelligence had been gathered to prepare for this expedition, and now even signs from the gods were being ignored. Marching overland from Dyrrachium, Crassus reached Syria in April or May 54 BCE and took over the command of Gabinius.

With the Syrian garrisons Crassus had an army of seven legions, to which were added mounted troops made available by Rome's allies, Abgarus of Osrhoene, the Arab Prince Alchaudonius, and Artavasdes of Armenia.[10] Help from these quarters, however, was unreliable and of doubtful quality. Alchaudonius quickly declared himself pro-Parthian, while Abgarus was acting as a double agent, pretending to be on Crassus's side while reporting back to the Parthians.[11]

THE INTELLIGENCE PROBLEM

Crassus arrived with a proper army but lacked hard strategic intelligence.[12] He knew little about Parthia and his most evident failure was not acquainting himself with his enemy. He thought the Parthians were like the Armenians and, misled by previous Roman victories, he was already anticipating his gilded laurels. Nor was intelligence difficult to obtain. Recent military operations conducted in the region, by Lucullus, Gabinius and Pompey among others, should have provided valuable information about the topography of Parthia, the strength of its armed forces, the type of weapons they used, weather conditions, and the willingness and ability of the Parthians to wage war. Instead, all of these factors were ignored, and Crassus mounted a major campaign against a formidable enemy from a position of relative ignorance.[13] It was solely to gratify his need for military glory that Crassus took advantage of his position to attack those whom Cicero described as a most peaceable folk.[14] His only fear seems to have been that easy success might diminish his glory.

Tactically, Crassus was in a better position because his subordinate officers did collect intelligence along their route. Once Roman troops had crossed the Euphrates and invaded Mesopotamia, they sent cavalry scouts (*prodromoi*) ahead of them to clear the route. They spent the first year on minor operations, the purpose of which is still not clear, although training troops and establishing supply bases in Mesopotamia are good guesses.[15] Another reason was waiting for the cavalry being brought by his son, now on the way from Caesar's army in Gaul with 1,000 picked horsemen. When he took up winter quarters in Syria, Plutarch criticized him for not having regular roll-calls or organizing athletic contests for his men.[16] Surely the collection of intelligence about Parthian strength, disposition and weaponry should have been his first priority. Instead, he was working out what revenue could be drawn from the various cities and letting discipline lag, not to mention giving his enemies time to prepare.[17]

The only resistance the Romans met came from the Parthian satrap, Silaces, whose forces were easily scattered when their leader was wounded. Greek cities in Syria, including Nicephorium, came over to the Roman cause, and Silaces retired to brief the Parthian King Orodes on the outcome of that early encounter with Crassus's army; the Parthian forces at hand were too small to offer further resistance.[18] Crassus did not follow up his initial success, and lost the momentum by not pressing home to his objective, Seleucia on the Tigris, nor did he winter at a forward location so as to monitor the situation in his area of interest, but retired to winter quarters in Syria.[19] At the time of Crassus's first campaign, Orodes was still vying with his brother Mithridates for the throne of their murdered father, and it would have been an opportune time for Crassus to exploit this fraternal conflict. Instead, his withdrawal for the winter allowed Orodes to eliminate Mithridates and make preparations to fight the Romans.[20] Crassus spent the winter stripping the Temple at Jerusalem of whatever money and gold Pompey had left, plundering the Temple of Atargatis at Hierapolis-Bambyce (Membodj), and recruiting a few more soldiers.[21]

The Parthians, meanwhile, were closely observing Roman movements. Orodes seemed well informed of developments on the political scene at Rome, and he apparently had grounds to believe that Crassus was waging the war on his own accord. We certainly cannot accept Dio's claim that the Parthians did not expect the Roman invasion.[22] Orodes knew what was happening, but as long as his throne was not entirely secure he was reluctant to bring together the nobles unless it was absolutely necessary, because together they might conspire to overthrow him. Crassus had encountered only light resistance because the Parthians had a rather small standing army and needed time to mobilize additional reserves. When Crassus halted his initiative and returned to Syria for the winter, Orodes directed two generals to harass Crassus's garrisons in the villages recently taken by the Romans, while Orodes himself continued to prepare for the impending struggle.[23]

Envoys from Orodes visited Crassus in Syria, probably in the early spring of 53 BCE.[24] They demanded to know the reason for this unprovoked invasion.[25] Here we see a diplomatic solution easily available, and a Roman commander not interested in it. If this dramatic confrontation is historical, then we see the situation clearly laid out by the Parthian envoys. They ask if the war was being waged without the consent of the Roman people, as the Parthians had been informed by their agents (i.e. on Crassus's own initiative). If so, the Parthians agreed to show mercy and take pity on Crassus's old age. If, on the other hand, the attack was formally authorized by the Roman Senate, then the war would be prosecuted without truce or treaty. The contents of Orodes's message to Crassus, if correctly reported, may be indicative of a Parthian intelligence capability to follow events at Rome.[26] The Parthians wanted to discover whether Crassus's campaign was an officially sanctioned one, or a private enterprise like some other military ventures of that period. It is significant that Orodes gave the impression of being fairly convinced the latter was the case, but refrained from stating this categorically and opted to put it in the form of a question to Crassus. The king was trying to test the Roman strength before committing himself to a final military decision.[27] Assuming that the Parthians did not determine conclusively that Crassus's campaign was indeed a private enterprise, the root of their doubts could be that whatever intelligence assets they did have at Rome were not sufficiently well placed to enjoy unfettered access to all the relevant information. If Orodes's message was calculated to give Crassus a diplomatic way out and help the Parthians pursue a course of containment, it failed.[28] The proposition infuriated Crassus. He replied that he would give his answer to Orodes in Seleucia when the Romans arrived at the Parthian capital, whereupon one of the Parthian envoys, Vagises, pointing to the palm of his hand, said, 'Sooner will hair grow here than you shall reach Seleucia.'[29]

Crassus had three possible routes open to him. Firstly, he could appeal for the support of Artavasdes the Armenian, who had recently succeeded his father Tigranes. This would mean that he could take the safe route through Armenia into Adiabene and then take the left bank of the Tigris to Ctesiphon. Artavasdes wisely counselled him that if he took the Armenian route, neither Abgarus nor Alchaudonius would be able to help the Parthians. If he took any of the other routes, he would need the alliance of both of them.

Secondly, he might follow the course of the Euphrates to Seleucia, then cross the narrow tract of the plain that separates the two rivers.

Thirdly, he might take the shortest but most dangerous line across the Belikh and Khabour rivers and directly through the Mesopotamian desert.

Crassus's mistake was refusing the good advice of King Artavasdes of Armenia who came to his aid with large body of foot and horse. He urged Crassus to invade Parthia by way of Armenia[30] (see Map 2). As pointed out in the first option above, this would prevent Abgarus or Alchaudonius from helping the Parthians very much. Crassus declined this invitation, explaining that his advanced posts were already established and he had already stationed garrisons in the territory conquered the previous summer. He would have to leave these personnel behind if he chose another invasion route. He was committed to following his original route back to Parthia. Artavasdes's suggestion had considerable merit, since Armenia's mountainous terrain was sure to frustrate any counteroffensive by the Parthian cavalry. But acceptance of Artavasdes's proposal would also have tied Crassus to a distant route, with an uncertain ally between himself and his base. Crassus's decision cost him the support of Artavasdes who, when his advice and assistance were rejected, rode away.[31] Crassus probably still expected Artavasdes to fulfil his obligations as Rome's ally, and evidently Orodes believed so too, as he was readying his forces for war on two fronts. Orodes resolved to conduct the offensive against Armenia himself, while entrusting his general Surenas with the defence of Mesopotamia against Crassus.[32]

Crassus crossed the Euphrates for the second time at Zeugma (see Map 2) and began his main offensive with a force about 42,000 strong, including 4,000 cavalry and an equal number of lightly-armed infantry.[33] Opposing him was the commander-in-chief, Surenas, the second most important man in Parthia, who had great wealth and a vast number of retainers.[34] He was assisted by the satrap, Silaces. Surenas's private army of mail-clad horsemen – the so-called cataphracts – and lightly-armed cavalry totalled 10,000.[35] Since archers could carry only a limited quantity of arrows with them, Surenas organized a troop of camels to transport a huge reserve of arrows.[36] The bulk of the Parthian infantry was still with Orodes, who had gone into Armenia to hold Artavasdes in check and wait for a Roman invasion from that route.

Some historians have suggested that, prior to Carrhae, the western world grossly underestimated the potency of Parthian weapons and tactics, and was ignorant of the geography and terrain of the area.[37] In the West, mounted archers did not count for much, although Cretan mercenaries did sometimes serve as archers. Roman historians such as Justin write that the Parthians could not fight a protracted battle, and even as late as Carrhae the Roman troops presumed that the Parthians would quickly exhaust their supply of arrows. This would suggest that Roman officers had no inkling of Surenas's ammunition resupply system, or, if they did know the truth, they hid it from their troops so as not to dampen their morale. The ability of Parthian arrows to pierce Roman armour may also have been unknown.[38] Or perhaps they just did not take bows and arrows seriously.[39] Whatever the explanation, if the Roman command completely underestimated Parthian capabilities, then this should qualify as a major intelligence failure, and an unforgivable one at that, because the information was at hand. Earlier, when Crassus's army was wintering in Syria, eyewitnesses escaped from the towns garrisoned during the first campaign in Mesopotamia in 54 BCE and described the capabilities of the Parthian mounted archers. For that very reason Cassius and other officers tried to persuade Crassus to reconsider the whole project,[40] but Crassus ignored their advice. Since he also failed to take into account the peculiarities of the desert terrain and climate, the intelligence breakdown seems to have been total.

Roman reconnaissance was not lacking. Cassius wisely suggested that the Roman army should rest in one of the garrisoned villages while scouts were sent to gather information about the enemy forces. He had argued that the advance should be made along the Euphrates right to the target – Seleucia. The scouts discovered tracks leading eastward from the river, which were assumed to indicate that the enemy had fled. Crassus then had to decide whether to continue along his original route or to strike out cross-country in pursuit of the supposedly retreating Parthians. According to Plutarch, while Crassus was considering which route to follow, Abgar of Osrhoene[41] arrived with the news that the Parthians were withdrawing and taking their goods with them and, moreover, that they had left only two subordinate officers to cover their flight. Eager to chase what he believed to be an enemy in flight, Crassus accepted Abgar's offer to guide the army. Without verifying the information, Crassus let enthusiasm cloud his judgement, and he immediately advanced across Mesopotamia. Roman historians labelled Abgar a traitor who lured Crassus into deviating from his safe route along the river, and led him through an open desert where the troops suffered from the barrenness and were thus vulnerable to cavalry attack. On the pretext of spying out the Parthians, Abgar is said to have met with Surenas, whom he informed of Roman movements.[42] The fact remains that he led the Romans into the immediate vicinity of the main Parthian force and, when the battle was imminent, made a pretext to ride away.

If Abgar indeed was a carrier of disinformation, the trick was effective but we cannot corroborate the charges of treachery.[43] In reality, Abgar may only have been leading the Romans along an old Arab road – a regular trade route dotted with oases and small settlements intended to supply Arab traders and their camel caravans. This particular track had a section of desert which took a day-and-a-half to cross before reaching the Belikh River.[44] The soldiers grumbled at the hardships of the march. Abgar's sarcasm was not unjustified. He reminded them that this was the border between Assyria and Arabia, not a route march through Campania with its 'fountains and streams and shades and baths ... and taverns'.[45] The troops – tired, thirsty and hungry – reached the Belikh River at a point below Carrhae (Harran) on 6 May 53 BCE[46] (see Map 2).

At Carrhae, scouts informed Crassus that Surenas was in the vicinity. They reported finding the tracks of large numbers of horses turning away from the Romans, but had encountered no actual people.[47] Cassius and the subordinate officers advised him to either make a fortified encampment from which he could safely reconnoitre, or else proceed along the river bank toward Seleucia, thus keeping his right flank covered and guaranteeing a line of supply by water.[48] Crassus did neither; he advanced almost immediately without allowing his men sufficient time to eat and drink while standing in ranks. He started southward when his scouts reported back that the Parthians were approaching. The allied cavalry promptly deserted.[49]

Crassus's best tactic would have been to pin the Parthians down and trap them into fighting on terrain which might be to their disadvantage. There is no evidence that he understood this. He seems to have believed that a search-and-destroy operation carried out by conventional Roman methods would work.[50] He had now located the Parthians; in his own mind, the only task left was to defeat them.

THE BATTLE OF CARRHAE

As the Parthians drew nearer, the first Romans prepared to advance to the encounter. On the advice of Cassius they formed up in a wide line with little depth, and the wings supported by cavalry. Crassus's son Publius had command of one wing and Cassius had command of the other, while Crassus took the centre. As the Parthians advanced, however, they formed up into a square.[51]

The Romans had no idea about the strength and size of the Parthian army. Its main body was invisible behind a vanguard, and the cataphracts concealed their armour under hides.[52] At a given signal, they discarded their camouflage coverings, and as the sun glittered on their helmets of Margian steel, they charged the Roman line to the roar of kettledrums.[53] This sound and fury caused the scouts and light-armed soldiers to withdraw into the square, and before he was aware of the manoeuvre, Crassus was swiftly surrounded. The Romans now understood the damage that could be wreaked by the Parthian archery. Their bows had a longer range than those in the Roman arsenal, and their arrows a more powerful impact, sufficient to penetrate Roman armour.[54] In addition, the Romans' close formation rendered them highly vulnerable to the barrage of Parthian arrows. Counter-attacks were futile since the Parthians simply withdrew, shooting backward from their mounts as they retired, the famous 'Parthian shot'.

A second Parthian deception resulted in another disaster for the Romans. Crassus had ordered his son Publius to lead a charge as the enemy was attacking and attempting to surround Publius's wing with the intention of getting at its rear. Publius charged and the Parthians feigned a retreat, which was a ruse to lure the younger Crassus and his cavalry farther from the main body of the

Roman army. Once he was far enough away, the Parthians turned and surrounded him. His entire force was destroyed; some soldiers survived to surrender. Most of the officers ordered their shield bearers to kill them, or else they committed suicide. Not more than 500 were taken alive.[55]

The Parthians cut off Publius's head, impaling it on a lance. Crassus was about to move to his son's aid when the Parthians arrived with their trophy. Despite heavy losses from the incessant hail of arrows, the square held until nightfall brought a respite and the Parthians withdrew. Once the pressure was off, Crassus broke down, and the order for retreat was given by his lieutenants, Octavius and Cassius. The army sought to escape in silence, but the Parthians were alerted by the cries of 4,000 Roman wounded who realized that they were being abandoned. The Parthians were not very adept in night fighting, so they did nothing to stop Crassus's retreat. By dawn, most of the survivors were walled up at Carrhae (Harran) where a Roman garrison could help them.[56] The Parthians spent the day capturing or killing Roman casualties and stragglers, including four cohorts under the command of the legate Vargunteius who had been separated from the main body.[57]

Once Parthian intelligence had determined that Crassus and his officers were present in Carrhae, elements of the Parthian army surrounded the town. The place offered little protection or security to the Romans; no provisions were available locally, nor were there Roman troops in Syria to come to their rescue. Armenia was near, and since the Parthians did not fight at night, it seemed that an escape by night was feasible. Crassus withdrew his troops northwards to Sinnaca, a town in the Armenian foothills, where the remnants of his army would be safe from the Parthian horsemen. Roman counterintelligence failed again and Crassus chose a Parthian agent named Andromachus to be his guide.[58] Andromachus led the retreating Romans through the night, to and fro over the hilly terrain to slow their march, wearing the soldiers down, and wasting time so that by daylight the Parthians would be close. For his trouble the agent was generously rewarded by the Parthians.[59] This theme of a Roman commander being purposefully and treacherously misguided is a common excuse for military disasters. One wonders why the Romans always relied on local guides and never seemed to possess adequate geographical information before they became involved in major foreign conquests.[60] Crassus's officer Octavius was better served by his own guides;

with 5,000 men he safely reached Sinnaca to await Crassus. When Crassus later appeared on a low ridge with only four cohorts surrounded by the enemy, Octavius went out to help. The united 7,000 held their own against the enemy.

Surenas, wanting to take Crassus alive, and fearing that the Romans might still escape since darkness was falling and the foothills were near, offered to discuss a truce and safe conduct. First, however, he set the stage with more disinformation. He released some Roman prisoners who had been deliberately allowed to overhear a conversation in which assurances of kind treatment for Crassus and a desire for peace were expressed. The Parthians ceased fighting and Surenas rode up to the knoll, where he offered Crassus safe passage and a treaty of peace. Crassus suspected treachery; scholars have widely debated whether the Parthian offer was genuine.[61] In any event, Crassus decided to accept Surenas's terms. A meeting was held between the two leaders, each accompanied by an equal number of men. The Parthians arrived on horseback, the Romans on foot. Surenas ordered a horse for Crassus, saying that a definitive treaty must be signed on the Euphrates frontier. But Octavius and some officers had followed Crassus and, when a horse was brought, they guessed that the Parthians intended to carry him off.[62] There was a scuffle, during which all the Romans were cut down, and in the commotion Crassus was killed. No one could ever tell with certainty how he died.[63] Later the headless bodies of the Romans were dragged around the walls of Sinnaca.[64]

THE AFTERMATH

Whether we accept the ancient interpretations blaming Crassus for a needless campaign, or see his invasion as a serious attempt to further Roman interests in the East, once undertaken, it is the commander's responsibility to carry out the campaign successfully. There is no doubt that Carrhae was one of the most humiliating defeats that the Roman army ever suffered. Of Crassus's 44,000 men, only 10,000 reached Syria; another 10,000 were made prisoners and resettled at Merv to protect the Parthian frontier.[65] The remaining 24,000 perished.[66] Surenas reportedly held a mock triumph in Seleucia, at which a Roman captive, C. Paccianus, who bore a resemblance to Crassus, was paraded in women's clothing and ridiculed with the title *Imperator*. Crassus's head and right hand were cut off and sent to Orodes, while his corpse was left unburied.[67] As a final insult, it was said that molten gold was poured down the dead man's throat to symbolize the downfall which he had brought upon himself by his excessive greed for riches.[68]

The explanation of the defeat has to do more with Crassus than with Cassius or his other senior officers. Crassus was a Roman general not untypical of his period. He was brave enough, obstinate, ordinarily competent, and conventional. He believed that if he brought the legions into contact with the enemy, the legions would then do the rest. He was unfortunate to meet, late in life, an enemy commander who had the imagination Crassus himself lacked. Now, advancing in age and trying to outrun his younger competitors, he made a number of serious military blunders, just when he could least afford it.[69] To attack an enemy whose main army is cavalry with a body of foot-soldiers, supported by an insignificant number of horse, is a rash and dangerous act. To direct such an attack on the more open part of the country where cavalry could operate freely, is to aggravate the danger even more. Having fallen into the trap and then to leave the protection of a city's walls once they had been taken seems even more reckless. If an ignorant and inexperienced commander ventures on a trial of arms with an enemy about whom he knows little or nothing, in the enemy's own country, without the support of allies, and neglects every caution suggested by his officers, marching straight into a trap prepared for him, then it is not surprising that a defeat will follow.[70]

Without the necessary intelligence upon which to base his decisions, Crassus had no idea of what he might encounter in the field. He may have assumed that a Parthia weakened by a civil war would be easy pickings, but the Parthians were no easy prey.[71]By the time he faced the enemy and discovered this, it was too late. He could have gathered and analyzed much more intelligence than he seems to have done; at the very least he should have consulted his own officers about the information they had. He was not, as one scholar suggested, just 'unfortunate in his advisers and guides'.[72] In fact, this is arguably Crassus's most damaging oversight in the sphere of intelligence – his failure to cultivate promising assets. There were, for instance, many Greeks in this area who knew the region well, yet Crassus altogether ignored these potentially valuable sources. He and his son Publius and the overwhelming bulk of his great army lay dead in the sands of Parthia – not so much the victims of the Parthian archers and executioners, but rather as victims of his unbridled ambition, greed and haste.

What would pertinent intelligence have taught him? It would have told him that the Parthians had developed a trained, professional force equipped with long-range weapons and carrying a large quantity of ammunition for a protracted fight. This alone, however, would not have been enough to defeat the Romans. The combination of heavy cavalry and mounted archers is said to have revolutionized ancient warfare, and it has further been argued that these two elements in concert also were the primary contributors to Crassus's defeat. In truth, the myth of Parthian military superiority was born at Carrhae.[73] But such a debacle was by no means inevitable. The Roman army at Carrhae was more than three times the size of the Parthian force. Had the Romans used their intelligence resources and not fallen for the Parthian ruse, they could have prevailed. The historian W.W. Tarn believed that even if Caesar had been there, with no more cavalry than at Crassus's disposal, he too would not have stood a chance.[74] But the Parthians were neither that numerous nor superior in arms, and later Roman commanders would find ways to defeat them. The Parthians at Carrhae simply knew what to expect and artfully lured the Romans into unfavourable positions. Reliable intelligence, surprise and speed gave the Parthian forces the edge over an army disproportionately larger.[75] Certainly, the Parthians had a superb military commander, but this was no 'secret weapon'. In fact, Surenas was executed the following year and his organization broken up.[76] There is nothing the Parthians did that was not used in eastern wars and of which the Romans were unaware.[77]

Nor did those long-range weapons and large amounts of ammunition truly revolutionize ancient warfare. The Romans developed long-range weapons of their own. When Antony invaded Parthia seventeen years later, he was accompanied by expert slingers whose weapons, with lead bullets, could outrange the bow. Carrhae demonstrated to the Romans the vulnerability of their legions to cavalry attack, and the need to strengthen the Roman cavalry that had been neglected ever since the military reforms of Marius a half-century earlier.[78] Carrhae should have impressed upon the Romans the importance of collecting intelligence and acting. Instead, the invincibility of the legions continued to remain an article of faith, a dogma that long precluded the establishment of a regular Roman cavalry or an intelligence arm. This resistance to change was distinctive of a people whose pride and confidence had served them well in the past. The late Republic was an age when senior commanders with tremendous individual powers were embroiling Rome in a clash of wills and authority characteristic of a decaying government. The resultant inefficiency is reflected in the nature of intelligence collection which, at the national level, was piecemeal and ineffective. Caesar's conquest of Gaul, Pompey's conquest of the East, and Octavian's conquest of Egypt, were all facilitated by these commanders' own privately-constituted intelligence networks, which also served each of them in the civil wars.

The Roman defeat had had a great political effect. The Parthians recovered Mesopotamia up to the Euphrates. Armenia was lost to the Romans, and thrown for a time into complete dependence on Parthia; and the Jews, always impatient of foreign domination, and recently aggrieved by the unprovoked spoliation of their temple by Crassus, flew to arms.[79] Crassus's fiasco placed Parthia on an equal if not superior plane with Rome in the minds of men all the way from the Mediterranean to the Indus.[80] This new attitude would influence Roman policy toward Parthia for decades. The Parthians were thus driven to abandon their pacific stance and take the offensive. There are still those who argue that both Gabinius and Crassus attacked Parthia to defend Rome against an imminent threat, but this case has yet to be proved.[81]

Although the Parthians were suffering from the usual internecine squabbles, they could put a formidable force in the field. The Parthians did not win because they were the more powerful empire, however; they won because they were fighting on familiar territory, and their intelligence service kept them well informed of the nature, strength, and location of the enemy. Orodes had tried for as long as possible to minimize the effects the Roman commanders had on his previously good relations with Rome. When this effort failed, he launched a successful counter-attack against the Romans. One can see by the humiliating way they treated Crasus that they were deeply alienated by the treachery of the Roman invasion in a period of formal peace. The remark that Suren made in his last meeting with Crassus was that the Romans were not too mindful of their verbal agreements.[82]

The aims of Parthian foreign policy toward Rome seem to have been fixing the Euphrates as the frontier and securing the border against its neighbours. But Crassus's death changed this intention drastically. The Parthians wanted revenge for this unprovoked invasion of their territory, and the Romans were forced to avenge the great blow to their prestige. Only a successful war against the enemy could restore Roman honour. The defeat required retaliation, and more than a century later Lucan would still bewail the civil wars that Rome waged while 'the ghost of Crassus wandered unavenged'.[83]

Rome might have learned much from the Parthians at Carrhae about effective intelligence operations, especially with more eastern campaigns being planned. Crassus's last remarks to his officers, which were meant to convey his loyalty and the loyalty of his army, also sum up equally well the Roman susceptibility to deception. 'But tell the world if you get safely home, that Crassus perished because he was deceived by his enemies, and not because he was delivered up to them by his countrymen.'[84] It is the commander's job to see that he is not deceived, and he does this with the use of timely and accurate intelligence. Intelligence is collected to enable commanders to make wise military decisions and win their battles and wars. If they do not collect ample, accurate intelligence and act on it properly, they leave themselves open to disaster. The Greek historian Polybius made it clear that a really experienced and responsible general should not move into a region about which he knew next to nothing without first having obtained thorough and detailed geographical, political and military intelligence.[85] This was Crassus's biggest mistake.

Crassus, like too many other Roman commanders in Parthia, in spite of their innate abilities in the field, found themselves at a great disadvantage if they tried to take short cuts when it came to collecting intelligence properly and adequately. Crassus was not a completely incompetent military commander; after all, he had saved Rome from the disaster of the Spartacus rebellion, and was held in high enough esteem to be appointed governor of Syria.[86] Nor was Crassus atypical of Roman generals. But like many of his type, he tended to make two major tactical mistakes. First, he assumed that if he delivered the army to the battlefield, the army would do the rest, and that the result would be a Roman victory. Secondly, in search of a great victory and the glory that attended it, he underestimated the enemy and failed to collect the proper intelligence that would have given him a better estimate of the enemy's strength and intentions. Like Caesar in Britain, he let his ambition override his common sense. In Crassus's case, however, the mistake was fatal.

In this first major encounter with the Parthians, the Romans lost the opportunity to develop peaceful relations with their eastern neighbour. The lands east of the Euphrates became definitely Parthian, and the Jewish population in Babylonia and Palestine turned to Parthia for liberation.[87] The capture of legionary standards by the Parthians was considered a grave moral defeat and evil omen for the Romans. It required a generation of diplomacy before the Parthians returned them. In the 20s BCE Horace and Propertius look forward to a victory against Parthia that will restore Rome to its pristine state of virtue after the demoralizing civil wars and avenge the defeat of Crassus.[88] Granted, Horace seems to wildly exaggerate the danger involved when he claims the Parthians were threatening Latium.[89] The loss of the battle did not create a security problem for Italy as much as it represented a loss of face and the appearance of weakness on the part of the Romans. Augustus would try very hard to rectify this situation without starting another war. He advertised the return of the standards very loudly, and the image of the kneeling Parthian became a common theme in the iconography of his reign.[90]

The most dangerous legacy of this campaign is that people began to recognize Parthia as a powerful state subsisting side by side with Rome, and indeed on a footing of equality.[91] This would become an intolerable situation for the Romans, who recognized no equals and certainly not one on their eastern border. Another result of the disaster for the Romans was the endurance of the idea that legionary armies could not successfully fight Parthian cavalry – a myth that even the sacking of the Parthian capital three times in the second century CE could not quash. Rather than realizing that Parthia was too large to defeat and occupy, and too foreign to assimilate, the Romans simply continued to chase the Parthian chimera.[92]

NOTES

1. Under the Lex Trebonia of 55 BCE, M. Licinius Crassus received Syria as his province for five years. On Crassus's campaign, see: Lucius Ampelius, *Lib. Mem.* 31, Appian, *BC* 2.18; Caesar, *BC*, 3.31; Cicero, *De Div.* 2.22; Dio 40.12–27; Eutropius, *Brev.* 6.18; Florus 1.46; Josephus, *BJ* 1.179–80 and Josephus, *AJ* 14.105 and 119; Justin 42.4; Livy, *Epit.* 106; Orosius 6.13; Plutarch, *Crassus* 16–33; Plutarch, *Cicero* 36; Plutarch, *Caesar* 28; Polyaenus, *Strat.* 1994), 7.41; Festus 17; Velleius Paterculus 2.46.2; Zonaras 5.7; Zosimus 3.32.

2. Plutarch, *Pompey* 52; Velleius Paterculus 2.46.2; Livy, *Epit.* 105; Plutarch, *Crassus* 16; Appian, *Parthia* 2; G. Rawlinson, *The Sixth Great Monarchy* (New York: Publishers Plate Renting Co., 1870), chapter 11, p.84. A. Keaveney, 'The Kings and Warlords: Romano-Parthian Relations circa 64–53', *AJPh*, 103 (1982), p.427, suggests that Crassus had formed his plan to invade Parthia even before Gabinius made his assault. T. Mommsen, *The History of*

Rome, trans. W.P. Dickson (New York: Scribner's, 1903), vol. 4, p.308, believed Crassus found a Parthian war already commenced. Once the Armenians sided with Rome, that was a declaration of war on Parthia; see, however, A.N. Sherwin-White, *Roman Foreign Policy in the East, 168 BC to AD 1* (Norman, OK: University of Oklahoma Press, 1983), p.279, who says: 'the Parthians had every reason to believe that they were formally at peace with Rome'.

3. Sherwin-White, *RFPE*, p.279. Cf. F. Cumont, 'Review of Dobrias', *Syria*, 6 (1925), p.282, n.1; H. Sonnabend, *Fremdenbild und Politik* (Frankfurt: Lang, 1986), p.16. K.-H. Ziegler, *Die Beziehungen zwischen Rom und dem Partherreich* (Wiesbaden: F. Steiner, 1964) pp.36–8, follows the conclusions of Dobrias and says the Romans considered the Parthians a 'negligible quantity'.

4. The people were angered over the levying of troops for a war that was viewed as unjust, illegal and designed solely to make Crassus rich. Plutarch also says his ambition did not stop at Parthia, but he planned to carry Roman arms to Bactria, India, and the Eastern Ocean. Velleius Paterculus 2.46.2–3; Livy, *Epit.* 105; Plutarch, *Crassus* 16.3: 'a large party arose which was displeased that anyone should go out to wage war on men who had done the state no wrong, but were in treaty relations with it' (Plutarch, *Lives*, trans. Bernadotte Perrin, 11 vols [Cambridge, MA: Harvard University Press, 1958–62]); Appian *BC* 2.18 on the unfavourable omens, also implies that Crassus's intention was known before he left Rome. Florus 1.46.2: 'Both gods and men were defied by the avarice of the consul Crassus, in coveting the gold of Parthia', E.S. Forster trans., Rawlinson, *Sixth Great Monarchy*, chapter 11, p.84. Keaveney, 'Kings and Warlords', pp.412–28, pp.417ff. on motive, opportunity and pretext. A.D.H. Bivar, 'The Political History of Iran under the Arsacids', in *CHI*, vol. 3, 1: *The Seleucid, Parthian and Sasanian Period*, ed. E. Yarshater (Cambridge: Cambridge University Press, 1983), p.50, believed Crassus was intervening in a Parthian civil war on the side of Mithridates, a Roman supporter as does C. Lerouge, *L'image des parthes dans le monde gréco-romain* (Stuttgart: Franz Steiner Verlag, 2007).

5. Cicero, *Ad Fam.* 1.9.20 and 5.8; Cicero, *Ad Att.* 4.13.2; Dio 40.12 on Crassus's quest for 'glory'. Plutarch, *Crassus* 16.3 on Caesar's approval of the project. On Crassus's political motivations, see Appian, *Parthia* 2; Keaveney, 'Kings and Warlords', pp.412–28; A.M. Ward, *Marcus Crassus and the Late Roman Republic* (Columbia, MO: University of Missouri Press, 1977), p.28; and A. Garzetti, 'M. Licinio Crasso', *Athenaeum*, 22 (1944), p.33.

6. The motive given by most ancient writers was greed. Plutarch, *Crassus* 1.2.2–8, 14.4; Appian, *BC* 2.18; Velleius Paterculus 2.46.3; Florus 1.46.2; Pliny, *HN* 33.57.134: 'nor was he satisfied without getting possession of the whole of the Parthian gold' (Pliny the Elder, *Natural History*, trans. H.H. Rackham [Cambridge, MA: Harvard University Press, 1958–62]); Seneca, *Quaes. Nat.* 5.18.10. It helped to put the blame on Crassus personally and not on the failure of Roman arms. For economic motives, see P. Giles, 'Rome and the Far East in 53 BC', *PCPhS*, 1 (1929), pp.1–4; cf. D. Magie, 'Roman Policy in Armenia and Transcaucasia', *Annual Report of the American Historical Association*, 1 (1919), p.297.

7. S. Mattern, *Rome and the Enemy* (Berkeley, CA: University of California Press, 1999), pp.153–4, 186.

8. Plutarch, *Crassus* 6.4–6; Eutropius, *Brev.* 6.18; Appian, *Parthia* 2. Several years later, the censor of 50, Appius Claudius Pulcher, who was also an augur, charged Ateius with having falsified the auspices, thereby bringing a terrible calamity upon the Roman people. Some find doubtful the story that curses were a part of Ateius's opposition. See A.D. Simpson, 'The Departure of Crassus for Parthia', *TAPA*, 69 (1938), pp. 532–41, who shows how the picturesque additions to the story came about because of a confusion among the consuls Crassus Mucianus and Crassus Divers, and the tribunes Atinius and Ateius.

9. Cicero, *De. Div.* 1.16.29 says that the catastrophe at Carrhae happened because Crassus neglected the formal report of unfavourable omens. See B.A. Marshall, *Crassus: A Political Biography* (Amsterdam: A.M. Hakkert 1976), pp.150–1, for the ominous signs; Plutarch, *Crassus* 16.

10. Plutarch, *Crassus* 19; Dio 40.20; Neilson C. Debevoise, *The Political History of Parthis*, reprint edn (New York, Greenwood Press, 1968), p.80.

11. Dio 40.20; Debevoise, *Political*, p.80. See Rawlinson, *Sixth Great Monarchy*, chapter 11, p.85, n.5, on the various forms of the name.

12. He did not lack for experienced officers. His quaestor was C. Cassius Longinus, and his legates were his son Publius Crassus, Varguntius and Octavius.

13. On Crassus's ignorance of the Parthian military capabilities, see most recently Lerouge, *L'image des Parthes*, p.282.
14. Marshall, *Crassus*, pp.144–6, claims that the unrest in Parthia represented a threat to Roman interests in the area. He cites Festus 17 and Zosimus 3.23.3, both later epitomizers, both inaccurate. The fact remains that the Parthians had been pacific and were likely to remain so. Tacitus, *Germania* 37, considered them much less important as opponents than the free Germans.
15. Debevoise, *Political*, p.81; W.W. Tarn, 'Parthia', in *CAH*, 9 (1963), p.606; Rawlinson, *Sixth Great Monarchy*, chapter 11, p.85.
16. Plutarch, *Crassus* 17; cf. Appian, *Parthia* 3.
17. Plutarch, *Crassus* 17.
18. The inhabitants of Zenodotium massacred some legionaries, but the Romans stormed the town – a minor exploit for which Crassus was hailed '*imperator*'. Plutarch, *Crassus* 17; Dio 40.13; Debevoise, *Political*, p.81; Tarn, 'Parthia', p.606. On Silaces, see Dio 40.12.2.
19. Dio 40.13.4; Plutarch *Crassus* 17.4–5. Matthias Gelzer, 'Licinius', no. 68 (Crassus), *RE*, no.13, 1 (1926), cols 232, suggests that he did not have enough cavalry for anything more than reconnaissance. Cf. E.S. Gruen, 'Crassus', *AJAH*, 2 (1977), p.125; W.W. Tarn, 'The Invasion of Crassus', in *CAH*, 9, p.606; Bivar, 'Political History of Iran', p.50; Sherwin-White, *RFPE*, p.284.
20. Plutarch, *Crassus* 17.4–5; Dio 40.13.4; Rawlinson, *Sixth Great Monarchy*, chapter 11, pp.84–5.
21. On the Temple at Jerusalem, see Josephus, *BJ* 1.179 and Josephus, *AJ* 14.105; cf. Orosius 6.13.1. On Hierpolis Bambyce see Plutarch, *Crassus* 17; Mommsen, *History of Rome*, vol. 4, p.310; Sherwin-White, *RFPE*, p.281.
22. Dio 40.12.
23. Ibid., 40.16.1–2; Plutarch, *Crassus* 21 on the two generals Surenas and Silaces. Debevoise, *Political*, p.81.
24. Plutarch, *Crassus* 18.1, when he was assembling his forces from their winter quarters. Cf. Dio 40.16.1. Florus 1.46.4 says the embassy came to him at Nicephorium, which could only have been in the campaign in 54 BCE.
25. Bivar, 'Political History of Iran', p.50, sees the Roman invasion as an attempt to relieve Mithridates in Seleucia and thus put a Roman sympathizer on the throne. If this was indeed the case, it has left no record in either Parthian or Roman sources. Keaveney, 'Kings and Warlords', p.418, says Orodes was undisputed ruler by the time Crassus arrived in the East, but Crassus still hoped to topple him. Dio 40.12.1. Marshall, *Crassus*, pp.144–6, claims that unrest in Parthia represented a threat to Roman interests in the area, but did not explain how. He bases this opinion on Festus 17 and Zosimus 3.23.3, but these sources are later, abbreviated and frequently inaccurate. If they were the only sources we might have to accept them. But we have fuller and more accurate sources in Plutarch and Dio. The Parthians had been up to this time pacific. Marshall cites Appian, *Syr.* 51 in support of the idea that the Romans thought there was a threat to the area when they appointed a consular governor to Syria, but this threat came from the Arabs, not the Parthians. As long as Parthia was weak or in turmoil, it posed no threat to Rome. Preoccupation with the internal disturbances presented Parthia from indulging in international adventures, but also provided a weakened target for a predatory neighbour or at least adventurers such as Gabinius and Crassus.
26. On the superiority of Parthian intelligence see Debevoise, *Political*, p.82. Cf. Keaveney, 'Kings and Warlords', p.424.
27. On Orodes's plans, see Plutarch, *Crassus* 21.5; Dio 40.16.2. This is why he kept his own forces in Media for an advance into Armenia by the Araxes valley, and dispatched his most experienced commander, Surenus, with the expeditionary force of 10,000 men into Mesopotamia. Sherwin-White, *RFPE*, p.287; Ziegler, *Die Beziehungen zwischen Rom und dem Partherreich*, pp.322, 338.
28. Keaveney, 'Kings and Warlords', p.425.
29. Dio 40.16.1–3. Cf. Plutarch, *Crassus* 18; Appian, *Parthia* 3; Bivar, 'Political History of Iran', p.50.
30. Plutarch, *Crassus* 19.1–2. In addition to the 6,000 horsemen who accompanied him to the camp, he is said to have offered 10,000 heavy-armed cavalry and 30,000 infantry. For a discussion of the route, see Rawlinson, *Sixth Great Monarchy*, chapter 11, p.85.
31. This was not an act of betrayal as portrayed in Plutarch's account, but a necessary defensive measure. He returned to Artaxata where he was confronted by an army led by

Orodes in person, and this prevented him from sending any help to Crassus. The betrayal came later when, after the news of the Roman disaster, Artavasdes came to terms with the Parthians. On Orodes attack, see Plutarch, *Crassus* 21.5, 22.2; Dio 40.16.2; Appian, *Parthia* 3; Sherwin-White, *RFPE*, p.286 and n.40; Bivar, 'Political History of Iran', p.53.

32. We do not know the personal name of the victor at Carrhae; only his hereditary title Suren survives. See Bivar, 'Political History of Iran', pp.50–1; Rawlinson, *Sixth Great Monarchy*, chapter 11, p.89.

33. On Zeugma, its history, importance, and the current state of the site, see http://www.zeugmaweb.com/zeugma/english/engindex.htm.

34. Rawlinson, *Sixth Great Monarchy*, pp.159–60, 164; Plutarch, *Crassus* 21; Tarn, 'Invasion of Crassus', p.607; Bivar, 'Political Hisory of Iran', pp.50–1.

35. Most Roman writers, with the exception of Velleius Paterculus, 2.46, never ascribe a large force to the Parthians. Plutarch, *Crassus* 20 gives the Roman force at seven legions with 4,000 horse and as many light-armed men. This is accepted by Bivar, 'Political History of Iran', p.52; Florus 1.46.2 speaks of eleven legions; Appian, *BC* 2.3.18 says 100,000. The legions are estimated at 35,000 by Rawlinson, *Sixth Great Monarchy*, chapter 11, p.87; 30,000 by P.M. Sykes, *History of Persia* (London: Macmillan, 1969), vol. 1, p.347; and 28,000 by Tarn, 'Parthia', p.608.

36. Plutarch, *Crassus* 21.6 mentions that Surenas's baggage train included 1,000 camels. See W.W. Tarn, *Hellenistic Military and Naval Developments* (Chicago: Ares Press, 1975), pp.160–1. On the use of archers by the Parthians, see A.D.H. Bivar, 'Cavalry Equipment and Tactics on Euphrates', *DOP*, 26 (1976), pp.281–5; Bivar, 'Political History of Iran', pp.52–3.

37. Rawlinson, *Sixth Great Monarchy*, chapter 11, p.88.

38. On the compound bow, see Bivar, 'Political History of Iran', p.52.

39. Justin 41.2.8. In two critical aspects the Romans underestimated the Parthian horse-archers. Their arrows could penetrate legionary armour, a fact probably unknown to the Romans who were unfamiliar with the composite bow. It was a more powerful weapon than the lighter bows found at that time in Europe. See A.D.H. Bivar, 'A Recently Discovered Compound Bow', *Seminarium Kondrakovianum*, 9 (1937), pp.1–10. The second miscalculation was that the Parthians would run out of arrows. But the camel train of Surenas made it possible to restock. Had this not been the case, the Roman square might have held its own against the Parthian cavalry. But the heat (the battle was fought in June) and the vast distances of the Mesopotamian plain would have put any infantry at a disadvantage. The Roman means of retaliation was also ineffective. The range of their javelins was limited, and the Gallic cavalry were lacking in defensive armour. See Bivar, 'Political History of Iran', p.53.

40. Plutarch, *Crassus* 18.3–4; Appian, *Parthia* 5; A. Garzetti, 'M. Licinio Crasso', *Athenaeum*, N.S., 22–3 (1944/45), p.43, who suggests that these two incidents show Cassius was not entirely devoted to his commander and the campaign, and suggests that the lack of devotion was due to the fact that he was a political opponent. Plutarch, on the other hand, draws the picture of Cassius to contrast with the hesitation and irrationality of Crassus. F.E. Adcock, *Marcus Crassus, Millionaire* (Cambridge: Heffer, 1966), p.59, suggests that the favourable picture of Cassius derives from Plutarch's use of Q. Dellius who served under Cassius later and knew his version of the campaign.

41. In Plutarch's account the information is provided by an Arab chief, whose name is given improbably as Ariamnes. Other sources call him Achar or Abgar, and some commentaries identify him as the king of the city of Edessa (Abgar of Osrhoene). Florus 1.46 says it was a Syrian named Mazaras; Bivar, 'Politcal History of Iran', p.53.

42. Dio 40.20; Rawlinson, *Sixth Great Monarchy*, pp.162ff; Tarn, 'Invasion of Crassus', p.608, believed Abgarus innocent. Debevoise, *Political*, pp.84–5. There are other traitors mentioned in the sources. Florus talks of a Syrian exile, Mazaras, who deceived Crassus and led him into open territory. Florus 1.46.6–7; Festus 17 follows Florus's story: J.W. Eadie (ed.), *The Breviarum of Festus* (London: Athlone Press, 1967), p.132, contra Rawlinson, *Sixth Great Monarchy*, p.166.

43. Abgar had been Pompeius's friend and owed his position as a client king to Pompey's settlement. It is not likely that he would have abandoned his Roman alliance that was protection against a takeover of his kingdom by the Parthians. It is possible that he lost his kingdom after Carrhae. Had he been on the Parthian side, why was he not rewarded? See Marshall, *Crassus*, p.155; Eadie (ed.), *Breviarum of Festus*, p.132.

44. Tarn, 'Parthia', p.608, identifies the description in Plutarch, *Crassus* 22 with the road of Strabo, 16.748.
45. Plutarch, *Crassus* 22.5, B. Perrin trans. It was the terrain not the climate that was giving the Romans the problem. Sherwin-White, *RFPE*, p.288.
46. Balissus in Plutarch, *Crassus* 23.4; Tarn, 'Parthia', p.609; Bivar, 'Political History of Iran', p.53. This site is the Haran of the Old Testament and the Mari letters. It was an important provincial capital, trading city, and fortress of the Assyrian empire.
47. Plutarch, *Crassus* 20.1. Plutarch is evidently referring to the *exploratores*, i.e. cavalry sent out for a reconnaissance. The Greek is *prodromoi*.
48. Plutarch, *Crassus* 20; C. Fair, *From the Jaws of Victory* (New York: Simon & Schuster, 1971), p.36. Rawlinson rejects the idea that Crassus led his army through a trackless desert and led it hungry and thirsty into the hands of the enemy. He points out that the topographical facts contradict this story and not even the classical writers are consistent in this point. Rawlinson, *Sixth Great Monarchy*, chapter 11, p.92.
49. Plutarch, *Crassus* 23.5. Abgar and Alchaudonius deserting. Plutarch, *Crassus* 22.6. Tarn, 'Invasion of Crassus', p.609.
50. Fair, *From the Jaws of Victory*, p.36. Crassus has been blamed for not going through Armenia or for not following the ordinary Parthian road from Zeugma to Nicephorium. It really does not matter, because if his object was Seleucia, sooner or later he had to cross open ground, and it was there that Surenas, with his superior mobility, would strike. See Tarn, 'Invasion of Crassus', p.608.
51. Appian, *Parthia* 6.
52. Plutarch, *Crassus* 23.6; Dio 40.21.2; Appian, *Parthia* 7. For a description of the armour and weapons, see Rawlinson, *Sixth Great Monarchy*, chapter 11, p.90; Debevoise, *Political*, p.86. Examples of armour were found at Dura Europos, *Illustrated London News*, 2 September 1933, p.362, but this was later than the time of Crassus. On the history of scale armour, see B. Laufer, *Chinese Clay Figures, I: Prolegomena on the History of Defensive Armor* (Chicago, IL: Field Museum Anthropological Series 13, 2, 1914), pp.271ff. Scale armour was first developed in Iran and spread rapidly eastward into China. It spread more slowly westward to the Roman army. See J.W. Eadie, 'The Development of Roman Mailed Cavalry', *JRS*, 17 (1967), pp.161–73, esp. 164–5.
53. The cataphracts were probably Saka tribesmen recruited on the eastern frontier of Parthia. See Bivar, 'Political History of Iran', p.53; Debevoise, *Political*, p.86; Lerouge, *L'image des Parthes*, pp.300–3.
54. Plutarch, *Crassus* 24.4; Dio 40.22.4; M.A.R. College, *The Parthians* (New York: Praeger, 1967), p.40; J.C. Coulston, 'Roman, Parthian and Sassanian Tactical Developments', in P. Freeman and D.L. Kennedy (eds), *The Defence of the Roman and Byzantine East: Proceedings of a Colloquium held at the University of Sheffield in April 1986*, British Institute of Archaeology at Ankara Monograph no. 8 (Oxford: British Archaeological Reports, International Series, 297, 1986), vol. 1, pp.59–75.
55. Plutarch, *Crassus* 25.2–5; Dio 40.12–13; Florus 1.46.10; Tarn, 'Invasion of Crassus', p.610, Debevoise, *Political*, p.88; Fair, *From the Jaws of Victory*, p.41; Bivar, 'Political History of Iran', p.54.
56. Mommsen, *History of Rome*, vol. 4, p.315.
57. Plutarch, *Crassus* 26; Dio 40.21.2–3; Florus 1.46.10; Appian, *Parthia* 11; Bivar, 'Political History of Iran', p.54–5; Tarn, 'Parthia', p.610.
58. Plutarch, *Crassus* 29.2–6; Appian, *Parthia* 11; Tarn, 'Parthia', pp.610–11; Bivar, 'Political History of Iran', p.55.
59. Plutarch, *Crassus* 23–6; Debevoise, *Political*, p.90; Tarn, 'Parthia', pp.610–11.
60. Note that both the expeditions of Crassus and Antony against Parthia went wrong because they took huge armies through unfamiliar territory without adequate preparation. B. Isaac, *The Limits of Empire: The Roman Army in the East* (Oxford: Clarendon Press, 1992), p.403, and more recently Mattern, *Rome and the Enemy*, pp.66–9; Fair, *From the Jaws of Victory*, p.40.
61. Plutarch, *Crassus* 30.1–5 says Surenas rode up to Crassus and made the invitation personally. Dio 40.26.1–4 says he sent an invitation to him. Dio also says that Crassus agreed to the parley out of anxiety for his men. Florus 1.46.9; Dio 40.26.2–27.2; Livy, *Periochae* 106; Orosius 6.13.4; Tarn believes he saw the trick. Tarn, 'Parthia', p.611; Bivar, 'Political History of Iran', p.55; Fair, *From the Jaws of Victory*, p.41.

62. Plutarch, *Crassus* 30.2; Dio 40.26 says that Crassus trusted Surenas without hesitation.
63. Debevoise, *Political*, p.92; it is said one of the supposedly 'unarmed' Romans struck the first blow. The whole incident could have been a tragic misunderstanding. It was even uncertain whether Crassus was killed by a Parthian or had one of his own men kill him. Plutarch has him killed by a Parthian named Pomaxaethres, but also confesses that the exact truth was unknown. Dio 40.27 gives both accounts.
64. Lucan, *de Bell. Civ.* 8.436ff; Strabo 16.1.23.
65. Pliny, *HN* 6.47; Rawlinson, *Sixth Great Monarchy*, pp. 96–7.
66. Pliny, *HN* 6.47.
67. Plutarch, *Crassus* 31.6–7; 32.1–2; Florus 46.10; Appian, *Parthia* 12; Some say his body was left unburied. Seneca, *Controversiae* 2.1.7; Lucan, *de Bell. Civ.*, 8.394ff; see Valerius Maximus 1.6.11 for the prodigies. Ovid, *Ars Ama.* 1.180 says both the Crassi were buried. Plutarch, *Crassus* 33 contains the melodramatic (and unlikely) story that Crassus's head was thrown on stage during a performance of Euripides's *Bacchae* being performed at the marriage feast of Orodes's son Pacorus and the sister of the Armenian King Artavasdes.
68. Dio 40.27.3. Note that the same story was told of the Roman governor of Asia Minor, Manius Aquillius (d. 89/88 BC), at the start of the First Mithridatic War: see Appian, *Mith.* 7, 19, 21; Livy, *Epit.* 77; Velleius Paterculus 2.18; Cicero, *Pro Lege Manilia* 5.
69. Fair, *From the Jaws of Victory*, pp.42–3.
70. Rawlinson, *Sixth Great Monarchy*, chapter 11, p.98.
71. See Keaveney, 'Kings and Warlords', p.427.
72. T.J. Cadoux, 'Marcus Crassus: A Revaluation', *G&R*, 3 (1956), p.160.
73. A few years after Carrhae it was shared by Cicero, *Letters to His Friends* 9.25.1. See Eadie, 'Development of Roman Mailed Cavalry', p.164, who points out that the Parthian feint and the Roman tactical mistakes, not the technological superiority of the Parthian cataphracts, defeated the Romans. Cf. E. Gabba, 'Sulle influenza reciproche degli ordinamenti militari dei Parti e dei Romani', in *La Persia e il mondo greco-romano (Per la storia dell'escercito Romana in età imperiale* (Bologna: Patron, 1974), pp.7–42, esp. 14–15; Bivar, 'Political History of Iran', p.55. On the armaments and tactics of the Parthians, see Lerouge, *L'image des Parthes*, pp.285–8; S. Shabazi, 'Army I. Pre-Islamic Iran', in *Encyclopedia Iranica* (London and New York: Center for Iranian Studies, 1987), vol. 2, pp.489–9.
74. Tarn, *Hellenistic and Naval Developments*, p.91.
75. Julius Africanus is one of the lone sources who openly questions Rome's military superiority to Parthia, a view shared by Dio 40.14.3 and Justin 41.1.7. See E.L. Wheeler, 'Why the Romans Can't Defeat the Parthians: Julius Africanus and the Strategy of Magic', in W. Groenman-van Waateringe, B.L. van Beek, W.J.H. Willems, and S.L. Wynia (eds), *Roman Frontier Studies, 1995* (Oxford: Oxbow Monograph 91, 1997), p.576.
76. Plutarch, *Crassus* 33.
77. Shabazi, 'Army I. Pre-Islamic Iran', pp.489–9 and Lerouge, *L'image des Parthes*, pp.288–95.
78. Eadie, 'Development of Roman Mailed Cavalry', p.164. Julius Caesar, a few years before Carrhae, had added Gallic and German *equites* together with Cretan and Numidian archers to his legions in Gaul. In the civil war he introduced mixed units of *equites* and *antesigniani* (elite infantrymen) that were employed against Pompey's cavalry. Caesar's successors, however, abandoned the *antesigniani* and relied exclusively on auxiliary *equites* to repel cavalry attacks. Cf. R. Ghirshman, *Iran from the Earliest Times to the Islamic Conquest* (London: Penguin Books, 1954), p.252; Wheeler, 'Why the Romans Can't Defeat the Parthians', pp.575–9.
79. Josephus, *AJ* 14.7.3.
80. Dio 40.14.3: '[The Parthians] finally advanced to so great glory and power as to wage war even against the Romans at that time, and ever afterward down to the present day to be considered a match for them.' Cf. Pliny, *HN* 5.88; Justin 41.1.7; Herodian 4.10.2. For its effect on the Jews see Debevoise, *Political*, pp.93–5. See also Bivar, 'Political History of Iran', p.55, and most importantly, D. Timpe, 'Die Bedeutung der Schlacht von Carrhae', *Museum Helveticum*, 19 (1962), pp.104–29.
81. Marshall, *Crassus*, pp.144–46, claimed that the unrest in Parthia represented a threat to Roman interests in the area.
82. Plutarch, *Crassus* 18.1, 31.4.
83. Lucan, *de Bell. Civ.* 1.2–12, J.D. Duff trans.
84. Plutarch, *Crassus* 30.5, B. Perrin trans.

85. Polybius 3.48; Vegetius 3.6, writing long after the time of Caesar; N.J.E. Austin and N.B. Rankov, *Exploratio: Military and Political Intelligence in the Roman World from the Second Punic War to the Battle of Adrianople* (New York and London: Routledge, 1995), p.13.

86. See R.M. Sheldon, 'The Spartacus Rebellion: A Roman Intelligence Failure?' *International Journal of Intelligence and Counterintelligence*, 6, 1 (1993), pp.69–84.

87. Debevoise, *Political*, pp.93–4; Sherwin-White, *RFPE*, p.288.

88. See M. Wisseman, *Die Parther in der Augusteichen Dichtung* (Frankfurt-am-Main: P. Lang, 1982), on the poetic tradition about the Parthians under Augustus and especially pp.128–31. See Horace, *Carmina* 1.2.21–4. In vv.50–2 he writes that Augustus will not allow the Medes to 'ride about unpunished'. In 3.2.1–6 he emphasizes the need to return to the ancient, warlike ways. In 3.5.1–12 he focuses on the humiliation of Crassus. Propertius, *Elegies* 4.1–10 and 3.5.47–8, encourages Augustus to expiate Crassus and his massacre. Cf. Lerouge, *L'image des Parthes*, pp. 44, 96–8, on the prominence of Parthia in the vision of later Romans.

89. Horace, *Carmina* 1.12.53; Mattern, *Rome and the Enemy*, p.187.

90. On Augustus's propaganda regarding the Parthian standards see E.S. Gruen, 'The Imperial Policy of Augustus', in K. Raaflaub and M. Toher (eds), *Between Republic and Empire: Interpretations of Augustus and his Principate* (Berkeley, CA: University of California Press, 1990), p.397; P. Zanker, *The Power of Images in the Age of Augustus* (Ann Arbor, MI: University of Michigan Press, 1988), pp.186–92; on the kneeling Parthian; Zanker, *Power of Images in the Age of Augustus*, pp.187–92, on the image of the defeated Parthian.

91. The fact is expressed in a remark of Strabo 11.515, who characterized the power of Parthia as a counterpoise to the power of Rome. Pompeius Trogus said that the world was now divided between Rome and Parthia: '*Parthi penes quo velut divisione orbis cum Romanis facta nunc Orientis imperium est*' (Justin 41.1.1); cf. J.G.C. Anderson, 'The Eastern Frontier under Augustus', in *CAH*, 10 (1963), pp.239–83.

92. See Ward, *Marcus Crassus*, p.280.

4

THE PARTHIAN RESPONSE

The unprovoked attack on Parthia created a rift between the two powers that would continue for the next two centuries. Parthia no longer saw its western border as safe, and the defeat of the foolhardy Crassus brought cries for revenge from the Romans. It also won recognition of Parthia as a world power equal, if not superior, to Rome.[1] A Roman army had been destroyed and the eagles of their legions now decorated Parthian temples.[2] The Parthian king, Orodes, had levered the Armenian king, Artavasdes, away from the Roman alliance. He sealed the arrangement by a marriage between his son Pacorus and the sister of the Armenian king. Parthian influences also began to grow among the Jews of Judaea who had maintained ties with their fellow Jews in Babylonia. They saw the rising power of Parthia as a possible counterbalance to Roman domination.[3]

The Roman East was devoid of troops, and the governors of the eastern provinces, Cicero, Bibulus, and Cassius, all girded, in turn, for the expected Parthian retaliation. The expected Parthian onslaught, however, never came in the form of a massive invasion. In 52 BCE a few weak bands passed the Euphrates in response to the Roman incursion, but Cassius speedily drove them back across the river.[4] The next year, a more determined effort was made. In October 51 BCE, a large Parthian army under Pacorus, son of Orodes, crossed the Euphrates and marched toward Antioch, but this too was repelled. Parthian aggression was not all that difficult to contain.[5]

CICERO'S INTELLIGENCE NETWORK

We get a unique glimpse into the events of these months because Cicero was appointed proconsular governor of Cilicia (see Map 3) from the summer of 51 BCE to the summer of 50. His frequent letters to family and friends and his dispatches to Rome allow us to piece together the events of his year waiting for the Parthian attack. He has left us his correspondence with details of what he did when faced with a possible Parthian invasion of his province. This gives us a rare inside view into the Roman intelligence process. Cicero's dispatches show how little information was provided by the Senate, and allows us to judge just how seriously he thought the danger was from Parthia. Cicero's main source of intelligence, besides local officials, was Roman allies, not his own agents or scouts. We can see from Sallust's letter to Cicero that no regular postal system existed, or Sallust would have used this instead of sending his own attendants.[6] He uses *statores* (runners) to deliver messages in his province. Once in Cilicia, he advised his brother Atticus to use the private post of the tax collectors when sending him news from Rome.[7] In letters to his friends he warns the consul and the Senate of the possible danger threatening Cilicia and Syria from the Parthians who seemed about to raid Roman territory.[8] We can track his progress as he leaves Rome and travels to Cilicia in southern Turkey.

Syria was an important frontier province now threatened with a Parthian invasion. The road to Syria lay through Cilicia which was also seriously threatened, and passed the city of Tarsus where Cicero was to be posted. Cicero's instructions gave him two tasks. The first was to keep Cappadocia friendly because the leanings of its new king, Ariobarzanes III, were unknown.[9] His other duty was to monitor the movements of the Parthians. He began gathering information even as he was travelling to his province. At Actium he received no news of Parthian movements;[10] at Tralleis he heard they were inactive.[11] He arrived in his province at Laodicea on 31 July, 51 BCE, and by 9 August reports were reaching him that the Parthians had cut up a Roman cavalry detachment.[12] Cicero's letters began warning his friends, the consuls, and the Senate of the possible danger threatening Cilicia and Syria from the Parthians who seemed about to invade Roman territory.

By the time Cicero arrived in camp at Iconium, his two legions were scattered and practically mutinous.[13] Cicero was whipping them into shape when on August 30, 51, he received a dispatch from Antiochus I of Commagene (see Map 3) informing him that Pacorus, the young son of King Orodes, supported by an experienced officer, Osaces, had reached the Euphrates boundary.[14] Most of this kind of intelligence came from Roman allies whose national interests would be endangered by an invasion from Parthians.[15]

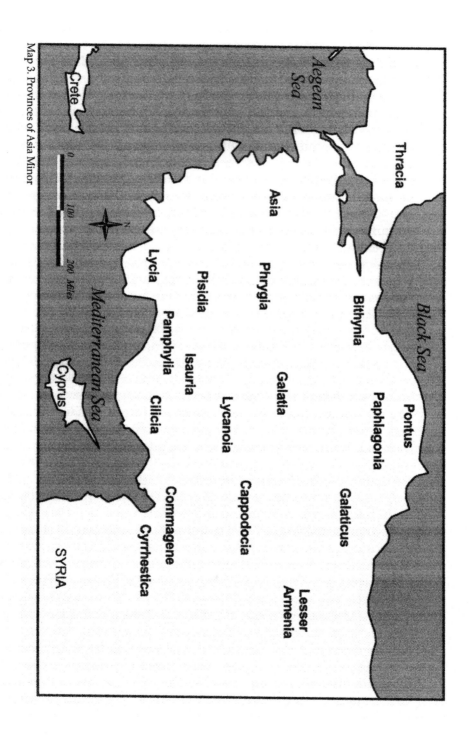

Map 3. Provinces of Asia Minor

The perception of this threat seems to have been taken much more seriously by the people on the ground than by the Roman Senate. It is rather ironic that the capital was taking very little interest in eastern affairs. They were so absorbed in the factional rivalries that would eventually destroy the Republic that they had no time for the remote problems in the East. The Senate took no steps to reinforce the army of Syria and to reassert Roman supremacy. Instead, Cassius was left to hold Syria with the battered remnants of the legions he had retrieved from the battlefield at Carrhae.[16]

The troops under Pacorus included a large detachment of Parthian cavalry and a considerable force of allies, some of whom may have been Arabs.[17] It was reported at the same time that Artavasdes of Armenia (Pacorus's brother-in-law) was also contemplating an attack on Cappadocia[18] (see Map 3). Cicero did not trust Antiochus as a source of information, and he decided to wait rather than take any rash actions, unlike his predecessor, Crassus.[19] The Parthian attack force from Syria was expected to pass through Cappadocia and strike at Cilicia. Cassius, the governor of Syria, with only the broken remains of Crassus's army, thought his force was too weak to take on a Parthian force in the open field. He contented himself with defending the towns while the Parthians overran the countryside.

Except for Deiotarus of Galatia and Ariobarzanes of Cappadocia, Rome had no allies on the Asiatic continent, according to Cicero.[20] Cappadocia was miserably weak and open to attack on the side of Armenia.[21] Had Orodes and Artavasdes acted in concert (Orodes sending his armies into Syria with Artavasdes leading the Armenian forces into Cappadocia and then into Cilicia, as he was expected to do), Roman possessions would have been in great danger.[22] The Roman provinces were not adequately supplied with Roman troops,[23] and the local inhabitants were, for the most part, disaffected and were more inclined to hail the Parthians as brethren and deliverers.[24]

Cicero advanced his legions into Cappadocia to a point where he could meet the expected attack. Information came in from the chief Roman ally in the region beyond the Taurus, Tarcondimotus, telling him Pacorus had crossed the Euphrates and camped at Tyba.[25] Cassius, meanwhile, shut himself up in Antioch and allowed the Parthian cavalry to pass him by, and even pass beyond the bounds of Syria into Cilicia.[26]

In spite of the panic these moves caused in the Romans, the

Parthians seem scarcely to have understood the situation of their adversaries, or to have been aware of their own advantages. Instead of spreading themselves wide, raising the natives, and leaving them to blockade the towns while they engaged the Romans in the open country, they instead engaged in the siege and blockade of cities which, for the most part, they were wholly unequipped to do. They confined themselves almost completely to the Orontes valley.[27]

A serious uprising, probably instigated by the pro-Parthian party, broke out in Syria in August. This news was supplied by Jamblichus, son of the Samsiceramus of Emesa, leader of the Arab allies. Cicero advanced to a camp near Cybistra at the foot of the Taurus, where he remained for five days. This position commanded the Cilician Gates, and was a point from which he could both block the Parthians and keep an eye on Artavasdes of Armenia, but he needed more manpower to do the job.[28] He sent a dispatch to the Senate, in which he explained his current actions and informed them of the military weakness of his army and the need for rapid reinforcement of the armies in Cilicia and Syria, since the Roman forces in the province were scarcely sufficient to maintain domestic order.[29] Rome's allies, Jamblichus, Tarcondimotus and Deiotarus, remained faithful, but Cicero wrote that only Deiotarus had dependable troops.[30] The native population, suffering from the greed and oppression of Roman governors, was only too ready to welcome the Parthians.[31]

By 20 September 51 BCE, Cicero heard that a substantial Parthian force under the young Prince Pacorus, supported by the veteran general Osaces, had made their way across the Euphrates and were raiding the suburbs and villas of Antioch. Cassius, with all of his troops, found himself surrounded in Antioch.[32] There was no news of the whereabouts of M. Calpurnius Bibulus, the next governor of Syria, who was on his way from Rome.[33] Parthian patrols began to penetrate beyond the frontiers of Cilicia, and a considerable body of Parthian cavalry was annihilated by squadrons of Roman horse and a praetorian cohort on garrison duty at Epiphanea.[34] Once Cicero learned that the Parthian offensive was directed at northern Syria, he marched through the Cilician Gates with the double purpose of holding the Amanus pass and giving any possible support to Cassius, since Bibulus had not yet arrived. Cicero proceeded by forced march through the Taurus and arrived in Tarsus on 5 October 51 BCE.[35]

While the Parthians moved on to Antigonea, the Romans showed that they could use irregular warfare as well as the Parthians, and set ambushes along the road.[36] They feigned a retreat with a small body of men, then turned to pursue their attackers. This was the same tactic that had been used to trap and kill Crassus's son. This time it was Osaces who was killed.[37] Cassius reported the victory to the Senate in the dispatch dated 7 October 51 BCE.[38] In his camp on 8 October, Cicero wrote to Appius Claudius Pulcher, the governor of Cilicia whom he had to succeed, about the Parthians. Cicero did not think that there were really Parthians present, but Arabs partially equipped as Parthians.[39] Cassius remained in Syria until M. Calpurnius Bibulus arrived to replace him.

The Parthians withdrew from the neighbourhood of the Syrian capital after his defeat and soon afterwards the Romans went into winter quarters in Cyrrhestica, or the part of Syria east of Amanus between Antioch and the Euphrates.[40] They remained here during the winter months guarding the Euphrates crossings. Cicero was led by his informants to expect a renewal of the invasion in the summer of 50.[41] He still took the threat of invasion seriously enough to place garrisons in the westernmost Anatolian cities such as Apamea. He himself remained in Laodicea, taking care of the civil administration there, and did not return to his military bases until early May, arriving in Tarsus a month later. There he remained at an unnamed camp, inactive but ready to support Bibulus in Syria until the emergency was over.[42]

THE GREAT PARTHIAN 'THREAT'

The Parthian army went back over the Euphrates in the summer of 50, and the 'great Parthian invasion' that Cicero had expected never materialized. By the middle of July Cicero felt that the Parthian danger had passed and that he could safely leave for Rome, now that his proconsulship was over.[43] Both Roman commanders, followed by Roman, Greek and modern historians, have misunderstood the Parthian tactics. No invasion was intended. These were merely cavalry raids made by comparatively small forces of swiftly moving horsemen whose object was not conquest, for which their numbers and equipment were inadequate.[44] They were after booty and the destruction of enemy property. This interpretation explains why they attacked the rich area around Antioch and not Cappadocia. It was an easy matter to cross the Euphrates, avoid contact with the small garrisons in the cities and descend upon the rich villages and suburbs of Antioch. Cassius shut himself up in the walled portion of the city and remained there until the Parthians left. Even Cicero admits that the Parthians probably left because they were finished plundering, not because of any action taken by the Roman troops.[45]

The garrisons in Apamea and elsewhere were withdrawn, an action that caused some criticism. Pacorus was allowed to live and later became one of Parthia's most capable generals. It is not known why the Parthians remained inactive during the next ten years. Perhaps their failure to invade Syria was due to events in the East, to internal dissensions, or to unrest among the Parthian nobility which provided the army. Perhaps there was simply no hostile intent toward the Romans or desire to take away Roman territory. Their actions seem to be geared toward keeping their borders safe. Orodes found it more profitable to foster civil war among the Romans than to pay for a full-scale invasion. Pompey eventually sent L. Hirtius as ambassador to Orodes.[46] The king offered an alliance provided that he receive the province of Syria in return. Pompey refused.

CAESAR AND THE CIVIL WARS

The one great Roman commander who did not get caught in a land war in Parthia was Caesar, but that was not for lack of trying. He had the plans on his desk in 44 BCE when he was assassinated. He had drawn up sixteen legions and 10,000 cavalry and made them available for service. Six of those legions together with light-armed troops and cavalry wintered in Apollonia (in Greece) under the command of M. Acillius Caninus while one legion went to Syria.[47] Gold was forwarded to Asia Minor to pay expenses and large quantities of arms were prepared and gathered at Demetrias in Thessaly.[48] The expedition was to proceed to Parthia by way of Lesser Armenia[49] (see Map 3). The extensive preparations reflect the new respect in which the Romans held the Parthians. If it was meant only as a show of force and not an invasion party, this is quite a large army.[50] We have no detail about Caesar's attention to intelligence gathering, and we will never know how it would have turned out, since his death on the Ides of March in 44 BCE put an end to his plans and saved the Parthians from another unprovoked attack from the Romans. Some scholars doubt whether Caesar would have been foolish enough to get caught up in a Parthian campaign.[51] He did have some campaigning experience in the East. In 47 BCE he visited Syria and Asia Minor partly in connection with the attempt of Pharnaces, son of Mithridates, to regain the kingdom of Pontus. Pharnaces had some initial success, but then Caesar took one legion, reinforced the beaten troops and boldly attacked Pharnaces at Zela. This swift victory is best known as being announced by Caesar to the Senate with the words: '*Veni, vidi, vici.*'[52]

THE DEFECTION OF LABIENUS

The Parthians took advantage of the Roman civil war that followed Caesar's death. In late 43/early 42 BCE, Brutus and Cassius sent Quintus Labienus to solicit aid from the Parthians against Antony and Octavian. After their defeat at Philippi invalidated his mission, Labienus offered his services to the Parthians.[53] He was not a great soldier, but his services were useful to the Parthians. Under the joint command of Labienus and Pacorus, the Parthian army crossed the Euphrates in the spring of 40 BCE and invaded Syria.[54]

Antony would have normally led the Roman troops but he had been called west to protect his interests against Octavian. Syria was left to his incompetent subordinate, L. Decidius Saxa. The Parthians drove out Saxa, captured him in Cilicia, and put him to death.[55] Saxa's brother lost most of his men through desertion to Labienus through a clever propaganda campaign. Pamphlets were wrapped around arrows and shot into the Roman camp. Apamea was then taken without resistance, and the two forces divided. Labienus turned north to penetrate far into Asia Minor, and Pacorus turned south along the coast through Syria. All the cities of the coast, as far to the south as Ptolomais (Acre) admitted the Parthians with the single exception of Tyre which was invincible except by sea.[56] Pacorus had notable successes in Palestine, strengthening the already strong Parthian influence there.[57] Practically all Rome's Asiatic possessions were either in Parthian hands or were seriously threatened by them.[58] The damage to Rome was immense both in prestige and property. For a moment, the whole of the Roman East seemed to be either in Parthian hands, or on the point of capture.

The conclusion of the Roman civil war, however, allowed the Romans to reunifiy and retaliate. By 39 BCE, Antony began a new campaign against the Parthians and sent Publius Ventidius into

Anatolia to oppose Labienus. Early in 39 BCE, Ventidius and his legate Poppaedius Silo embarked for the East with eleven legions and a strong force of slingers.[59] Now that the Romans were familiar with the deadly Parthian bowmen, they knew they had to take countermeasures. There is nothing magical about the Parthian use of the bow, it just took some planning to counteract the effect of the Parthian archers. Ventidius or Antony rightly realized that the sling with leaden bullets would outrange the Parthian bows. What they did not seem to account for were the heavily armed cataphracts that had supplanted the archers of Surenas. As usual, Roman intelligence on the Parthians seems to have been a little out of date. No Parthian archers are mentioned in Ventidius's campaigns and his battles show clearly that Pacorus was relying on heavy cavalry. [60]

THE TRIUMPH OF VENTIDIUS

Ventidius shared Caesar's skill in surprise and speed. He immediately attacked Labienus after landing in Anatolia, even before Labienus knew he had arrived. Certainly this reflects an intelligence failure on Labienus's part. The suddenness of the attack terrified Labienus, who had only a small body of troops, none of them Parthian. Labienus retreated into Syria where he received Parthian reinforcements of cavalry. Ventidius, after recovering Cilicia, remained there to organize the administration of the distracted provinces.

Ventidius finally overtook Labienus and his Parthian allies on the Syria slope of the Taurus Mountains. The retreating Parthians made a stand at the Amanus Gates on the border between Syria and Cilicia (see Map 3). By combining the accounts of Dio and Frontinus, who give somewhat divergent stories, the ensuing battle can be reconstructed. Ventidius took the Amanus Pass by trickery. He sent his lieutenant Pompaedius Silo ahead with a small force to lure the Parthians from their strong position. Then, while the Parthians were in hot pursuit of the fleeing Roman cavalry, Ventidius's infantry and slingers struck the surprised Parthians from a flank ambush.[61]

Ventidius remained on high ground, but the Parthian cataphracts, because of their numbers and their scorn for the Romans, did not even bother to join forces with Labienus; rather they rode uphill at dawn, intending to destroy the Romans. Ventidius held his men back until all the Parthians were on a steep slope, then he ordered his legions to fire and charge. A sudden hail of lead from the Roman slingers threw the Parthians into confusion. Then down the incline poured the Roman legions and the rush routed the cavalry. The surviving Parthians fled not to Labienus but to Cilicia, and Labienus was killed trying to escape. Most of his forces joined Ventidius's army.[62]

By this victory Ventidius also recovered Syria without a battle, for Pacorus withdrew from the province late in 39 BCE. Ventidius continued southward through Syria and occupied Palestine without difficulty before the end of 39. His two victories had, in fact, cleared Roman Asia of Parthians almost as quickly as it had been overrun. It is illustrative of how a Roman commander, using a bit of guile and having good intelligence about the enemy, could easily defeat the Parthian forces. There was no magic involved.

Early in spring of 38, while Ventidius's legions were still in winter quarters, Pacorus gathered his army and again invaded Syria. There was, however, real cause now to fear a general uprising. Dio says the eastern cities had not yet become pacified and many of the Roman governors had mistreated their eastern subject peoples. Under adverse conditions, Ventidius acted with extreme caution, since he wanted to make his foe delay in order to win time to gather his own scattered forces.[63] To gain this time, he resorted to another stratagem. By good intelligence gathering, he knew that Prince Pharmaeus of Cyrrhestica, who pretended to be a Roman ally, was really a Parthian spy who was reporting the Roman preparations to them. Ventidius therefore used Pharmaeus to spread a bit of disinformation. He honoured Pharmaeus and confided secrets to him like a true confidant. Ventidius pretended to be afraid that the Parthians might abandon the place where they usually crossed the Euphrates near the town of Zeugma and use some other crossing farther downstream. The downstream crossing was, he said, a plain that would be very useful to the Parthian cavalry. The crossing at Zeugma, on the other hand, was over a deep stream and the terrain was hilly, affording the Roman troops protection from the Parthian archers. Pharmeaus, deceived, relayed the false information to Pacorus who acted on it. Pacorus avoided the short route by Zeugma and led his troops by the long route through Cyrrhestica (see Map 3). Furthermore, he also spent forty days gathering materials and in constructing a bridge over the Euphrates.[64]

Ventidius utilized this time to reunite his scattered forces and was ready for action in Cyrrhestica three days before the Parthians arrived. The Parthians found the crossing unopposed. The Romans did not attack as soon as this crossing was made, but remained on high ground. Pacorus and his men, having been made over-confident now, boldly attacked the fortified Roman camp near Gindarus. [65]

Ventidius did not lead out his soldiers until the Parthians were within fifty paces. Then, by a rapid advance, he came so near to the enemy that he escaped the Parthian arrows. This sudden Roman sally easily drove the attacking Parthian cavalry down the hill in confusion. At the foot of the Hill, the cataphracts made a valiant stand, but they were confused by the suddenness of the attack and stumbled over one another. They were especially harassed by the Roman slingers with their deadly leaden pellets. In the midst of this mêlée, while the heavily-armed Romans were still fighting with the cataphracts, Pacorus and his bodyguard were killed.[66] As soon as the Parthians saw their leader dead, most of them fled, although a handful fought to the death in a vain attempt to retrieve his corpse.[67] The loss of his son Pacorus proved a great shock to the aged King Orodes. With thirty sons to choose from, Orodes found it difficult to make up his mind. His selection of Phraates, the eldest of his eligible children, was unfortunate, as later events would prove.[68]

The Romans regarded Pacorus's death and the destruction of his army as a severe blow to Parthia and as a Roman victory that went far to redeem the disgrace of Carrhae.[69] The Roman tradition held that the battle was fought on the same day as the battle of Carrhae, but the claim was probably an invention to satisfy Roman patriotism. The battle was still celebrated in later poetry and prose by Ovid in the *Fasti*, Velleius Paterculus in his *History* and Tacitus in the *Germania*.[70] To writers of the first century CE, Ventidius was indeed a great military hero – a man Plutarch praised as the only Roman ever to have triumphed over the Parthians.[71] It need not have been that way. His stratagems were innovative, and his intelligence gathering good. The connection between these facts and his success should be obvious.

OF WHAT BENEFIT?

Both Rome and Parthia were expanding empires whose treaty arrangements had kept them from war during the scrambling for territory during the crumbling of the Seleucid kingdoms.[72] Crassus's bold but ultimately foolish and unsuccessful attempt to invade Parthia created a hostile situation between the two kingdoms that could have been avoided. Rome struck first, seemingly without provocation. Parthia staged raids in 52 and 51 that caused some damage and put the Romans on the defensive when Pacorus surrounded Antioch. Cassius inflicted a defeat, but a Parthian army still wintered in northern Syria and the province remained in turmoil. This was the closest the Parthians would come to taking Roman territory and, as often happened, dissension within the Parthian royal family ended the invasion, and the Parthian threat disappeared. Once Parthia and Rome were set on this hostile road, it would lead to periodic strikes and retaliations that would continue on for the next 200 years. Had Crassus not arrogantly pushed his way into Parthia, it is doubtful any of this scenario would have followed.

NOTES

1. A.D.H. Bivar, 'The Political History of Iran under the Arsacids', in *CHI*, vol. 3, 1: *The Seleucid, Parthian and Sasanian Period*, ed. E. Yarshater (Cambridge: Cambridge University Press, 1983), p.55.
2. Horace, *Epistles* 1.18.56–7 and *Odes* 4.15.6–8; N.C. Debevoise, *The Political History of Parthia* (New York: Greenwood Press, 1968), p.96.
3. An anti-Roman party took shape under Aristobulus, but their attempt to revolt was soon suppressed by the Roman governor, Cassius, who marched down from Syria.
4. Dio 40.28; G. Rawlinson, *The Sixth Oriental Monarchy* (New York: Publishers Plate Renting Co., 1870), p.100.
5. On the Parthians taking the initiative, see C. Lerouge, *L'image des Parthes dans le monde gréco-romain* (Stuttgart: Franz Steiner Verlag, 2007), pp.83–9.
6. Cicero, *Ad Fam.* 5.15, 5.16.1. Cicero mentions news from Asia being delivered by the agents of Roman financial speculators and tax farmers. Most political and military intelligence was transmitted to Rome by private letter-bearers on private expense accounts. See F. Dvornik, *The Origins of Intelligence Services* (New Brunswick, NJ: Rutgers University Press, 1974), p.78. In his letter to his brother Atticus, Cicero advises him to use the private post of the tax collectors when sending him political news of Rome (*Ad Att.* 5.15). See also his speech on 'The Appointment of Gnaeus Pompeius' (chapters 11, 12, 17) on pirates barring communications both public and private until Pompey wiped them out.
7. Cicero, *Ad Att.* 5.15. See M. Beard, *The Roman Triumph* (Cambridge, MA: Harvard University Press, 2007), p.203, on the use of 'laurelled letters'.
8. Cicero, *Ad Fam.* 15.1. It is generally assumed that Pompey's annexation of Syria as a Roman province in 64 BCE represented the first official step by which Rome gained control of Syria. Some think the annexation had been preceded by an attempt to turn what was left of the Seleucid realm into a client kingdom. See J.M. Cobban, *Senate and the Provinces 78–49 BC* (Cambridge: Cambridge University Press, 1935), pp.135–6, and G. Downey, 'The Occupation of Syria by the Romans', *TAPA*, 82 (1951), p.149, who updates the evidence and recounts the occupation of Syria from 83 BCE by Tigranes of Armenia. For the coin evidence that shows when Pompey annexed Syria after the surrender of Tigranes, see H. Seyrig, 'Antiquités syrienne 42: Sur les ères de quelques villes de Syria', *Syria*, 27 (1950), pp.5–15. The ultimate reasons for the annexation of Syria have been discussed by J. Dobrias, 'Les premiers rapports des Romains avec les Parthes', *Archiv Orientalni*, 3 (1931), pp.215–56.

9. Plutarch, *Cicero* 36.1. Debevoise, *Political*, 96. Cf. Cicero, *Ad Fam.* 2.17.
10. Cicero, *Ad Att.* 5.16.
11. Ibid., 5.14, *primum otium Parthcium*.
12. Ibid., 5.16.4, *concisos equites nostros a barbaris nuntiabant*.
13. Cicero, *Ad Fam.* 15.4.2; Debevoise, *Political*, p.97; A.N. Sherwin-White, *Roman Foreign Policy in the East, 168 BC to AD 1* (Norman, OK: University of Oklahoma Press, 1984), p.291, notes that the province contained a garrison of two depleted and discontented legions, supported by even less satisfactory local militia which had been serving in Cilicia since 56 when the province became consular. Many were due for discharge and their pay was in arrears.
14. Dio 40.28; Cicero, *Ad Fam.* 15.1.1–2.
15. F. Dvornik, *Origins of Intelligence Services*, p.79.
16. Sherwin-White, *RFPE*, p.292; C. Lerouge, *L'image des Parthes*, p.85.
17. Cicero, *Ad Fam.* 15.4.7: '*magnas Parthorum copias atque Arabum*'.
18. Ibid., 15.3.1.
19. Ibid., 15.1.1–2.
20. Ibid., 15.1.
21. Ibid., 15.1.
22. Ibid., 15.3; Cicero, *Ad Att.* 5.20.
23. See the complaints of Cicero, *Ad Fam.* 15.1. Cicero himself had for his large province only two legions: *Ad Fam.* 3.6.
24. Dio 40.28.
25. Cic. *Ad Fam.* 15.1.2. Debevoise, *Political*, p.98. On Tarcondimotus, see *RE*, *s.v.* col. 2297–8. On the location of Tyba (possibly Ain Deba) see 'Syria', in *RE*, col. 1624.
26. Cicero, *Ad Fam.* 15.4 tells us that his cavalry defeated a Parthian detachment within the limits of Cilicia.
27. Dio 40.29.
28. Cicero, *Ad Fam.* 15.2.1–2.
29. Ibid., 15.1.3–5; cf. the letter from Caelius in Rome, *Ad Fam.* 8.5.1; Sherwin-White, *RFPE*, p.293.
30. Cicero, *Ad Fam.* 15.1.2 and 6; *Ad Att.* 5.18.1–8. Deiotarus received praise from the Senate for his loyalty. Lucan, *de. Bell. Civ.* 5.54ff. and Cicero, *pro rege Deiotaro* 1.2. Debevoise, *Political*, p.99; Sherwin-White, *RFPE*, p.293.
31. Dio 40.28; Cicero, *Ad Fam.* 15.1.5; Dvornik, *Origins of Intelligence Services*, p.79, on Rome's allies.
32. Cicero, *Ad Att.* 5.18.1. On the passage through Commagene, see the letter from Caelius in Cicero *Ad Fam.* 8.10.1; see also Dio 40.29; Cicero, *Ad Att.* 5.20.3.
33. Bibulus, became governor of Syria in 51 BCE and succeeded Cassius. While governor, he would turn to diplomacy rather than arms in an attempt to stave off this invasion. He plotted with Ornodapates, a satrap hostile to Orodes, to put Pacorus on the throne, but word of the conspiracy reached Orodes and Pacorus was recalled. Pacorus felt he had no option but to obey. See Dio 40.30.
34. Cicero, *Ad Fam.* 15.4.7; 'Epiphaneia', in *RE*, no. 2, col. 192.
35. Cicero *Ad Att.* 5.20.2.
36. On the ambush, see Dio 40.29.3. On Antigonea, see Malalas 8; Strabo 16.2.4; 'Antigoneia', in *RE*, no. 1, col. 2404; R.J. Braidwood, *Mounds in the Plain of Antioch* (Chicago, IL: University of Chicago Press, 1937), p.38, n. 2; Debevoise, *Political*, p.101. P.M. Sykes, *History of Persia* (London: Macmillan, 1951), vol. 1, p.352, says he 'played Parthian tactics', as if an ambush could only be an eastern tactic.
37. Cicero, *Ad Att.* 5.20.3–4, who says he was mortally wounded and died later; cf. Dio 40.29.3, who states that he was killed in the fighting. On the victory, see also Frontinus, *Strat.*, 2.5.35. Cicero, *Ad Fam.* 2.10.
38. Cicero, *Ad Att.* 5.21.2; Dio 40.29.
39. Cicero, *Ad Fam.* 3.8.10.
40. Cicero, *Ad Att.* 5.21; 6.1.
41. Ibid., 5.21; cf. ibid., 6.1; Cicero, *Epi. ad Div.* 2.10.
42. Sherwin-White, *RFPE*, p.294.
43. Bivar, 'Political History of Iran', p.56.
44. Ibid., p.56.

45. Cicero, *Epi. ad Att.* 5.21.2.
46. Caesar, BC 3.82; Dio 41.55; Lucan, *de Bell. Civ.* 2.633, 637ff.
47. Appian, BC 3.24; Dio 45.3.
48. Plutarch, *Brutus* 25.
49. Suetonius, *Div. Jul.* 44; Plutarch, *Caesar* 58.
50. Dio 44.15; Appian, *BC* 2.110; Plutarch, *Caesar* 60; Cicero, *de Div* 2.54; Suetonius, *Div. Jul.* 79, all of whom repeat the story that the Sibyl reported that the Parthians could only be defeated by a king. This is obviously propaganda, but it shows in what respect the Parthians were held by the Romans. On the change of perspective, see D. Timpe, 'Die Bedeutung der Schlacht von Carrhae,' *Museum Helveticum*, 19 (1962), pp.104–29; Some modern historians believe Caesar was not planning an invasion of Parthia but simply wanted to conduct a show of force along the Euphrates. See, for example, J. Malitz, 'Caesars Partherkrieg', *Historia*, 33 (1984), pp.21–59, and W.C. McDermott, 'Caesar's Projected Dacian-Parthian Expedition', *Ancient Society*, 13/14 (1982/1983), pp.223–31.
51. Sykes, *History of Persia*, vol. 1, p.355, believes Caesar would have won. His assassination was, in fact, connected to his Parthian campaign. They wanted Caesar dead before he could leave Rome on an extended tour or, worse, return as an even bigger war hero. Cf. P.A. Brunt, 'Roman Imperial Illusions,' in P.A. Brunt, *Roman Imperial Themes* (Oxford: Clarendon Press, 1990), pp.450–1.
52. Sykes, *History of Persia*, vol. 1, p.355. Pharnaces's illegitimate brother, with Rome's support, succeeded to the throne.
53. Not only did Romans fight with Parthians, but a Parthian force fought with Cassius at Philippi. It was the only appearance of a Parthian force in Europe. Sykes, *History of Persia*, vol. 1, p.357; Bivar, 'Political History of Iran', p.57.
54. Anderson, in *CAH*, 10, 2.4 (1963), p.47, calls the invasion of Syria in 40 BCE little more than a raid. Cf. K. Butcher, *Roman Syria and the Near East* (Los Angeles, CA: Getty Publications, 2003), p.37.
55. It was Labienus who killed Saxa in a second battle. Velleius Paterculus 2.78.1; Plutarch, *Antony* 30.1; Dio 48.24.4–25.4; Florus 2.19.3–4; Justin 42.4; Livy, *Periochae* 127; Festus 18; Rawlinson, *Sixth Great Monarchy*, p.106; Sykes, *History of Persia*, vol. 1, p.357.
56. Bivar, 'Political History of Iran', p.57.
57. The rapidity with which Malchus, king of the Nabataean Arabs, obeyed Parthia orders to expel Herod from their territory is a good example. Josephus, *BJ* 1.276; *AJ* 14.370–5.
58. Pacorus ruled jointly with his father and he struck coins which may point to his intention to hold Syria permanently. Anderson, *CAH*, 10, 2.4, p.48.
59. Dio 48.39; Plutarch, *Antony* 33.
60. Sources for the Parthian campaign of Ventidius are numerous. Dio 48.41ff. and 49.19–22; Josephus, *AJ* 14.394ff. and *BJ* 1.288–292; Appian, *BC* 5.65 ff; Aulus Gellius, *The Attic Nights of Aulus Gellius*, with English translation by John C. Rolfe (Cambridge, MA: Harvard University Press, 1978–84), 15.4; Aurelius Victor, *de vir. ill.* 85; Eutropius, *Brev.* 7.5; Florus 1.29ff; Frontinus, *Strat.* 1.1.6 and 2.5.36; Tacitus, *Germania* 37; Justin 42.4.7–11; Juvenal, *Sat.* 7.199; Livy, *Epit.* 127; Orosius 6.18.23; Pliny, *HN* 7.135; Plutarch, *Antony* 33ff; Festus 18; Strabo 12.2.11; 14.2.24 and 16.2.8; Valerius Maximus 6.9.9; Velleius Paterculus 2.78; Zonaras 10.18 and 22ff. Plutarch derived information on Antony from Quintus Dellius. It is doubtful whether Dellius covered the campaign of Ventidius. See O. Hirschfeld, 'Dellius ou Sallustius?' in *Mélanges Boissier* (Paris: Albert Fontemoing, 1903), pp.293–5.
61. Dio 48.41ff; Frontinus, *Strat.* 2.5.37; Plutarch, *Antony* 33; Zonaras 10.23. The exact site is uncertain, but it has been suggested that the scene was 'north of the Taurus watershed' because the defeated Parthians retreated 'not towards Labienus, but *into* Cilicia'. Sherwin-White, *RFPE*, p.303, n.16.
62. Dio 48.39.1ff; Strabo 14.2.24; Debevoise, *Political*, p.115; Rawlinson, *Sixth Great Monarchy*, chapter 12, p.107.
63. Dio 48.24ff. and 49.19, 20.
64. Ibid., 49.20ff.
65. Bivar, 'Political History of Iran', p.58.
66. Eutropius, *Brev.* 7.5; Bivar, 'Political History of Iran, p.58.
67. Strabo 16.2; Dio 49.20.3; Frontinus, *Strat.* 2.2.5; Florus 2.19.6; Josephus, *BJ* 1.317. A slightly different version is given in Justin 42.4.7–10. Cf. Strabo 16.2.8 (751) for the battle site. W.W. Tarn, 'The Parthian Invasion', in *CAH*, 9 (1963), pp.47–50, believed Ventidius could

defeat the Parthians because Orodes relied solely on his cataphracts and retained the
archers at home. Sherwin-White, *RFPE*, p.305, disagrees.

68. Justin 42.4.11–16; Dio 49.23; Debevoise, *Political*, p.120.
69. Dio 49.20; Florus 2.19; Plutarch, *Antony* 34.3; Arrian, *Parthica* fr.25; Strabo 16.2.8; Festus 18.1; Eutropius, *Brev.* 7.5, who says the battle was fought on the same day as Carrhae. Bivar, 'Political History of Iran', p.58.
70. Ovid, *Fasti*, 12 May; Velleius Paterculus 2.78; Tacitus, *Germania* 37.4–5.
71. Plutarch, *Antony* 34.1–2; Dio 49.19.1–20; Tacitus, *Histories* 5.9; Florus 2.19.7; Eutropius, *Brev.* 7.5.2; Orosius 6.18.23. Cf. J.E. Seaver, 'Publius Ventidius – Neglected Roman Military Hero,' *CJ*, 47 (1951–52), pp. 275–80.
72. On the crumbling of the Seleucid kingdoms and Rome's annexation of Syria, see Butcher, *Roman Syria*, pp.19–31.

THE CAMPAIGNS OF ANTONY[1]

Mark Antony became the heir not only to Caesar's papers (and therefore his intelligence on Parthia), but he also inherited the idea of a Parthian campaign. He was already considering an attack on Parthia when he passed through Asia Minor after the battle of Philippi.[2] It was the accession of a new Parthian king, however, that finally handed him the opportunity. In the end, his movements would become much more complex and confused than those implied by Caesar's plan.[3]

Phraates IV came to power shortly before 37 BCE and had his father put to death.[4] He then exiled his brother together with a large number of Parthian nobles including military men from the recent war.[5] One of these soldiers, Monaeses, went to Rome and promised Antony that he would lead the Roman army and win over much of Parthia.[6] Induced by this promise, Antony prepared for war against the Parthians. He epitomized the Roman military attitude that the eastern boundary must be secured and that an able Roman general could triumph over any oriental barbarian.[7] For Phraates, the expedition of Antony was a major threat to his empire as well as his personal position.[8] In 36 BCE Phraates had only been king for a year and the immediate background to his accession had been the defeat and ejection of Parthian armies from Syria. Phraates, through his agents, persuaded Monaeses to return to Parthia. Antony did not try to stop Monaeses and even sent envoys along to request the return of the standards and any survivors captured from Crassus in 53 BCE.[9] He probably also assumed Monaeses would mislead the Parthians as to the Roman plans. Some commentators, however, maintain that Monaeses was a double agent and had been acting in the Parthian interest all along and was reporting to Phraates all the details of the Roman military preparations.[10] While these negotiations were underway, Antony continued to prepare for war and especially to secure allies who could supply cavalry. His most powerful ally in this regard was Artavasdes of Armenia.[11]

Antony headed one of the largest armies ever to undertake operations against the Parthians. It was estimated at around sixteen legions – more than double that of Crassus's ill-fated force. He was a good cavalry leader but he had never planned a major campaign before. What kind of intelligence did he have? He had Caesar's papers and could claim to be carrying out Caesar's plans. Certainly he knew that Crassus's error in crossing the deserts and open steppes had to be avoided.[12] After securing Anatolia behind him, he wasted no time in occupying Armenia in the early spring and then pressed towards Media Atropatene (see Map 2). His goal was to lay siege to the capital so he pressed forward, leaving his siege train and baggage wagons to follow. He was impatient to realize his dream of eastern conquest but the impression left by Crassus after the battle of Carrhae meant that he no longer found it easy to win allies among the Armenians, the Medes, or the people of Elymais who hesitated to betray their own common cause.[13] And with Asia closing its ranks, the Armenians could not well hold aloof for long. For this reason alone Antony had failed before he started. Caesar would never have left an uncertain but powerful ally between himself and his base; even Crassus had been wise enough not to do that.

ANTONY'S FIRST CAMPAIGN

In late April or early May, Antony advanced to the Euphrates with about 100,000 men.[14] It seems that his original intention was to cross the Euphrates into Mesopotamia and advance almost exactly in the footsteps of Crassus.[15] The whole area was strongly garrisoned by the Parthians, however, so Artavasdes, King of Armenia, advised Antony to attack Media Atropatene instead while their king and all of his troops were with the Parthians on the Euphrates. Since he needed the cavalry that would be furnished by his northern allies, he turned up the Euphrates to Zeugma[16] (see Map 4). He marched up the Euphrates to Carana (near modern Erzerum) where Artavasdes joined him with a force of 6,000 armoured cavalry and 7,000 foot soldiers.[17]

The guide who had led the Romans northward from Zeugma to the border, and also the king of Media Atropatene himself (also named Artavasdes), would later stand accused of being Parthian agents.[18] The charge may have been intended to shift the blame for the defeat that followed. The Romans frequently blamed their guides for misleading them and being enemy agents, and they loved accusing easterners of sneakiness. But whose responsibility was it to judge the bona fides of the guides? The failure to investigate these guides definitely implies that active counterintelligence was not a recognized duty of Roman commanders. In reality, the problem was that Antony was marching blind. He had no idea where the Parthian army might be, while Monaeses had accurate information about Roman movements. This seems to confirm that Artavasdes had an understanding with Phraates.[19]

As he approached Praaspa, the capital city of Media Atropatene,[20] Antony proceeded with only cavalry and infantry and left the slow-moving baggage train behind including 300 wagons, all the beasts of burden, and the siege engines.[21] The main Parthian force, under the personal command of King Phraates himself, was scouting his movements. With their excellent intelligence they were also able to keep their own whereabouts secret until the last moment. They attacked the Roman baggage train with their light cavalry, overcame its escort, and plundered and burnt the siege engines. Artavasdes of Armenia, whose troops formed the greater part of the escort, deserted just before the battle, which might account for the completeness of the Roman defeat.[22] The two legions were annihilated and their eagles added to the Parthian collection. All their food was burnt or carried off and thus Antony found himself in mid-August helpless before Praaspa, a strong fortress that was well garrisoned and provisioned. Deprived of his siege engines and supplies, Antony could not take the strong and stoutly defended city.[23] Then more bad news arrived. The Roman commander with the rear force, Oppius Statianus, was caught off guard, surrounded by enemy cavalry, and was killed together with all 10,000 of his men.[24] Antony rushed back to the scene with reinforcements but found only 10,000 corpses.[25]

Antony, being too proud to retreat, threw up a mound against the city wall, but the machines he improvised for the siege were useless. His attacks were repulsed. His army soon ate up all the food in the neighbourhood, and when foraging parties were sent out, they were ambushed by Parthians squadrons.

To restore the spirit of the legionaries, Antony led out his main force of ten infantry legions to offer battle to the Parthians. By a skilful manoeuvre, the Roman commander marched his infantry back across the Parthian front, where the horse archers were in a crescent. The Parthians were impressed by the discipline and silence

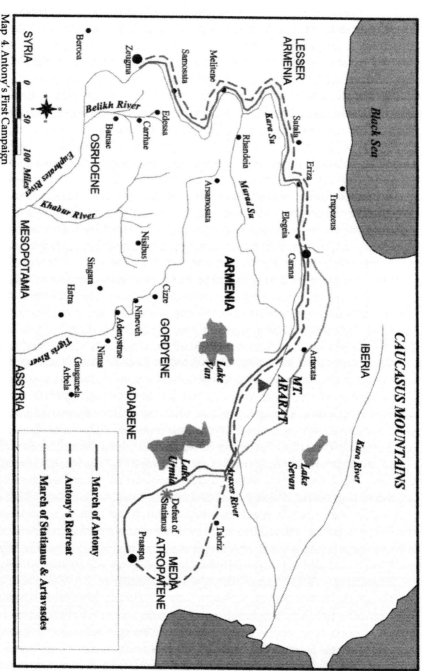

Map 4. Antony's First Campaign

of the Roman troops as they passed at regular intervals. They interpreted the display as a retreat, not an attack. Then the Gallic cavalry came on at full speed, and as soon as the attention of the Parthians had been diverted in their direction, the legionaries also charged and engaged at close quarters. The Parthian cavalry was put to flight. The legionaries maintained the pursuit for a distance of five miles, and the Gallic cavalry kept it up for nearly fifteen. Yet, when the Romans came to count the Parthian losses, they found that no more than eighty Parthians had been killed and thirty captured.[26] This damage was trivial compared with what had happened to them in the previous encounter. On the following day they marched back to Praaspa. The Parthian horse-archers had regrouped to harry them, and it was only with great difficulty that the retreat was finally accomplished.[27]

As the siege dragged on, Antony was in a difficult position. To obtain food he sent out foraging parties, but the Parthians massacred small ones and large parties reduced the strength of the besiegers.[28] Whenever the siege lines were weakened in this way, the defenders of Praaspa made successful sorties to destroy the siege works. The legionaries, though protected by slingers, took the brunt of the attack from the Parthian archers and their run-and-fight tactics. An eyewitness remarked that, in these skirmishes, the Romans lost many men when they were victorious, even more when they were defeated.[29] When the defenders made a successful sally and put the Romans to flight, Antony used an outdated punishment, decimation, to punish his men for cowardice, and he fed the rest on barley.[30]

The Parthians and their allies followed him closely, impeded his movements and cut off his stragglers, but carefully avoided engaging him in a pitched battle. If he could have forced the city to surrender, he would have been able to go into winter quarters in the city and remain in comparative safety until the spring when he could renew his campaign. But now he was in no position to do anything but negotiate a safe exit. Antony made one last attempt to secure the lost standards and captives before ending the siege, but negotiations proved abortive and the Parthians remained derisive.[31] With the winter advancing, Antony made the decision to retreat. No doubt the Parthian king was also anxious that the onset of the Azerbaijan winter would mean his feudal levies would return to a warmer climate and he would be left without adequate troops to sustain the campaign. As good a public speaker as Antony was, he assigned Domitius Ahenobarbus the task of telling the men they would be retreating. Many of them were incensed at having to leave without a victory, but the rest accepted the fact that it was their only recourse.

Phraates expected the Romans to return by the same route by which they had come, but a friendly Mardian advised Antony to follow the hills and thus to hamper the Parthian archers rather than to cross the open, treeless plain.[32] The hill route was reportedly better provisioned and had the additional advantage of passing through many villages. Antony took the route suggested by his Mardian guide. Showing some inkling of the importance of counterintelligence, Antony must have questioned the fidelity of this guide. He made the Mardian pledge his good faith. The Mardian, in turn, offered to let himself be put in fetters until he brought the army safely to Armenia. This seems to have convinced Antony.

For two days all went well. On the third day, however, when he relaxed his guard and was marching in open order, he reached a point where the road was flooded by a recently breached dike. Warned by his Mardian guide that this was the work of the Parthians, Antony ordered his men into battle array. These orders were scarcely executed when enemy cavalry enveloped the Romans. Charges by light-armed troops simply caused the Parthians to withdraw momentarily, but Antony's Celtic horsemen were able to attack more effectively. Having thus learned what he needed to do, Antony adopted a formation consisting of a hollow square whose flanks were covered by slingers and javelin-throwers, while horsemen broke up the Parthian attacks with charges. The column proceeded slowly forward in this manner.[33] He gave orders to his horsemen to rout the enemy if they attacked but not to pursue them any further. Because of this change in tactics, the Parthians suffered greater loss than they inflicted when they attacked. This made them less eager to attack the Roman column.

On the fifth day, Flavius Gallus asked for some of the light-armed troops from the rear. When the usual Parthian attack came he used these troops to press toward the enemy rather than drawing the Parthians back toward the legionaries, contrary to Antony's orders. The leaders of the rearguard, seeing that he was being cut off from them, tried to call him back, but he refused. Titius, the quaestor, tried to grab hold of the unit's standards and lead the men back, heaping abuse on Gallus for wasting the lives of so many good men. Gallus kept his men together and attacked the enemy but after only a few moments he found himself surrounded. He sent for aid, but Canidius made the mistake of sending a small force to help rather than wheel around the entire army to attack the enemy. The small detachment was cut to pieces. Antony arrived with the III Legion trying to push his way through the fugitives and rescue the survivors, but not before 3,000 Romans had been killed with another 5,000 wounded.[34]

The Parthians, although tired, were so elated by their victory, that they bivouacked for the night near the Romans, expecting to plunder the rearguard again. At daybreak they gathered for an attack in far greater numbers than ever before. Forty thousand horsemen were joined by the king's personal guard, although Phraates himself was not present.[35] Antony harangued the troops, who even offered themselves up for decimation if they failed him. On the sixth day, 40,000 Parthians tried to destroy Antony's forces, but the legions rallied and met the attack by forming a *testudo*.[36]

The Parthians, seeing the wall of shields, supposed that the Romans were giving up the struggle. They dismounted and charged on foot. When they were within a short distance, the legionaries met them with their short swords and cut the front ranks to pieces. They put the remainder of the Parthians to flight and then continued their weary retreat. Much of the suffering on the retreat came from the weather: blinding snow and driving sleet. They not only lacked provisions, but the Romans had abandoned their mills with the baggage train, and the little amount of grain that they had was difficult to grind. Many of the beasts of burden had died, and the ones remaining had to carry the sick and wounded. The wild plants they tried to eat made them sick or even resulted in derangement and death.[37]

The Parthians continued to follow the Romans, but did not attack. Instead they lulled them into a false sense of security by saying they were only following to protect the outlying villages from the Romans. A man named Mithridates came from the enemy camp. He was the cousin of Monaeses, who had been with Antony before.[38] He asked for a translator, and a certain Alexander of Antioch was produced. Mithridates warned Antony not to leave the hill country unless he wanted to suffer the fate of Crassus, and be ambushed. He told them that marching through the hills might involve thirst and hard labour, but the plain offered only the fate of Crassus.[39] After providing this information, Mithridates left and Antony consulted with his friends and his Mardian guide.[40] They were all in agreement to stick to the hills even though it meant spending a day without water. The march would be at night, and the men were ordered to carry all the water they could in skins if they had them, or even in inverted helmets if necessary.

Word was brought at once to the Parthians that the Romans were advancing, and contrary to their usual practice, they set out on a night pursuit. They came up on the rearguard of the Romans just as the sun was rising. The Romans were tired from the night march of 30 miles, and were not expecting any Parthians in the vicinity. In spite of their thirst and fatigue, they had to fight off a Parthian attack while still making forward progress. Those in the front arrived at a river which was clear and cold but turned out to be salty and poisonous. The Mardian guide had warned them not to drink from this river, but they disobeyed even Antony's pleas that there was a better river up ahead. Those who drank became even more thirsty and ill. Furthermore, the road ahead was too rough for the Parthian cavalry so it was important to move ahead. Eventually, Antony called his men back from the fighting and had them pitch their tents to create at least a modicum of shade. [41]

Once the Romans had pitched their tents, the Parthians withdrew and Mithridates reappeared. Through the same interpreter, Alexander, he told Antony to let the army sleep only a little while and to get under way quickly to the next river. He assured Antony that the Parthians would pursue them up to the river but would under no circumstances cross it. As a reward for this intelligence, Mithridates was given as many gold vessels as he could conceal in his garments. While it was still daylight, the Romans broke camp and proceeded on their march. Ironically, during the night they were not attacked by the Parthians, but an outbreak of looting occurred among their own troops. Anyone carrying gold or silver was robbed and killed. Goods were plundered from the beasts of burden, and even Antony's baggage-carriers were attacked and plundered.

The Roman army was in total disorder because they thought they were being attacked by the Parthians. When the real Parthians attacked, Antony was so sure they might not survive that he called a freedman in his bodyguard, named Rhamnus, and made him swear that before he could be captured, Rhamnus would run him through with his sword and cut his head off so that he might neither be taken alive nor recognized when he was dead. The Mardian guide encouraged him, however, by saying the river was near. He could already feel a cool moist breeze blowing that enabled them all to breathe more easily. There was little of the night left and word had been brought to him that most of the tumult had been caused by the looters, not the Parthians. In order to stop the chaos and regroup his men, he gave the signal for encampment.[42] Day no sooner dawned than the Parthians attacked the Roman rearguard as they were forming up for their march to the river. The light-armed troops were ordered to engage while the infantry formed a *testudo*. The front ranks advanced little by little until the Araxes River came into sight. Antony drew up his horsemen on the banks of the river to confront the enemy, while allowing his sick and wounded to cross the river first. Even the Romans who were fighting finally got the chance to drink. Once the Parthians saw the river, they retreated, bidding the Romans farewell and, according to Plutarch, praising them for their courage.[43] Thus, six days after the last battle with the Parthians, the Romans crossed the Araxes River, the border between Media and Armenia, twenty-seven days after leaving Praaspa.

Antony did a review of his troops and found that the expedition had cost the lives of approximately 24,000 men. Not all died by the hands of the enemy, but more than half by disease. In eighteen defensive engagements, Antony had managed to preserve his army from total annihilation but it was a Pyrrhic victory at best.[44] Phraates celebrated his victory by re-striking with his own types the *tetradrachms* of Antony and Cleopatra captured as part of the spoils.[45]

ANTONY'S SECOND CAMPAIGN

The army wanted to take revenge on the Armenian king who had betrayed them, and Antony knew that Artavasdes's betrayal had cost him dearly. But he also knew he was forced to treat the king of Armenia with respect while his own troops were passing through Armenia, because he was short of troops and the ones he had needed supplies from the region. From Armenia, Antony proceeded to the Syrian coast, hampered by the weather all the way, and he lost another 8,000 men on the march.[46] He stayed there until Cleopatra joined him with money and clothing for the troops. Because these were insufficient, Antony had to make up the difference out of his own pocket with contributions from the allies.[47] Although Antony's wife Octavia offered to bring clothing for the soldiers, beasts of burden, money and gifts he refused her help and stayed with Cleopatra.[48]

Antony wintered in Alexandria with Cleopatra. Meanwhile, Sextus Pompey, son of Pompey the Great, offered his services to the Parthians, but Antony's men intercepted the envoys and sent them back to Egypt.[49] Antony planned to return to Syria in the spring of 34 BCE, advance through Media Atropatene, join the king of Armenia at the Araxes River and invade Parthia once again. He tried to cement the alliance by marrying off one of the Armenian king's daughters to Alexander, his son by Cleopatra.[50] Antony went to the border of Armenia where he negotiated further for the marriage alliance. When Artavasdes did not appear, Antony moved toward the Armenian capital, Artaxata. Eventually, the Armenian king was lured into the Roman camp, seized and chained, and the Armenians treated his arrest as a permanent grievance against Rome.[51]

Antony rapidly overran the Armenian countryside without difficulty. Artaxias, the king's eldest son, whom the Armenians had made king in place of his father, was defeated and forced to take refuge with the Parthians. In 33 BCE, Antony had penetrated as far as the Araxes River (see Map 4), where he made a treaty with the Median king, an alliance against Octavian and the Parthians. Troops were exchanged, the Median king received a part of Armenia, and the king's daughter, Iotape, was betrothed to Antony's son, Alexander.[52] The standards taken at the defeat of Statianus were returned.

The region was garrisoned and Antony returned to Egypt. The Armenian king, his wife and children were given along with substantial booty to Cleopatra as presents. The king eventually graced a triumph and was later put to death.[53] Antony's son, Alexander, became king of Armenia, Media and Parthia – all the land from the Euphrates to India. This was, of course, only propaganda since Rome was not in possession of all these territories.[54] What kind of message did it send to the Parthians about Roman intentions?

The Parthian king, Phraates, must have watched these events with amusement. He watched as Artavasdes was punished, having first sided with the Romans but later betraying them. It must also have gratified him to observe how Antony was injuring his own cause by exasperating the Armenians and teaching them to hate the Romans even more than they hated Parthia.[55] While Antony's troops held both Syria and Armenia, and the alliance of Rome and Media Atropatene continued, Phraates could not afford to take any aggressive steps, but merely guarded his own frontier. But once

Antony withdrew into Asia Minor to prepare for his contest with Octavian, Phraates took the offensive. He combined with Artaxias, the new Armenian king, and attacked Antony's ally Media. The Median king was able to fight off this attack with the help of the Roman troops sent to him by Antony.[56] Soon afterwards, however, Antony recalled these troops without restoring to the Median king his own contingent. Once Antony recalled his troops, Artavasdes was removed by the Parthians and forced to seek refuge with the Romans. The Parthians and Armenians combined and attacked again. This time they were successful; the Median king was defeated and taken prisoner.[57] Artaxias recovered Armenia and massacred all the Roman garrisons which he found in it.[58] Both Armenia and Media were thus lost to Rome. They became totally independent and probably returned to their old alliances with Parthia.[59]

WHAT DID THE ROMANS ACHIEVE?

Antony's second campaign was no more successful than his first. One historian describes it as ending in 'an ignomious retreat with no positive achievement.'[60] He was saved only by the fact that internal strife broke out in Parthia, weakening their defence. Antony had planned his campaign in an area that had been invaded previously by Lucullus, Pompey, Gabinius and Crassus. He had avoided the flatlands of northern Mesopotamia, so favourable to the Parthian cavalry, and yet Antony failed to achieve his objectives and he sustained huge losses – greater indeed than those of Crassus. This demonstrated that the Romans could be defeated, even on their chosen mountainous ground, by avoiding pitched battle in favour of more appropriate hit-and-run tactics.[61] Thus what started out as a Parthian setback in 34 BCE caused by Antony's establishment of a favourable king in Armenia, and the defection of Media to his side, proved to be short-lived. By 32 BCE, Antony's troops had been withdrawn from Armenia, which quickly became independent, and Media reverted to Parthian vassalage.

Unfortunately for the Parthians, Phraates's military successes abroad produced some ill consequences at home. Assuming his position was safe, he renewed the cruel behaviour towards his subjects that had been interrupted by his war with Rome. He pushed them so far that an insurrection broke out and he was forced out of the country.[62] From 31 to 25 BCE, Phraates had to contest his throne with the rebel Tiridates.[63] Both sides sought aid from Octavian who was too busy with his war against Antony and Cleopatra to get involved either clandestinely or openly with a Parthian power struggle. Soon Octavian would be the only Roman left to whom they could appeal – Cleopatra and Antony were defeated in battle at Actium in 31 BCE and both chose to take their own lives; Antony to escape capital punishment and Cleopatra not to appear in Octavian's triumphal parade.

Phraates, who had fled to Scythia to enlist the aid of the nomads, returned to recover his throne. He was successful, and Tiridates was driven out, but not without carrying off with him Phraates's youngest son. Tiridates presented himself before Octavian, who was in Syria after his return from Egypt in 30 BCE. Tiridates offered the young hostage to Octavian and tried to enlist his aid in helping him recapture the throne. Octavian accepted the valuable hostage but, with his usual caution, he declined to pledge himself to furnish any help to Tiridates. Octavian did, however, allow Tiridates to stay in Syria.

Only several years later in 23 BCE, when Phraates demanded the surrender of both his young son and the rebel Tiridates, did Octavian answer that he would restore his son to him without ransom, but not Tiridates. In return Octavian expected Phraates to deliver the standards taken from Crassus and Antony, together with all of the Roman captives still alive. Phraates gladly received his son back but made no move to return the standards, his trophy and proof of the Parthian victories over Rome. The return of the standards would not occur until 20 BCE when Octavian, now called Augustus, visited the East and war seemed the probable alternative if Phraates remained obstinate (see chapter 5).

There was another unintentional change in Roman–Parthian relations caused by Antony's adventure, but it would only become evident in hindsight. Until 36 BCE the focus of Romano-Parthian confrontation had been south of the Taurus. Gabinius's invasion had threatened Mesopotamia. Crassus had advanced into Mesopotamia with the intention of marching on Babylonia. Both empires would now see a shift of the action to the north. The Romans had proven to the Parthians their commitment to retaining Syria, and Syrian topography had suited Roman armies well. Antony and his lieutenants had demonstrated the ability of Rome to overrun western Anatolia, to exercise control over Armenia, and its ability to destabilize Parthian vassals in Media Atropatene or even the heartlands of Media. For the next two-and-a-half-centuries, the disputes between Rome and Parthia would shift away from the Syria/Mesopotamia region to a struggle for supremacy east of the Upper Euphrates[64] The seat of war would be in Armenia rather than Cappadocia. Rome was now firmly in charge of Anatolia and Syria, but Armenia would never be converted into a direct and permanent administration by Rome. Armenia would remain a Parthian vassal most often in the hands of the Arsacid family. Parthia, however, had lost its influence in Syria, and her influence over Commagene and the Arab powers further south was gradually lost, as was its control over northwest Mesopotamia.

To return once again to the late republic, the result of the twenty-year struggle between Rome and Parthia had been to instil both empires with a wholesome dread of each other. Both had triumphed on their own ground; both had failed when they ventured into enemy territory. Each now stood on its guard, watching the movements of its adversary across the Euphrates. For the time being, both powers remained pacific.

NOTES

1. The most substantial description of this campaign comes from Plutarch's *Antony*. Dio, Velleius Paterculus and Florus all add details. The principal source of all these versions was probably the account of Quintus Dellius, a Roman officer who took part in the expedition, and whose descriptions of the terrain are also mentioned by Strabo 11.13.3. See A.D.H. Bivar, 'The Political History of Iran under the Arsacids', in *CHI*, vol. 3, 1: *The Seleucid, Parthian and Sasanian Period*, ed. E. Yarshater (Cambridge: Cambridge University Press, 1983), p.59.
2. Plutarch, *Antony* 25.1.
3. See the comments of A.N. Sherwin-White, *Roman Foreign Policy in the East, 168BC to AD 1* (Norman, OK: University of Oklahoma Press, 1984), p.307.
4. Plutarch, *Crassus* 33; he first tried poisoning him with aconite and later strangled him. Debevoise, *The Political History of Parthia* (New York: Greenwood Books, 1968), p.121, n.2, believes the poisoning incident is a later Greek or Roman addition.
5. There is no agreement in the sources as to the time of these murders. Justin, 42.5.1 gives no time; Plutarch, *Antony* 37 has Phraates putting Orodes to death; Dio 49.23 has Orodes die of grief and old age before the murder of the sons. Cf. G. Rawlinson, *The Sixth Great Monarchy* (New York: Publishers Plate Renting Co., 1870), p.196 and n.1.
6. Horace, *Odes* 3.6.9; Plutarch, *Antony* 37; Debevoise, *Political*, p. 122. A. Günther, *Beiträge zur Geschichte der Kriege zwischen Römern und Parthern* (Berlin: C.A. Schwetschke, 1922), p.58, n.1, suggests that his reputation was won in the attack on Statianus.
7. Preparations included having P. Canidius Crassus force Armenia to become a Roman ally in late 37 or early 36 BCE. He then turned northward to defeat the Iberians and Albanians to remove the threat of attack from the rear on the proposed expedition. Rawlinson doubts whether it took a Monaeses to put the idea of a Parthian campaign into Antony's head. Rawlinson, *Sixth Great Monarchy*, chapter 13, p.112.
8. D.L. Kennedy, 'Parthia and Rome', in D.L. Kennedy (ed.), *The Roman Army in the East* (Ann Arbor, MI: *Journal of Roman Archaeology*, Supplementary Series, 18, 1996), p.81.

9. Dio 49.24; Plutarch, *Antony* 37. Debevoise, *Political*, p.123.
10. Bivar, 'Political History of Iran', p.61.
11. Dio 49.25; Plutarch *Antony* 37; Strabo 11.13.4; 16.1.28; Debevoise, *Political*, p.124.
12. Suetonius, *Div. Jul.* 44, i.e. by way of Lesser Armenia. Cf. W.C. McDermott, 'Caesar's Projected Dacian Parthian Expedition', *Ancient Society*, 13/14 (1982/1983), pp.223–31, who doubts Caesar would have been foolish enough to get caught up in a Parthian campaign. J.G.C. Anderson, 'The Invasion of Parthia', in *CAH*, 10 (1963), 3.2, p.72, argues the same.
13. Plutarch, *Antony* 37 blames Antony's haste on his need to return quickly to Cleopatra. Rawlinson states that after Ventidius's successes, it should not have been difficult to defeat the Parthians; that their prestige in war was gone; and that the weaknesses and strength of their military system was now well known. Rawlinson, *Sixth Great Monarchy*, chapter 13, p.113.
14. Antony's force was twice the size of Crassus's. K. Butcher, *Roman Syria and the Near East* (Los Angeles, CA: Getty Publications, 2003), p.38; According to Plutarch, *Antony* 53 and Justin 42.5.3 there were 60,000 infantry (sixteen legions), 10,000 Iberian and Celtic cavalry, 30,000 allies, both horsemen and light-armed, including 7,000 foot and 6,000 horse furnished by Artavasdes. For varying figures, see Florus 2.20; Aurelius Victor, *de vir ill.* 85.4; Livy, *Epit.* 103, Velleius Paterculus 2. 82. J. Kromayer, 'Kleine Forschungen zur Geschichte des zweiten Triumvirats', *Hermes*, 31 (1896), p.71, says Antony did not feel strong enough with the army he had assembled at Zeugma to confront the Parthians on the Mesopotamian plain and therefore took the route through Armenia. H. Delbrück, *History of the Art of War*, vol. 1: *Warfare in Antiquity* (Lincoln, NE, and London: University of Nebraska Press, 1990), p.49, disagrees. Cf. W.W. Tarn, 'Antony's Legions', *Classical Quarterly*, 26 (1932), p.80, who argues that the light-armed forces could not have exceeded 10,000–12,000; Bivar, 'Political History of Iran', p.58; Sherwin-White, *RFPE*, p.311.
15. Dio 49.24.5–25.1 expressed surprise that Antony would try and follow Crassus's route into Mesopotamia. Modern historians reject the whole story because the scale of the Roman preparations could not have been concealed from the Parthians. The subsequent Median campaign can hardly have been a sudden improvisation. The Euphrates approach could not have been a feint unless a substantial force maintained pressure on the south while the main army initiated an invasion in the north. W.W. Tarn, 'The Parthian Invasion', in *CAH*, 9 (1963), pp.47–50, does not explain the march to the Euphrates. T. Rice-Holmes, *The Architect of the Roman Empire* (Oxford: Clarendon Press, 1928–31), vol. 1, p.125, supports a diversion; see Sherwin-White, *RFPE*, p.309 and n.30 for the discussion. Cf. Plutarch, *Antony* 37.2–3; Florus 2.20.2.
16. On the route, see J. Kromayer, 'Kleine Forschungen zur Geschichte des zweiten Triumvirats', *Hermes*, 31 (1896), pp.70–86; Rice-Holmes, *Architect of the Roman Empire*, pp.124ff; Delbrück, *Warfare in Antiquity*, p.444; Debevoise, *Political*, p.124.
17. Strabo 11.13.4 and 16.1.128; Debevoise, *Political*, p.125; Bivar, 'Political History of Iran', p.359.
18. Strabo 11.13.4 and 16.1.28; Debevoise, *Political*, p.125.
19. J.G.C. Anderson, 'The Invasion of Parthia', in *CAH*, 10, 3.2 (1963), p.73; Sherwin-White, *RFPE*, p.314, points out that Tarn, Rice-Holmes and their followers treat this campaign as if it were doomed from the start, but he disagrees. He rather sees Antony's failure as a 'misapplication of the methods of Caesar in Gaul' (p.315).
20. Praaspa is the classical Vera mentioned by Strabo 11.13.3, the modern Takht-i-Sulaiman, capital of ancient Media Atropatene in north-western Iran. Praaspa was designated a world heritage site by UNESCO in July 2003; the archaeological site includes the principal Zoroastrian sanctuary partly rebuilt in the Ilkhanid (Mongol) period (thirteenth century) as well as a temple of the Sasanian period (sixth and seventh centuries CE) dedicated to Anahit; P.M. Sykes, *History of Persia* (London: Macmillan, 1951), vol. 1, p.360 and n.1; H.C. Rawlinson, 'Memoir on the Site of Atropatenian Ecbatana', *Journal of the Royal Geographic Society*, 10 (1841), pp.113–15; Bivar, 'Political Hisory of Iran', p.59; Praaspa: 'US scientists survey big Parthian citadel where Rome's march to the east was stopped in 36 BC', *Life*, 4, 17 (25 April 1938), pp.28–9.
21. Two legions under Oppius Statianus were left behind with the task of bringing up the equipment as soon as possible. Dio 49.25; Plutarch, *Antony* 38 says 10,000 men.
22. On the siege of Praaspa see Plutarch, *Antony* 38.2–40.5; on the loss of two legions see

Velleius Paterculus 2.82.2; Plutarch, *Antony* 42.2-4; Florus 2.20.3; Livy, *Periochae* 130; Dio 49.25; On the desertion of Artavasdes, see Plutarch, *Antony* 39 and Rawlinson, *Sixth Great Monarchy*, p.114; Debevoise, *Political*, p.126.

23. Because there was no heavy timber in the area they were crossing, they could not construct more siege engines in the field. The battering ram was seventy feet long according to Appian, *Parthia* 14. Debevoise, *Political*, p.125.

24. Plutarch, *Antony* 38 mentions the loss of 10,000 men. Livy, *Epit.* 103 and Velleius Paterculus 2.82 say two legions; Debevoise, *Political*, p.126; Rawlinson, *Sixth Great Monarchy*, p.114.

25. Plutarch, *Antony* 38 and Appian, *Parthia* 15; whereas Livy, *Epit.* 103 and Velleius Paterculus 2.82 mention two legions. Bivar, 'Political History of Iran', p.59; Debevoise, *Political*, p.126, n.21.

26. Plutarch, *Antony* 39.6-7; Sherwin-White, *RFPE*, p.317.

27. Plutarch, *Antony* 39, and Bivar, 'Political History of Iran', p.60.

28. Dio 49.26; Eutropius, *Brev.* 7.6; Rawlinson, *Sixth Great Monarchy*, p.114.

29. Plutarch, *Antony* 39; Debevoise, Political, p. 127 identifies the eyewitness as Dellius.

30. Plutarch, *Antony* 39; Frontinus, *Strat.* 4.1.37; in Dio 49.27 barley was given to the entire army. On barley used as a punishment, see Suetonius, *Augustus* 24; Dio 49.38.4; H.M.D. Parker, *The Roman Legions* (Oxford: Clarendon Press, 1928), pp.232-4; Debevoise, *Political*, p.127; Rawlinson, *Sixth Great Monarchy*, p.114.

31. See Plutarch, *Antony* 40 for the stratagem he used to demoralize Antony; cf. Dio 49.27, and Rawlinson, *Sixth Great Monarchy*, p.115.

32. Plutarch, *Antony* 41; Velleius Paterculus 2.82 and Florus 2.20.4 identify him as Roman survivor of Crassus's expedition who had been settled in Margiana. See Rawlinson, *Sixth Great Monarchy*, chapter 13, p.115 and notes, on the location of the route; Bivar, 'Political History of Iran', p.61.

33. On the retreat, see Frontinus, *Strat.* 2.13.7.

34. Among the wounded was Gallus who died shortly thereafter. Plutarch, *Antony* 42ff; Tacitus, *Histories* 3.24; Appian, *Parthia* 17; Bivar, 'Political History of Iran', p.62.

35. Plutarch, *Antony* 44-5.

36. Ibid., 45; Dio 49.29; Frontinus, *Strat.* 2.3.15. For another example of its use see Tacitus, *Annals* 13.39.

37. Plutarch, *Antony* 45; Appian, *Parthia* 18; Debevoise, *Political*, p. 130. Rawlinson, *Sixth Great Monarchy*, p.115. The good news was that the antidote was wine. The bad news was that they did not have any wine.

38. Plutarch, *Antony* 37.1.

39. Ibid., 46.

40. The Mardians were an Iranian mountain tribe occupying the area of the Alburz Range. See Bivar, 'Political History of Iran', p.61 and n.3, p.62; Tacitus, *Annals* 14.23. Why Parthian subjects were guiding the Romans is unclear. Plutarch claims he was an Italian survivor of Crassus's campaign who had taken a Median wife.

41. A cousin of the Monaeses who had been with Antony came to camp and warned him through an interpreter that the same fate that had befallen Crassus awaited him if he left the hill country. Appian, *Parthia* 18; Debevoise, *Political*, p.130.

42. Plutarch, *Antony* 48.

43. Plutarch, *Antony* 49. Frontinus, *Strat.* 2.3.15; 2.13.7. G. Rawlinson, *Parthia* (London: T. Fisher Unwin, 1893), p.213, suggests the Julfa ferry crossing. On the retreat see H.C. Rawlinson, 'Memoir on the Site of Atropatenian Ecbatana', *Journal of the Royal Geographic Society*, 10 (1841), pp.113-17. On copper and silver medals with Antony's portrait on them, see J.G. Taylor, 'Travels in Kurdistan with Notices of the Sources of the Eastern and Western Tigris, and Ancient Ruins in their Neighbourhood', *Journal of the Royal Geographic Society*, 35 (1865), pp.21-58, esp. p.25; Debevoise, *Political*, p.131.

44. Plutarch, *Antony* 50 puts the loss at 20,000 infantry and 4,000 cavalry but apparently does not include the 10,000 men lost under Statianus. See Rawlinson, *Sixth Oriental Monarchy*, p.205, n.2; Velleius Paterculus 2.82 says that losses amounted to not less than one-fourth of all his soldiers, one-third of the camp followers and slaves and all of the baggage. Cf. Florus 4.10, who says one-third of the legions remained.

45. Dio 49.31; Plutarch, *Antony* 51.

46. Plutarch, *Antony* 51. He proceeded to 'the white village' (*Leuke kome*) somewhere

between Beirut and Sidon on the Syria coast, where he waited for Cleopatra to bring him clothing and money for the troops.

47. Dio 49.31. Cf. Plutarch, *Antony* 51, who insists Cleopatra only brought clothing and Antony provided the money from private funds. During this period, a quarrel arose between Phraates and his Median ally over the booty taken from the Romans. The Median, fearful for his throne, sent an emissary, Polemon, to Antony with an offer of alliance which Antony accepted. Antony later gave the kingdom of Lesser Armenia to him as a reward for his services. Dio 49.33; Debevoise, *Political*, pp.132–3.

48. Plutarch, *Antony* 53.

49. Appian, *BC* 5.133 and 136; Dio 49.18; Livy, *Epit.* 131; Debevoise, *Political*, p.33.

50. Debevoise, *Political*, p.133.

51. Dio 49.39 claimed the chains were of silver and afterwards (49.40) of gold; Velleius Paterculus 2.82; Tacitus, *Annals* 2.3. The fact that Octavian has tried to enlist the aid of Artavasdes might have motivated Antony's action. See Dio 49.41.5; Debevoise, *Political*, p.134; Bivar, 'Political History of Iran', p.65.

52. Rawlinson, *Sixth Oriental Monarchy*, p.117 who does not name the monarch to avoid confusion because he had the same name as the Armenian monarch, Artavasdes.

53. Plutarch, *Antony* 50; Josephus, *BJ* 1.363 and *AJ* 15.104ff; Strabo 9.14.41.

54. Plutarch, *Antony* 54.4; Tacitus, *Annals* 2.3. Horace, *Odes* 3.8.19 mentions internal strife among the Parthians; Plutarch, *Antony* 53.6; Dio 49.41.

55. Tacitus, *Annals* 2.3.

56. Horace, *Odes* 3.8.19; Plutarch, *Antony* 53.6.

57. Dio 49.44.

58. Ibid., 51.16.

59. Debevoise, *Political*, p.135.

60. B. Campbell, 'War and Diplomacy: Rome and Parthia, 31 BC – AD 235', in J. Rich and G. Shipley (eds), *War and Society in the Roman World* (New York: Routledge, 1993), p.214.

61. Kennedy, 'Parthia and Rome', p.81.

62. Justin 13.5.4; Rawlinson, *Sixth Great Monarchy*, p.117 and n.43.

63. Justin 52.5.4; Dio 51.18ff; See also Horace, *Epistles* 1.12.27–8 and *Odes* 1.26.5. See also 'Tiridates', in *RE*, no. 4, cols. 1439–40.

64. Kennedy, 'Parthia and Rome', p.81.

6

THE DIPLOMATIC SOLUTION: AUGUSTUS AND TIBERIUS

The reign of Augustus was a crucial stage in the history of Roman-Parthian relations. While Rome was engaged in the civil war between Antony and Octavian (later Augustus), Tiridates had claimed the throne of Parthia by deposing Phraates who escaped and sought aid from the 'Scythians'.[1] The story of Antony consolidating his rule and the Parthian king trying to establish his own rule, therefore, run concurrently. From Egypt, Octavian returned through Syria to the province of Asia where he spent the winter of 30/29 BCE. Meanwhile Phraates and his Scythian allies drove Tiridates from Parthia, whence he fled to Syria where Octavian permitted him to live in peace.[2] Before leaving Parthia, however, Tiridates had been able to steal Phraates's young son whom he took with him to Syria. Phraates IV, now sole ruler of Parthia, sent envoys to Octavian in Asia Minor requesting the return of his son and the surrender of Tiridates. Octavian did not accede to the request, but left for Rome with Tiridates and the son of the Parthian king with him. They were brought before the Senate, which turned the matter over to Octavian for settlement. Octavian bartered well with the Parthians: we will send you back your son if you will send us back the standards lost at Carrhae. The king agreed, although it would be a number of years before the Romans actually received the standards. The son of Phraates was then returned to his father.[3]

The Romans could achieve all they wanted from Parthia by diplomatic means, but that did not stop certain interests groups from urging another Parthian campaign. There was no military threat that made a renewal of the conflict essential, but Roman losses at the hands of the Parthians were not forgotten. War in the East remained on Augustus's list of priorities. The first indication of this was the reconnaissance agents sent to the East.[4] We know one by name, Lycotas.[5] There are clear echoes of this kind of intelligence gathering in the lines of Propertius 4.3:

I teach myself where the Araxes flows,
that river you must conquer,
and inquire as to the mileage of Parthian horses,
between the water holes,
and I study the world as laid out on the maps,
the location of high Dahan.[6]

But although Augustus may have toyed with the idea of conquering Asia, he was no fool. He realized that those who sought conquests east of the Euphrates had pursued mistaken policies, and therefore he sought a compromise.[7] The embassies from Augustus to Parthia and back had led to better relations between the two powers; Parthia was not menacing Rome,[8] and this made it possible for Rome to adopt a friendlier attitude. An entente between the two powers would benefit both, if only through commercial ties. Their intelligence on each other seems to have improved and no one was about to make any rash moves.[9]

THE RETURN OF THE STANDARDS

This change of policy bore fruit.[10] By negotiation, Phraates IV restored to Augustus the Roman standards captured from Crassus and Antony. The prisoners and standards were surrendered on 12 May 20 BCE to Tiberius, who was commissioned to receive them.[11] Of course, Augustus treated the whole affair as if he had conquered the Parthians in a war. We are told he took great pride in the achievement, and declared that what had previously been lost in battle, he had recovered without a struggle.[12] It is hard to appreciate today how large this event loomed in the eyes of contemporaries. The negotiated treaty of 20 BCE was celebrated in Roman poetry and iconography as the submission of the Parthians to the 'right rule of Caesar'.[13] In the centre of the cuirass of Augustus's famous Prima Porta, a statue shows a bearded and trousered Parthian handing over the standards to a Roman amid symbols of world rule.[14] Ovid celebrated the victory by saying: 'You [Parthian] no longer hold proofs of our shame.'[15] The event was commemorated on Roman coinage from Syria to Spain.[16] The standards themselves were dedicated in a new, hastily improvised temple to Mars Ultor (the Avenger).[17]

The Augustan poets show themselves to be acutely aware of the defeat suffered by the Romans legions. The idea that all the dishonours of the past could be wiped away with one large-scale military expedition began to appear. Horace regularly speaks of the Parthian problem. In 28 BCE he urged to start a new war against the Parthians,[18] and he expressed his expectations of a great military campaign against the Parthians in another poem dated to 20 BCE.[19] In another poem he calls the Parthians *'feroces'* and urges the necessity of creating a Roman cavalry corps equipped with long lances, which could be a match for the rapid Parthian horsemen with their bows and arrows.[20] The fact that the importance of cavalry was emphasized shows a fundamental change in the Roman strategic conceptions. The basic strategy, in which only the legions of infantry were thought to be invincible without any support from cavalry squadrons, had now been changed and abandoned. In a letter dated to 20 BCE, Horace describes how many foreign peoples subjected themselves to the Roman power, including Phraates, king of Parthia, who accepted *'ius et imperium'* from Augustus while kneeling as a suppliant.[21] This poem expressed the same idea in words that were portrayed by the kneeling Parthian on the denarii from the Roman mint of 19 BCE. Once the Parthian problem was solved, however, Horace's last poem, dating to about 13 BCE, evokes the feelings of a poet who is completely convinced that the Augustan policy of peace was the right solution to the political problem. Horace celebrated in his poem the closing of the shrine of Janus near the Roman Forum because there were no more wars to be waged.[22]

The single most important result of the military defeats by Parthia was that it put Rome and Parthia on the same level as world powers. Pompeius Trogus, a freedman of Pompey the Great, says that a deal was contemplated to *share the world between Parthia and Rome*.[23] Augustus thought the event important enough to mention it in his record, a copy of which is preserved and called the *Monumentum Ancyranum*.[24] And yet, the return of the standards was accomplished, not through military means, but through clandestine bartering, kidnapping and blackmail that went on behind the scenes. The return of the standards may have been celebrated with a triumphal arch in Rome and coins, but there had been no battle other than the covert one. And at least some of Augustus's contemporaries felt the emperor's policy was insufficiently forceful. Horace may have been convinced that Augustus's decision to solve the Parthian problem without waging an expensive and risky war was correct, but others were not happy with the decision. They felt the only effective way to retaliate for Crassus's defeat was with violence.

On the death of Artaxias (20 BCE), Augustus,s who was then in the East, sent Tiberius into Armenia to arrange matters and Tiberius placed upon the throne a brother of Artaxias named Tigranes II, who had spent ten years in Rome and who now received the crown from Tiberius's hand, just as Tiberius had personally received the standards when Phraates handed them over.[25] Phraates acquiesced to this replacement. The Parthians stayed out of the Armenian succession problem, yet their conciliatory attitude and Rome's bloodless intervention were ignored at Rome.[26] In 19 BC, Augustus's coins celebrated 'the return of the standards' (*signis receptis*) and 'the conquest of Armenia' (*Armenia capta*).[27]

It suited Augustus to minimize direct Roman military intervention in the East so he could concentrate resources elsewhere. It was on the eastern frontier that Augustus made most use of client kings (*reges socii*), the most important of whom were Herod of Judaea, Archelaus of Cappadocia and Polemo of Pontus.[28] Suetonius rightly stressed that he treated them as members and parts of the empire, encouraging ties of marriage and friendship among them, appointing regents for such as were minors or incapacitated, and bringing up their children with his own.[29] But even as a client kingdom Armenia was less tractable than most and Augustus's policy amounted only to a sound provisional measure. On the border of two empires, Armenia was effectively subject to the influence of one or the other of its neighbours, even if the autonomous kingdom did not become an integral part of either. Its natural connection was to Parthia, not to Rome, since the royal families of Parthia, Armenia and Media Atropatene were all intermarried.[30] This dynastic interconnection was an insuperable obstacle to any Roman policy involving a protectorate over Armenia. The Arsacids regarded the Roman claims to Armenia as an encroachment and a standing threat to the security of their realm. The Romans could not enforce their own claims since their capital and administrative centres were so remote and no Roman troops were stationed nearby.

The remainder of Phraates's reign was almost unbroken by any event of importance.[31] After yielding to Augustus in the matter of the standards and prisoners, Phraates appears for many years to have studiously cultivated Augustus's good graces. Between 11 BCE and 7 BCE, distrustful of his subjects and fearful of their removing him in order to place one of his sons on the Parthian throne, Phraates resolved to send these possible rivals out of the country, and he paid Augustus the compliment of selecting Rome for his children's residence. Two of these sons were married with children. They resided at Rome for the remainder of their father's lifetime, and were treated in a manner commensurate with their rank. The Roman writers speak of these as 'hostages' given by Phraates to the Roman emperor, but they were supported at public expense in magnificent style.[32] The good relations between these two rulers might have continued undisturbed until the death of one or the other had not a revolution broken out in Armenia.

A PREGNANT INTERVAL

The feudal hierarchy in Parthia kept Phraates IV constantly vulnerable to powerful cliques of nobles. The surrender of the standards aroused animosity against him and provided additional fuel for existing discontent. Strong central government was rare among the Parthians and the Parthian royal family was increasingly dependent on Rome during this period. While the relations remained friendly, Augustus sent a present to Phraates – an Italian slave girl named Musa.[33] Augustus knew that having influence at the Parthian court was the most efficient way to control Parthian events. Scholars have debated whether Musa was placed in a strategic position as a source of information or with the hope that she might influence the king; we will never know for sure.[34] Phraates married a slave girl in spite of the fact that some considered her a Roman agent assigned to spy on the king and perhaps to influence him to cooperate with Rome. Phraates had a son by Musa named Phraataces (little Phraates, Phraates V). After the birth of an heir to the throne, Musa was raised from the status of concubine to queen, with the name Thea Urania Musa.

When Phraataces attained sufficient age to become a candidate for the throne, Musa persuaded her husband to send his older children to Rome, leaving the field clear for her own son Phraataces. Phraates contacted the governor of Syria M. Titius and arranged a conference where he turned over his four eldest sons as well as two of their wives and four of their sons.[35] These political hostages gave Augustus nominal custody of the Parthian succession. As long as the legitimate heirs were in Italy, Phraates had a compelling reason to support Roman foreign policy in the East.

In 2 BCE, Musa took the final step toward securing the throne of Parthia for her son – she had her husband poisoned.[36] Thus her husband, Phraates IV, the parricide and fratricide was, after a reign of thirty-five years, himself assassinated by a wife whom he loved and a son whom he esteemed and trusted. (So much for Parthian politics.) Phraates had been a successful Parthian monarch. His conduct in the campaign against Antony showed him to be a master of guerrilla warfare. His dealings with Augustus show that he had admirable diplomatic ability, and the fact that he stayed on his throne for thirty-five years testifies to his powers of management. He did not advance the Parthian frontiers, but neither did they contract. He did not cede anything to the Scythians for helping to put him back on the throne. He maintained the Parthian supremacy over northern Media, and he ceded not one inch to the Romans. He considered it a prudent step to soothe the irritated vanity of Rome by a surrender of useless trophies and scarcely more useful prisoners. This did as much to produce a peace between the two empires as any fear of Parthian arms. This peace lasted unbroken for ninety years from the campaign of Antony (i.e. from 36 BCE to the commencement of the war between Vologases I and Nero 58 CE (see Chapter 6). If Phraates felt that on the whole Rome was a more powerful state than Parthia, and that Parthia had nothing to gain but much to lose in any war against its western neighbour, he did well to allow no sentiment of foolish pride stand in the way of a concession that made a prolonged peace between the two empires possible. It was a balancing act to maintain one's frontiers and one's dignity and not be dragged into a war based only on national vanity.[37]

THE ARMENIAN SUCCESSION PROBLEM

With Phraataces reigning as Phraates V, Rome had its candidate on the throne and the rest of the heirs were safely tucked away. Phraataces did have one short run-in with Augustus, however, over another snag in the Armenian succession. In 6 BCE, Tigranes II died and the Armenians, without waiting to hear what the will of Rome might be, conferred the royal title on his sons – a reasonable decision since their father had paved the way for this by sharing governmental responsibilities with them in his lifetime.[38]

The Armenians had no doubt that the Romans would interfere with this new display of independence, so they called the Parthians in to help them with the resistance. Armenia was too weak to ever fight a war alone – one or other of the two big empires on her border always had to be called in. They do not seem to have had much political foresight, considering how this situation always ended. They constantly fluctuated between the two great powers according to how the 'feelings of the hour' dictated.[39]

Phraates V could not bring himself to reject the Armenian overtures. It was a Parthian policy generally to keep Armenia dependent, and even if it meant risking a rupture with Rome, Phraates responded to the appeal made to him. Perhaps he was gambling that since Augustus was now in his old age, he might let this latest affront slip by. He had just lost the services of his best general, Tiberius, who had gone into retirement at Rhodes. He had no one he could employ except his grandsons, but they were still quite young and inexperienced. If these were indeed his thoughts, he miscalculated. From the moment that Augustus received the intelligence about Armenia and the support given to it by Parthia, he was determined to enforce Rome's claims to control Armenia.

Phraataces, by supporting Tigranes IV rather than a Roman nominee for the Armenian throne, was publicly taking a strong line against Augustus. Such strong Parthian involvement in this matter is rather surprising because it violated the treaty of 20 BCE, and because the heirs to the throne were still at Rome.[40] Enraged at this assumption of independence, Augustus sent an expedition into Armenia in 5 BCE, deposed the sons of Tigranes and established Artavasdes on the throne, a man whose birth and parentage are not known.[41] The Armenians were no more inclined to submit to foreign interference than they ever were. They rose in revolt against Artavasdes, defeated his Roman supporters, and expelled him from the kingdom. Tigranes IV was made king.[42]

The crisis in Armenia was serious enough to provoke a special command for Rome's most prestigious general. In sending Tiberius, Augustus was responding as he thought the situation required. Tiberius would eventually refuse the commission and retire to Rhodes, but his presence nearby in the meantime was enough of a threat to the Parthians to keep a lid on things between 6 and 2 BCE.[43] Augustus then sent the elder of his two adopted sons, Gaius, to the East in 2 BCE to impose a solution. The theme of Gaius's expedition was revenge. 2 BCE was also the year in which Augustus consecrated his new, famous temple of Mars the Avenger, an event that was preceded by a mock naval battle recreating the defeat over the Persians by the Greeks[44] Ovid anticipated Gaius's triumph and wrote: 'Parthian, you will pay the penalty.'[45]

Gaius's commission was to secure advance information about

the East and, with due preparations and a very capable staff to accompany him, he set out.[46] Gaius's presence in the East was supposed to dramatize the continuity and stability of Roman frontier policy in the East. The absence of a truly critical situation explains both Augustus's willingness to send his adopted son and the long duration of Gaius's journey from Rome to Syria.[47]

When news of Gaius's advance reached Parthia, Phraataces sent an embassy to Rome to explain matters to Augustus and to request the return of his brothers. Augustus replied with ridicule; he refused to address Phraataces as king and told him to get out of Armenia. Continuing the game of one-upmanship, Phraataces sent Augustus a letter in which he referred to himself as king-of-kings, a favourite Parthian title, and referred to the Roman emperor simply as 'Caesar'.[48] The insults would have escalated had they continued to write letters, but Augustus took active measures. Gaius showed himself in Syria with all the magnificent surroundings of the Imperial dignity, and news of his arrival reached Phraataces who now realized he was in trouble. Acceptance of the Roman nominee for Armenia was Augustus's quid pro quo for the return of the legitimate heirs. By retaining the heirs and reaffirming his plans for Armenia, Augustus left Phraataces no choice but to back his threats with action.[49]

The two sides were preparing for war late in 2 CE, when Gaius received news of his brother's death, and domestic unrest in Parthia caused Phraataces to end war preparations.[50] This opened the way for a diplomatic settlement. A meeting was arranged in late September or early October between the two men on an island in the Euphrates where the terms of the arrangement between the two empires was discussed.[51] The armies of the two chiefs were drawn up on the opposite banks of the river, facing one another; and the chiefs themselves, accompanied by an equal number of attendants, proceeded to deliberate in the sight of both hosts. Satisfactory pledges having been given by the Parthian monarch, the prince and the king in turn entertained each other on the borders of their respective dominions.[52] The duration of the conference was not reported, but the official celebrations at its conclusion seemed to have lasted for two days, since on one evening Phraataces banqueted among the Romans, and on the next Gaius among the Parthians.[53]

A strange side note concerning Roman security deserves attention. To demonstrate his good faith, Phraataces reported that M.

Lollius, Augustus's hand-picked *comes et rector* for Gaius,[54] was in the pay of local rulers. The veracity of the charges was never proved, but Lollius, expelled from Gaius's camp, was found dead a few days later. It was never established whether the cause of death was a murder, suicide, or natural causes.[55]

Gaius returned to Syria with a promise from the Parthians to abstain from any further interference in Armenian affairs. The arrangement seems to have been honourably kept, and the Parthians do not seem to have been involved when Gaius was killed shortly thereafter. Dio says that in exchange for a secure border along the Euphrates, Phraataces would cease to demand the return of his half-brothers and recognize the Roman claims in Armenia.[56] The peace was on Roman terms and Phraataces's demands, which had precipitated the crisis, were withdrawn. It was agreed that the Parthians should drop all claims to Armenia and that the four Parthian princes should stay in Rome.[57]

Although Phraataces withdrew direct support, the Parthian-aligned faction in Armenia, even with its platform jeopardized by his concessions, refused to disarm following the Euphrates agreement. Armenia was divided between a submissive majority more or less open to the Roman nominee and a Parthian-aligned nationalist opposition commanded by a certain Addon with headquarters at Artagira.[58] Addon's decision to fight without Parthian support marks the formal opening of Gaius's Armenian campaign. Minor engagements with the rebels brought Rome victories in the spring and summer of 3 CE, but none was decisive until the fall of Altagira.[59]

Again a Roman commander fell victim to an ambush. Addon summoned Gaius to a personal meeting (on the pretext of revealing secrets about Phraataces).[60] Gaius's general staff no doubt regarded this meeting as preliminary to Addon's surrender, since the Parthian secrets represented his negotiating strength and were meant to be taken as a sign of good faith. The cautions of the previous Euphrates conference were not practised. Addon's invitation was bait, and Gaius was careless.[61] He was wounded by a sword while distracted by a document that Addon had handed him. The sources agree that Addon himself struck the blow.[62] The Roman army ended the campaign soon after the city walls of Altagira were razed.[63] Augustus's appointee, Ariobarzanes, was installed on the throne of Armenia but did not last long.[64] Gaius died from the effects of his wound the year after. There are some indications that this Armenian campaign was but a preliminary to an attack on the Parthians themselves. The situation in the Near East was probably much more complicated than Augustan propaganda suggests.[65]

Phraataces had a hard time establishing his rule at home, not only because he had ascended the throne himself by killing his father, but the Parthian nobles distrusted him because he was the son of an Italian concubine sent by Rome.[66] The Parthian Senate did not tolerate foreigners, especially those with Roman connections. Even when Phraataces put her effigy upon his coins and gave her absurd titles it did not cover the fact of her low birth and foreign origin. Within a few years of his obtaining the throne, an insurrection broke out against his authority and, after a brief struggle, he was deprived of his crown and put to death.[67] Orodes III was placed on the throne but shortly thereafter he was assassinated for his alleged cruelty.[68] An embassy was sent to Rome in 6 CE requesting the return of one of the sons of Phraates IV. The eldest son, Vonones, was sent, and installed as Vonones I (7/8–12 CE).[69] The Parthians, however, were dissatisfied with their new king. They disliked his western manners and the friends he had acquired in Rome. His dislike for the hunt and traditional feasts went against Parthian custom. He was disarmingly informal, and he failed to show interest in horses; all these things caused the nationalists to call for another candidate.[70] An army was raised under another Arsacid, Artabanus III (12–38 CE), king of Media Atropatene. Artabanus was defeated, but he returned to his own country, raised a larger army, and returned to make a second invasion.[71] This time he was successful and Vonones was driven from the kingdom.[72] He escaped on horseback to Seleucia with a small body of followers, while his defeated army, following behind him, was attacked from behind by Artabanus's troops and they suffered great losses. Artabanus entered Ctesiphon in triumph and was immediately proclaimed king.[73]

Vonones eventually made his way to Armenia which was then without a king because Artavasdes III had been murdered and Tigranes IV, a grandson of King Herod the Great, sent by Augustus to succeed him, had been deposed after a brief reign.[74] Vonones seized the Armenian throne, but owing to pressure from the Parthian king Artabanus, he was forced to abdicate in 15 or 16 CE.[75]

There was no way Artabanus was going to submit to this arrangement and have Vonones next door in a position to cause him constant annoyance. He therefore let his displeasure be known both in Armenia and at Rome. Since the Romans claimed the right of investiture of the Armenian monarchs, Artabanus sent an embassy to Tiberius and threatened war if Vonones were acknowledged. Augustus had died in 14 CE just before Vonones abdicated from the throne of Armenia, and his adopted son Tiberius succeeded him. At the same time he wrote to the Armenians and demanded the surrender of Vonones. Tiberius drew back from supporting Vonones because of the Parthian threats.[76] Vonones still felt too threatened to remain in Armenia and took refuge among the Romans in Syria where the Roman governor, Creticus Silanus,[77] allowed him to live in Antioch and to retain the pomp and name of king, but there was always the threat that Rome would use him as a covert operator against Parthia.

COVERT OPERATIONS UNDER TIBERIUS

When Artabanus of Parthia sent his son Orodes to fill the vacant throne of Armenia, Tiberius felt it incumbent upon himself to take action. He wanted to send to the East someone of sufficient importance and bearing to command the respect of the Parthians and impose upon them the will of Rome. In 18 CE he sent Germanicus, his nephew, the eldest son of his deceased brother Drusus and now his own adopted son, with full authority to act as a free agent.[78] He was given command over all Roman dominions east of the Hellespont, which rendered him a sort of monarch of Roman Asia. Full powers were granted to him for making peace or war, for levying troops, annexing provinces, appointing subject kings and performing other sovereign acts without referring back to Rome for instructions.[79] This, and the magnificent entourage that accompanied him, would convince the Parthians that this was no common negotiator.

Germanicus proceeded to Artaxata, the Armenian capital (see Map 1), with an impressive retinue, where he discovered the people wanted Zeno, son of Polemon, king of Pontus, as their leader.[80] Since Zeno was also friendly to the Romans, Germanicus decided he was a suitable candidate and crowned him before a huge crowd who hailed him as king of Armenia, with the adopted name of Artaxias.[81]

Germanicus returned to Syria, where an embassy from the Parthian king reached him requesting that previously friendly relations between Rome and Parthia be restored.[82] Artabanus said that he would be willing to come as far as the Euphrates, the

traditional meeting place for Roman and Parthian, and the boundary between the two great empires. He specifically requested,
however, that Vonones be removed from the neighbourhood of the
frontier because he was fomenting discontent among the Parthians.
Germanicus replied with politeness but did not accept the terms;
the conference never took place and he opened negotiations with
surrounding states that were Parthian vassals.[83] Germanicus, did,
however, transfer Vonones to the coastal city of Pompeiopolis
(ancient Soli) in Cilicia[84] (see Map 3).

The next year, 19 CE, Vonones bribed his guards and attempted
to flee while on a hunt. He was stopped by the destruction of
a bridge that had been torn up to prevent his escape. He was
arrested by Vibius Fronto, prefect of the cavalry, and later assassinated by the man who had been put in charge of him at Pompeiopolis, probably to cover up his own complicity in the escape.[85]
In this same year, 19 CE, Germanicus died, and for the next decade
the East remained at peace.[86] Between the years 19 and 32 CE, only
one governor, L. Vitellius, was sent to Syria, and even he served
only a short term. Tiberius was criticized for leaving that position
vacant and putting the Armenian frontier in jeopardy.[87]

Bolstered by his recent military successes on his borders, and
the fact that his intelligence told him the aging Tiberius was in self-
exile on Capri, the Parthian king gambled that the Romans would
leave him alone. On the death of Artaxias (Zeno) of Armenia in 34
CE, Artabanus seized the opportunity to place his eldest son,
Arsaces on the throne.[88] His position must have been secure if he
thought he could 'push the envelope' with the aging Tiberius. He
wrote to the emperor claiming the treasure left by Vonones in Syria
and Cilicia, and threatening to add to his domain all the lands of
the Achaemenids and Selecids.[89] He is said to have even commanded operations against Cappadocia, which was an actual portion of the Roman Empire.[90] Tiberius sent instructions to Vitellius
to cultivate peaceful relations with Parthia, or at least to seek
a diplomatic solution to any problems.[91] Tiberius was in a good
position to use covert action because his timely intelligence told
him that Artabanus's subjects were greatly dissatisfied with his rule
and that it would be easy to foment discontent, to bring about a
revolution.[92] Some of the Parthian nobles even went in person to
Rome in 35 CE to suggest that if Phraates, one of the sons of
Phraates IV, were to appear under Roman protection upon the
banks of the Euphrates, they would back him.

Tiberius decided that encouraging rivals to the thrones of both Armenia and Parthia was a good idea. Artabanus also faced an Iberian invasion of Armenia that he failed to stem, and fled to Hyrcania (see Map 5). Later he won his way back to Seleucia and, somewhat chastened, he met L. Vitellius on the Euphrates and accepted Rome's settlement in Armenia in return for recognition of his sovereignty in Parthia.[93]

Artabanus III had a long reign, suggesting that he was both powerful and able and had restored central authority in Parthia over the nobility. Yet clandestine plotting by nobles continued, and Rome was the obvious place for them to look for support. A prominent Parthian noble, Sinnaces, and a eunuch named Abdus, with a position at the Parthian court, went secretly to Rome, where they reported that if a Parthian prince were to come to the frontier, Parthia would rise to his support. Tiberius chose to send such a prince – Phraates, the youngest son of Phraates IV, who had been living in Rome for nearly half a century and was of advanced age. But Phraates died suddenly after his arrival, either because of his age and the fatigue of the journey, or because Artabanus had his own operatives and had him poisoned before he could make a move for the throne.[94] Artabanus let Tiberius know he had discovered the mission of the two ambassadors, then had Abdus poisoned and kept Sinnaces occupied with other missions and pretences.[95]

Not discouraged by this first attempt, Tiberius intensified his efforts by digging up another Parthian heir, this time a grandson of Phraates IV named Tiridates (III).[96] He appointed Lucius Vitellius as governor of Syria, and to make Vitellius's job easier, he planned to set up a rival king in Armenia. A large bribe convinced Pharasmanes, the king of Iberia (see Map 5), to put his brother Mithridates on the Armenian throne.[97] Arsaces, the son of Artabanus, was murdered by his attendants who had been bribed, and Pharasmanes took Artaxata without resistance.[98] When this news reached the Parthian court, Artabanus immediately sent his son Orodes to recover the lost dependency.

Orodes was unable to raise enough mercenary troops to secure the passes they needed to travel through, which were controlled by the Iberians.[99] The Parthian forces consisted wholly of cavalry, whereas the Iberians had a force of infantry. Orodes was unwilling to risk a battle against superior odds and prudently evaded the issue until forced by his men to give battle.[100] When Orodes was defeated in personal combat by Pharasmanes, his troops supposed

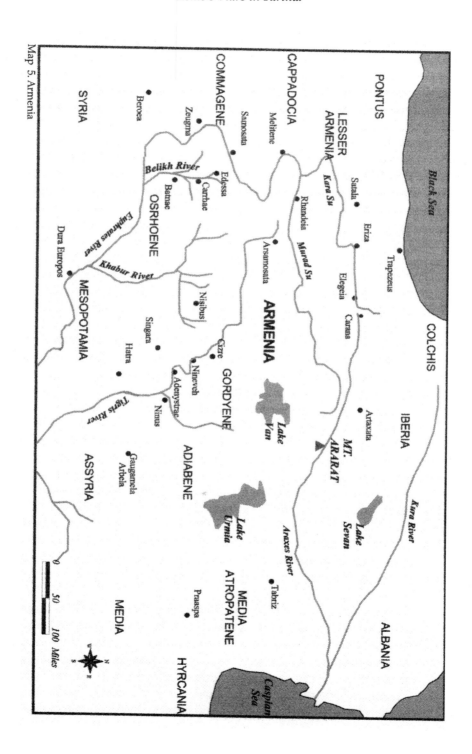

Map 5. Armenia

him dead, and fled from the field.[101] A rout followed. If we may believe Josephus, many 'tens of thousands' were killed.[102] Armenia was wholly lost, and Artabanus found himself left with diminished resources and a tarnished image at home.

In 36 CE, the Parthian king, Artabanus, levied a larger force and took to the field against the Iberians in the hope of recovering his lost province.[103] They were attacked along the way by the Alani who may have been bribed by Roman agents; covert funding was doing its work well. Before Artabanus could force a decisive engagement, Vitellius took the field, headed toward the Euphrates and threatened to invade Mesopotamia. Not willing to fight a war on two fronts (Romans and Alani), Artabanus withdrew from Armenia and returned home to defend his kingdom, Parthia. The Romans had thus obtained their objective, and by means of bribes and disinformation encouraged disaffection within the Parthian kingdom. This undercover work was so successful that Artabanus was compelled to retire to his eastern frontier into Hyrcania with only a band of foreign mercenaries.[104]

The Romans, always willing to capitalize on the weakness of a Parthian ruler, had Vitellius deliver Tiridates into his kingdom, and urged him to seize control while the opportunity offered itself.[105] They conducted him with legions and allies to the banks of the Euphrates. Sacrifices were made and the omens were favourable. A bridge of boats was thrown across the river and an army passed over to Parthian territory. There they were met by Ornospades, satrap of Mesopotamia, a Parthian who had served under Tiberius and had thus won Roman citizenship.[106]

Shortly afterwards, Sinnaces arrived with more troops, and his father, Abdagases, brought the royal treasure and ornaments. The Greek cities of Mesopotamia such as Nicephorium and Anthemusia, and Parthian cities like Halus and Artemita, all welcomed Tiridates.[107] He seems to have been acceptable to the Greeks, some of the Parthian nobility and to the pro-Romans, because he was received in Seleucia with acclaim and his supporters were rewarded with control of the city government, replacing the more aristocratic group that had supported Artabanus.[108] The coronation was delayed pending the arrival of two nobles, Phraates and Hiero, who in the end never attended and sided with Artabanus who was installed in the far eastern portion of the empire.[109] Tiridates was restrained by a lack of funds from attacking Artabanus, so instead he besieged a fort in which the former ruler had stored his treasure and his concubines. The possession of the royal harem was vital to his recognition by the country at large.[110] This tactic, however, would lose him the throne.[111]

Although the Romans were successful in putting their nominee on the throne, kings who held their crowns by virtue of Roman support never had popular support very long. The disaffected party found Artabanus hiding in Hyrcania, clothed in dirty rags and living off the land. When first discovered, he was suspicious of a trap, but they convinced him that Tiridates was sufficiently unpopular for Artabanus to be returned to the throne. Still in rags, he raised an army and headed for Seleucia.[112] Once he became aware of the move on his throne, Tiridates consulted his chief advisor, Abdagases, who suggested he retreat across the Tigris into Mesopotamia to delay any action until Roman forces could arrive with reinforcements from Armenia or Elymaea. Tiridates took his advice and agreed to the withdrawal. Unfortunately, his retreat took on the aspect of a flight when his troops deserted him rapidly and went over to Artabanus. Tiridates fled to Syria where he arrived with scarcely more than a handful of men.[113]

The flight of Tiridates put Parthia back into the hands of Artabanus. He reoccupied the throne, apparently without having to fight a battle.[114] For the time being, he was not yet strong enough to take revenge on the Armenians, or to retaliate in any way upon the Romans for their support of Tiridates. Mithridates, the Iberian, was left in possession of Armenia, and Vitellius found himself unmolested on the Euphrates.

Tiberius wanted the struggle formally ended, and having failed in his attempts to fill the Parthian throne with a Roman nominee, was ready to acknowledge Artabanus and sign a treaty with him. Tiberius instructed Vitellius to that effect late in 36 or early 37 CE.[115] He invited Artabanus to an interview on the Euphrates, and Artabanus expressed his willingness to meet with the Romans. A bridge of boats was put up across the Euphrates and each representative was escorted by a guard. The Romans persuaded the Parthian king to terms that were regarded as highly honourable to themselves, and not degrading to Parthia. We do not know the terms agreed upon, but peace was established between the two empires, probably by having Rome promise not to back any more pretenders to the Parthian throne, and by having Parthia give up any claim to Armenia. He was also induced to throw a few grains of frankincense on the sacrificial fire which burnt in front of the Roman standards and the imperial images, an act which was accepted at Rome as one of submission and homage.[116] Artabanus was persuaded to send his son, Darius, with some other Parthians of rank to Rome as hostages for his good behaviour.[117]

THE DIPLOMATIC SOLUTION

Augustus resisted the temptation to retaliate against Parthia, and this restraint set a pattern. He recognized that prudent diplomacy and a discreet display of force were preferable to expensive and hazardous ventures across the Euphrates. Indirect suzerainty in Armenia and a *modus vivendi* with Parthia represented a means to preserve prestige and protect security.[118] All of his diplomatic successes were accomplished by means other than overt military operations. Parthia as well as Rome had reasons for avoiding war. Rome found that its military successes in the East were short-lived. Parthia, torn by dissensions of rival claimants to its throne, and continually menaced by Asian migrations, was in no position to attack the Romans, and willingly endured a diplomatic defeat rather than risk actual conflict. Struggle after struggle between contenders for the throne over a half century had reduced Parthia to a state of anarchy, and the good effects of the strong rule of Artabanus had been largely negated by his contest with Tiridates.[119] Artabanus was forced to recognize the virtual independence of large areas in the north, and Parthian troops and officials frequently found themselves helpless. Of course, when the Romans thought they were strong enough to defeat the Parthians by force, then force was used. As we will see in the next three chapters, the campaigns under Nero, Trajan and Septimius Severus were just that – straightforward military campaigns. They were, in the long run, spectacularly unsuccessful. The only thing they accomplished was to weaken Parthia sufficiently for a takeover by the Sassanid Persians. Although the eastern frontier remained a focus of military activity throughout the fourth century, it was always at great expense. From the Roman perspective, covert action was a much better way to achieve their goals than expensive military action.

By the use of diplomacy under Augustus, each side was able to escape the shackles of its own military propaganda and lay the foundations of a relatively stable peace. J.G.C. Anderson commented about this very issue in *The Cambridge Ancient History*: Augustus took a sane view of Rome's Eastern question, and if he could have freed himself from the shackles of political tradition, he might have brought about an understanding that would have saved the empire endless trouble and bloodshed without sacrificing 'any real Roman interest'.[120]

The peaceful outcome he achieved was at once a tribute to the patience and judicious foresight characteristic of Augustus as a policy maker. By building a degree of confidence between two monarchs of antagonistic powers, Phraates would be able to uphold the integrity of his kingdom despite having to face down the wealthiest and most effectively organized military power of the ancient world.[121] How unfortunate that success by these means did not bring the military glory that later Roman emperors and commanders so often craved.

NOTES

1. Among the Greek inscriptions from Susa is a much-mutilated metric one which Cumont has dated to Phraates IV. See F. Cumont, 'Nouvelles inscriptions grecques de Suse', *CRAI*, (1930), pp.211–20. Cumont suggested that the rebel Tiridates might be the general mentioned in these verses, perhaps a commander who won fame in victory over Antony. See N.C. Debevoise, *The Political History of Parthia* (New York: Greenwood Press, 1968), p.136.

2. Dio 51.18.1. There are no known dated tetradrachms of Phraates IV for 30/29 BCE. See R.H. McDowell, *Coins from Seleucia on the Tigris* (Ann Arbor, MI: University of Michigan Press, 1935), p.185. Horace, *Odes* 2.2.17, mentions Phraates's restoration. On the problem of Tiridates and Phraates see Debevoise, *Political*, pp.135–6.

3. Dio 51.18.3 has this happen just after Actium, and Dio 53.33.1 clearly suggests he is recalling earlier events. The interval between Octavian's stay in Asia Minor and the reappearance of Tiridates in Parthia in May 26 BCE. Justin 42.5.6 says Tiridates, Phraates's son, and the envoys were received by Octavian in Spain. This is rejected by Debevoise, *Political*, pp.137–8, who discusses the numismatic evidence; cf. A.D.H. Bivar, 'The Political History of Iran under the Arsacids,' in *CHI*: vol. 3, 1: *The Seleucid, Parthian and Sasanian Period*, ed. E. Yarshater (Cambridge: Cambridge University Press, 1983), p.66.

4. D. Magie, 'The Mission of Agrippa to the Orient in 23 BC', *CP*, 3 (1908), pp.145–52, who suggests that while Agrippa was at Mytilene in 23 BCE, his officers may have been negotiating for the return of the standards. Horace, *Odes* 1.12.53.

5. J.H. Dee, 'Arethusa to Lycotas. Propertius 4.3', *TAPA*, 104 (1974), pp.81–96.

6. Cf. Propertius, *Elegies* 3.1.16; 4.1.19; 5.48; 9.25ff. Debevoise, *Political*, p.139, n.50; J.G.C. Anderson, 'The Eastern Frontier under Augustus,' in *CAH*, 10 (1934), p.262.

7. See the comments of Bivar, 'Political History of Iran', p.66, that the growing concentration of troops may have been for propaganda effect: a very expensive effect.

8. The idea that the Parthians might establish a foothold in the Mediterranean by means of Syria and threaten Rome is put forth by F. Cumont, 'Review of Dobrias', *Syria*, 6 (1925), p.282, n.1; cf. J. Dobrias, 'Les premiers rapports des Romains avec les Parthes', *Archiv Orientalni*, 3 (1931) pp 215–56, esp. 217.

9. See C. Lerouge, *L'image des Parthes dans le monde gréco-romain* (Stuttgart: Franz Steiner, 2007), p.76, who points out that our sources on what the Romans and Parthians thought of each other also improve with the time of Augustus.

10. His negotiated settlement with Parthia did not please the more militaristic elements of the Roman world and so he had to carefully justify it by edicts and coins. Dio 54.8.1–3. On the restitution of the standards, see Lerouge, *L'image des Parthes*, pp.103–4.

11. On the return of the standards, Suetonius, *Augustus* 21.3; Suetonius, *Tiberius* 9.1; Justin

42.5.11ff; Livy, *Epit.* 141; Velleius Paterculus 2.91.1; Florus 2.34.63; Ovid, *Fasti* 5.545ff; Eutropius, *Brev.* 7.9; *CIL*, 1, pp.229 and 318. The event was celebrated in Rome by the erection of a triumphal arch, see H. Mattingly and E.A. Sydenham, *Roman Imperial Coinage* (London: Spink, 1923–94), vol. 1, nos. 46, 61, no. 17 and no. 63; no. 37; Dio 54.8.

12. Dio 54.8.
13. Ovid, *Fasti* 5.580–94.
14. P. Zanker, *The Power of Images in the Age of Augustus* (Ann Arbor, MI: University of Michigan Press, 1988), pp.188–92 on the Prima Porta statue. See also A. Hannestad, *Roman Art and Imperial Policy* (Aarhus: Aarhus University 1988), pp.50–6.
15. Ovid, *Fasti* 5.580–94.
16. The propaganda slogan *signis receptis* appeared especially on gold and silver coins that circulated among the upper classes. Mattingly and Sydenham, *RIC*, vol. 1, p.46; nos. 46ff; p.70, nos. 98ff; p.84, no. 256; p.86, nos. 302ff.
17. Zanker, *Power of Images*, pp. 187–196; Dio 54.8.3. On the poets as heir to Republican aspirations and the spokesmen for public opinion, see P.A. Brunt, 'Roman Imperial Illusions', in P.A. Brunt, *Roman Imperial Themes* (Oxford: Clarendon Press, 1990), p.443. On the temple of Mars Ultor and its location see J.W. Rich, 'Augustus's Parthian Honours: The Temple of Mars Ultor and the Arch in the Forum Romanum', *PBSR*, 66 (1998), pp.71–128.
18. Horace, *Odes* 1.2.51–2 (winter of 28 BCE).
19. Ibid., 3.3.43–4 (between 30 and 20 BCE).
20. Ibid., 3.2.3–6 (between 30 and 20 BCE).
21. Horace, *Epistles* 1.12.26–8.
22. Horace, *Odes* 4.15.6–9. The same attitude can be found in *RGDA*, chapter 13. Virgil, *Aeneid* 7.601ff. stresses the shrine being open.
23. Justin 41.1.1. On Parthia being on equal footing with Rome, see Lerouge, *L'image des Parthes*, pp.119–22.
24. *RGDA*, 5.29.
25. Tacitus, *Annals* 2.3; Suetonius, *Tiberius* 9.1; Dio 54.9. Velleius Paterculus 2.94 gets it wrong by calling the new king Artavasdes. Suetonius, *Augustus* 21.3; Justin 42.5.11ff; Livy, *Epit.* 141; *RGDA*, 27; Florus 2.34.65; Magie, 'Mission of Agrippa', pp.145–52; Horace, *Odes* 4.15.6–8; Horace, *Epistles* 1.12.27–8; 18.56; Propertius 4.6.79–86; Ovid, *Fasti* 5.580–98; 6.465–8; *RGDA*, 29.2; Eutropius, *Brev.* 7.9; Orosius 6.21.29. Rawlinson, *Parthia*, p.223.
26. Dio 54.9.5–7; Suetonius, *Tiberius* 9.1; Josephus, *AJ* 15.105; Festus 19; Tacitus, *Annals* 2.3.2, 4.1. We are told that around 20 BCE, the Armenians became so dissatisfied with him that they requested that Tigranes be sent in his place. By the time Tiberius arrived with an army to drive him out, Artaxes had already been killed by the Armenians themselves. F.E. Romer, 'Gaius Caesar's Military Diplomacy in the East', *TAPA*, 109 (1974), p.200.
27. The restoration of the standards was recorded on coins struck in Asiatic, Spanish, senatorial and imperial mints. Most of the coin legends that related to contemporary events mentioned the Parthians. Augustus mentions the incident in *RGDA*, 5.29. Mattingly and Sydenham, *RIC*, vol. 1, p.63, n.46–8; p. 70, no. 98–100; p.84, no 256; p.86, nos. 302–4; pp. 86–7, nos. 305–10; p. 87, nos. 311–13.
28. Archelaus of Cappadocia was given Lesser Armenia as well as certain lands in Cilicia. Ariobarzanes, son of the former king of Media Atropatene, was appointed to rule over his father's lands. Strabo 12.1.4 and 3.29; Dio 54.9.2. On Rome's influence on Media Atropatene see E. Dabrowa, 'Roman Policy in Transcaucasia from Pompey to Domitian', in D.H. French and C.S. Lightfoot (eds), *The Eastern Frontier of the Roman Empire: Proceedings of a Colloquium held at Ankara in September 1988*, British Institute of Archaeology at Ankara Monograph no. 11 (Oxford: British Archaeological Reports, International Series, 553, 1989), pp.67–75.
29. Suetonius, *Augustus* 48.
30. Note that Tigranes's coins bear Parthian titles. See E.T. Newell, *Some Unpublished Coins of Eastern Dynasts*, Numismatic Notes and Monographs (New York: The American Numismatic Society, 1926), pp.13–15.
31. G. Rawlinson, *The Sixth Great Monarchy* (New York: Publishers Plate Renting Co., 1870), p.118.
32. Among the Latin writers, this idea begins with Velleius Paterculus 2.94. From him it passes to Suetonius, *Octavian* 21; Justin 13.5, Eutropius, *Brev.* 7.5, Orosius 6.21. Tacitus does not accept this interpretation. See Rawlinson, *Sixth Oriental Monarchy*, p.620, n.54.

33. Josephus, *BJ* 18.40, 'Thesmusa', variant reading 'Thermousa'. 'Thea Musa' on coins. Bivar, 'Political History of Iran', p.67, n.3.

34. See, for example, Debevoise, *Political*, p.143.

35. Josephus, *AJ* 18.42. Titius was governor from 10 to 9 BCE. See 'Syria' in *RE*, col. 1629. The four sons were Seraspadanse, Phraates, Rhodaspes, and Vonones. We are told they were treated with respect due to their rank, but they were nevertheless hostages. Debevoise, *Political*, p.144; A.F. von Gutschmid, *Geschichte Irans und seiner Nachbarländer von Alexander der Grosse bis zum untergang der Arsaciden* (Tübingen: H. Laupp, 1888), p.116. They are mentioned in *RGDA*, 6.32, and in Latin inscriptions, *CIL*, 6.1799, 14.2216.

36. Phrataaces and Musa were married – an act that horrified the Greeks and Romans. The act suggests a possible connection with the changes that Zoroastrianism was then undergoing. Customs confined solely to the Magi, like next-of-kin marriages, were now being adopted by the rulers. Debevoise, *Political*, p.143. W. Wroth, *A Catalogue of Greek Coins in the British Museum: Catalogue of the Coins of Parthia* (Bologna: Arnaldo Forni, 1964), pp.xl–xlii.

37. Rawlinson, *Sixth Great Monarchy*, p.122.

38. Dio 55.9; Romer, 'Gaius Caesar's Military Diplomacy', p.201; Rawlinson, *Parthia*, p.224.

39. Rawlinson, *Sixth Great Monarchy*, p.120.

40. Romer, 'Gaius Caesar's Military Diplomacy', p.201.

41. Rawlinson, *Sixth Great Monarchy*, p.120. Coins of the year 5 BCE have the legend *ARMENIA RECEPTA*. Ibid., p.620, n.57.

42. According to Rawlinson, this Tigranes is mentioned only once in a fragment of Dio 55.11.

43. See Romer, 'Gaius Caesar's Military Diplomacy', p.202.

44. Dio 55.10.7; Ovid, *Ars Ama.* 1.179. On the Mars Temple see Dio 55.10.1–8; Suetonius, *Augustus* 29.1; Zanker, *Power of Images*, pp.194–5; C. Nicolet, *Space, Geography and Politics in the Early Roman Empire* (Ann Arbor, MI: University of Michigan Press, 1991), pp.41–4.

45. Ovid, *Ars Ama.* 1.177–228: the quotation is v.179. See R. Syme, *History in Ovid* (Oxford: Clarendon Press, 1978), pp.8–13 on Ovid and the expedition of Gaius; and G. Williams, *Change and Decline: Roman Literature in the Early Empire* (Berkeley, CA: University of California Press, 1978), pp.77–80.

46. On the information gathering, see Pliny, *HN* 6.141; M.I. Rostovtzeff, 'The Sarmatae and the Parthians', in *CAH*, 11 (1936), p.126, who identifies Isidore to the time of Pliny; Romer, 'Gaius Caesar's Military Diplomacy', p.202.

47. He made a grand tour lasting over a year-and-a-half, through Greece, the lower Danubian region, and Anatolia. The tour culminated in his consulship for 1 CE.

48. Dio 55.10.20.

49. Romer, 'Gaius Caesar's Military Diplomacy', p.204; Syme, *History in Ovid*, p.11.

50. A.M. Ramsay, 'The Speed of the Imperial Post,' *JRS*, 15 (1925), p.72; the distance from Massilia, where Lucius died, to an unspecified point in Syria exceeds that from Limyra to Pisa. Even allowing for seasonal variance in the speed of travel, word did not reach Gaius until mid-September, perhaps not much more before October, 2 CE, when he was preparing for a Parthian war. See Romer, 'Gaius Caesar's Military Diplomacy', p.209, n.30 and n.31.

51. Romer, 'Gaius Caesar's Military Diplomacy', p.209; Velleius Paterculus 2.101–2; Dio 55.10a.4. Velleius served as a military tribune during the conference but leaves only details of the formalities. Some commentators date the meeting to 2 CE, but it seems unlikely that Gaius would have delayed for so long the main purpose of his visit.

52. See G.V. Sumner, 'The Truth about Velleius Paterculus: Prologomena,' *HSCP*, 74 (1970), p.266, who believes Velleius was on the island himself. Romer, 'Gaius Caesar's Military Diplomacy', p.210, does not.

53. Velleius Paterculus 2.101; Romer, 'Gaius Caesar's Military Diplomacy', p.210; Syme, *History in Ovid*, p.12.

54. Velleius Paterculus 2.102.1.

55. Pliny, *HN* 9.118; Velleius Paterculus 2.97.1 on Lollius's rapacity; Romer, 'Gaius Caesar's Military Diplomacy', p.210.

56. Dio 55.10a.4; Romer, 'Gaius Caesar's Military Diplomacy', p.210.

57. Debevoise, *Political*, p.148. At this meeting was a young officer, Velleius Paterculus, a tribune with Gaius who would go on to write a military history of Rome. He describes

Phraataces in his history, 2.101.1.

58. 'Donnes', in *RE*, col. 1548. The spelling is uncertain. Debevoise, *Political*, p.149, no. 26, suggests Dones or Addus as better choices. Dio 55 10a.6 and Vellius Paterculus 2.102.2 have the Altagira campaign following the Euphrates conference. On the chronology see Romer, 'Gaius Caesar's Military Diplomacy', p.211.

59. For the siege of Altagira, *CIL*, 9.5290; Velleius Paterculus 2.102.2; Florus 2.32; Festus 19. Defended by 'Donnes', Florus 2.32, 'Adwr', Strabo 11.14.6 529C; 'Adduus', Valerius Maximus 2.102.2; 'Addwn', Dio 55.10a.6. He was probably the Parthian satrap for the area.

60. Dio 55.10a.6.

61. Velleius Paterculus 2.102.2; Florus 2.32.44; Dio 55.10a.6–7; Festus 19. The conference was on 9 September 3 CE. *CIL*, 9.5390, and Romer, 'Gaius Caesar's Military Diplomacy in the East', p.211.

62. Dio 55.10a.6–7; Velleius Paterculus 2.102.2, and Florus 2.32.44; Romer 'Gaius Caesar's Military Diplomacy', p.212.

63. Strabo 11.14.6. The spelling and date is fixed by *CIL*, 9.5290.

64. His place was taken by his son, Artavasdes III. *RGDA*, 27; Dio 55.10a.7; Tacitus, *Annals* 2.4; Romer, 'Gaius Caesar's Military Diplomacy', p.212; Debevoise, *Political*, p.150.

65. Romer 'Gaius Caesar's Military Diplomacy', p.214.

66. Josephus, *AJ* 18.43.

67. On Vonones I, see Debevoise, *Political*, pp. 65–6, 144, 151–5, 157, 172, 270; Rawlinson, *Parthia*, pp.231–6.

68. Josephus, *AJ* 18.44–5; Tacitus, *Annals* 2.2–3. Tacitus contrasts the soft lifestyle of King Vonones, who was raised in Rome, with that of his challenger Artabanus, whom the Parthians preferred because he was raised amongst the Scythian Dahae.

69. Tacitus, *Annals* 2.1–2; Josephus, *AJ* 18.46; Debevoise, *Political*, p.151.

70. Josephus, *AJ* 18.47; Tacitus, *Annals* 2.2.

71. Vonones commemorated this victory by striking coins that bear on one side the legend *BASILEUS VONONES* and on the other a Victory with *BASILEUS VONONES NEIKEISAS ARTABANON*. D. Sellwood, 'Parthian Gold Coins', in *Proceedings of the Eleventh International Numismatic Congress, Brussels, 8–13 September 1991* (Louvain-la-Neuve, Belguim: Association Professeur Marcel Hoc, 1993), 60.5; E. Rtveladze, *The Ancient Coins of Central Asia* (Tashkent: Izd-vo lit-ry i iskusstva im. Gafura Guliama, 1987), no. 13. This coin is generally not recognized as authentic.

72. Josephus, *AJ* 8.48–50; McDowell, *Coins from Seleucia*, p.187. Artabanus was king of Atropatene, but he had connections on one side of his family with the Dahae. Tacitus, *Annals* 2.3, 6.36 and 42; See also 'Hyrcania', in *RE*, col. 507ff., and W. Schur, 'Die Orientpolitik des Kaisers Nero', *Klio*, 15 (1923), pp.70ff. Vonones's existing coins are dated 9/10 CE, 11/12 CE and 12/13 CE.

73. Josephus, *AJ* 18.48.

74. *RGDA*, 5.27; Tacitus, *Annals* 2.3ff; Josephus, *AJ* 8.140, and *BJ* 2.222. See also 'Tigranes', in *RE*, no. 5, col. 980; and Debevoise, *Political*, p.153.

75. Tacitus, *Annals* 2.4; cf. Josephus, *AJ* 18.50–2; W.E. Gwatkin, *Cappadocia as a Roman Procuratorial Province* (Columbia, MO: University of Missouri Press, 1930), p.13; McDowell, *Coins from Seleucia*, p.187; Debevoise, *Political*, p.151.

76. Josephus implies this broadly in *AJ* 18.51.

77. Q. Caecilius Metellus Creticus Silanus, 'Caecilius', in *RE*, no. 90, col. 1212; Debevoise, *Political*, p.153; Tacitus, *Annals* 2.4.

78. Tacitus, *Annals*, 2.5. On the diplomatic overtures to the Caucasian countries by Tiberius for help in the Armenian crisis, see E. Dabrowa, 'Roman Policy in Transcaucasia', pp.67–75.

79. Tacitus *Annals* 2.60.

80. Ibid., 2.56.

81. Ibid., 2.56; cf. Suetonius, *Gaius* 1.2, and Strabo 12.3.29. Coins were struck in Caesarea of Cappadocia with the legend *GERMANICUS ARTAXIAS* and with the coronation scene: see Mattingly and Sydenham, *RIC*, vol. 1, 104, no. 8, although Mattingly suggests that perhaps these were struck by Caligula. Contra Debevoise, *Political*, p.154, and D. Magie, 'Roman Policy in Armenia and Transcausasia and its Significance', *Annual Report of the American Historical Association*, 1 (1919), pp.298–9. On the choice of his new name, see Rawlinson, *Sixth Great Monarchy*, p.621, n.28.

82. Tacitus, *Annals* 2.58.

83. Germanicus sent Alexander, perhaps a Palmyrene merchant, on a mission to a certain Orabazes in Mesene. We do not know the nature of the message. Mesene, a former Parthian vassal state, might have been independent by this time – not surprising in view of the weakness of the central government. Debevoise, *Political*, p.155.

84. Tacitus, *Annals* 2.58. The contemporary Strabo 16.1.28 confirms the fact that the Euphrates was still the boundary. Debevoise, *Political*, p.155; Bivar, 'Political History of Iran', p.69.

85. Tacitus, *Annals* 2.68; Suetonius, *Tiberius* 49.2. On Remmius, see *RE*, *s.v.*, no. 3, cols 595–6; Debevoise, *Political*, p.155.

86. The details of Parthian history in this period are not known to us. It seems that Artabanus was engaged in wars with nations on his borders, rather successfully. Rawlinson, *Sixth Great Monarchy*, p.129.

87. Suetonius, *Tiberius* 41.

88. Tacitus, *Annals* 6.31. Cf. Philostratus, *Vita Apoll.* 2.2. Debevoise, *Political*, p.157.

89. That is, the domains of old Macedonia and Persia. Tacitus, *Annals* 6.31. Dio 58.26; Suetonius, *Tiberius* 66.

90. Tacitus, *Annals* 6.31; Dio 58.26.

91. Josephus, *AJ* 18.97, 99.

92. Tacitus, *Annals* 6.32.

93. J.G.C. Anderson, 'The Eastern Frontier from Tiberius to Nero', in *CAH*, 10 (1963), p.749.

94. For the poison theory, see Rawlinson, *Sixth Great Monarchy*, p.130.

95. Debevoise, *Political*, pp.157–8. On the letter Artabanus supposedly wrote to Tiberius at this time, see Suetonius, *Tiberius* 66.

96. Tacitus, *Annals* 6.37.

97. This candidate was suggested by Tiberius, according to Tacitus, *Annals* 6.32. Mithridates was eventually removed, imprisoned and then banished by Caligula. Dio 60.8; Seneca, *De tranquillitate animi* 11.12. See E. Dabrowa, 'Roman Policy in Transcaucasia', p.69.

98. Tacitus, *Annals* 6.33; Bivar, 'Political History of Iran', p.73.

99. Although the Sarmatians were willing to sell their services to either side, the Iberians guarded the main passes through the Caucasus. The Derbend Pass, between the mountains and the Caspian, was, according to Tacitus, impassable during summer because it was flooded by the sea. Tacitus, *Annals* 6.33.

100. Ibid., 6.34, talks about the soldiers being exasperated by the reproaches of the enemy troops for not engaging.

101. Tacitus, *Annals* 6.35; Josephus, *AJ* 18.97ff.

102. Josephus, *AJ* 18.98.

103. Tacitus, *Annals* 6.36.

104. Ibid., 6.36, and Rawlinson, *Sixth Great Monarchy*, p.132; Bivar, 'Political History of Iran', p.73.

105. Tacitus, *Annals* 6.37.

106. Ibid., 6.37. Cf. Rawlinson, *Sixth Great Monarchy*, p.234. Ornospades was not yet satrap of Mesopotamia, an honour which he received after he rejoined his king.

107. A number of ancient authors make this distinction between Greek and Parthian cities. The cities are given in Tacitus, *Annals* 6.41; Isidore of Charax, *Parthian Stations* 1–3 names Ichnae, Nicephorium, Artemita and Chala as Greek cities. Artemita is called both Greek and Parthian. On its location, see Debevoise, *Political*, p.160.

108. Tacitus, *Annals* 6.42; McDowell, *Coins from Seleucia*, p.225, suggests that his supporters in Seleucia were the native elements, consistently pro-Roman. This idea cannot be reconciled with information from Tacitus which clearly indicates that the three groups behind Tiridates were the Greeks, the nobility, and the pro-Romans, unless we assume the last to be the native elements. Debevoise, *Political*, p.161.

109. It was suggested by F. Cumont, 'Une lettre du roi Artaban III', *CR* (1932), pp.249ff., that this Phraates may have been the satrap of Susiana.

110. Phraates IV had murdered his women rather than allow them to fall into the possession of the pretender, Tiridates. Debevoise, *Political*, p.161.

111. Tacitus, *Annals* 6.43; Rawlinson, *Sixth Great Monarchy*, p.133.

112. Josephus, *AJ* 18.100; Tacitus, *Annals* 6.44.

113. Debevoise, *Political*, p.162; Rawlinson, *Sixth Great Monarchy*, p.135.

114. Josephus, *AJ* 18.101–3; Tacitus, *Annals* 6.44.
115. Josephus, *AJ* 18.101–3.
116. Suetonius, *Caligula* 14; Dio 59.27.
117. Josephus, *AJ* 18.101–3 uses the word hostage as do Suetonius, *Caligula* 14 and Suetonius, *Vitellius* 2.4. All of these sources either place this incident in the reign of Gaius or leave the question unsettled. See E. Täubler, *Die Parthernachrichten bei Josephus* (Berlin: Druck von E. Ebering, 1904), pp.39ff. See Debevoise, *Political*, pp.165–78, on the pretenders to the throne of both Parthia and Armenia. On page 163 he points out that the coinage from the beginning of the common era to 40 CE shows frequent intervals for which no royal coins are known. The kings were either not in possession of the mint cities or were too poverty-stricken to be able to coin money. Cf. Magie, 'Roman Policy in Armenia and Transcausasia', pp.298–9.
118. E.S. Gruen, 'The Imperial Policy of Augustus', in K.A. Raaflaub and Mark Toher, *Between Republic and Empire* (Berkeley, CA: University of California Press, 1999), pp.395–9.
119. Debevoise, *Political*, p.163; Magie, 'Roman Policy in Armenia and Transcausasia', pp.295–304.
120. Anderson, 'The Eastern Frontier under Augustus', p.256.
121. Bivar, 'Political History of Iran', p.67.

7

THE CAMPAIGNS OF CORBULO AND THE NERONIAN SETTLEMENT

As long as Parthia remained weak, Augustus and his successors pursued a policy of Roman suzerainty over Armenia with a Roman nominee on the throne. In 51 CE, however, the powerful and ambitious Vologases I became a Parthian king and Rome suddenly needed to take a more vigorous policy to retain its previous influence in the region.[1]

Vologases made the first move. When the Emperor Claudius was poisoned in 54 CE, the youthful Nero came to the throne and this seemed like an opportune moment to take advantage of Roman weakness. So, when the Roman client king of Armenia was killed by the neighbouring Iberians (see Map 5), Vologases put his brother Tiridates on the throne without consulting Rome.[2] His intelligence staff may have informed him that the mere youth of 18 now on the throne at Rome was not ready to fight a major campaign. Nero was a lover of music and of the arts, who might just possibly ignore the loss of a remote province. Vologases acted as if Rome had no history of responding to this situation, established his brother at Artaxata, and did not so much as send an embassy to Nero to excuse or explain his acts.

News of the events in Armenia reached Rome by December and Nero, or his advisors at least, made preparations immediately for war.[3] They applied themselves at once to a series of vital military and political decisions. All the Roman provinces bordering upon Armenia were placed under new governors.[4] The eastern legions were brought up to full strength and sent toward Armenia.[5] The allies, Antiochus IV of Commagene and Agrippa II of Calchis, were instructed to collect troops and hold them ready to invade Parthia, and bridges were constructed over the Euphrates.[6] Gnaeus Domitius Corbulo was recalled from Germany and given command of Cappadocia and Galatia with the eastern forces and charged with recovering Armenia.[7] He was a seasoned veteran and a career man whose appointment shows how seriously Rome took the situation. The X Fretensis, the XII Fulminata and some auxiliaries were left in Syria with its governor, Ummidius Quadratus. An equal number of allies, the III Gallica, and the VI Ferrata were assigned to Corbulo, who was also given the cohorts that were wintering in Cappadocia.[8] Corbulo moved to Cilicia where he met Quadratus, who was more afraid of his popular colleague stealing his shot at military glory than he was of what the Parthians might do.[9]

The Roman commanders sent envoys to Vologases, suggesting that he make concessions and apparently giving him the understanding that something less was required of him than the restoration of Armenia to the Romans.[10] The Parthian king listened favourably to these overtures and tried to avoid war by surrendering some important members of his family as hostages. At the same time, he withdrew his troops from Armenia.[11] The motive for the Parthian king's actions is obvious. The Parthian throne, as usual, was not totally secure. Vologases's son Vardanes had revolted a little while earlier, and no doubt he preferred to come to an agreement with the Romans, rather than have an internal revolt and an all-out war with the Romans at the same time.[12] Even Tacitus cynically comments that Vologases complied not from terror of the Romans, but in order to prepare for war at his convenience, or that he might remove those whom he suspected of jealousy under the name of hostages. Thus Rome did not achieve its main goal here.[13]

The struggle for power between Vologases and his son Vardanes seems to have lasted for three years, from 55 to 58 CE. Its details are unknown to us, but Vologases must have been successful and we may assume that the pretender, who disappears from the record, was put to death. No sooner was this contest settled than Vologases began taking a higher tone in his communications with Corbulo and Ummidius. He declared that not only must his brother Tiridates be left in the undisturbed possession of Armenia, but it should be distinctly understood that he held it as a Parthian possession, not a Roman protectorate.[14] At the same time, Tiridates began to exercise his authority over the Armenians with severity, and especially punished those whom he suspected of favouring the Romans.[15]

Corbulo now began prosecuting the war in earnest. The condition of the eastern legions was poor. He needed to tighten discipline over these poorly trained and ill-equipped troops. Tacitus says that many of the veterans scarcely knew arms when they saw them, and in some instances the troops were not even supplied with armour (a familiar theme in America's war in Mesopotamia as well).[16] Those who were too old or incapacitated were sent home, and the strength of the legions was increased by levies from Galatia and Cappadocia. To these was added the X Fretensis, which was relieved in Syria by the IV Scythica from Moesia.[17]

CORBULO AND THE CAMPAIGN OF 57–60 CE

By late 57 CE, Corbulo felt the troops' condition had improved enough to mobilize them and to move into Armenia. The winter of 57/58 CE was bitterly cold and the army was bivouacked in tents. Many of the men suffered from frostbite, and some died while on guard duty. Corbulo paraded among his troops bareheaded and tried hard to keep up their morale. Still, many deserted. A man who had left the standards was executed. The Romans normally did not inflict the death penalty until the third offence, but in this case, Corbulo inflicted it on the first offence. Paccius Orfitus was given command of the auxiliaries who were distributed in garrison posts at strategic points. He had been given strict orders not to engage the enemy, but the leading centurion disobeyed and was badly defeated.[18]

In the spring of 58 CE, when weather conditions improved, the campaign was resumed.[19] Large parts of Armenia were overrun and put to fire and sword. Vologases sent a contingent of troops to the assistance of the Armenians, but was unable to proceed to their relief in person because of a revolt that had broken out in Hyrcania (see Map 5). This event occurred in the same year that the rebellion of Vardanes was suppressed.

Not seeking his own intelligence, and misled by his experiences in Germany, Corbulo expected a native army to attack his forces en masse. Instead, Tiridates invaded from the direction of Media Atropatene and began a guerrilla war.[20] In a hostile, unknown and intricate country, Corbulo thought it highly imprudent to separate his forces into several columns. A month or two of vain pursuit, however, proved to him that Tiridates did not intend to risk his fortunes on one battle. The elusive king flouted the mobility of his army with its horsemen vastly superior to the slow-moving Roman infantry. Tiridates's active guerrilla warfare compelled the Roman general to change tactics. Corbulo divided his men into bands to pillage the country. The punitive expeditions he organized succeeded in reducing some strongholds. Simultaneously he arranged with various allies to make raids into Armenia from the south-west and north-east. Antiochus of Commagene attacked the districts closest to his kingdom, and Pharasmanes of Iberia attacked his neighbours.[21]

The larger Roman force marched down the valley of the Araxes, its left flank resting on the foothills. Tiridates's forces tried to induce the Romans to break formation and expose themselves to cavalry attack, but when Corbulo's ranks stood firm, this tactic failed and Tiridates fled. The capital city of Artaxata had to open its gates, and the city surrendered in 58 CE without a struggle.[22] The inhabitants' lives were spared but the walls were pulled down and the city burned. Two other strongholds that resisted were reduced, one by storm and the other by siege.[23] With the fall of Artaxata the campaign of 58 appears to have ended.[24]

In the spring of 59 CE Corbulo made the long march south-westwards past Lake Van to take the second capital of Armenia, Tigranocerta.[25] Ambassadors from Tigranocerta were sent out before he arrived with a gold crown for Corbulo, and they informed him that the city was prepared to surrender.[26] When the army arrived at Tigranocerta, however, the city gates were closed. To discourage a lengthy defence and the need for the Romans to besiege such a large city, Corbulo executed an Armenian noble whom he had captured and shot his head into the city. We are told it fell into the midst of a council of war (a very lucky shot indeed) and this hastened the surrender of the city without further resistance.[27] Corbulo took one more fort by storm, Legerda, and then wintered in Tigranocerta.

In the spring of 60, Tiridates made a final attempt to invade Armenia from Media Atropatene, but he was repulsed and forced to abandon his struggle. The previous status quo was restored, and a reliable client prince, Tigranes, was duly appointed king of Armenia.[28] Parts of Armenia were put under client kings in order to make control of the newly subdued territory easier, because many people still favoured rule by the Parthians.[29] Leaving 1,000 legionaries with 3,000 or 4,000 cavalry and infantry auxiliaries to support the new ruler, Corbulo returned to Syria, where he succeeded Quadratus who had died.[30]

In 61 CE, Tigranes attacked Adiabene, a Parthian dependency. The Parthian nobility pressured Vologases to make peace with the Hyrcanians and send Parthian levies to counter-attack. He himself threatened the Euphrates crossings to deter Corbulo from sending help to Armenia.[31] Corbulo sent two legions, perhaps the IV Scythica and the XII Fulminata, to Armenia under Verulanus Severus and Vettius Bolanus.[32] He brought up the III Gallica, the VI Ferrata and the X Fretensis to the Euphrates, all augmented by levies. All the crossings were defended and the water supplies carefully guarded. Because of the seriousness of the situation, Corbulo requested that Nero send an additional commander to take charge in Armenia.

Tigranes anticipated trouble with the Parthians and therefore withdrew into Tigranocerta, the seat of government now that Artaxata was destroyed. Monaeses and his Parthian forces cut off convoys carrying food to the city, and then appeared at the city walls. An attempt to storm it proved unsuccessful, and a siege was begun. Vologases himself proceeded to Nisibis from where he could threaten Armenia and Syria at the same time.[33] When Corbulo heard of these events, he threatened Vologases with an invasion of Mesopotamia unless the siege was raised. Corbulo's messenger delivered his message to the Parthian king at Nisibis. Vologases decided to seek peace rather than take on a Roman army that was so well prepared and a well-fortified city like Tigranocerta. Foraging would also be a problem since a recent plague of locusts had destroyed local crops.[34] For these reasons, the king decided to reach an agreement, and it was announced that Vologases was sending ambassadors to Rome to request control of Armenia. He ordered Monaeses to abandon the siege of Tigranocerta, and the Parthian monarch returned to his own country.[35]

The Roman concessions were not immediately disclosed. Tigranes and the Roman legions that supported him were told to withdraw from Armenia. The soldiers spent the winter of 61/62 in temporary quarters on the Cappadocian frontier.[36] At the time, most people considered the Parthian withdrawal a triumph, but the terms of agreement led some to suspect that Corbulo had made a secret pact with the Parthians. The embassy failed for reasons that are unknown, and further conflict became inevitable.

PAETUS AND THE DISASTER AT RHANDEIA

In response to Corbulo's request, L. Caesennius Paetus was appointed governor of Cappadocia in 62 CE and given command of the eastern front. Corbulo confined himself to the care of Syria, careful not to invoke Nero's jealousy. Together they set to work building an army of invasion.[37] An equitable division of troops was made, and each commander got three legions.[38]

The truce that had been established in the early summer, when Vologases sent his envoys to Nero, now expired in the autumn on the return of the envoys without a definite reply.[39] Vologases marched to the Euphrates, and the Roman commanders entered upon an autumn campaign, the second within the space of a year. Corbulo crossed the Euphrates in the face of a large Parthian army facing him. He forced the Parthians to withdraw from the eastern bank of the river by means of bringing up ships of considerable size, furnished with towers on which were placed *ballistae* and catapults that cleared the hills on the opposite side of the river. A bridge was completed, and he then advanced and occupied a strong position in the hills at a little distance from the river, and ordered his troops to construct an entrenched camp. This success caused the Parthians to abandon their thoughts of a Syria invasion and to turn all of their forces against the Romans in Armenia.[40]

Paetus did not like the slow, temporizing policy of his rival. He wanted the war to be carried on with more dash and vigour: storm the cities, plunder the country and make severe examples of the guilty. The object of the war should be changed from using shadowy client kings to reducing Armenia into the form of a province.[41] Ignoring the bad omens, Paetus took the offensive. Without waiting for troops being sent from Moesia, with no provisions made for the supply of grain, and without his winter quarters adequately protected, he crossed the Euphrates probably near Melitene. He entered Armenia from Cappadocia with two legions.[42] He hurried the army across the Taurus range with the intention of recovering Tigranocerta and devastating the districts that Corbulo had left untouched. He overran districts that were impossible to retain and much of the grain he captured was ruined.

With winter approaching, and the enemy nowhere in sight, he led his troops back across the mountains and, regarding his campaign as finished, he wrote a dispatch to Nero boasting of his successes. Tacitus describes it as being 'as grandiloquently phrased as it was void of content'.[43] He sent one of his three legions to winter in Pontus, and placed the other two in quarters between the Taurus and the Euphrates, at the same time granting furloughs to as many soldiers as chose to apply for them.

His choice of winter quarters was Rhandeia on the Arsanias

River (Murad Su), a tributary of the Euphrates.[44] He had pitched his camp some forty or fifty miles from the Isoghli crossing on the northern bank of the river (see Map 6). A position on the *south* bank of the river Murad Su would have allowed him to secure communications with the Isoghli crossing in the event of an attack by the enemy. He chose instead a site on the northern bank. It is hard to understand what fragile tactical advantage Paetus thought justified sacrificing the elementary rules of defence. His great impatience had driven him to march to war with an unfinished base camp behind him. Not only did he lack Corbulo's wise patience and imagination, but he showed himself entirely incapable of grasping the patent facts of his military situation. Paetus had greatly weakened his legions by granting leaves to all who applied for them. In addition, his troops were not those who had been whipped into shape by Corbulo; his best men were with the V Macedonica in Pontus. An entire cohort was dispatched to guard his wife and small son who were placed, for safety, in a fortress at Arsamosata.[45]

Defying the severities of winter, the Parthians saw the chance to take Armenia away from the Romans by a surprise attack in a season when normally wars were not carried out. Thanks to his mobility and his position, Vologases engaged Paetus long before Corbulo had news of it. When news of the approaching Parthians reached him, Paetus again made bad decisions. Instead of setting his troops to finishing the fortifications, he boasted to them that the Romans did not need ramparts, and he then marched off to find Vologases. Vologases's scouts reported the positions of the Roman forces, so that he could easily crush the Roman vanguard when they got to the pass, and drive their cavalry from the plain. Even Arsomasata, where Paetus had placed his wife and child in the fortified camp of the legions, was besieged.[46]

The attack caught Paetus unsuspecting and unprepared. His camp was indefensibly located and not even fully fortified because of the furloughs he had granted to a large number of his men when he thought that year's campaign had ended. Once his scouting party was cut off, he fled back to Rhandeia where he divided his vanguard into two isolated detachments. One group of 3,000 men he sent to guard the nearby passes of the Taurus, while the other he kept in the camp.[47] This left his main force across the river at a point at least twenty-five miles away, and he had put the river between his main army and his advanced guard holding the pass. He would therefore be sacrificing his vanguard while cutting off his own communications with Cappadocia, now defenceless against the enemy. After some hesitation, Paetus reluctantly decided to make Corbulo acquainted with his position, but his message simply said that he was expecting to be attacked.[48] When Corbulo received the news, he dispatched 1,000 men from each legion, 800 cavalry, and put an equal number of auxiliaries on notice to be prepared to march immediately.

Once Vologases began besieging Rhandeia, a second Roman messenger broke through enemy lines to warn Corbulo that the attack had begun. Corbulo began his march.[49] Leaving a part of his forces to maintain the forts along the Euphrates, he moved by the shortest and best-provisioned route through Commagene, Cappadocia and then Armenia. To avoid such difficulties as Paetus had encountered in securing positions, Corbulo carried wheat on camels that followed the army. Before long he began to meet fugitives from the besieged Roman camp, and he speeded up his army by forced marches. He finally arrived two days after Rhandeia had surrendered.[50]

Paetus had had enough supplies in his camp to hold out for months, but because of his own cowardice and the bad morale of his troops, he did not await Corbulo's arrival; he capitulated and entered into negotiations with the Parthians immediately. No doubt the Parthians were aware of the proximity of the relieving column and were glad to arrange a peace. The Roman commission was forced to negotiate with Vasaces, the Parthian cavalry commander. An agreement was reached on the second day, when Corbulo was within a three-day march from the scene. Monobazus of Adiabene acted as witness to the treaty thus concluded, the terms of which were naturally highly favourable to the Parthians.

The siege of the camp was to be abandoned, and all Roman soldiers were to be withdrawn from the confines of Armenia. All forts, supplies and provisions were to be turned over to the Parthians. When these conditions had been fulfilled, Vologases was to be free to send ambassadors to Nero to negotiate the Armenian question.[51] In addition, the Romans were forced to build a bridge over the Arsanias River (Murat Su) which ran in front of their camp, as a visible symbol of their defeat.[52] These stipulations were carried out faithfully, but not without further difficulties for the vanquished. Even before the Roman troops left the entrenchments, the Armenians entered and seized the arms and clothing of the legionaries, who dared not protest lest a general massacre ensue.[53]

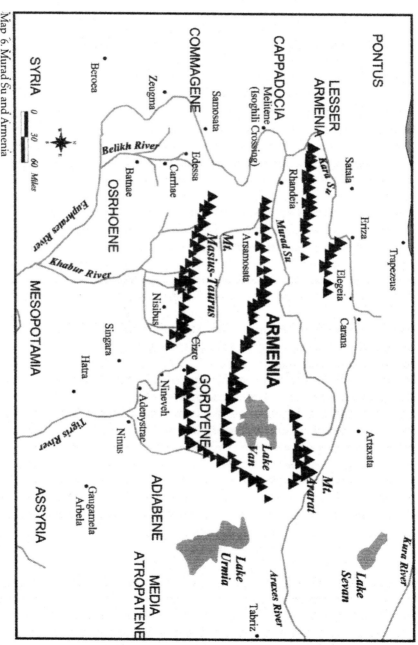

Map 6. Murad Su and Armenia

Paetus proceeded with unseemly haste to the Euphrates, abandoning his wounded and stragglers along the way.[54] When he met up with Corbulo, he attempted to persuade him to return and resume the attack. Corbulo sensibly refused to adopt this foolish plan. He returned directly to Syria to protect his province while Paetus spent the winter in Cappadocia. Corbulo's wrath with the defeated general was extreme. The fruit of his own labours had seemed wasted by Paetus's incompetence and cowardice. In his report home, Corbulo lashed Paetus, pointing out he was amply provisioned and could easily have held out. Paetus had surrendered when the relieving army was within a three-days' march, although he probably did not know this when he surrendered. Roman intelligence gathering, bad as usual, failed to detect the approaching army – information easily and simply signalled, for example, by heliograph or other means. Prompt information might have saved the army at Rhandeia from destruction. The defeat was an embarrassment for the Romans but Vologases had prudently not totally humiliated them, so a major war did not become inevitable.

Monaeses was sent by Vologases to Corbulo with a request that the forts on the east side of the Euphrates be abandoned by the Romans. Negotiations were conducted on the bridge which Corbulo had built over the river, but only after the central portion had been destroyed. The Roman commander agreed to evacuate the forts if the Parthians would withdraw from Armenia, a condition to which they agreed.

The ambassadors sent by Vologases arrived in Rome in the spring of 63 CE.[55] They proposed that Tiridates should receive the crown of Armenia at Roman headquarters, explaining that only his duties as a Magus prevented him from coming to Rome for the investiture.[56] The request was denied. The ambassadors were sent back with presents – an action from which they might infer that if Tiridates appeared in person at Rome, the appeal would be granted. Another consideration might have been that Rome did not want to make peace immediately after a disaster, but wanted time to retrieve its reputation by one last show of power. Having finally read all the dispatches and realized who had been at fault, Paetus was at once recalled and the whole direction of the new campaign was given to Corbulo with widespread authority.

RESUMPTION OF THE WAR

Preparations were made to continue the war. The administration of Syria was given to C. Cestius Gallus, and the military forces, augmented by the XV Apollinaris from Pannonia under Marius Celsus, were entrusted to Corbulo. With Paetus called back to Rome, theauthority of Corbulo was now increased until it was such that Tacitus compared it with that of Pompey under the Manilian Law.[57] The IV Scythica and the XII Fulminata, which had lost the best of their men and were in low morale, were sent to Syria. Picked troops were then gathered at Melitene, ready to cross the Euphrates.[58] There were also picked detachments from Illyria and Egypt, the latter probably part of the XXII Deiotariana, and auxiliaries from allied kings.

Corbulo advanced into Armenia over the route followed by Luculllus and Paetus against the combined Armenians and Parthians led by Tiridates and Vologases respectively. His 30,000 man army particularly took vengeance on the Armenian nobles who had been active in opposing Tigranes, the late Roman puppet-king.[59] His march led him near the spot where the capitulation of Paetus had occurred in the preceding winter. Proposals of peace arrived from Tiridates and Vologases, and the ambassadors were accompanied on their return by some Roman centurions who carried messages of a conciliatory nature. Vologases craftily proposed that a meeting be arranged at Rhandeia, where Paetus had been forced to surrender. Tiberius Alexander and Annius Vinicianus, son-in-law of Corbulo, went to the camp of Tiridates as pledges against ambush. The leaders, each accompanied by twenty horsemen, met and agreed that Tiridates was to receive Armenia, but only from the hands of Nero. Since Corbulo was at the head of an intact army and held possession of Armenian territory, the terms would not seem to have been extorted by fear, and the Parthians were getting what they wanted. In a formal ceremony some days later the Armenian monarch removed the crown from his head before the assembled Roman and Parthia troops and laid it at the feet of a statue of Nero erected for that purpose. This agreement was reached late in 63 CE, but it was not until 66 that it was consummated.[60] In the interval, Tiridates's daughter and also his kingdom remained as hostages in Roman hands. The troops on the eastern front were kept ready for action, and there is evidence that the crossing near Melitene was used by troops that were pushed forward into Armenian territory.[61]

DEFERENCE TO ROME

A part of this period was no doubt occupied by a long trip that Tiridates took to visit his mother and his brothers Pacorus, king of Atropatene, and Vologases, the Parthian monarch, who was in Ecbatana. Besides his own sons, Tiridates took with him those of his two brothers and of Monobazus. The queen also was a member of the party and rode beside her lord, wearing a helmet in lieu of the usual veil. They were escorted by 3,000 Parthian cavalry.[62] This triumphal procession passed through two-thirds of the empire, and was warmly welcomed everywhere it stopped, and lavishentertainments were provided. Every city along the route was decorated to receive the procession, and crowds loudly acclaimed this magnificent spectacle. On the long journey to Rome, Tiridates took care to observe the Zoroastrian regulations that were his duties because of his priestly office.[63] The entire trip was made by land to avoid defiling the sea, and the large sums of money required to support the 3,000 horsemen who accompanied the Armenian king were drawn from the Roman state treasury. It was said to have cost the treasury 800,000 sesterces a day.[64] This outlay went on for nine straight months.

In Italy, Tiridates travelled in a two-horse carriage sent by Nero, which conveyed him by way of Pisenum to Neapolis, where he was met by the emperor. Here Tiridates did obeisance and paid homage to Nero, saluting the emperor as 'Lord'. But, like the warrior that he was, he refused to remove his dagger, preferring to fasten it to its sheath with nails.[65]

A gladiatorial exhibition was given at the nearby city of Puteoli, after which the party proceeded to Rome. The imperial city was decorated for the occasion, and great crowds gathered to watch the ceremony. Tiridates again humbled himself before Nero, who then declared him king of Armenia and placed the diadem on his head.[66] After a stay of some duration in Rome, Tiridates returned home partly by land and partly by sea, for he crossed from Brundisium to Dyrrachium and then passed through Asia Minor. He brought back with him many costly gifts and numbers of artisans in order to rebuild the capital city of Artaxata.[67]

Nero had already erected a triumphal arch in Rome while the war was still in progress. Now that the struggle was concluded, he issued a series of coins to commemorate the closing of the Temple of Janus.[68] The period of peace that followed the temporary settlement of the Armenian question is responsible for the dearth of information on Parthia. There is even considerable doubt as to the length of the reign of Vologases I; it probably extended to 79/80.[69]

More military preparations on a large scale were made by Rome again in the years 66 and 67. A new legion, the I Italica, was created.[70] Another seasoned legion, the XIV Gemina (Martia Victrix), was started on the journey to the eastern front.[71] At the time of his death in 68, Nero was engaged in plans for a great expedition that had as its objective the Iron Gates of the Caucasus.[72] Possibly its ultimate aim was the Alani, as has been suggested, or it might have been a feint to keep the Parthians occupied and thus prevent their sending aid to the Jews.[73] In any case, the hostilities with the Parthians could hardly have been avoided. The troublesome times that followed Nero's death put a stop to all such preparations.

PARTHIAN COOPERATION

In 69 CE, Vespasian declared himself emperor. Vologases, informed of the event, sent ambassadors to Alexandria the next year to offer him 40,000 Parthian horse.[74] It has been suggested that the salutation of the letter making the offer was an insult to Vespasian and that this had something to do with the polite refusal which followed.[75] More likely, Vespasian felt he had the situation in hand. Sohaemus of Emesa and Antiochus of Commagene joined forces with Vespasian, and embassies were sent to the Parthians and Armenians so that peaceful relations might be established with them.[76] In 71, Vologases sent his congratulations to Titus at Zeugma on the Roman victories over the Jews and presented him with a gold crown. The gift was accepted, and the messengers who brought it were feasted before their return.[77]

PAETUS STRIKES AGAIN

An incident occurred in 72 CE that threatened to break the established peace.[78] L. Caesennius Paetus, the unsuccessful general in the last Armenian war, seemed to have suffered no setback because of his incompetence, and was now made governor of Cappadocia and Galatia.[79] He informed Vespasian that he had discovered a plot by which Commagene, one of Rome's subject kingdoms, was planning an alliance that included Antiochus of Commagene and his son Epiphanes with Vologases against Rome. We are not told Paetus's intelligence sources. The union would have been dangerous because Samosata, the capital of Commagene, lay on the Euphrates at one of the best crossings. By this alliance, the Parthians would have gained an excellent base for operations in Syria and Cilicia. Vespasian seems to have trusted Paetus, and he gave the proconsul full liberty to proceed as he thought best, which he did with all possible speed. Moving forward with the X Fretensis and some auxiliaries furnished by Aristobulus of Chalcis and Sohaemus of Emesa, Paetus took Antiochus of Commagene by surprise. Antiochus did not want to be part of his sons' rebellion, so he gathered his wife and children and retired before the Roman advance, which swept into Samosata without a struggle. Although Antiochus himself was not disposed to contest the matter by force of arms, his two sons, Epiphanes and Callinicus, with such troops as they could muster, barred the passage. An all-day battle resulted in a draw at nightfall. When news reached them that the king had defected, it so disheartened his troops that they deserted and the princes fled for refuge to Parthia with a guard of only ten men.[80] Vologases received them with courtesy and hospitality due to their royal rank, but since he was no part of their rebellion, he made no effort to reinstate them. He did, however, write a letter on their behalf to Vespasian, in which he declared them guiltless of the charges that had been brought against them by Paetus.[81] Had Paetus made up the story just to have an excuse for a military campaign or was his intelligence as bad as usual? Among the Parthians the princes were well treated, but they were later surrendered to Velius Rufus, who had been sent by Vespasian to secure them. Antiochus was placed under arrest by the Romans, but was allowed to live in Sparta, where he was furnished with sufficient money to maintain an estate such as befitted a king.[82] Lesser Armenia and Commagene were then made into provinces and garrisoned accordingly.[83]

HANDLING THE EASTERN SITUATION

A contrast is drawn in Tacitus between the general Caesennius Paetus, who is portrayed as weak and lax, and Corbulo, the stern disciplinarian. Paetus was forced to negotiate a truce with the Parthians and this involved a loss of face for the Romans. Paetus requested the peace himself after a military defeat. He agreed to withdraw entirely from Armenia. A rumour even circulated that his troops had been subjected to the ritual humiliation of the yoke. Armenian soldiers had snatched back the spoils and slaves the Romans had captured.[84] This was not the way the Romans were supposed to conduct themselves. Romans were expected to defeat their enemies decisively and dictate the peace (see Chapter 10). When given the choice between a dangerous war (*bellum anceps*) or a disgraceful peace (*pax inhonesta*), Nero chose to go back to war.[85] The treaty ultimately negotiated by Corbulo, and approved by Nero, exacted signs of deference from the Parthians. Tiridates was forced to acknowledge the authority of Rome by going there as a suppliant and, like Artabanus before him, he sacrificed before an array of Roman military standards, and a statue of the emperor where he deposited his crown.[86]

Thus, although a perfectly sensible diplomatic solution had been reached, this did not serve all of Rome's needs. Since deference from the enemy was a critical goal in the conduct of Roman foreign relations, Corbulo's success, like Augustus's, left something to be desired. Corbulo had inflicted no military defeat on the Parthians to counterbalance or retaliate for what they had done to Paetus. Tacitus cynically comments on this fact (*Annals* 15.29) showing that members of the aristocracy were not fooled by Nero's spectacular ceremonial humiliation of Tiridates at Rome. Cassius Dio wrote disparagingly that by the end of the visit, the Parthians despised Nero's weakness but respected the more martial Corbulo.[87] Nero made the mistake of giving Tiridates huge amounts of money and valuable artisans which was a concession to the Parthians, not something demanded of them.[88]

The final compromise reached by Nero was reasonable from a diplomatic point of view. It saved Roman prestige, satisfied the well-founded claim of the Parthian Empire and led to a stable peace on the eastern frontier for half a century. The settlement suited the hostile terrain of remote Armenia and acknowledged its social, cultural, and dynastic ties to Parthia.[89] Interposed between two great empires, Armenia was bound to be under the effective influence of one or the other, if it did not actually form an integral part of either. But beyond a doubt its natural connection was with Parthia, not with Rome. Here was an insuperable obstacle to the success of the policy of making it a Roman protectorate. Roman claims to Armenia were regarded by the Arsacids as an encroachment on their domain and a standing threat to the security of their realm. It was wholly incompatible with lasting peace between the two empires. It was a claim that Rome could not enforce when its capital was so far away and it had no troops nearby.

The Romans had only four possible political/military solutions for the Armenian problem: first, complete surrender by the Romans; second, whole-hearted annexation of Armenia and military defeat of the Parthians; third, actual Roman suzerainty with a Roman nominee on the throne and military defeat of the Parthians; or fourth, nominal Roman suzerainty with a Parthian candidate on the throne, and either a military stalemate or a Parthian victory. The first was impossible for Roman prestige and the second for military reasons. A weak Parthia allowed the Romans to pursue the third possibility. But, when Vologases acceded to the throne and heartened the Parthians, only the fourth proved viable.

Some modern authors argue that Nero's policy was directed consistently from the beginning towards the fourth goal which became the reality.[90] Supposedly Seneca and Burrus shaped this policy with full cooperation between Nero and Corbulo, but the ancient sources are closer to the truth. No ancient writer attributes statesmanship of this kind to Nero; nor would I. The portrait of Nero as a conceited play actor who cared nothing for the state except as a stage for his own megalomania is, I believe, an accurate one. His policy of conquering the East, in the manner of Alexander the Great, was designed both to flatter the Roman people and to put the Parthians in the wrong. Serious aims attributed to him by modern historians rest largely on modern hypotheses, and the divergence of scholarly opinion testifies to the weakness of modern findings. Four specific problems which the ancient accounts present are not explained by assuming a consistent policy on Nero's part.

First, there is the contrast between the return to Augustan policy after the successful campaigns of 58/59 and Paetus's avowed intention in 62 to annex Armenia. Since individual Roman commanders had usually tried to extend their conquests as far as possible, Paetus's arrogance about Roman invincibility was not an anomaly. Secondly, the lack of cooperation between Corbulo and Paetus, after the former had been sent out in response to the urgent appeals of the latter, suggests that they were acting under different orders with different intentions. Thirdly, Rome returned to a policy of nominal suzerainty in Armenia after Paetus's defeat anyway. And lastly, Corbulo was executed by Nero after the general had pulled victory out of a defeat.

The events in Armenia demonstrate an insufficient under-standing of problems in the East due to a lack of hard intelligence. The situation exemplifies what was wrong with Roman political and military intelligence and also with its field communications in general. Knowledge of the region was poor; inadequate or inappropriate proposals, based on poor intelligence, could not be implemented, and the military execution of those policies was haphazard and often ineffective. Individual commanders made the best decisions on the spot and did so with little or no communications with the capital or other Roman armies. They could only hope their decisions would be pleasing to the emperor. The logic of supporting a Paetus and punishing a Corbulo escapes me.

A consistent policy based on better intelligence would have pointed to the discreet accommodation which was eventually reached. Instead, it was not until eight years had been used up in the shifting alternatives of action and delay, of policies invented and discarded, of diplomacy and even warfare, that a compromise emerged: a prince of the Parthian royal family might reign in Armenia but Rome must decide and confirm his investiture. This device satisfied mutual interests in regional stability and prevented war. If anyone pursued a consistent policy it was Corbulo himself, since he was willing to risk Nero's displeasure for the only sound policy, a half-century of peace in the East. The Roman annexation of Armenia could never have ensured a lasting eastern peace.

NOTES

1. Tacitus, *Annals* 12.44; Josephus, *AJ* 20.2, 4; Dio 63.5.
2. Tacitus, *Annals* 12.50. The first invasion of Vologases falls into the latter part of 51 CE which was the year that he became king according to the coins. Nero was 17 years old on 16 December 54 CE.
3. Ibid., 13.6. Tacitus describes the anxiety felt by some over Nero's potential performance in this situation. Note that Tacitus assumes that the decision about Armenia would be made personally by the emperor in close consultation with his advisors. Cf. S. Mattern, *Rome and the Enemy* (Berkeley, CA: University of California Press), p.7.
4. Tacitus *Annals* 13.7. Lesser Armenia was assigned to Aristobulus, a son of Herod of Chalcis, and a first cousin of Agrippa II. Sophene, the more southern portion of Greater Armenia, was entrusted to a certain Sohaemus. See A.A. Barrett, 'Sohaemus, King of Emesa and Sophene', *AJPh*, 98, 2 (Summer 1977), pp.153–9.
5. Tacitus, *Annals* 13.7.
6. N.C. Debevoise, *The Political History of Parthia* (New York: Greenwood Press, 1968), p.179.
7. Tacitus, *Annals* 13.8.
8. On the legions see 'Legio', in *RE*, both the general section and those on the individual units. See also the article on Domitius Corbulo, no. 50, in *RE*, Suppl. 3, cols. 394–410; Frontinus, *Strat.* 4.2.3, refers to the beginning of this campaign. R.F. Evans, *Soldiers of Rome* (Cabin John, MD: Seven Locks Press, 1986), on the XII Fulminata, pp.104–5; on the X Fretensis, pp.96–8; on the III Gallica, pp.99–101; on the VI Ferrata, pp.102–4.

9. Tacitus, *Annals* 13.8. Rawlinson suggests this as a motive for their not staging the invasion sooner, and accepting the hostages in lieu of repossessing a Roman province. G. Rawlinson, *The Sixth Great Monarchy* (New York: Publishers Plate Renting Co., 1870), p.153; J.G.C. Anderson, 'The Eastern Frontier from Tiberius to Nero', in *CAH*, 10 (1963), p.759.

10. Tacitus, *Annals* 13.9 does not say this, but see Rawlinson, *Sixth Great Monarchy*, p.624, n.14.

11. Tacitus, *Annals* 13.7; A.D.H. Bivar, 'The Political History of Iran under the Arsacids', in *CHI*, vol. 3, 1: *The Seleucid, Parthian and Sasanian Period*, ed. E. Yarshater (Cambridge: Cambridge University Press, 1983), p.81.

12. Whether he ever succeeded in displacing his father, even temporarily, and making himself king, is doubtful. Vologases seems to have been successful in putting down the revolt. Debevoise, *Political*, p.180 and n.4, 5; J.G.C. Anderson, 'The Eastern Frontier under Augustus', in *CAH*, 10, pp.759, 879, for a discussion and a bibliography on this pretender to the throne. The relationship between the two depends upon the acceptance of an emendation of Tacitus, *Annals* 13.7.2; Debevoise, *Political*, pp.50–2; W. Wroth, *A Catalogue of Greek Coins in the British Museum: Catalogue of the Coins of Parthia* (Bologna: Arnaldo Forni, 1964), pp.l–lii. Rawlinson interprets the coin evidence to mean Vardanes was on the throne as early as 55 CE: Rawlinson, *Sixth Great Monarchy*, p.624, n.16.

13. Tacitus, *Annals* 2.1; Mattern, *Rome and the Enemy*, p.179.

14. Tacitus, *Annals* 13.31. This is in contradiction to the message delivered when the hostages were given in 55 – that Tiridates must either relinquish Armenia or consent to receive it at the hands of the Romans and hold it as a Roman fief. Cf. Dio 62.20.

15. Tacitus, *Annals* 13.37.

16. Ibid., 13.35. On the language of this passage, see K. Gilmartin, 'Corbulo's Campaigns in the East: an Analysis of Tacitus' Account', *Historia*, 22 (1973), pp.592–4. E.L. Wheeler, 'The Laxity of Syrian Legions', in D.L. Kennedy (ed.), *The Roman Army in the East* (Ann Arbor, MI: *Journal of Roman Archaeology*, Supplementary Series, 18, 1996), pp. 229–76, identifies the laxity of the Syrian legions as a literary *topos*. Bivar, 'Political History of Iran', p.81.

17. Tacitus, *Annals* 13.35 states that the IV Scythica came 'ex Germania'. See 'Legio' art. in *RE*, 'Legio', IIII Scythica, cols 1558–64.

18. Debevoise, *Political*, p.181; Anderson, 'Eastern Frontier Under Augustus', p.760.

19. Tacitus, *Annals* 13.35.

20. Ibid., 13.37; 14.26.

21. Anderson, 'Eastern Frontier under Augustus', p.761.

22. Tacitus, *Annals* 14.23–4. In the course of the march, the army suffered more from hardships than from the attacks by the Armenians. They complained about being reduced to a 'flesh diet'. Normally, the legionary diet was mainly grain. The allotment was a bushel of unground wheat a month. For the objection to too much meat, see Caesar, *BG* 7.17; Pliny, *HN* 18.74, on barley.

23. Tacitus, *Annals* 14.24.

24. Tacitus does not tell us where Corbulo spent the winter, but it seems likely that the army wintered in Artaxata and then destroyed it before leaving. Anderson, 'Eastern Frontier under Augustus', p.763.

25. 'Tigranokerta', in *RE*, cols 981–1007; Tacitus, *Annals* 14.23.1. On the conflict among Greek and Roman historians as to the location, see Bivar, 'Political History of Iran', pp.45–6, and B.W. Henderson, 'Controversies in Armenian Topography: I: The Site of Tigranocerta', *AJPh*, 28 (1903), pp.99–121; and the sagacious Sir Ronald Syme, 'Tigranocerta: A Problem Misconceived', in S. Mitchell (ed.), *Armies and Frontiers in Roman and Byzantine Anatolia* (Oxford: British Archaeological Reports, 1983), pp.61–70.

26. Tacitus, *Annals* 14.24. On the route the army took to reach Tigranocerta, see Anderson, Eastern Frontier under Augustus', p.763.

27. Frontinus, *Strat.* 2.9.5. Cf. Tacitus, *Annals* 14.24.6. For army discipline during this campaign, see Frontinus, *Strat.* 4.1.21 and 28. On other famous 'head shots', see Crassus's son's head, Hannibal's brother's head, etc.

28. Tigranes was the great-grandson of Archelaus, the last king of Cappadocia. Debevoise, *Political*, p.185; Tacitus, *Annals* 14.26. Rawlinson says he is the grandson: *Sixth Great Monarchy*, p.154; Bivar, 'Political History of Iran', p.83.

29. The client kings were Pharsamanes of Iberia, Polemon of Pontus, Aristobulus of Lesser

Armenia and Antiochus of Commagene. Tacitus, *Annals* 14.26 on the loyalties of the population.

30. Ibid., 14.26; Josephus, *AJ* 18.140, and Josephus, *BJ* 2.222; Anderson, 'Eastern Frontier under Augustus', p.765.

31. Tacitus *Annals* 15.2–3; Dio 62.20. Monobazus, the ruler of Adiabene, wanted to surrender to the Romans rather than be captured by Tigranes. The Parthian king sent his own cavalry under the Parthian noble, Monaeses, to Adiabene to cooperate with Monobazus. Debevoise, *Political*, p.186; Rawlinson, *Sixth Great Monarchy*, p.134.

32. Tacitus, *Annals* 15.3; Anderson, 'Eastern Frontier under Augustus', p.766.

33. Tacitus, *Annals* 15.5.

34. Ibid., 15.5; Bivar, 'Political History of Iran', p.84.

35. Tacitus, *Annals* 15.5.

36. Ibid., 15.6; Dio 62.20; Debevoise, *Political*, p.187.

37. Tacitus, *Annals* 15.6–7; Anderson, 'Eastern Frontier under Augustus', p.768, says that a worse choice (than Paetus) could not have been made. He describes Paetus as 'an incompetent soldier, an insufferable braggart, and an absolute poltroon'.

38. Paetus got the IV Scythica, the XII Fulminata and the V Macedonica (which had recently been withdrawn from Moesia), and certain auxiliaries from Pontus, Galatia, and Cappadocia. Corbulo retained the Syrian auxiliaries; Corbulo took the III Gallica, the VI Ferrata and the X Fretensis. Tacitus, *Histories* 3.24 and *Annals* 15.6. See also *CIL*, 14. 3608 = *ILS*, 986. The troops were paid in silver that had been specially struck at Caesarea in Cappadocia. H. Mattingly and E.A. Sydenham, *Roman Imperial Coinage* (London: Spink, 1923–94), vol. 1, 15, no. 4, and p.147, coins nos. 37ff. See plate 10, no. 159: the reverse bears the legend *ARMENIAC* and a Victory holding a palm and a wreath.

39. Tacitus, *Annals* 15.7; Dio 62.20.

40. Debevoise, *Political*, p.189.

41. Tacitus, *Annals* 15.3; Rawlinson, *Sixth Great Monarchy*, p.156 and n.39.

42. Tacitus, *Annals* 15.7. With him were his two legions, the IV Scythica under Funisulanus Vettonianus and the XII Fulminata under Calavius Sabinus; the V Macedonica was left in Pontus for the winter.

43. Ibid., 15.8.

44. Dio 62.21; B.W. Henderson, 'Rhandeia and the River Arsanias', *Journal of Philology*, 28 (1903), pp.271ff., placed it north of the Murad Su; Debevoise, *Political*, p.188. See Tacitus, *Annals* 15.7 on the *hiberna* or winter quarters built on the Cappadocian Euphrates by Paetus in 62, with a ditch and a moat (*Annals* 15.10). In the same year, Corbulo crossed the Syrian Euphrates and occupied the opposite bank, building first auxiliary forts and then a legionary camp (*castra*) (*Annals* 15.9.2). See D.L. Kennedy and D. Riley, *Rome's Desert Frontier from the Air* (London: Batsford; Austin, TX: University of Texas Press, 1990), p.95.

45. Debevoise, *Political*, p.189.

46. Tacitus, *Annals* 15.10.

47. Ibid., 15.10. The infantry had the support of some troops of Pannonian horse which fled, however, on the approach of Vologases.

48. Ibid., 15.11, makes no mention of how the message was sent. Debevoise, *Political*, p.189.

49. Some have suggested that Tacitus attempted to cover up deliberate negligence on the part of Corbulo, in not hastening to the relief once he knew of Paetus's predicament.

50. Rawlinson, *Sixth Great Monarchy*, p.157, accused Corbulo of holding back so that he could arrive at the last moment and be hailed as the saviour of the situation. But even if Corbulo guessed where the Parthians were going, his troops could not reach Paetus faster than the Parthian horse travelling by a shorter distance. Since Corbulo's task was to defend Syria, he could not set out to look for the other Roman army, because he did not know where it was and had not been asked to reinforce it.

51. Tacitus, *Annals* 15.14; Dio 62.21; cf. Suetonius, *Nero* 39.1.

52. Dio 62.21; cf. Tacitus, *Annals* 15.15.

53. Tacitus, *Annals* 15.15.

54. Ibid., 15.16.

55. Ibid., 15.24.

56. Bivar, 'Political History of Iran', p.84–5; Debevoise, *Political*, p. 194.

57. Tacitus, *Annals* 15.25; *CIL* 3. 6741–42a = *ILS*, 232. J.G.C. Anderson, 'Cappadocia as a

Roman Procuratorial Province', *CR*, 45 (1931), p.190; Debevoise, *Political*, p.192.

58. They consisted of the III Gallica and the VI Ferrata from Syria, the V Macedonica, and the recently arrived XV Apollinaris. An inscription from Bithynia honours Sulpicius Asper of the VI Ferrata and refers to the legion's wintering in Cappadocia. See F.W. Hasluck, 'Inscriptions from the Cyzicus District, 1906', *JHS*, 27 (1907) p.64, no. 5. This is the Asper of Tacitus, *Annals* 15.49ff.

59. Tacitus, *Annals* 15.27.

60. Ibid., 15.29. Cf. Josephus, *BJ* 2.379, speech of Agrippa in 66. T. Mommsen, *Provinces of the Roman Empire: From Caesar to Diocletian* (New York: Barnes & Noble, 1996), vol. 2, p.64; Anderson, 'Eastern Frontier under Augustus', pp.770–3; Debevoise, *Political*, p.193.

61. The III Gallica under Titus Aurelius Fulvus was stationed at Ziatra (Harput) where it apparently built a fortress at the command of Corbulo: see *CIL*, 3.6741–42a = *ILS*, 232. Debevoise, *Political*, p.194.

62. Dio 63.1.2.

63. Pliny, *HN* 30.16ff; Tacitus, *Annals* 15.24; Debevoise, *Political*, p.194; Bivar, 'Politcal History of Iran', p.85; Anderson, 'Eastern Frontier under Augustus', p.771.

64. Suetonius, *Nero* 30. Dio 63.2 disagrees.

65. Dio 63.2.

66. Ibid., 62 (53.1.2–6.1), Suetonius, *Nero* 13. Debevoise, *Political*, p.195.

67. For an interpretation of this trip of Tiridates, see F. Cumont, 'L'iniziazione di Nerone da parte di Tiridate d'Armenia', *Rivista di filologia*, 61 (1933), pp.145–54.

68. Tacitus, *Annals* 15.18.1. The arch is probably represented on coins. See Mattingly and Sydenham, *RIC*, vol. 1, p.156, n.1, and coins nos.159ff. Debevoise, *Political*, p.194.

69. Wroth, *Coins of Parthia*, pp.xlixff; R.H. McDowell, *Coins from Seleucia on the Tigris* (Ann Arbor, MI: University of Michigan Press, 1935), p.192; Debevoise, *Political*, p.196.

70. Suetonius, *Nero* 19; Dio 55.24.2; R.E. Evans, *The Legions of Rome* (Cabin John, MD: Seven Locks Press, 1986), pp.118–19.

71. Tacitus, *Histories* 2.11; W. Schur, *Die Orientpolitik des Kaisers Nero* (Leipzig: Dieterich, 1923), pp.107ff; Debevoise, *Political*, p.196.

72. Tacitus, *Histories* 1.6; Suetonius, *Nero* 19; Dio 62.8.1; Pliny, *HN* 6.40; Anderson, 'Eastern Frontier under Augustus', pp.773–8. See also E.M. Sanford, 'Nero and the East', *HSCP*, 48 (1937) pp.75–103.

73. Mommsen, *Provinces of the Roman Empire*, vol. 2, 65ff. and n.3; Debevoise, *Political*, p.197.

74. Suetonius, *Vespasian* 6; Tacitus, *Histories* 4.51. On a revolt in Seleucia in 69/70 see McDowell, *Coins from Seleucia*, p.192.

75. The letter was addressed from 'The King of Kings, Arsaces, to Flavius Vespasianus, greetings'. Dio 65 (66.11.3).

76. Tacitus, *Histories* 2.81.ff., 5.1. In 70 CE the same allies appear reinforcing his son Titus in the Jewish War. See A.A. Barrett, 'Sohaemus, King of Emesa and Sophene', *AJPh*, 98, 2 (Summer 1976), pp.153–9; Anderson, 'Eastern Frontier under Augustus', p.758.

77. Josephus, *BJ* 7.105ff.

78. See 'Syria', in *RE*, col. 1629; Debevoise, *Political*, p.198.

79. R. Syme, 'Flavian Wars and Frontiers', *CAH*, 11 (1969), chapter 4, 2, p.140.

80. *CIL*, 3.14387 I = *ILS*, 9200; Josephus, *BJ*, 7.233–7.

81. Dio 66.11.

82. Josephus, *BJ* 7.234–43.

83. F. Cumont, 'L'Annexation du Pont Polémoniaque et de la Petite Arménie', *Anatolian Studies Presented to Sir William Mitchell Ramsay* (London and New York: Longmans Green, 1923), p.114 and notes; E. Dabrowa, 'Roman Policy in Transcaucasia from Pompey to Domitian', in D.H. French and C.S. Lightfoot, *The Eastern Frontier of the Roman Empire: Proceedings of a Colloquium held at Ankara in September 1988*, British Institute of Archaeology at Ankara Monograph no. 11 (Oxford: British Archaeological Reports, International Series, 553, 1989), pp.71–2.

84. Tacitus, *Annals* 15.13–15; Dio 62.21.2 for Paetus peace and 62.23.2 on the rumour that the Romans had been led under the yoke. The story is repeated by Suetonius in *Nero* 39.1.

85. Tacitus, *Annals* 15.25.

86. Ibid., 15.29; Dio 62.23.3–4 'Tiridates was in this way, practically a prisoner, to be a spectacle to the people'. Cf. Tacitus, *Annals* 15.29.

87. Dio 62.1–6; Suetonius, *Nero* 16. On Tiridates despising Nero, Dio 62.6.4 and 6.

88. On using money for diplomacy, see Mattern, *Rome and the Enemy*, pp.159–60, 179–80.
89. R. Ghirshman, *Iran from the Earliest Times to the Islamic Conquest* (London: Penguin Books, 1954), p.256.
90. See, for example, B. Henderson, *The Life and Principate of the Emperor Nero* (London: Methuen, 1903), pp.193–5, and W. Schur, 'Untersuchungen zur Geschichte der Kriege Corbulos', *Klio*, 19 (1925), pp.112–14; R. Syme, *Tacitus* (Oxford: Clarendon Press, 1958), p.237.

8

TRAJAN'S PARTHIAN ADVENTURE: WITH SOME MODERN CAVEATS

Of all the Roman campaigns conducted in Parthia, Trajan's is the most massive, the least successful and the most poorly documented. The times, the places and even the purpose of Trajan's campaign remain obscure.[1] The evidence is scattered, fragmentary, and much of it is of inferior quality. Had Trajan written an account of his eastern campaign as he did with his Dacian wars, we would be in a better position to know what he was thinking and what really happened during the campaign. Classical scholars have mostly occupied themselves with the close dating of the coinage and the unravelling of Trajan's titles on coins and inscriptions.[2] For military historians, however, the real mystery is why such a well-trained Roman army, led by a competent general, suffered such a disaster. With numerous unsuccessful campaigns as a warning, what did this ambitious emperor hope to gain in Mesopotamia?

A series of Roman commanders had already tried to mount successful campaigns against the Parthian Empire. Was it not enough warning that Crassus had lost three legions and the Roman legionary standards ended up decorating Parthian temples in 53 BCE? Did Trajan not know that in eighteen defensive engagements the great Mark Antony lost 35,000 men? Had he not heard that in 63 CE Nero's General Corbulo had saved his colleague Paetus from near disaster and set up the arrangement that had held until Trajan's day? With these historical events in mind, why would any Roman commander try again? What made Trajan think he would succeed where these others had failed?

THE STATUS QUO BROKEN

Trajan's attack on Parthia seems unnecessary, since he had the diplomatic solution to the problem right in the palm of his hand, but he chose not to use it. The two powers had agreed to terms negotiated by Augustus and confirmed under Nero, that the ruler of Armenia was to be nominated by Parthia, but Rome alone had the power to approve the choice and effect the installation. This arrangement had worked well for eighty years. Those who believe Parthia broke the pattern point out that when Osroes took the Parthian throne in 109 CE, he invaded Armenia and placed his nephew, Exedares, on the Armenian throne.[3] Trajan was attending to the subjugation of Dacia and did not acknowledge the insult.[4] But the event did not evade the emperor's notice, and by 110/111 CE there is evidence that Trajan already had a Parthian campaign on his agenda.[5]

WAS TRAJAN PLANNING AN INVASION?

The evidence for premeditation on Trajan's part comes in five groups of events.[6]

1. Trajan's general (and soon to be the next emperor), Hadrian, was given command of the eastern provinces from April 112, a commission perhaps connected with the logistical preparations for a war with Parthia. The preparations must have begun the previous year at the very latest. His departure from Italy in the autumn of 111 can be deduced from his election as eponymous archon of Athens that winter.[7] It has also been suggested that Julius Quadratus Bassus, appointed to command Cappadocia at this time, was charged with organizing the northern armies in readiness for an eastern campaign.[8]

2. There were the military themes that characterized the coins minted in 111/12–13, announcing the emperor's imminent departure on campaign. For example, towards the end of 111, Trajan issued a series of coins with *FORT[una] RED[ux]* (May fortune return you safely), which some think heralds an impending imperial journey overseas.[9] It is natural to associate this coin with more ominous reverse types of the same period, all usually held to be harbingers of war. They show Mars with his spear and trophy, eagles and legionary standards. Victory is paired with a representation of the great equestrian statue in the recently dedicated Forum, showing the emperor trampling upon his vanquished enemies.[10]

3. Towards the end of 111, a series of coins was issued commemorating Trajan's deification of his father, Ulpius Traianus, *triumphator* over the Parthians when he was governor of Syria. His father was one of the few Roman generals to receive triumphal decorations for an eastern campaign.[11]

4. Probably not coincidentally, the Via Egnatia, the main route from Italy to the eastern provinces via the Greco-Balkan peninsula, was ordered to be restored in the course of 112. It was a substantial undertaking. One milestone records that work was necessary on the entire 250-mile-long route, from Dyrrachium in the west to Acontismaa in the East, and was brought about by the circumstance that the road had 'long been neglected'.[12]
5. One coin type commemorates the 'taking of Arabia'. Both Eutropius and Festus also talk of Trajan forming Arabia into a province. The claim is usually treated as a *post eventum* reference to the earlier assimilation of Nabataean Arabia in 106.[13] Certainly Trajan would want Arabia secured behind him if he invaded Parthia.

When all these activities are considered together they suggest preparations for an Eastern campaign. The public inscriptions and coinage have been seen as an attempt to prepare the national will towards recognizing and approving Trajan's familial duty to subordinate Rome's last remaining enemy.[14] Such a suggestion is not unlike that from critics who accused George Bush of having an Iraqi campaign on the agenda long before 9/11. Perhaps it is not impossible that the Parthians made the move to choose an Armenian king more likely to be able to mount a defence against a pre-emptive strike by the Romans.[15]

The fact that active hostilities did not actually break out until the spring of 114, after Parthia had twice offered a diplomatic solution, only serves to confirm the thesis that the war was premeditated as early as 111, and merely awaited a suitable and felicitous *cassus belli*. Trajan was conveniently delivered a motive by another intervention of the Parthian king into the Armenian succession in 113 CE. Trajan's precise motives in attacking Parthia have been much discussed, but Dio Cassius gives us a viable argument when he says Trajan wanted to annex Armenia as an extension of his policy in Dacia and Arabia.[16] His passion for glory and extending Roman power overcame any hesitation caused by doubts about the feasibility of the adventure. Whether there were Weapons of Mass Destruction or not, Trajan was going to invade Iraq.

Trajan's explanation of his war plans seemed specious even to a Roman senator like Dio Cassius because Rome and Parthia had, in effect, a diplomatic solution at hand. The only bone of contention was the actual coronation of the agreed-upon candidate. Not giving this prerogative to Rome had offended Trajan's sense of dignity. We should not downplay the role that slights to dignity, image, or challenges to power play in decisions to go to war. Such factors could then, as they do now, result in violent and quite unnecessary armed conflict in place of reasoned diplomacy. There certainly seems to have been no strategic need for a war with Parthia at this time. The treaty between the two powers had worked thus far to the advantage of both sides, and none of the admittedly few and fragmentary sources even hints that Parthia was making threatening moves against Rome. This is not to say Trajan was a pathological warmonger, but we cannot rule out the possibility that Trajan wanted to follow up his Dacian success, and the dedication of his Forum and Column, with an eastern campaign to conquer what all other conquerors had failed to take except Alexander. Those senatorial advisors who argued against such a policy may have suffered.[17]

THE PREPARATIONS OF 113 CE

Trajan left Rome in the autumn of 113 on the sixteenth anniversary of his adoption by Nerva.[18] He travelled along the Via Appia and the Via Traiana to Brundisium (see Map 7). By ship, he sailed to Corinth, then overland to Athens where he was met by an embassy from Osroes, who proposed that since his nephew Exedares was 'satisfactory to neither the Romans nor the Parthians, Parthamasiris should be allowed to retain the Armenian throne'.[19] He suggested that the solution of the problems was for Trajan to offer Parthamasiris the royal diadem as had been the practice since Nero's time. Trajan ignored him and refused to discuss the matter; he also refused to accept any of the gifts sent to him by Osroes. The embassy was sent packing with the words that 'friendship and diplomacy were determined by deeds, not words' and that Trajan would review the matter after he arrived at his forward base in Syria.[20] Dio saw this as further confirmation that Trajan had decided on war already.

Trajan continued his journey by crossing the Aegean to Ephesus, and from there travelled overland to Aphrodisias. He continued from there on ship, by the way of the coastal towns of Asia Minor to Seleucia-in-Pieria, the seaport of Antioch and the principal base and imperial residence for the campaign.[21] Hadrian met him late in December and together they went to nearby Mt Kasios where the emperor dedicated spoils from the Dacian War to Zeus. Trajan entered Antioch on 7 January 114.[22]

The passes in Armenia reach altitudes of 6,000 feet and were probably still blocked with winter ice and rock falls.[23] So while Trajan was waiting for the spring thaw, he entered into diplomatic negotiations with the kingdoms of the border marches. He received an embassy from Abgarus of Osrhoene who baulked at coming in person in hopes of remaining neutral, and instead sent gifts and a message of friendship.[24] Embassies came from Mannus, king of the Scenite Arabs, and Sporaces, ruler of the adjacent kingdom of Anthemusia.[25] Another embassy was sent from Osroes to receive Trajan's decision on the terms proposed in Athens. Trajan responded to Osroes that he had no desire for war, but that the terms were unsatisfactory and he rejected them.[26]

THE CAMPAIGN OF 114 CE

In the spring, Trajan left with his army for Satala, which would be his campaign base for the 114 campaign year (see Map 8). He made the journey from Antioch to Satala in two stages: he proceeded by way of Beroea (Aleppo, Syria) to the fortress of Zeugma (Bireçik), headquarters to the Legio IV Scythia. From Zeugma he probably followed a regular route along the right bank of the Euphrates River as far as Samosata, the base of the Legio VI Ferrata.[27] From Samosata, the easiest route north for a large army was directly across the Malatya Daglari to Melitene and its fortress, at this time garrisoned by the Legio XII Fulminata.[28]

About this time, Trajan received a letter from the Armenian pretender, Parthamasiris, suggesting that the fait accompli of his own enthronement be accepted and that he should come to Trajan and be formally presented with the Armenian royal diadem. Trajan considered this letter peremptory in tone because Parthamasiris had the audacity to sign it as 'King of Armenia', a status not yet recognized by the Romans. Trajan did not even deign to reply.[29] A second, more conciliatory, letter was brought for the emperor's consideration. This one left out the royal title and asked that the governor of Cappadocia, Marcus Julius Homullus, be empowered to open negotiations on behalf of Trajan. The emperor would not agree to this, but instead dispatched Marcus Junius's son to verify the terms being offered by Parthamasiris.[30]

He continued north through the Pülümur Pass, crossed the Euphrates again, probably at Eriza. A day's march from there brought him to Satala, the headquarters of the Legio XVI Flavia

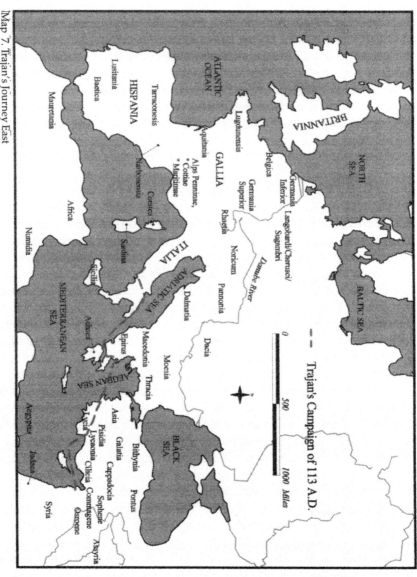

Map 7. Trajan's Journey East

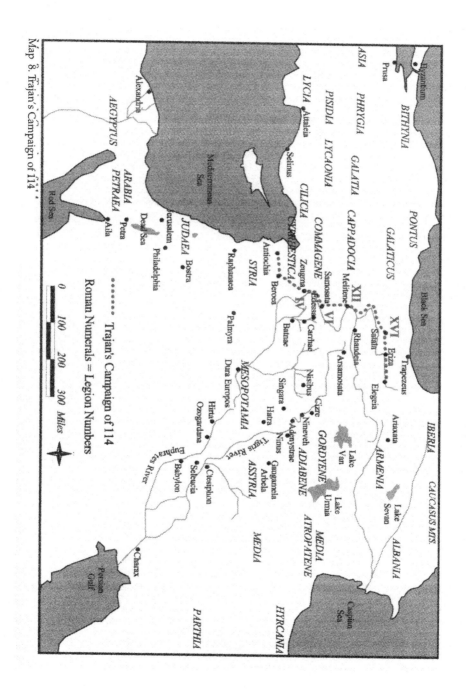

Map 8. Trajan's Campaign of 114

Firma where he arrived late in May 114.[31] At Satala, Trajan had assembled the greatest concentration of Roman legions ever known. Seven legions from the eastern armies were present in full or slightly reduced strength.[32] There were contingents from the Danubian armies, some of whom had travelled overland from the Balkans by way of Ancyra (Ankara) in the winter of 113/114.[33] Logistical supplies had been sent by water from Tomis along the coast of the Black Sea to Trapezus, and then overland through the Zigana Pass to Satala.[34] Trajan thus had eight fully supplied legions totalling 80,000 men.

After receiving the homage of local kings, Trajan advanced into Armenia.[35] His destination was the Armenian capital Elegeia, 110 miles east of Satala and 180 miles west of Parthamasiris's capital at Artaxata. Parthamasiris and the leading Armenian nobility were supposed to meet Trajan at Elegeia, but they arrived late, claiming they were held up by bands of Exidares's supporters.[36] Not a good tactical move by Parthamasiris under the circumstances.

Coming before Trajan seated upon his throne, Parthamasiris removed his diadem and laid it at the emperor's feet in confident expectation it would be returned. Trajan left it on the ground, whereupon his soldiers declared him *imperator* for having deposed a monarch without striking a blow.[37] Parthamasiris's retainers were told they were now Roman subjects and as such would remain in camp. Parthamasiris himself was escorted by Roman troops outside the city walls where he was promptly murdered.[38] Even Fronto remarked that killing a man who had come in good faith to a conference damaged Rome's credibility in diplomatic terms.[39]

Roman armies now swarmed over Armenia. Lusius Quietus descended the Araxes and destroyed the Mardi, then garrisoned the area near the Caspian Gates south of Lake Van, which controlled access to the Bitla Pass.[40] A second division under C. Bruttius Praesens, legate of the VI Ferrata, operated in the Armenian highlands where his men adopted the native snowshoes to get around as they campaigned late in the year in wintry conditions.[41] A third division advanced far to the east; it might well have been the IV Scythica, known to have stayed in Armenia until the spring of 116.[42] A fourth division, which included the historian Arrian himself, advanced beyond Armenia as far as the Caucasian Gates (the Dariel Pass).[43]

The Romans used the same tactics that had proved successful in other mountainous areas. They advanced up the valleys of navigable rivers, occupied key points at their head and systematically isolated the mountain masses by a network of roads and forts drawn round them on every side. By the end of 114, all of Armenia had been consolidated, and it was declared a Roman province, with L. Catilius Severus as its first governor.[44] Dio reports that once Armenia was subdued, more local satraps submitted to him.[45] Trajan remained at Elegeia for the summer, receiving delegations, and he may also have been developing the network of permanent garrisons in the Caucasian hinterland. He probably was also making a concentrated effort to exercise Roman supremacy over the tribes that occupied the eastern Black Sea Coast.[46]

On account of these military successes, in the summer of 114 the Roman Senate voted Trajan the title *Optimus*, a title he formally adopted into his nomenclature. With a successful first year of campaigning behind him, Trajan spent the winter of 114/115 at Elegeia or Artaxata.[47]

THE MESOPOTAMIAN CAMPAIGN OF 115

In the Spring of 115, Trajan began his Mesopotamian campaign (see Map 9). First he marched south with his army over the central Taurus Mountains to consolidate the territory between the Euphrates and the Upper Tigris. Permanent garrisons were left at opportune points along the way to secure the regions. We are told he travelled with his men, on foot, fording rivers, and that he used his time during this unopposed advance to practise manoeuvres and marching dispositions.[48] By mid-summer, Trajan had reached Upper Mesopotamia and was ready to annex it.

From what little detail we have, Trajan was planning to take Mesopotamia with a large-scale pincer movement. One part was led by Lusius Quietus who had finished subduing the Mardi, and now proceeded south into Adiabene, where he fought and defeated King Mebarsapes, and then advanced into eastern Mesopotamia. Trajan himself skirted Osrhoene and set about the reduction of the western part of the territory.[49]

Trajan took Batnae (Incidere or Batnan), the capital of Anthemusia, to punish King Sporaces for not offering fealty to Rome.[50] Then the Romans struck at the main strategic centre, Nisibis, which they then used as their own base.[51] Mebarsapes of Adiabene was driven back into his kingdom beyond the Tigris. Abgarus VII of Osrhoene found himself surrounded on three sides and made the

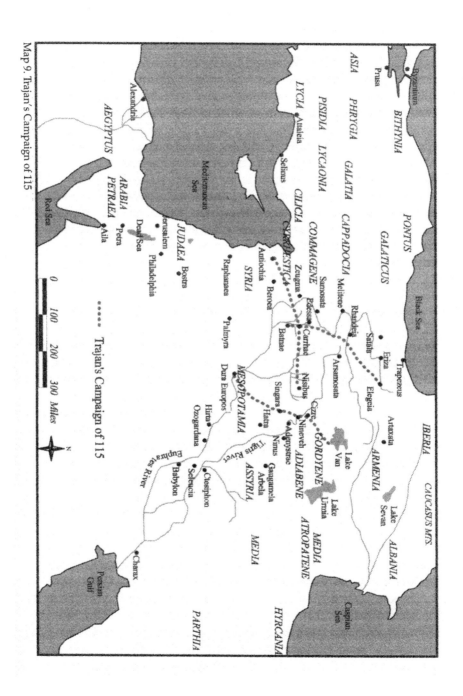

Map 9. Trajan's Campaign of 115

best of the situation. On the approach of the Romans, King Abgarus, prompted by his son Arbandes, offered homage to Trajan to make amends for not doing so the year before. Trajan met Abgarus outside his capital at Edessa (Sanliurfa). With the Romans in full force before him, Abgarus had little choice but to come over to the Roman side. He sent out gifts and weapons and troops to Trajan as a sign of fealty; Trajan returned them. Nevertheless he pardoned the King, granted Osrhoene the status of protectorate, and left it autonomous for the time being.[52]

The two sides of the pincer movement met as Trajan joined Lusius Quietus in Adiabene for a prearranged meeting. Lusius was allowed to possess the Scenite Arab town of Singara and from there move down to Hatra and possibly even Libana and a corresponding thrust down the Euphrates to Dura Europas. This completed the occupation of Mesopotamia.[53] Not surprisingly, a lot more envoys came to pay obeisance. Some opportunists even offered to fight with Rome against the Parthians.

The intensity of the fighting during this period can be gauged by the fact that Trajan received five imperial salutations between Autumn 114 and December 115. By the end of the year, Trajan dispatched a laurelled letter to the Senate on 21 February 116, announcing annexation of both Armenia and Mesopotamia. Shock and awe had succeeded. Coins were minted announcing the territories as 'subjugated to the power of Rome' and prayers were offered for his safety.[54]

Trajan garrisoned Edessa and returned for the winter of 115/116 to Antioch, where he nearly lost his life in a devastating earthquake. He lived out of doors in the hippodrome to keep from having a roof collapse on him.[55]

THE TIGRIS CAMPAIGN OF 116

Early in 116, Trajan marched out of Antioch for the Tigris on his third and final campaign against the Parthian confederation (see Map 10). Trajan could have taken the two new provinces, organized and garrisoned them, and just gone home, but this would not have sufficed for his imperial designs on Parthia. Perhaps he was lured on by the seemingly total lack of Parthian resistance and the opportunity for acquiring more war booty.[56]

Trajan struck hard across the Tigris at the Jewish kingdom Adiabene, with the intent of breaking the resistance of Mebarsapes.

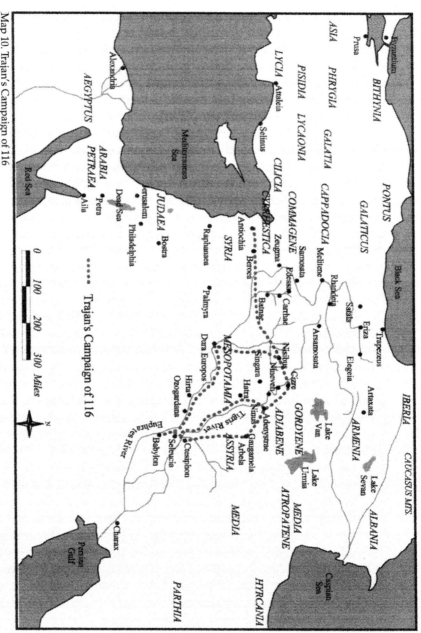

Map 10: Trajan's Campaign of 116

To reach the Adiabenean capital, Arbela, he had to cross the Tigris, which he did by bringing a wagon with prefabricated pontoons built the previous winter at Nisibis, which had lots of wood available from the forests of Mt Massius (Tur Ab'din) north of the city. The river was eventually crossed, but with some difficulty because of fast water and no doubt fighting Adiabenians. They crossed in the vicinity of the modern city of Cizre, and at least part of the province was taken.[57] Singara, Libana and possibly Thebeta were taken without fighting. All of the troops furnished to Mebarsapes by Mannus of Arabia were lost.[58]

The next part of the narrative is confused because there is an abrupt transition in Dio/Xiphilinus's account, and there are places named that we cannot yet locate on the map.[59] One division, it is suggested, swept south along the Euphrates using the route taken by Alexander, capturing Ninus (Nineveh), Arbela and Gaugamela, where Alexander had defeated Darius III in 331 BC The parallels with Alexander the Great's campaigns are attractive, but others have pointed out that no general would use the Euphrates route if he could use the Tigris instead.[60] The same division then seized Adenystrae which fell without a fight.[61] A Roman centurion named Sentius being held prisoner there escaped and, along with his escaped comrades, killed the garrison commander and opened the gates to the Roman forces outside.[62] Adiabene was formally occupied, probably the occasion for Trajan's twelfth imperial salutation.[63] It is believed by some that he formed the territory into the new province of Assyria. Others believe that despite the taking of Nisibis, Singara, and Hatra, most of Adiabene remained in enemy hands, thus no 'Adiabene capta' coins.[64]

The army moved west and occupied Edessa. Most accounts try to bring Trajan back from Adiabene by the most expeditious route so that he could take command of the second force. Trajan then marched at the head of a force down the Euphrates to Dura Europus where another army, supported by a supply fleet, awaited him. They proceeded down the western bank of the Tigris as far as Babylon, meeting no opposition on the way. Dio says there were civil conflicts which kept the Parthians busy.[65] Arrian's *Parthica* lists towns along the Euphrates.[66] A similar itinerary can be deduced from Dio's account. Trajan visited the asphalt wells at Hit, where the building materials for Babylon had been obtained. Ammianus Marcellinus records in the fourth century how people visited Trajan's tribunal at Ozogardana, even further down the Euphrates.[67]

Trajan was accompanied by a river fleet on the Euphrates. Arrian lists fifty ships, three squadrons; four vessels carrying the imperial vexilia. The largest craft was the emperor's flagship decorated in gold, with the emperor's name on the sails.[68] They reached the artificial canal called Naharmalcha (Royal River), which ran from Falluje to the Tigris some distance south of the point where Seleucia and Cteiphon faced each other on opposite banks of the river.[69] Trajan intended to cross the Tigris and attack Ctesiphon, south of modern Baghdad. He proposed cutting a canal between the Tigris and the Euphrates at Sippar (Abu Abba), where the two rivers flow within twenty miles of each other. Since the Euphrates flowed at a higher level than the Tigris, however, they feared that one river would drain and flood the other, and instead Trajan elected to have his fleet dragged overland by means of capstan devices and rollers.[70] Trajan took Seleucia on the west bank and then crossed the Tigris unopposed and entered the city of Ctesiphon without a fight.

Osroes and his entourage had fled, leaving behind his daughter and golden throne to be captured by the emperor.[71] Trajan's army saluted him as *imperator* and he established his right to be acclaimed *Parthicus*. Trajan issued coins with the legend *PARTHIA CAPTA*.[72] The capture of Ctesiphon marked the official culmination of Trajan's third campaign and of the war. And yet, during the entire time, Trajan had not once encountered any resistance from King Osroes or his cavalry. Osroes had used traditional tactics against his enemies; he withdrew over the Zagros Mountains in the face of a superior enemy.[73]

Trajan set out to review and consolidate the territory he had captured. Some have suggested he was attempting to form a province of 'Babylonia'. It seems plausible that the later references which talk of Trajan establishing a frontier along the banks of the Tigris were inspired by a belief that he intended to form a province out of the fertile territory of the lower Euphrates and Tigris.[74]

Using ships from the Euphrates fleet, Trajan sailed down the Tigris to the Persian Gulf. After nearly losing his life in a tidal bore, the emperor eventually arrived at Spasinu Charax (Basra) located at the river's mouth. We are told that Trajan arrived there just in time to see a merchant ship sailing for India, and he publicly lamented that he was no longer young enough to follow in Alexander's footsteps.[75]

This episode signalled Trajan's personal consummation of the

Parthian war. He dispatched another laurelled letter to the Senate, announcing his accomplishments, and erected a statue marking the limit of his advance. He left his ships behind with the intention of a future campaign eastwards. The Senate voted him a triumph over as many nations as he wished and he got his thirteenth imperial salutation. Coins were issued with the legend *FORT(una)* *RED(ux)*, wishing the emperor a safe return to Italy.[76]

THE UPRISING

When he arrived back in Babylon, Trajan discovered that a widespread rebellion had broken out in northern Mesopotamia. His capture of Ctesiphon had galvanized the Parthians, who now put aside their internal differences and incited a widespread insurgency. With the Romans over-extended and the commander far from the centre of action, Osroes's brother Mithridates began recapturing large tracts of Roman territory.[77] When Mithridates was killed in an equestrian accident, his son, Sanatrukes, continued to incite pro-Parthian resistance. Sanatrukes was also nominated by the Parthians as king-in-exile of the Armenians in place of Parthamasiris.[78]

Sanatrukes seems to have been able to organize a rebellion simultaneously in many places. He coordinated it at a time when Trajan had advanced too far and too quickly without making sure he had sufficient resources to consolidate his gains. This took advance planning, suggesting they had been watching Trajan's advance very closely. Trajan had absented himself from the lower Euphrates without properly securing his perimeters.[79] There were Parthian invasions of both Mesopotamia and Armenia, and many occupied towns drove out or massacred their Roman garrisons. Even Osrhoene rose while Trajan himself was threatened by the revolt of Seleucia and the prospect of all of Babylonia following its lead.

Trajan ordered three divisions against the rebels. The first one was led by Appius Maximus Santra. His force was defeated and he was slain by the rebels.[80] The second force was led by Trajan's best general, Lusius Quietus, who recovered Nisibis and a number of cities including Edessa, which he sacked and burned either because of Abgarus's treachery or because he had been replaced by a pro-Parthian substitute. He was promised a consulship in the following year.[81] A third force, under the joint command of two legates, Erucius Clarus and Julius Alexander, captured Seleucia in Babylonia and burned it. Trajan himself joined this group.[82] The three commanders then went on to defeat a Parthian host somewhere in the vicinity of Ctesiphon, after which Sanatrukes was killed.[83]

Armenia was now threatened by a Parthian army under Sana-trukes's son, Vologases.[84] The situation must have been critical, for when an armistice was offered in return for part of the territory, Trajan quickly agreed and granted him a portion of Armenia in exchange for peace. In an effort to avoid further insurrection in Babylon, and perhaps to assert some authority over Vologases, Trajan went to Ctesiphon and appointed Parthamaspates, son of Osroes, king of Parthia. He personally crowned him with a royal diadem, after which Parthamaspates did obeisance to Trajan in the traditional manner in full view of the assembled population, confirming his subordinate status.[85] The status of Parthamaspates was advertised on coins issued late that year bearing the legend *REX PARTH* [*ic*]*US DATUS*: 'A King is given to the Parthians.'[86]

Trajan had to justify his action to the Senate because some thought he was abandoning Roman territory. His reply encapsulates the problem of having adequate strategic intelligence: 'So vast and infinite is this domain, and so immeasurable the distance that separates it from Rome, that we do not have the compass to administer it. Let us then [instead] present the people with a king who is subject to Rome.'[87]

With both Parthia and a major part of Armenia restored to client-kings, Trajan hurried north to recover what he could of Mesopotamia. A priority was the reduction of Hatra, which controlled the central route from Nisibis to Ctesiphon and which was still in revolt.[88] Trajan needed to possess Hatra to restore Roman rule beyond the Tigris and he accordingly began a siege. Dio describes Hatra as being neither large nor prosperous; this is incorrect.[89] What Hatra does *not* have is water in the surrounding desert, nor timber or fodder for a besieging army. The Roman army was plagued by flies which swarmed over their food and water and brought discomfort and even disease to the troops.[90] Still Trajan persisted with the siege. He even managed to breach the defences with a cavalry charge using his own *equites singulares*, during which his distinctive 'majestic grey head' attracted the attention of the Hatrian archers. They missed him but hit a trooper in his escort.[91]

Winter was setting in and Mother Nature turned on the be-siegers. They had to put up with sudden cloud bursts, hail storms and thunderstorms in addition to their other troubles. Trajan lifted the siege, and returned west to Antioch.[92]

THE JEWISH REVOLT

Trajan's troubles were not yet over. The Greek-speaking Jews of the diaspora began a separate, bloody revolt. It would seem that religious tensions between the Jewish and pagan communities flared into open riot and there was widespread destruction of pagan shrines by the Jews.[93] The canonical date for the revolt is 115–117 CE, and it started in Cyrene, although at least one scholar has suggested it started in Mesopotamia and spread west.[94] It is not clear whether the Jewish Revolt began as part of the Parthian *revanche* or separately. As one eminent Jewish scholar has pointed out, Parthian international intelligence was excellent, and their connections could have been used to arouse Jewish rebellion in Alexandria, Cyrenaica and Cyprus.[95] The Jews had never forgiven the Romans for destroying the Temple in Jerusalem, and this might be an opportune time to strike back. Perhaps the Jews in Adiabene were fighting for independence or in the hopes of re-establishing another messianic state. A second reason might have been to keep the Romans from rearranging the international trading routes and cutting Babylonia off by diverting commerce through Armenia via the northern routes.[96] Whatever the cause, the revolt was very bloody and Trajan had to expend more manpower to put it down.[97] Marcus Turbo was dispatched to Alexandria to help subdue the uprising there.[98] Renewed disturbances between Greeks and Jews continued even after the Roman intervention.[99]

Despite all of this, Trajan held on and intended to march into Mesopotamia again in 117, but was dissuaded by his ill-health, as opposed to just the futility of the idea.[100] The gaunt features of the bronze bust of Trajan displayed at the public baths in Ankara (if they are indeed Trajan), do not suggest a young or healthy man.[101] Trajan suffered a stroke which left him partially paralyzed. The symptoms suggest congestive heart failure brought on by hypertension. Certainly marching through the Anatolian Mountains and crossing the Arabian desert at 60 years of age did not help.[102]

Daily news arrived of fresh disturbances across his *imperium*. There was insurrection in Mauretania, threat of war from the Roxolani and Iazyges. There were raids by British brigands in the north and signs of rebellion in Judaea (which would result in the Bar Kokhba revolt in 135).[103] Parthamaspates, the Roman appointee to the Parthian throne, was fighting a civil war (not unlike the Iraqi ruling council and the rebels). Faced with more Jewish revolts throughout the East, having Armenia already lost, and with the fate of Mesopotamia hanging in the balance, Trajan, already in pain due to his illnesses, decided to return to Rome and celebrate his Parthian triumph. He appointed Hadrian to the overall command of the armies in the East and left.[104]

In the summer of 117, Trajan boarded his royal yacht at Seleucia-in-Pieria when the climate was favourable for sea travel. Sick and in his sixty-third year, Trajan became suspicious and began to think his illness was due to poison. This is not surprising since at the same time, his wine and table steward and taster, M. Ulpius Phaedimus, contracted similar symptoms and died; he was only 28.[105] As they coasted along the shores of rough Cilicia, Trajan's condition got worse. The ship pulled into the nearest harbour, Selinus, where he took to his bed and died.[106]

Hadrian immediately abandoned the Eastern campaign (see Map 11). He justified his action by quoting the dictum of Cato, that those who could not be subject should be made free.[107] Trajan's more aggressive officers were replaced or died under suspicious circumstances, including A. Cornelius Palma, C. Avidius Nigrinus, and Lusius Quietus, governor of Judaea.[108] They probably resented Hadrian's policy of giving back territory they had fought hard to conquer. All the territory east of the Euphrates was immediately relinquished, as was the Syrian pre-desert. Dura Europas was abandoned before 30 September 117, although there is some evidence to show that Hadrian's withdrawal from Trajan's conquest of Mesopotamia did not signify a total relaxation of Roman control beyond the Euphrates.[109] The client kingdom of Mesene (Charax) seemed to have retained its loyalty to Rome. Roman officials remained present on the Euphrates, and a temple to the Augusti was built by a Palmyran merchant right in the Parthian capital of Vologesia.[110]

ROME'S IMPERIAL FOLLY

Trajan was a great general and no fool. He did not blunder into Parthia as Crassus had done and lost three legions and their standards. He did not go into Armenia with poor logistical support as Antony had done. Nor did he lack good intelligence gathering skills.[111]

Plague did not strike the army as it would under Lucius Verus. Yet, by the end of the campaign, he had nothing to show for his efforts in a major campaign some have characterized as a 'fiasco'.[112] But there is as much reason to believe he was pulling himself out of a situation that was degenerating daily. Dio, in his justly famous passage, said that conquering Mesopotamia was a constant source of war that became a great financial burden to the Roman economy. This seems borne out by Trajan's actions as well as Hadrian's.[113]

Trajan's Parthian campaign is, in many ways, the climax to the story of two centuries of political posturing and bitter rivalry. Trajan was the first emperor to successfully carry out an invasion of Mesopotamia itself. Yet Trajan's grand scheme for Armenia and Mesopotamia would ultimately be cut short by circumstances created by an incorrect understanding of the strategic realities of eastern conquest and an underestimation of what insurgency can do. The lasting results of this endgame could only be failure. Rome gained not one inch of territory for its efforts, and by creating unnecessary problems on the eastern front, he made it necessary to take security forces from elsewhere. By 117 CE, Trajan was dead in Cilicia, the new provinces had risen in revolt, and so had the Jews in a vast arc from Cyrene to Mesopotamia, with catastrophic results in Cyrene, Egypt and Cyprus. Parthamaspates, who had been placed in Ctesiphon as a Roman client king, was losing control, and the lesser client kings were either losing their thrones or their imposed Roman allegiance. The only thing that remained for Rome was the claim to suzerainty over Armenia and Osrhoene. Hadrian did not abandon provinces that could be held. After all, where were the armies when Trajan died? In Syria[114] (see Map 11). The extent of Trajan's military disaster together with the existing threats elsewhere were not propitious to a second Parthian war. This did not stop Roman writers like Fronto from criticizing Hadrian's decision not to proceed with Trajan's policy of expansion.[115] It may very well have been that Hadrian gave up Mesopotamia because he realized he could not afford to reconquer it.[116] Whatever their hopes, Trajan's successors never again extended the empire to the boundaries he had achieved and they never held more than a fraction of his Mesopotamian bastion.

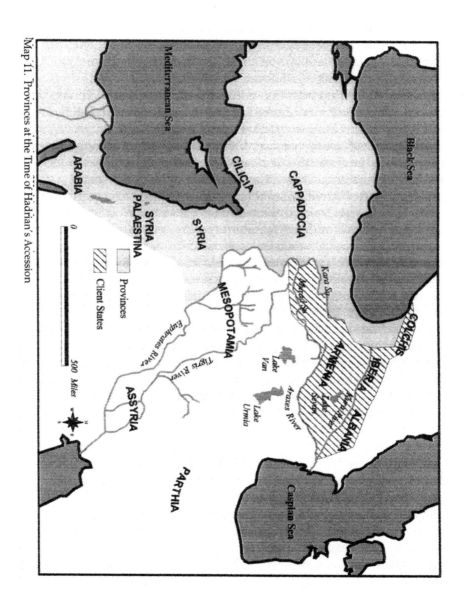

Map 11. Provinces at the Time of Hadrian's Accession

NOTES

1. For the major studies on Trajan's Parthian War, see F.A. Lepper, *Trajan's Parthian War* (London: Oxford University Press, 1948); J. Bennett, *Trajan Optimus Princeps* (Bloomington, IN: Indiana University Press, 2001); N.C. Debevoise, *The Political History of Parthia* (New York: Greenwood Press, 1968); J. Guey, *Essai sur la guerre parthique de Trajan*, Bibliothèque d'Istros, no. 2 (Bucharest: Imprimerie nationale, 1937); C.S. Lightfoot, 'Trajan's Parthian War and the Fourth Century Perspective', *JRS*, 80 (1990), pp.115–26; R.P. Longden, 'The Wars of Trajan', in *CAH*, 11 (1936), pp.236–52; R.P. Longden, 'Notes on the Parthian Campaigns of Trajan', *JRS*, 21 (1931), pp.1–35; R. Paribeni, *Optimus Princeps*, reprint of Messian, 1926–27 (New York: Arno Press, 1975); H.H. Sills, *Trajan's Armenian and Parthian Wars* (Cambridge: Cambridge University Press, 1897); R. Hanslik, 'M. Ulpius Traianus', in *RE*, Suppl. 10, cols 1035–102.

2. On the coin evidence, see G.G. Belloni, *Le Monete di Traiano: Catalogo del civico Gabinetto numismatico* (Milano: Museo Archaeologico, 1973); P.L. Strack, *Untersuchungen zur römischen Reichspragung des zweiten Jahrhunderts* (Stuttgart: W. Kohlhammer, 1931), vol. 1, *Reichsprägung zue Zeit des Trajan*. On the chronological problems, see T. Frankfort, 'Trajan Optimus – Recherche de Chronologie', *Latomus* 16 (1957), pp.333–4; J. Guey, 'Le problème chronologique que soulève la guerre de Trajan contres les Parthes', *CRAI* (1934), pp.72–4; H. Mattingly *et al.*, *Coins of the Roman Empire in the British Museum*, 5 vols (London: Trustees of the British Museum, 1932–62) (BMC).

3. The series of events is unclear. G. Rawlinson, *The Sixth Great Monarchy* (New York: Publishers Plate Renting Co., 1870), p.170, has Tiridates dying in 100 CE; Pacorus succeeds him and puts his son Exedares (var. Axidares) on the throne. Others, like Debevoise, *Political*, pp.217–18, have Exedares put on the Armenian throne by Osroes, c. 110.

4. The Dacian War occupied Trajan from 101 CE to 106 CE. The year 107 CE was spent taking possession of Dacian territory. Rawlinson, *Sixth Great Monarchy*, p.627, n.3; Bennett, *Trajan Optimus Maximus*, pp.85–103.

5. On premeditation in the American war, see M. Danner, 'The Secret Way to War: The Downing Street Memo', *New York Review of Books*, 52, 10 (9 June 2005), p.70, which shows that an invasion of Iraq was already being discussed by the Bush Administration by 21 November 2001, when the President ordered the Secretary of Defense, Donald Rumsfeld, to look at what it would take to remove Saddam Hussein.

6. On the premeditation of Trajan, see Guey, *Essai sur la guerre parthique*, p.27. Bennett, *Trajan Optimus Maximus*, pp.85–103; R. Paribeni, *Optimus Princeps*, vol. 2, p.281, who believes Trajan had a Parthian war planned before he even invaded Dacia. He bases this on one passage in Ammianus Marcellinus. O. Cuntz, 'Zum Briefwechsel des Plinius mit Trajan', *Hermes*, 61 (1926), pp.192ff., believed that the correspondence of Pliny showed clearly that Trajan had this war in mind as early as 111, when Pliny was sent to Bithynia; Lepper, *Trajan's Parthian War*, pp.164–90.

7. Hadrian's appointment to the assignment is substantiated by a single documentary source, Dio 89.1.1; *SHA, Hadrian* 4. The possibility that Hadrian was appointed as interim governor is reasonable. There is a *lacuna* in the Syrian *fasti* between L. Fabius Justus, whose term of office ended 111/112, and C. Julius Quadratus Bassus, appointed 114/115. See W. Eck, 'Jahres-und Provinzialfasten der senatorischen Statthalter von 69/70 bis 138/139', *Chiron*, 12 (1982), pp.353–7; E.M. Smallwood, *Documents Illustrating the Principates of Nerva, Trajan and Hadrian* (Cambridge: Cambridge University Press, 1966), no. 108. There were Roman troops under Hadrian's control at Hyssus, Apsarus, Phasis and Dioscurias to control the coast. *Periplus* 3.1, 6.1–2, 9.3, 10.3–4. Cf. *CIL*, 10.1202 = *ILS*, 2660;

8. R.K. Sherk, 'Roman Galatia: The Governors from 25 B.C. to A.D. 114', in *ANRW*, 2, 7.2 (1980), p.1006.

9. On the *Fortuna Redux* coins minted in 111–113 heralding Trajan's journey overseas, see Bennett, *Trajan Optimus Princeps*, pp.183–4; Strack, *Untersuchungen*, pp.215–16; H. Mattingly and E.A. Sydenham, *Roman Imperial Coinage* (London: Spink, 1923–94), nos. 253, 254, 302, 308, 318, 319, 320, 321. H. Cohen, *Description historique des monnaies frappés sous l'Empire romain* (Paris and London: Rollin et Feuardent, 1880–92), nos. 148, 149, 150, 152, 153; Mattingly and Sydenham, *RIC*, no. 315.

10. Mars with his spear and trophy, eagles and legionary standards: Strack, *Untersuchungen*, nos. 332, 336, 429; Cohen, *Description historique*, nos. 373, 374, 375; Strack, *Untersuchungen*,

nos. 217, 225, 230, 243, 252, 326; Cohen, *Description historique*, nos. 103, 190, 270, 271, 626.

11. *Ulpianus pater* coins, Strack, *Untersuchungen*, nos. 199–202; Belloni, *Le Monete di Traiano*, p.14.

12. Smallwood, *Documents Illustrating the Principles of Nerva, Trajan and Hadrian*, 415, on the milestone. M. Fasolo, *La Via Egnatia* (Roma: Istituto grafico editorial romano, 2003), vol. 1, pp.1–9; F. O'Sullivan, *The Egnatian Way* (Harrisburg, PA: Stackpole Books, 1972), p.136; See *CIL*, 9.6003 = *ILS*, 291. The milestone was found six miles from Thessaloniki and is in St George's Church in Thessaloniki. It dates to 107 CE. The section from Macedonia to Acontisma dates to 112 CE. The coins only celebrated the completion of the work in 112, Strack, *Untersuchungen*, 1.211.

13. Dio 68.14 says Trajan appropriated the Nabataean kingdom at or about the time of the Second Dacian War, which means either 105 or early 106. G.W. Bowersock, *Roman Arabia* (Cambridge, MA: Harvard University Press, 1983), p.79. On the *Arab Adquis* coins see Strack, *Untersuchungen*, 408, 409, 410, 422; Belloni, *Le Monete di Traiano*, no. 79, p.8; Mattingly *et al.*, *Coins of the Roman Empire*, vol. 3, 296; 474–6; J. Eadie, 'Artifacts of Annexation: Trajan's Grand Strategy and Arabia', in *The Craft of the Ancient Historian: Essays in Honor of Chester G. Starr* (Lanham, MD: University Press of America, 1985), pp.407–23; M. Sartre, *The Middle East under Rome* (Cambridge: Harvard University Press, 2005), p.133.

14. America, on the other hand, had town meetings with Condoleeza Rice and UN briefings with Colin Powell. 7 August 2003: Rice tells a group of African American journalists that Americans must press forward with the struggle for democracy in Iraq even in the face of opposition, in the same way that African Americans resisted their opponents during the civil rights era – *St Petersburg Times* (St Petersburg, FL), 8 August 2003, p.6A. On 10 October 2004, Rice, appearing on *Fox News Sunday*, defended the invasion of Iraq, citing the need to topple Saddam Hussein and saying the debate over weapons of mass destruction was irrelevant – CNN.com, 10 October 2004.

15. G. Rawlinson, *The Story of Parthia* (London: T. Fisher Unwin, 1893), p.299 writes: 'Pacorus II was succeeded upon the throne by Chosroes, his brother, whom the Parthian Megasthenes preferred over the head of Exedares and Parthamasiris, Pacorus's two sons, as more fit to rule under the difficult circumstances of the period.' With Trajan raising an expedition against the East, it seemed necessary to entrust the government of the Parthian state to a man of mature age and sound judgment. The sons of Pacorus were young and considered too rash and incompetent to cope with so dangerous an antagonist as Trajan. Parthamasiris probably replaced Exedares in Armenia for the same reason.

16. M.A.R. College, *The Parthians* (New York: Praeger, 1967), p.53, and others discuss Trajan's frontier policy as a rude and costly interruption of a process of careful and economical stabilization which had been begun by the Flavians and to which Hadrian wisely returned. Lepper, *Trajan's Parthian War*, pp.106, 191–204, disagrees. On contemporary Roman criticism of Trajan's Parthian campaign, see W.C. McDermott, 'Homullus and Trajan', *Historia*, 29 (1980), p.118.

17. Junius Homullus may have done so and this cost him the governorship of *Armenia maior* to Catilius. McDermott, 'Homullus and Trajan', p.119.

18. Arrian, *Parthica* fr.35, on the day. The chronological problem is discussed in Lepper, *Trajan's Parthian War*, pp.28–30.

19. Dio 68.17.3, E. Cary trans.

20. Dio 68.17. A similar arrogance was displayed by the Romans in the spring of 53 BCE when the Parthians demanded the reason for Crassus's unprovoked invasion and were told he would tell them the causes when the Romans reached Seleucia. Plutarch, *Crassus* 17–18. A. Keaveney, 'The Kings and the Warlords: Romano Parthian Relations circa 64–53 BC', *AJPh*, 103 (1982), p.425.

21. Denis van Berchem, 'La port de Séleucie de Piérie et l'infrastructure lofistique des guerres parthiques', *BJ*, 185 (1985), pp. 47–87. The route from Athens to Seleucia in Pieria is generally confirmed by Dio 68.17.2–3. Bennett, *Trajan Optimus Princeps*, p.191, suggests stops at Attaleia (Antalya) or Side (Selimiye). Pliny *Ep.* 10–15 admits it was not a comfortable or easy journey even in late summer. See R.P. Duncan-Jones, *Structure and Scale in the Roman Economy* (Cambridge: Cambridge University Press, 1990), pp.8–29, for times and seasons involved in ancient sea travel in general and pp.25–29 for passage across the eastern Mediterranean in particular.

22. John Malalas, *Chronographia* 2.272. For a discussion of Malalas's dates, see M.I.

Henderson's review of Lepper's *Trajan's Parthian War*, in *JRS*, 39 (1949), pp.122–4.

23. See V.W. Yorke, 'A Journey in the Valley of the Upper Euphrates: Part I, The Journey', *Geographical Journal*, 8,4 (1896), pp.325, 333.

24. Embassy from Abgarus of Osrhoene, Dio 68.18.1; Bennett, *Trajan Optimus Princeps*, p.191.

25. Embassies from Mannus, king of the Scenite Arabs, and Sporaces, ruler of the adjacent kingdom of Anthemusia. Dio 68.21.1, which Bennett, *Trajan Optimus Princeps*, p.191, n.37, believes belongs to this time.

26. On the damage Trajan's actions did to the development of diplomatic channels, see B. Campbell, 'War and Diplomacy: Rome and Parthia, 31 BC – AD 235', in J. Rich and G. Shipley, *War and Society in the Roman World* (New York and London: Routledge, 1993), pp.234–5.

27. On Trajan's route from Antioch to Samosata, see Bennett, *Trajan Optimus Princeps*, p.192. Samosata was the base of the Legio VI Ferrata. For the military dispositions in the area, see J. Crow, 'A Review of the Physical Remains of the Frontiers of Cappadocia', P. Freeman and D.L. Kennedy (eds), *The Defence of the Roman and Byzantine East: Proceedings of a Colloquium held at the University of Sheffield in April 1986*, British Institute of Archaeology at Ankara Monograph no. 8 (Oxford: British Archaeological Reports, International Series, 297, 1986) vol. 1, pp.79–81 and 84; and E. Dabrowa, 'Les rapports entre Rome et les Parthes sous Vespasien', *Syria*, 58 (1981), p.199. The remains of Samosata were completely inundated by the building of the Atatürk Dam, as will be Zeugma by the Birecik Dam downstream.

28. Melitene was the base of the Legio XII Fulminata, a legion founded by Vespasian to control the Euphrates crossing on the main trade route between Armenia and Cappadocia. It commanded the southern approaches to the Caspian Gates. On the legionary fortress there see T.B. Mitford, 'The Euphrates Frontier in Cappadocia', in *SMR 2*, pp. 504–5. On the route through Melitene, see Bennett, *Trajan Optimus Princeps*, p.192.

29. Dio 68.19–20; Bennett, *Trajan Optimus Princeps*, p.192 and n.42.

30. Dio 68.19.1; Bennett, *Trajan Optimus Princeps*, p.192. Marcus Junius Homullus was the governor who commanded the XVI Flavia Firma. T.B. Mitford, 'Cappadocia and Armenia Minor: Historical Setting of the *Limes*', in *ANRW*, 2, 7.2 (1980), p.1196. Homullus's son was serving under his father as *tribunus laticlavus*. A.R. Birley, *Hadrian: The Restless Emperor* (London and New York: Routledge, 1998), p.69.

31. Satala was the headquarters of the XVI Flavia Firma; on the archaeology of Satala, see C.S. Lightfoot, 'Satala Survey 1989', *Anatolian Studies*, 40 (1990), pp.13–16; C.S. Lightfoot, 'Satala Survey [1990]', *Anatolian Studies*, 41 (1991), pp.14–17; Dabrowa, 'Les rapports entre Rome', p.195.

32. See Mitford, 'Cappadocia and Armenia Minor', pp.1196–8 for a listing of the legions epigraphically or otherwise attested in the Parthian War. Bennett, *Trajan Optimus Princeps*, p.192; Debevoise, *Political*, pp.220–1. On Satala and the Euphrates frontier, see Mitford, 'Euphrates Frontier', pp.501–10.

33. The reinforcements from the Danubian provinces had marched some 475 miles through difficult country. The journey probably took about seven weeks. Bennett, *Trajan Optimus Princeps*, p.192; Sherk, 'Roman Galatia', pp.1196–8; Smallwood, *Documents Illustrating the Principles of Nerva, Trajan and Hadrian*, no. 215, whose content Bennett thinks is 113/14.

34. The Greek city of Trapezus controlled access to Armenia across the Zigana Pass once fortified by Corbulo to command the approaches from the eastern end of the Black Sea and the short route from Iberia. See Mitford, 'Euphrates Frontier', p.503; Bennett, *Trajan Optimus Maximus*, p.192.

35. Anchialus, ruler of the Heniochi, and Machelones of the Coruh Nehri are mentioned in Dio 68.19.2; Bennett, *Trajan Optimus Princeps*, p.194, n.46; Eutropius, *Brev.* 8.3; Festus 20, and J.W. Eadie (ed.), *The Breviarum of Festus* (London: Athlone Press, 1967), p.139. Trajan appointed a new ruler to the Iberi and Albani. Julianus of the Apsilae was confirmed in his kingdom. Sherk, 'Roman Galatia', p.1198. The ceremony at which the kingdoms were assigned (*regna Adsignata*) was duly celebrated on the imperial coinage. Three men in short tunics and trousers are portrayed standing before Trajan who is wearing a breastplate and seated at a tribunal with a lector and the Guard Prefect at his side. He is extending his right hand to the foreign rulers in the foreground who raise both arms in salute.

36. Arrian, *Parthica* frs.38–40; Bennett, *Trajan Optimus Princeps*, p.194.

37. Dio 68.19.2–20 describes the main events at Elegeia. Sherk, 'Roman Galatia', p.1198.
38. On the death of Parthamasiris, see Arrian, *Parthica* fr.40; Fronto, *Princ. Hist.* 18; Eutropius, *Brev.* 8.3; Sherk, 'Roman Galatia', p.1198; Bennett, *Trajan Optimus Princeps*, p.194. On the Rex Parthus coins which show on the reverse the humiliation of Parthamasiris at Elegeia, see Strack, *Untersuchungen*, no. 209 = Mattingly and Sydenham, *RIC*, 312; Mattingly et al., *Coins of the Roman Empire*, vol. 3, 103; Lepper, *Trajan's Parthian War*, p.46. On the scandal the murder caused, see Rawlinson, *Sixth Great Monarchy*, p.174.
39. Fronto *Epist. ad Verum* 2.2, vol. 2 of the Loeb edition, pp.212–14, and the comments of Campbell, 'War and Diplomacy', pp.235–6.
40. Debevoise, *Political*, p.224; Dilleman, *HM*, locates the Mardi among the mountains south and west of Artaxata in the foothills of Mount Ararat. See Sherk, 'Roman Galatia', p.1198; Birley, *Hadrian*, p.70. Lepper, *Trajan's Parthian War*, p.137, admits: 'The literary accounts of the operations after Elegeia are so extremely inadequate that no one can say what may have taken place.'
41. C. Bruttius Praesens, legate of the VI Ferrata. See E. Dabrowa, 'The Commanders of the Syrian Legions 1st–3rd c. AD', in D.L. Kennedy (ed.), *The Roman Army in the East* (Ann Arbor, MI: *Journal of Roman Archaeology*, Supplementary Series, 18, 1996), pp. 277–96. See Dilleman, *HM*, p.278. Bennett, *Trajan Optimus Princeps*, p.194; the snowshoes incident is recorded in Arrian, *Parthica* fr.85; *AE* (1950), p.66. Melitene, at 3,000 feet has a month of snow. Satala, at 6,000 feet, has snow from December to March. See Mitford, 'Euphrates Frontier', p.503 on the suffering of Corbulo's army in the same area.
42. Inscriptions put the IV Scythica in Armenia at least until the spring of 116 when it was building a stone fortress at Artaxata. A huge inscription was erected by the IV Scythica in 116, perhaps marking the completion of the preliminary organization of the new province. *ILS*, 1062; Sherk, 'Roman Galatia', p.1196 and n.67. See J.G. Crow, 'A Review of the Physical Remains of the Frontiers of Cappadocia', in Freeman and Kennedy (eds), *Defence of the Roman and Byzantine East*, pp.80–1; Eutropius, *Brev.* 8.3 and Festus 20 speak of the Cardueni and Marcomedi as being subdued; these exploits cannot be exactly located but they have been associated with the extreme eastern end of Armenia where it projects towards the shore of the Caspian. Lepper, *Trajan's Parthian War*, p.138; Guey, *Essai sur la guerre parthique*, pp.72ff.
43. On the importance of the Dariel Pass, see Pliny, *HN* 6.40 and Treidler, 'Portae Caspiae' in *RE*, 22, cols 325–6. See Arrian, *Parthica* frs5, 85 and 87; Dilleman, *HM*, p.276. For Arrian's possible involvement see P.A. Stadter, *Arrian of Nicomedia* (Chapel Hill, NC: University of North Carolina Press, 1980), pp.142–3.
44. L. Catilius Severus, the distinguished ex-consul of 110 CE and 120 CE, was the first governor of Armenia. Debevoise, *Political*, p.225 with references. Under him as *Procurator Aug. Armeniae Maioris* was T. Haterius Nepos. *ILS*, 1338, 1041. See Sherk, 'Roman Galatia', p.1026 (and p.1199, n.87). For other evidence of the Roman establishment in Armenia, see M.L. Chaumont, 'L'Armenie entre Rome et L'Iran', in *ANRW*, 2, 9, pp.138–9; J. Crow, 'A Review of the Physical Remains of the Frontier in Cappadocia', in Freeman and Kennedy (eds), *Defence of the Roman and Byzantine East*, pp.80–1, with *CIL*, 3, 13627a. Note that the garrisons were placed at the same points that were considered important during Corbulo's campaign.
45. Some people place the submission of the kings of the Pontic Iberians, the Crimean Bosporus and the Colchi at this point in the narrative. Festus 20; Eutropius, *Brev.* 8.3. Pliny, *Ep.* 10.63, 64, 67 makes it clear that the Crimean Bosphorans were already in some form of allied status with Rome. Bennett, *Trajan Optimus Princeps*, p.283, n.55. The Iberians probably provided Trajan with a detachment of soldiers since a nephew of the king, Amazaspos died the following year while on campaign with the emperor.
46. One satrap supposedly brought as a gift a horse trained to do obeisance by kneeling on its forelegs: Dio 68.18.2 and 3; Bennett, *Trajan Optimus Princeps*, p.194. Arrian reports that the kings of three tribes along the Pontic coast – the Lazi, the Abasci and the Sanigae – all received their authority from Rome. On the Black Sea coast, see B. Isaac, *The Limits of Empire: The Roman Army in the East* (Oxford: Clarendon Press, 1992), pp.42–50. If it was Trajan's goal to control the area, he did not complete the task. Arrian chides Hadrian about the importance of the region. A.B. Bosworth, 'Arrian and the Alani', *HCSP*, 81 (1977), p.240. Some of the Caucasian kingdoms had been clients of Rome since the time of Pompey. Rome had on occasion dispatched troops to the Causasian

kingdoms for engineering works and other duties. Tacitus, *Annals* 6.31–6. For Roman troops in the Caucasus, see *SEG*, 20.112 of AD 75 from Harmozica near Tbilisi, Georgia and *AE* 1951, 263 near Baku dating to the reign of Domitian. Perhaps Trajan was trying to formalize the ad hoc arrangements and might even have developed a network of permanent garrisons in the Caucasian hinterland. Arrian, *Periplus* 6.1–5 cf. M. Speidel, in *SMR 3* (1986), pp.657–60, on the units, and Bennett, *Trajan Optimus Maximus*, p.194.
47. Dio 68.23.1. The Senate votes Trajan the title of *Optimus*. The arguments over the date of this event are summarized by Lepper, *Trajan's Parthian War*, pp. 34–9, esp. Table 1 and p. 38. The winter of 114/115 at Elegeia or Artaxata is obscured by the Dio/Xiphilinus account. The Mesopotamian campaign then begins in 115 including the events which lead to Trajan's receiving the title Parthicus which the *Fasti Ostienses* firmly dates to 115. Bennett, *Trajan Optimus Princeps*, p.195. See also *ILS*, 299, in which Trajan's titulature included IMP IX and TRIB POT XIX indicating the ninth imperial salutation being awarded before December 115. Lepper, *Trajan's Parthian War*, p.26.
48. Dio 68.23.1–2. Some have suggested the 'travelling on foot through the snow' story is a *topos*. If so, it would go along with the character assessment in 68.6.1–8.
49. These movements are inferred from his known activities around Lake Van and the events described in Dio 68.22.2. His success was rewarded by his adlection into the Senate as praetor. Dio 68.32.5; Bennett, *Trajan Optimus Princeps*, p.195 and no. 64. On the resistance of Mebarsapes see Lepper, *Trajan's Parthian War*, p.130.
50. On Trajan taking Batnae, see Arrian, *Parthica* fr.54–6; Dio 68.23.2; Eutropius, *Brev.* 8.3; Festus 20; Bennett, *Trajan Optimus Princeps*, p.196.
51. On Nisibis, see J. González, 'La Guerra Pártica de Trajano', in J. González (ed.), *Imp. Caes. Nerva Traianus Aug.* (Sevilla: Ediciones Alfar, 1993), p.154.
52. Arrian, *Parthica* fr.42–8 says there was a faction in Edessa that objected to the reappointment of Abgarus. Arrian also adds the details about Arbandes wearing gold earrings. According to Dio 68.21, Trajan had met Arbandes on an earlier occasion (presumably as a member of the Osrohenian embassy dispatched to Antioch in 114) and had become deeply enamoured of him. At the conclusion of the agreement, a banquet was held where the royal youth performed a 'barbaric dance'. If the evidence of the so-called acts of Sharbil and Barsamyes is to be believed, Odessa was in a tributary relationship with Rome before this date. W. Cureton, *Ancient Syriac Documents* with a Preface by W. Wright (Piscataway, NJ: Gorgias Press, 2005), no.41, and Lepper, *Trajan's Parthian War*, pp.93–4.
53. On these events see Dio 68.22.1; Lepper, *Trajan's Parthian War*, pp.208–9; Bennett, *Trajan Optimus Princeps*, p.196. A milestone north of Singara with the appropriate imperial titulature for the spring of 116 at the earliest, shows the territory was being consolidated before then. *AE* (1927), p.161. On the site of Singara, see Kennedy and Riley, *Rome's Desert Frontier from the Air*, pp.125–31. On the extent of the new province of Mesopotamia, see Lepper, *Trajan's Parthian War*, pp.141–8.
54. A fragment of the *Fasti Ostienses* first published in 1934 gives a virtual fixed point for the title *Parthicus* on Trajan in February 116. Lepper, *Trajan's Parthian War*, pp.39–43. Laurelled letters to the Senate were received 21 February 116. At this time of year, it could take as long as ten weeks or more for official letters between Rome and the eastern Mediterranean to arrive at their destination. See F. Millar, 'Trajan: Government by Correspondence', in González (ed.), *Imp. Caes. Nerva Traianus Aug.*, pp.363–88. Smallwood, *Documents Illustrating the Principles of Nerva, Trajan and Hadrian*, 23, lines 9–12; *Parthicus* coins: Strack, *Untersuchungen*, no. 246. Coins announcing territories subjugated to the power of Rome, Mattingly *et al.*, *Coins of the Roman Empire*, 1033–40. Coins with *Armenia et Mesopotamia in Potestatem PR Redactae*, Strack, *Untersuchungen*, nos. 472, 473, 474; Cohen, *Description historique*, no. 39.
55. For a description of the earthquake, see Dio 68.24–5. Lepper, *Trajan's Parthian War*, pp.65–87, discusses the problems with the chronology and Malalas's dating, as does Longden, 'Notes on the Parthian Campaigns of Trajan', pp.2–4; Bennett, *Trajan Optimus Princeps*, p.196.
56. Lepper, *Trajan's Parthian War*, p.129, notes that Trajan had accomplished so much in 115 that one begins to wonder why he went on in the following year to attack Adiabene and Ctresiphon at all.
57. Dio 68.26.1 for the pontoon bridges built at Nisibis, and who notes at 68.26.2 that the

crossing was dominated by the Gordyaean Mountains, thus the location of the crossing at Cizre. Lightfoot, 'Trajan's Parthian War', p.120, does not believe the story. Cf. J.G. Taylor, 'Travels in Kurdistan', *Journal of the Royal Geographical Society*, 35 (1865), p.56 on the forests of Nisibis.

58. The taking of Singara, see Arrian, *Parthica* fr.50; Dio 68.22; of Libana, see Arrian, *Parthica* fr.7; of Thebeta, see Arrian, *Parthica* fr.11. Debevoise, *Political*, p.226.

59. On Xiphilinus's account, see Lepper, *Trajan's Parthian War*, pp.134–5.

60. Paribeni, *Optimus Princeps*, vol. 2, pp.298ff., believes in the Alexander parallel as does Lepper, *Trajan's Parthian War*, pp.132–3 and n.2. Ammianus Marcellinus 24, 2.3, 6.1 and Zosimus 3.15.24, associate Trajan with this route and it is the route the emperor Julian would later follow; A.D.H. Bivar, 'The Political History of Iran under the Arsacids', in *CHI*, vol. 3: 1: *The Seleucid, Parthian and Sasanian Period*, ed. E. Yarshater (Cambridge: Cambridge University Press, 1983), p.90.

61. On Alexander's route, Dio 68.22.3. The location of Adenystrae remains unknown. See Lightfoot, 'Trajan's Parthian War', p.118, n.20, for two possibilities. Bennett, *Trajan Optimus Princeps*, p.284. Dilleman, *HM*, p.285, rejected the identification with Dunaisir, and equated it with Ad Herculem, which Aurel Stein placed at Jaddalah. Recent excavations have cast doubt on this identification, see S. Gregory and D. Kennedy (eds.), *Sir Aurel Stein's Limes Report: The Full Text of M.A. Stein's Unpublished Limes Report: His Aerial and Ground Reconnaissances in Iraq and Transjordan in 1938–39* (Oxford: British Archaeological Reports, 1985), p.399. A portrait head found at Hatra and attributed to Trajan suggests a brief period of Roman occupation in the area. See J.M.C. Toynbee, 'Some Problems of Romano-Parthian Sculpture at Hatra', *JRS*, 62 (1972), pp.106–7; Lightfoot, 'Trajan's Parthian War', p.118, and M.G. Angeli-Bertinelli, 'I Romani oltre l'Euphrate nell II secolo dC', in *ANRW*, 2, 9.1 (1976), pp.14–15. M.L. Chaumont, 'A propos de la chute de Hatra', *AAASH*, 27 (1979), p.227.

62. On the Sentius story, see Dio 68.22; Bennett, *Trajan Optimus Princeps*, p.198.

63. Trajan's twelfth salutation can be dated between 20 February and 9 December 116. *CIL*, 2.5543, from Azuaga. Lepper, *Trajan's Parthian War*, pp.44–5.

64. Eutropius, *Brev.* 8.3. Not all scholars are convinced such a province existed. For those who think it did, see Longden, 'Notes on the Parthian Campaigns of Trajan', pp.13–14; D. Magie, *Roman Rule in Asia Minor* (Princeton, NJ: Princeton University Press, 1950), p.608; Dilleman, *HM*, pp.288–9; College, *The Parthians*, pp.54–5; M.L. Chaumont, 'L'Armenie entre Rome et L'Iran', in *ANRW*, 2, 9, p.140; W. Eilers, 'Iran and Mesopotamia', in Bivar, 'The Political History of Iran under the Arsacids', in *CHI*, vol. 3, 2, p.496; Debevoise, *Political*, p.230. For dissenters, see A. Maricq, 'La province d'Assyrie crée par Trajan: A propos de la guerre parthique de Trajan', *Syria*, 36 (1959), p.254; Lightfoot, 'Trajan's Parthian War', pp.121–4; Lepper, *Trajan's Parthian War*, pp.152 –3; Eutropius, *Brev.* 8.3.2 and 8.6.2, and Festus 14 and 20, talk of Trajan forming Arabia into a province about this time. The claim is usually dismissed as a substantially *post eventum* reference to the earlier assimilation of Nabataenan Arabia, but it has also been interpreted as a formal, if short-lived, integration of the Scenite Arabs and *Arabia Deserta* within the proposed Provincia Arabia. See Bennett, *Trajan Optimus Princeps*, pp.284–5, n.74; there is no celebration of a foundation of *Assyria Provincia* on the coinage on Trajan. Mariq's attempt to explain this absence on coins by saying that those with the legend *Parthia capta* are in fact proclaiming the annexation of Assyria is not convincing. While there is a name for the governor of Armenia, there is no record of any Roman official appointed to Assyria. There is no trace of Roman occupation around Djebel Singara in the second century. If there was a province in Assyria, it was so transitory that it left no trace in contemporary records. Lightfoot suggests the references in Eutropius and Festus may be regarded as a misconceived reference to Adiabene.

65. Dio 68.26 on civil conflicts.

66. Arrian, *Parthica* fr.2–17.

67. Ammianus Marcellinus 24.2.3 on Trajan's tribunal at Ozogardana on the Euphrates. Arrian, *Parthica* frs8, 10, 64. On the asphalt wells at Hit, see Dio 68.27.1; Arrian, *Parthica* fr.13. For the debate over whether these or similar wells at Kirkuk are meant, see the discussion and references supplied by Lepper, *Trajan's Parthian War*, pp.134–5; Lightfoot, 'Trajan's Parthian War', p.120. Lightfoot does not accept this reference as proof that the Romans advanced far into Adiabene or that they marched from there

down to Babylon and so on to Ctesiphon. Lepper, *Trajan's Parthian War*, p.9–10. The placing of the excerpt depends on the location of Adenystrae. Boissevain assumed it must be in Adiabene, Mebarsapes's kingdom, and therefore put the Sentius embassy after or just before Trajan's invasion of that country: Dio 68.22.3. On the other hand, an earlier occasion in which Mebarsapes was defending Mesopotamia is suggested by Hoffman's identification of Adenystrae with medieval Dunaisir, about fifty miles west of Nisibis, on which see *RE*, Suppl. 1.10; Londgen, 'Notes on the Parthian Campaigns of Trajan', p.11, n.5. Guey, *Essai sur la guerre parthique*, pp.113ff., believed Dio mentioned both in his original account.

68. Trajan's river fleet down the Euphrates. Arrian, *Parthica* fr. 67.
69. Lepper, *Trajan's Parthian War*, p.133. On Naharmalcha, see F.H. Weissbach in *RE*, 16.2, cols 1440ff.
70. Trajan dragging ships overland with capstan devices, Arrian, *Parthica* fr.67.
71. Hadrian later restored the daughter c. 128 and at the same time promised to return the throne, but failed to do so. Antoninus Pius later refused a direct request for it. *SHA, Hadrian* 13.8 and *SHA, Antoninus Pius* 9.7; Bennett, *Trajan Optimus Princeps*, p.285, n.80.
72. *Parthia capta* coins. Belloni, *Le Monete di Traiano*, p.xxxvi. On the title *Parthicus*, Dio 68.28.2–3. This should be the twelfth salutation. See Lepper, *Trajan's Parthian War*, pp.44–5 for the problems.
73. Osroes retreats in face of a superior enemy. See the remarks of Bennett, *Trajan Optimus Princeps*, p.199.
74. Trajan forming a province in Babylonia: Lepper, *Trajan's Parthian War*, pp.146–7. Later references talk of Trajan establishing a frontier along the banks of the Tigris. Festus 14. For Trajan's personal activities in forming the province see Fronto's comment that the emperor spent some time 'making more stringent the ferry dues for camels and horses on the Euphrates and Tigris', Fronto, *Princ. Hist.* 19. Bennett does not believe this was a *topos*: *Trajan Optimus Princeps*, p.285, n.82. There is no evidence of Roman occupation under Trajan anywhere along the Euphrates below the city of Dura Europas.
75. Arrian, *Parthica* fr.70, on Spasinu Charax. For the events after the taking of Cteisphon, see Dio 68.28–9; Bennett, *Trajan Optimus Princeps*, p.199. On the province of Characene and Charax, see J. Black, 'The History of Parthia and Charactene in the Second Century AD', *Sumer*, 43, 1–2 (1984), pp.230–4; Lepper, *Trajan's Parthian War*, p.10.
76. Thirteenth imperial salutation, Bennett, *Trajan Optimus Princeps*, p.199; Jordanes, *Rom* 268, on the statue marking his advance. The statue was apparently still standing in AD 569 when recorded by John of Ephesus in his Ecclesiastical History: Bennett, *Trajan Optimus Princeps*, p.285, n.83. Lepper, *Trajan's Parthian War*, p.14, n.2. More coins were issued with the legend FORTUNA REDUX; Cohen, *Description historique*, nos. 157, 2158, 159, 160. Strack, *Untersuchungen*, nos. 454, 459; Mattingly and Sydenham, *RIC*, no. 652.
77. Insurrection breaks out instigated by Osroes's brother Mithridates. Dio 68.30–2 and 75.9; John Malalas 11.273–20–274.
78. Mithridates is killed in an equestrian accident and his son Sanatrukes continues the insurgency. Sanatrukes is also nominated by the Parthians as king-in-exile of the Armenians in the place of Parthamasiris: Debevoise, *Political*, p.235 and n.111 on the sources.
79. Securing perimeters. Bennett, *Trajan Optimus Princeps*, pp.199–200.
80. Division one led by Appius Maximus Santra, *legatus legionum*. See Fronto, *Princ. Hist.* 209; R. Syme, *Tacitus* (Oxford: Clarendon Press, 1958), p.239, n.9; Dio 68.28 and 29.
81. Division two led by Lusius Quietus. He reconquers Nisibis and Edessa. Dio 68.32.5. The end of Abgarus's reign and presumably the fall of Edessa can be closely dated to between 6 June 116 and 1 July 117. See Lepper, *Trajan's Parthian War*, pp.92–5, 262, n.62, but this still does not tell us when the Parthian *revanche* began as Bennett, *Trajan Optimus Princeps*, p.285, n.88, points out.
82. Third division under the joint command of two legates, Erucius Clarus and Julius Alexander, captures Seleucia in Babylonia and burns it. Trajan himself joined this group. Bennett, *Trajan Optimus Princeps*, p.200.
83. Ibid., p.200.
84. Vologases II. Bennett, *Trajan Optimus Princeps*, p.200; Dio 68.30; Debevoise, *Political*, p.237.
85. Dio 68.30. Parthamaspates, son of Osroes, King of Parthia. Bennett, *Trajan Optimus Princeps*, p.200 and p.285, n.89.
86. The statue of Parthamaspates was advertised on coins issued late that year bearing the

legend REX *PARTH*[ic]*US DATUS*: 'A King is given to the Parthians', Mattingly *et al.*, *Coins of the Roman Empire*, no. 1054. Belloni, *Le Monete di Traiano*, pp.xxxv, xxvi, 48; Mattingly and Sydenham, *RIC*, vol. 2, nos. 310, 311, 312, 66; Mattingly and Sydenham, *RIC*, vol. 2, nos. 667, 668. Strack, *Untersuchungen*, no. 476; Cohen, *Description historique*, no. 328.

87. Bennett, *Trajan Optimus Princeps*, p.200.
88. For the strategic importance of Hatra, see A. Maricq, 'Les dernières années de Hatra: l'alliance romaine', *Syria*, 34 (1957), pp.288ff., and M. Bonaria, 'Hatra', in *RE*, Suppl. 10 (1965), col. 1101.
89. Dio 68.31 for the events at Hatra. Hatra was a rich caravan city. The city walls enclose an area of about 1,000 acres. Kennedy and Riley, *Rome's Desert Frontier from the Air*, pp.106–7 and plates 53 and 54. Isaac, *Limits of Empire*, pp.152–6; Bennett, *Trajan Optimus Princeps*, p.200 and p.285, n.90; S. Bergamini, 'Parthian Fortifications in Mesopotamia', *Mesopotamia*, 22 (1987), p.201.
90. Dio 68.31.4 on the swarming flies.
91. Ibid., 68.31.3 on Trajan's majestic grey head.
92. Trajan lifts the siege of Hatra. Cloudbursts and hailstorms. Bennett, *Trajan Optimus Princeps*, p.201; Dio 68.31.4.
93. M. Pucci ben Ze'ev, 'Greek Attacks against Alexandrian Jews during Emperor Trajan's Reign', *JSJ*, 20 (1989), pp.31–48. For the evidence of the revolt on papyri, see A. Fuks, 'The Jewish Revolt in Egypt (AD 115–117) in the Light of Papyri', *Aegyptus*, 33(1953), pp.131–58; J. Neusner, 'The Jews East of the Euphrates and the Roman Empire, I: 1st–3rd centuries AD', in *ANRW*, 2.9.1, pp.57–9.
94. T.D. Barnes, 'Trajan and the Jews', *JJS*, 40 (1989), pp.145–62.
95. Neusner, 'The Jews East of the Euphrates', p.58.
96. On this theory, see ibid., p.58.
97. The statistics given seem highly inflated. We are told that in Cyrene, 220,000 Greeks and Romans perished and had their flesh eaten, and their entrails were used to make belts. This last detail is certainly unlikely if it was a crowd of religious Jews; human flesh is not kosher. There is more documentation for destruction of property than there is for atrocities, especially in Cyrene. See A. Fuks, 'Jewish Revolt in Egypt', p.156, and S. Applebaum, 'The Jewish Revolt in Cyrene in 115–117 and the Subsequent Re-Colonization', *JJS*, 2 (1951), pp.177–81. Marcus Turbo was dispatched to Alexandria to put down the revolt. Dio says Trajan sent Lusius 'among others'. Turbo was prefect of the Misenum fleet.
98. On Marcus Turbo's prefecture in Egypt see Fuks, 'Jewish Revolt in Egypt', p.152. On Lusius Quietus being sent to Jerusalem to head off any potential revolt by the Jews there, see S. Applebaum, 'Notes on the Jewish Revolt Under Trajan', *JJS*, 2, 1 (1950), pp.26–30.
99. Fuks, 'Jewish Revolt in Egypt', p.153.
100. Trajan's intent to march back into Mesopotamia: Dio 68.33.1.
101. Not everyone agrees this is a portrait of Trajan. See R. Winkes, *Clipeata Imago: Studien zu einer römische Bildnisform* (Bonn: Habelt, 1969), pp.73–80. Cf. L. Budde, 'Imago Clipeata des Kaisers Traian in Ankara', *Antike Plastik*, 4 (1965), pp.103–17. Bennett, *Trajan Optimus Princeps*, p.286, n.93, observes that the likeness bears comparison with other depictions of the general period, while the claim that it is Trajan's father can be rejected on account of the laurel wreath on his head. This symbol is appropriate to the emperor alone.
102. On Trajan's stroke and ailments, Bennett, *Trajan Optimus Princeps*, p.201, who lists bad circulation, stroke and dropsy. Cf. Dio 68.33.3. Eutropius suggests there was haemorrhaging and bloody diarrhoea. Among the various diseases that have been suggested are dropsy (peripheral oedema – fluid in the limbs), arteriosclerosis and haemostasis in the nether regions (no blood due to vaso-constriction).
103. Insurrection in Mauretania, *SHA*, *Hadrian* 55; Bennett, *Trajan Optimus Princeps*, pp.201–2; Roxolani and Iazyges, *SHA*, *Hadrian* 6.6; British brigands, *SHA*, *Hadrian* 5.1; signs of rebellion in Judaea, *SHA*, *Hadrian* 5.1; E.M. Smallwood, 'Palestine AD 115–118', *Historia*, 11 (October 1962), pp.500–10, discusses the unrest in Palestine, the possibility of a revolt and Lusius Quietus's being sent there to quell the uprising.
104. Hadrian gets overall command in the East, Dio 68.33.1; Bennett, *Trajan Optimus*

Princeps, p.202.

105. Dio 68.33.2ff; Eutropius, *Brev.* 8.5. For an attractive if unprovable theory concerning the events surrounding the death of Trajan and Phaedimus and the matter of Hadrian's succession, namely that Trajan was assassinated, and Phaedimus murdered to assure silence, see Paribeni, *Optimus Princeps*, 2.310, no. 16, and Syme, *Tacitus*, p.240, n.7; Bennett, *Trajan Optimus Princeps*, p.202; *ILS*, 1792, and *SHA, Hadrian* 4.7.

106. Trajan's death in Selinus: Dio 68.33.3; Bennett, *Trajan Optimus Princeps*, p.202. The date of his death is not certain, but it was before 11 August 116.

107. *SHA, Hadrian* 5.1–5, and Eutropius, *Brev.* 8.6, on Hadrian abandoning the eastern conquests. The speech by Cato was supposedly given in the Senate in 167 B.C. after the defeat of Perseus, the last king of Macedonia at Pydna. See Livy 14.17–18. Tacitus, *Annals* 1.11 on the non-expansion of the empire.

108. A. Cornelius Palma, former commander in Asia, Hispania Ulterior and Syria; C. Avidius Nigrinus, governor of Dacia at Faventius; Lusius Quietus, Governor of Judaea and L. Publilius Celsus at Baiae. Bennett, *Trajan Optimus Princeps*, p.203. On the plot to kill Hadrian hatched by these four generals and their condemnation by the Senate see *SHA, Hadrian* 7.2–3.

109. All territory east of the Euphrates was given back. *SHA, Hadrian* 5.3, 9.1; Bennett, *Trajan Optimus Princeps*, p.203; Dura Europas was abandoned before 30 September 117. Smallwood, *Documents Illustrating the Principles of Nerva, Trajan and Hadrian*, 53, with the inscription. Bennett, *Trajan Optimus Princeps*, p.203, no. 104; M.I. Rostovtzeff, 'Deux notes sur des trouvailles a Doura-Europos', *CRAI* (1935), pp.285–90. Rostovtzeff modifies his views in a later article, making the abandonment of Dura take place in two stages: 'Kaiser Trajan und Dura', *Klio*, 31 (1938), pp.285–92; Lepper, *Trajan's Parthian War*, pp.148–9. On the site itself, see Kennedy and Riley, *Rome's Desert Frontier from the Air*, pp.111–14.

110. See J. Teixidor, 'Un port romain du désert: Palmyre', *Semitica*, 34 (1984), C.R. Whittaker, 'Where are the Frontiers Now?', in Kennedy (ed.), *Roman Army in the East*, p.37.

111. He not only collected intelligence, he was said to have used disinformation. Arrian, *Parthica* fr.41, says: 'But Trajan always releasing false messages through spies, was accustomed both to advance and not to be upset at frightening matters.'

112. Campbell, 'War and Diplomacy: Rome and Parthia', p.215.

113. Dio 68.3.2–3. Longden, 'Notes on the Parthian Campaigns of Trajan', pp.27–8, on the contrary, believed Trajan had no intentions of annexing Mesopotamia.

114. Dio 78 (77.12.1); Debevoise, *Political*, p.263. See comments of Isaac, *Limits of Empire*, p.25.

115. Fronto, *Princ. Hist.* 10; Aurelius Victor 14.1; Eutropius, *Brev.* 8.6.2; Festus 14.4; 20.3.

116. Isaac, *Limits of Empire*, p.25.

9

FROM HADRIAN TO CARACALLA

At the accession of the new emperor Hadrian in 117 CE, Roman foreign policy temporarily underwent a change. Claims to the new provinces that Trajan had attempted to add were dropped, and the frontier was once more to be limited to the old Euphrates boundary.[1] To honour the activities of Trajan in the East, Hadrian established the Parthian games, which were celebrated for many years.[2] Parthia was suffering from territorial losses because it was reported that the kings of Bactria sent envoys to Hadrian to seek friendship, suggesting that Bactria had become independent from Parthia.[3]

HADRIAN'S NEW STRATEGY

Parthamaspates, who had been rejected by the Parthians soon after the departure of the Roman troops, was given Osrhoene by Hadrian.[4] Around 123, Hadrian himself went personally to the eastern front, where he managed to settle difficulties that threatened to break out into actual hostilities.[5] Perhaps these were connected with the struggle for power between Osroes and Vologases II, which was almost continuous from the time of the Roman withdrawal under Trajan. Vologases was gradually able to overcome his opponent, who struck no more coins after 128/129.[6] During that year Hadrian returned to Osroes, his daughter, who had been captured when Trajan took Ctesiphon, and in addition promised to restore the golden throne.[7]

In the years 131–132 CE, another Jewish revolt was simmering, and there is just a suggestion that the Parthians may have been expected to lend them assistance.[8] By 136, however, they were tied down with a conflict with the Alani. At the insistence of Pharasmanes of Iberia, this tribe from the north-east invaded Albania, Media Atropatene, and finally Armenia and Cappadocia.[9] A hostile force invaded Gorduene (see Map 6) but was met by 20,000 foot troops raised in Ctesiphon by Vologases. They were trapped in a valley, but the heroic efforts of one of their generals saved them. The Parthians were forced to withdraw and the way into Mesopotamia was open to the invaders, but fortune favoured the Parthians because the Alani homeland was invaded while they were away, and they were forced back eastward to repel the attack. According to another account, Vologases was forced to bribe the Alani to leave, but Flavius Arrianus, the Roman historian, Arrian, who was governor of Cappadocia, finally forced them to halt. Vologases complained to the emperor Hadrian about the behaviour of Pharasmanes in starting all this trouble. Pharasmanes was 'invited' to Rome to answer the charges, but he refused, and insults were exchanged between him and Hadrian.[10]

In 138 Hadrian died and was succeeded by Antoninus Pius. There were no difficulties on the Parthian frontier that the western historians deemed worthy of mention.[11] In May 148 CE, there appear coins of Vologases IV, who seems to have succeeded to the throne without a struggle and who ruled until March 192.[12] Vologases seems to have planned a campaign against the Armenians, but some ancient writers say it was forestalled by warnings from Antoninus Pius.[13] Roman troops were sent to Syria in preparation for a Parthian war.[14] Parthian weakness is suggested by several events during these years. Abgarus VII of Osrhoene was returned to his kingdom after having been exiled after Trajan's campaigns, and the Hyrcanians and the Bactrians sent an embassy to Antoninus Pius as independent kingdoms.[15] Antoninus refused to return the throne of Osroes which had been captured by Trajan.[16] Firm action had backed the diplomacy, the Syrian army was reinforced, and war with Parthia was averted.[17]

This policy would be reversed over the next century, however, as Marcus Aurelius and Lucius Verus, Septimius Severus and Caracalla mounted imperial expeditions on an unprecedented scale. They were designed to do great damage to Parthian power and prestige. They were also aimed at extending Roman control over lands belonging to former Parthian vassals.

MARCUS AURELIUS AND LUCIUS VERUS

It was not until 162 CE, just after Antoninus Pius died and was succeeded by Marcus Aurelius and Lucius Verus, that Vologases III, bolstered by Roman inactivity, invaded Armenia.[18] He took advantage of the accession of the new rulers to launch his long-threatened campaign. He marched into Armenia and expelled Sohaemus, the king protected by the Romans, and established in his place Pacorus, a member of the Parthian royal family.[19]

THE CAMPAIGN OF 161

C. Sedatius Severianus, the Gallic legate of Cappadocia, took the field against Vologases III in 161 CE.[20] He had considerable military experience, but he was led to believe he could deal easily with the situation and that he would win himself military glory. Severianus took one of his legions[21] and probably followed Trajan's route northward into Armenia, when he was caught by the Parthian forces under a commander named Osrhoes and forced into Elegeia beyond the frontiers of his province, high up by the headwaters of the Euphrates. After a short attempt to fight back, he decided that further resistance was futile, and he committed suicide. His legion was massacred. The whole affair lasted only three days.[22] The Parthian forces turned southward and crossed the Euphrates into Syria. We are told they spread terror everywhere, and the danger of a general revolt was imminent since there were many Parthian sympathizers. L. Attidius Cornelianus, governor of Syria, attempted to oppose the invaders but he was driven back, thus making the situation even more critical.[23] Even the Syrians toyed with the idea of revolting against the Romans.[24] The Parthians passed through Syria into Palestine, and almost the whole East seemed to lie open to their incursions.

Once the intelligence of this serious situation reached Rome, it was decided that one of the emperors must go to war in person. Lucius Verus, the younger co-emperor, took command of the operations. Since his military talents were suspect, he was supplied with the best generals Rome could produce: Avidius Cassius, Statius Priscus, G. Julius Severus, and Martius Verus.[25] The frontier armies had not fought a full-scale war under direct imperial direction for forty-five years – since Trajan's death in 117 CE.

Marcus Aurelius accompanied him as far as Capua, then Verus set off in a ship from Brundisium to Syria, where he arrived at Antioch in the summer of 162.[26] Troops were gathered from the eastern provinces, and three legions were brought from the Rhine and the Danube.[27] Parts or all of several other legions may have been mobilized.[28] This made the northern frontier defences weakened at strategically placed intervals, but the governors of the northern provinces were instructed to avoid hostilities and deal with disturbances by diplomacy whenever possible.[29]

Avidius Cassius, a stern disciplinarian and a native Syrian, was given command of the army and the task of whipping the legions into shape.[30] We are told the generals found the Syrian legions in low morale through decades of inertia, just as Corbulo had found them a century before (see Chapter 6). The same description is given of the eastern troops: they were ill-equipped and some were not all that familiar with their weapons.[31] Evidently, an army in Mesopotamia without proper equipment is not an entirely new phenomenon.[32] Cassius drilled and exercised the army, and in 163 CE the Romans were ready to take the offensive.

Verus was greatly worried about his own predicament.[33] He made an attempt to settle the issue diplomatically, but the suggestion was refused by Vologases, who interpreted this concession as an admission of weakness or cowardice.[34] With his military headquarters established in Antioch, Verus preferred to enjoy the shade and the running waters at Daphne in the summer, and winter in comfort at Laodicea while his lieutenants were given the task of recovering Syria.[35] There is no record of his ever taking an active part in the campaign, except for one rapid trip to the Euphrates, which he made at the insistence of his staff.[36] The Augustan history (*SHA, Marcus Aurelius* 8.14) claims that Marcus Aurelius, although in Rome, planned and executed everything necessary for the prosecution of the war. Verus spent his time in Syria taking a Syrian mistress, and is accused by the Augustan history of 'adulteries and love affairs with young men'.[37]

THE CAMPAIGN OF 163

Operations began in 163 with Statius Priscus invading Armenia.[38] He seized the capital, Artaxata, and although he did not destroy it, he founded a 'new city', Kaine Polis (Kainopolis) (see Map 12), not far away.[39] It was strongly garrisoned with Roman troops, and news of his success was sent to Rome. Priscus then reinstalled Sohaemus, the pro-Roman Arsacid prince, back on the throne of Armenia. The fact that he had been a senator and even a consul shows he must have been in exile in Rome for a long period of time waiting for this to happen.[40] The event was celebrated on the coinage of the year, which bore the legend REX ARMENIIS DATUS, and depicted

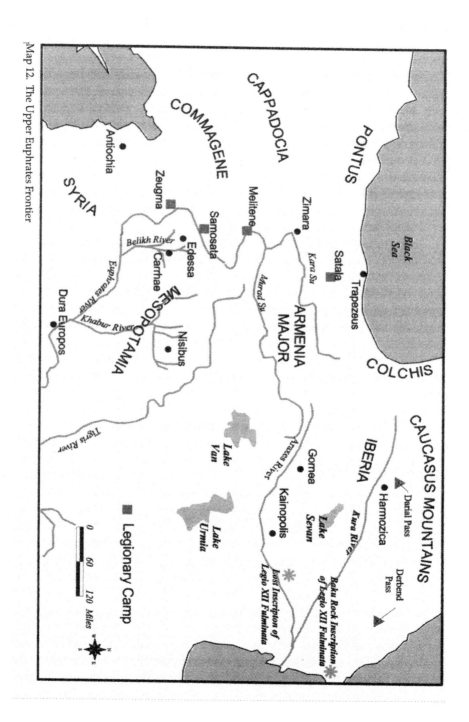

Map 12. The Upper Euphrates Frontier

Lucius sitting on a platform surrounded by his officers, with Sohaemus standing in front of him being saluted. Both emperors
were given the title Armeniacus.[41]

THE CAMPAIGN OF 164

There was at least a one-year lull in military operations between
Priscus's advance into Armenia and Avidius Cassius's three-pronged
attack on Mesopotamia.[42] The time was spent on preparation for the
assault on the Parthian homeland. After Cassius had cleared Syria
of invaders he was made by Marcus Aurelius into a sort of *gener-
alissimo*,[43] and being thus free to act as he chose, he determined to
carry the war into the enemy's country, perhaps in an
attempt to rival or outdo the exploits of Trajan fifty years earlier
(showing he had learned nothing from the disaster there). We have
no continuous narrative of the campaign, but we can trace its
course in general outline, based on various fragmentary writings
which bear upon the history of the time.

Meanwhile, the Romans invaded north Mesopotamia and
occupied Osrhoene and Anthemusia[44] (Map 6). In the north Edessa
was besieged, captured and returned to its former pro-Roman
ruler, Mannus. The Parthian appointee disappears from the principality of Osrhoene in 165.[45] A Roman army pursued the Parthians
eastwards to Nisibis which was also captured. When the retreating
enemy reached the Tigris, their general, Chosroes, only escaped by
swimming the river and taking refuge in a cave. This part of the
campaign may have been led by Martius Verus.[46]

A battle was fought at Sura (above Circesium) in which the Romans were victorious.[47] Cassius crossed the Euphrates.[48] Once
across, he turned southward along the river and took Dausara and
Nicephorium (Map 1),[49] near the junction of the Belik with the
Euphrates.[50] He then won a bloody engagement near Dura-Europus,
which remained in Roman hands from then on.[51] This was a hard-
fought victory for the Romans, but it forced the Parthians into an
armistice.

By the end of 165 Cassius brought his men far to the south and
moved across Mesopotamia at its narrowest point to attack the
twin cities on the Tigris: Seleucia on the right bank and the Parthian
capital, Ctesiphon, on the left.[52] The Roman army advanced into
Babylonia and was received at Seleucia in a friendly manner.
Seleucia welcomed the Romans and opened its gates. The vast city,

with a population of almost 400,000, still retained its Hellenistic characteristics.[53] Shortly afterward, however, someone broke the armistice and the Roman legions stormed the city and destroyed much of it by fire.[54] How this came about is not recorded in detail. Some blame Avidius Cassius for not maintaining the discipline of his troops, which seems unlikely considering his reputation for severity with lapses in discipline.[55] Not surprisingly, the Roman version was to claim that the 'Seleuceni had broken faith first'. What the truth is we will never know, but the action marked the end of one of the major outposts of Greek civilization in the East, not quite 500 years after its foundation.[56]

The Romans then moved on to Ctesiphon, where they took the city and destroyed the summer palace of Vologases.[57] Various temples were plundered, and there was much searching for secret places where treasure might be hidden. This was, after all, one of the benefits of such a campaign. A large amount of booty was carried off by the invaders. The Parthians, who had been worsted in every encounter, now ceased to resist. The Romans recovered all the territory lost by Trajan.

At the moment of success, however, an unforeseen disaster struck the Romans almost as Nemesis striking the over-fortunate. As the legionaries were looting Seleucia, plague swept through the army.[58] Much of the booty was left behind. Their sufferings were further aggravated by the failure of supplies, which caused many men to die of famine.[59] The survivors carried the disease throughout the Roman world.[60] The plague ravaged Italy, and spread as far as the Rhine and the Atlantic Ocean in the west, and took its toll in the Parthian Empire in the East.[61] Nevertheless, Cassius led a united force back in good order. Laurelled dispatches were sent to Rome announcing the victory. Lucius took the title of Parthicus Maximus, 'greatest conqueror of Parthia', and he and Marcus became Imperator III.[62]

By 166 the war was virtually over. Lucius was jubilant and was making arrangements for Fronto to write the official history. He directed Avidius Cassius and Martius Verus to draw up memoranda for him which he promised to send to Fronto.[63] In 166 came the final demonstration of Roman might, when the Parthian kingdom was invaded again. This time an assault was made across the northern Tigris, into Media, homeland of the ancient rulers of the East. The new victories of Cassius's armies led Lucius to take a further title, Medicus; meanwhile, Marcus accepted the title won in

165, Parthicus Maximus, and both became Imperator IV.[64] Cassius's victories in the far-off lands beyond the Tigris set people in the East talking. It was rumoured that he had crossed the Indus with one of the Syrian legions, the III (Parthica?) and some German and Moorish auxiliaries. Lucian, one of the many writers who cashed in on the war by producing histories of it, actually included such an episode.[65]

The date of Lucius's return and the exact circumstances of the conclusion of hostilities are not recorded. The Misenum fleet was still lying off the mouth of the Orontes at the end of May 166, so it was later than this.[66] Lucius would not have left until peace had been made. Rome could have annexed Mesopotamia. There was certainly some expectation that the empire would be enlarged.[67] We know that the province of Syria was increased to include Dura Europus. Garrisons were left in several strong points beyond the frontier, including Kainopolis in Armenia and Nisibis in northern Mesopotamia.[68] To ensure the Parthians kept the peace, the man who had gained the major victories in the war, Avidius Cassius, was installed as governor of Syria. The triumph for the eastern victories was held on 12 October. Rome had not seen a triumphal procession for over fifty years.

The expedition of Cassius was the first invasion of Parthia in which the Romans were entirely triumphant, in their own definition of a campaign. Trajan had overrun territory and had brought about the submission of Armenia to the Romans, but it did not deprive Parthia of any portion of her actual possessions. Trajan's gains had been lost almost immediately and caused his retreat. These reverses were so severe that it was generally believed Hadrian's concessions were prudent. The war of Lucius Verus, on the contrary, produced the actual cession to Rome of a Parthian province that remained for centuries an integral portion of the Roman Empire. Western Mesopotamia between the Euphrates and the Khabur rivers passed to Rome at this time, and although it was never actually made into a province, it was absorbed by Rome and was considered a loss to Parthia.[69] Lucius Verus's success enabled Rome to move the frontier of Syria after 165 as far as Dura-Europos, which was not only the scene of a battle but was also besieged by the Romans as attested by the discovery of a Roman trench.[70] In the Euphrates Valley, Rome also gained control of the outlet of one of the great caravan routes linking Palmyra and Mesopotamia. For Rome, the territorial gain was minimal although strategically important, but the acquisition reassured the network of clients along the Euphrates.[71]

The results of the three campaigns of Lucius were not decisive because the war ended in a compromise.[72] Yet Rome had penetrated Parthia more deeply than ever before and this had serious consequences for the Parthian regime. The war with Rome had ended in 166 CE. Vologases survived for another twenty-five years, but he never ventured to renew the struggle except for one further attempt to regain the Parthian losses.[73] In contending with Rome, the Parthians were fighting a losing battle. It added to their sense of defeat that they were crushed by a mere general who was a man of no great eminence and certainly did not have all of Rome's immense resources at his disposal. Not only had Parthia lost any ability to be an aggressive power, but now it was losing territory by the revolt of its own subjects and by losing the ability to protect itself from attacks by a foreign assailant.[74] The conclusion of the war marks a further step in the decline of Parthia. The territory west of the Khabur River remained permanently in Roman hands. Roman territory and influence now spread deeper into northern Mesopotamia than ever before. Dura Europus was Roman, and Carrhae and Edessa came more and more under the sway of Roman influence.[75] In spite of the lavish public celebration, Marcus must have realized that the four-year-long war had been an expensive and ultimately unnecessary interlude.

THE REVOLT OF AVIDIUS CASSIUS

In 175, Avidius Cassius, the conqueror of Seleucia and Ctesiphon, declared himself emperor while Marcus Aurelius was far away on the Danube (and incorrectly reported dead).[76] The news of Cassius's rebellion reached Marcus like a bolt from the blue. Marcus was totally unprepared and extremely disturbed by the intelligence which reached him in the form of a dispatch from Martius Verus, governor of Cappadocia. Both Dio and the Augustan History assert that Cassius proclaimed himself emperor at the wish of Faustina. Knowing that her husband was in bad health, she did not want the empire to fall into the hands of Commodus, who was too young and naive to handle the duties. She secretly persuaded Cassius to make his preparations, so that if anything should happen to Marcus, he might take over both her and the empire.[77] While he was considering his options, news came of Marcus's death and, without waiting for confirmation, he laid claim to the empire. Having found out the truth, however, he did not change course. Cassius was declared a public enemy by the Senate as soon as the news reached it, and ordered that his property be confiscated

In view of the possibility of a civil war among the Romans, Vologases threatened to take back his lost territory.[78] He was probably dissuaded when Marcus Aurelius turned up alive, and appeared on the scene and defeated Cassius. He sent ambassadors to the emperor with friendly assurances, who were received favourably by the philosopher emperor.[79] Four years later Marcus Aurelius died and was succeeded to the purple by his son, Commodus. The accession of a young, inexperienced and soon to be dissolute youth might have provided a good opportunity for the Parthians to attempt a recovery of Mesopotamia. What little we know of the period (and it is little indeed) shows no trace of Vologases entertaining any such design. Perhaps his advanced age made it impractical. Vologases died in 190, having reigned for at least ten years contemporaneously with Commodus, and yet Rome was never troubled by its eastern border and retained its Parthian conquests.[80]

THE CAMPAIGN OF SEPTIMIUS SEVERUS

Rome found itself in an unstable position in 193 CE when no less than three emperors declared themselves. Among the claimants to the throne was Pescennius Niger in Syria, who was backed by the eastern vassals of Rome and the western dependants of Parthia.[81] Vologases himself offered congratulations and support. Niger politely declined with thanks when his outlook was bright. Later, when Septimius Severus was acknowledged emperor in Rome and started marching eastward, Niger suddenly changed his mind and sought aid. In 193, he sent legates to rulers east of the Euphrates, especially those in Hatra, Armenia and Parthia, entreating them to sent troops to his aid.[82] By that time, however, the eastern vassals had assessed the situation correctly and most declined to become involved. Abgarus of Edessa and the ruler of Adiabene actually sent Niger troops, and Vologases promised to order the satraps to collect forces, but refrained from dispatching any body of distinctly Parthian troops.[83] Hatra, the chief city of central Mesopotamia, with a large Arab community, made a solid commitment.[84] Barsemius, its king, not only received envoys from Niger favourably, but actually sent to his aid a body of archers.[85]

After being defeated by Severus, Niger attempted to escape to the Parthians but failed. Some of his more successful followers gave military advice to Parthia.[86] It has been suggested that this could not have been done without Parthian permission, and that Vologases was behind the move because he thought it prudent to secure the friendship of the pretender whom he expected to be successful. Using the Hatrians as proxies merely gave him plausible deniability if the struggle did not turn out the way he expected. Sending his own troops to the camp of Niger would have committed him irretrievably, but the actions of a vassal might be disclaimed in the future.

While the Romans were distracted with the struggle between Severus and Niger, Vologases fomented a revolt in Osrhoene and Adiabene, and troops from these districts besieged Nisibis.[87]After the death of Niger, they sent ambassadors to Severus to lay claims before the Emperor by virtue of the aid they had given him in attacking a city that had sheltered his opponent's sympathizers. They also promised to restore what spoils remained, as well as the Roman prisoners. They refused to surrender, however, the cities that they had captured, or to receive garrisons, and they demanded that the Romans completely evacuate that territory and restore to them their independence.[88] Ever since Marcus's Parthian campaign, the Romans had regarded control of Osrhoene and Mesopotamia as necessary for the security of Syria and the other eastern provinces.[89] Severus was not about to surrender Roman territory without a fight; thus war was at once declared. His campaign would be punitive and demonstrative in nature.[90] Although he was attacking the petty kings of Osrhoene, Adiabene and Hatra, in the background loomed the massive Parthian Empire which may have instigated the fighting, and would probably not be indifferent to the fortunes of its vassal kings.

Late in the spring of 195 CE, Severus, at the head of his troops, crossed the Euphrates and advanced into enemy territory. At Edessa Abgarus IX, ruler of the surrounding area, joined Severus, gave his sons as hostages, and assumed the name Severus.[91] The next advance was to Nisibis, which the Mesopotamians had been unable to capture, and Severus established his headquarters there. The legionaries suffered greatly on this long march, especially because of the scarceness and badness of the water.[92] It was possibly at Nisibis that envoys were sent from 'the Arabians' (of Hatra?) with more reasonable offers than they had previously made. The offers were refused since the rulers had not come themselves. Severus only went as far as Nisibis, but he sent his army in three separate divisions under three separate generals to attack his different enemies. The generals chosen were Claudius Candidus, Julius Laetus and T. Sextius Lateranus.[93] He latter divided his army again, but changed commanders. Among the second group were three divisions under Anullinus, Probus and Laetus, which were sent to one of the districts of Mesopotamia called Arche (unidentified).[94] They had no trouble reducing Mesopotamia. Once subdued, they made Nisibis the capital and raised it to the position of Roman colony.[95] With this done, the troops then crossed the Tigris into Adiabene and, although the inhabitants offered strong resistance, the province was taken.[96] The Parthian king made no effort to defend the occupation of this province. He stayed in his capital and watched the events unfold.

Severus received three imperial salutations and took the titles 'Parthicus Arabicus' and 'Parthicus Adiabenicus'.[97] He declined the title of Parthicus Maximus since he had not yet conquered the Parthian capital as Trajan had done.[98] This campaign was useful in helping the emperor to take over the armies of Niger, and to forge the links of loyalty between his soldiers and himself.[99] But Severus could not afford to remain east very long because he still had one more rival in the West to take care of, Clodius Albinus, who might invade Italy in his absence. In early 196, therefore, Severus was forced to leave the eastern front before a direct attack could be made on Parthia.

Albinus was defeated and killed in 197 CE, but with the emperor absent and the Romans weakened by civil war, Vologases took the opportunity to attack again. He swept rapidly northward through Mesopotamia and, according to one writer, even crossed the Euphrates into Syria.[100] Nisibis was saved only by the desperate defence of Laetus who was besieged within the city, and even Armenia may have been retaken.[101]

Parthia's allies were not standing firm at home either. Narses, king of Adiabene, had not only refused to join with Vologases in his eastern campaign, but he showed signs of becoming friendly with the Romans. A revolt of Medes and Persians in his rear jeopardized his success and required hard fighting in eastern Iran. This done, Vologases restored his control over Adiabene after pillaging several of its cities and drowning its pro-Roman monarch, Narses, in the Greater Zab.[102] Vologases advanced with a large army against the revolters, and met them at Khorasan. After crossing a small river, his forces found themselves surrounded on all sides. Taken by surprise, they were forced to abandon their horses and retreat, but the rebels cornered them in the mountains and killed a great number of them. The loyal Parthian troops managed to reorganize, attack the pursuers and drive them to the sea. As Vologases's army was returning home, they met up with a rebel contingent that had become separated from the main body. After two days of hard fighting, the forces opposing the king slipped away during the night and Vologases returned with his troops in triumph.[103]

The success of any expedition against Parthia depended greatly on the dispositions of the semi-dependent princes, who possessed territories bordering the two great empires. The two most important of these were Armenia and Osrhoene. Armenia had been approached by emissaries of Niger when he began his attempt on the throne, but the Armenians refused to take any part in the civil war.[104] But the Armenian king must have done something to offend Severus, because when he reached the East again, he regarded Armenia as a hostile state requiring instant subjugation.[105]

It seems to have been in the summer of 197 CE, soon after his first arrival in Syria, that Severus dispatched a force against the Armenian king (confusingly named Vologases, the same as the Parthian monarch). The Armenian king mustered his troops and met the invaders at the frontier of his kingdom. A battle seemed imminent, but the Armenian king requested a truce and was granted one by the Roman leaders. A breathing space having been gained, Vologases sent ambassadors with presents and hostages to the Roman emperor in Syria, and professed to be a friend of the Romans. He entreated Severus to allow him terms of peace. Severus was persuaded and a formal treaty was made in which the Armenians even got an enlargement of their territory.[106]

Severus must have delighted in these events because it gave him undisturbed possession of western Mesopotamia as far as the junction of the Khabur with the Euphrates.

THE SECOND CAMPAIGN OF SEVERUS[107]

Severus was forced, therefore, to resume his eastern campaign later in 197, in order to regain his lost territory and justify the titles which he had taken. On his first arrival in Syria, he contented himself with expelling the Parthians from the province. It was not until the end of the year that he was able to cross the Euphrates into Mesopotamia.[108] In preparation for the attack on Parthia itself, he created three new legions – the I, II, and III Parthica.[109] At least part of the III Augusta may also have served.[110] His offers probably included Statilius Barbarus, L. Fabius Cilo, Q. Lollianus Gentianus, and C. Fulvius Plautianus.[111] In the latter part of 197, Severus and his army left Brundisium and sailed directly to Syria. In the spring he advanced to relieve Nisibis, but the Parthians withdrew before him without a struggle.[112]

Severus planned to invade Parthia by the Euphrates route,[113] while he sent detachments under other leaders to ravage Eastern Mesopotamia and Adiabene,[114] which had evidently been reoccupied by the Parthians. To solve the supply problem, Severus followed Trajan's lead and built a fleet of ships in Upper Mesopotamia where timber was plentiful. Accompanied by the brother of the Parthian king, he marched his army down the left bank of the Euphrates into Babylonia while his transports carried supplies and descended the course of the river.[115] By the fall of 198, the capital city was reached. He easily captured the two abandoned cities of Babylon and Seleucia that had both been evacuated by their garrisons.[116]

He then proceeded to Ctesiphon using either one of the canals uniting the Tigris and the Euphrates or else (like Trajan) he conveyed the ships on rollers across the narrow neck of land that separates the two rivers. Vologases took up his own position outside of Ctesiphon, determined to defend his capital. Some authors believe Severus's arrival surprised the Parthian king.[117] In any event, he seems to have made a poor showing. We are told by one author that he met the Romans in the open field, which is always a bad idea, and then allowed himself to be shut up in Ctesiphon, another bad idea.[118] The Romans loved engineering warfare, and had no trouble punching through city walls. Once the city was invested it appears to have been taken quickly. They did not offer the kind of resistance that we see later at Hatra.

Severus's soldiers stormed Ctesiphon on the first assault. The Parthian monarch took to flight accompanied by a few horsemen.[119] Septimius did not even take the trouble to pursue him. The capital thus fell into the hand of a foreign invader for the second time within the space of eighty years. The male population was slaughtered, and the Roman soldiers were allowed to plunder both the public and

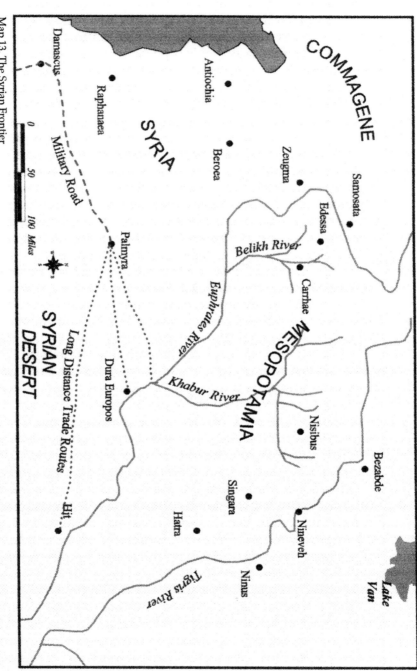

Map 13. The Syrian Frontier

private buildings at their pleasure. They seized the precious metals accumulated in the royal treasury and carried off all the ornamentation from the palace. The women and children were led into captivity in numbers close to 100,000.[120] On 28 January Septimius proclaimed that he had conquered Parthia and took the title that Trajan had first held; he assumed the title of Parthicus Maximus.[121] The date was chosen carefully. It was the exact centenary of Trajan's accession.

Dio suggests that he departed as if his only purpose had been plunder, but that his real reason for abandoning Ctesiphon was 'lack of supplies' and inadequate military intelligence.[122] Eventually they became short of food as well as intelligence and his soldiers were forced to exist on roots for some days, which gave them a dangerous form of dysentery.[123] He found himself unable to pursue Vologases, and recognized the necessity of retreating before disaster overtook him.[124]

He did not return by the route of the Euphrates, probably because his army had completely exhausted the resources of that region on their way downriver.[125] Severus withdrew by way of the Tigris, which brought him directly to Hatra, the city which had given its support to Niger.[126] Not only did he feel the city should suffer because of its audacity in backing the wrong pretender, but storming it successfully would give him the opportunity to eclipse the fame of Trajan, who had not been successful in storming that town.[127] Realistically, with Nisibis and Singara loyal to his cause, an easy line of communication with Syria could be established but for Hatra, which stood in the way (see Map 13).[128] So Severus stopped his march in order to lay siege to the place on 28 January 198 CE.[129] This was no easy target. Hatra was defended by a massive double wall, four miles in circumference. He used every siege engine he had and every trick in the book known to the Romans, but his first attempt was easily repulsed.[130] The walls of the town were too strong, and its defenders brave and resourceful. Their long-range archery was also effective. They burned the siege engines and created as much havoc among the besiegers as they could. It seems to have worked because mutiny broke out among the Romans and the emperor himself had to repress it. He put to death two of his chief officers, and then had to deny that he had given execution orders for one of them. One of them had been executed for complaining about the pointlessness of the siege.[131] He moved his camp farther away, and while there he had fresh engines in increased numbers built, collected an abundant supply of provisions and made every preparation for renewing the siege as quickly as possible.[132] Cupidity played a role in the decision since the accumulated wealth in the Temple of the Sun would make a splendid trophy.[133] Nothing was accomplished in the end and Severus retired to Nisibis. He probably spent the spring and summer of 198 reorganizing the eastern frontiers.

In 199 CE, Severus returned to Hatra with more provisions and better siege engines. Still his success was no greater. The Hatrene cavalry attacked his foraging parties and the defenders destroyed almost all his engines. They also harassed the soldiers by hurling down jars of insects and Hatrene fire – a burning, bituminous naphtha – upon the attackers.[134] Hatrene engines fired two missiles simultaneously with great force and these even endangered the emperor's life. Two imperial guards were shot down.[135]

When the soldiers at last breached the outer wall, the soldiers demanded to be led in an assault, confident in the power to force an entrance and carry the place.[136] Instead, Severus signalled retreat and hoped his show of mercy would entice their surrender; but his soldiers found themselves robbed of their booty when the Hatrenes held out and rebuilt their walls at night.[137] The Roman legionaries refused, under the circumstances, to renew the fighting, and the Syrian troops that were driven to the attack were slaughtered miserably. At the end of twenty-four fruitless days, Severus withdrew to Syria.[138] During the siege, Laetus, the commander who had so successfully defended Nisibis, was killed by the soldiers, possibly at the emperor's command.[139] He was extremely popular with his men, but was suspected of being too politically ambitious. Severus withdrew from Hatra a second time, after having besieged it for twenty days, and returned – by what route we are not told – into Syria.[140] There is no way to reconcile the disagreements in the ancient accounts, but one thing is certain, both sieges failed. This did not stop Septimius Severus from counting these events among the successes of his reign. The fourth panel of his arch in the Roman Forum depicts his siege of Hatra.[141] The emperor chose to stress his new alliance with the Hatrenes rather than the failed siege.

The most surprising thing about this campaign is the apparent apathy of the Parthians. Vologases, after withdrawing from Ctesiphon, seems to have made no effort to hamper or harass his Roman adversary. Considering the resistance of Hatra, the sufferings of the Romans, their increasing difficulties with respect to provisions and the injurious effect of the summer heat would all have been irresistible temptations to a commander with any spirit or energy. The Parthians could have pursued the Romans when they retreated; they could have harassed their rear lines, cut off their supplies and rendered their retreat difficult, if not disastrous. Parthia must have been weak and in decline, unable to gather the troops needed for a spirited defence, and thus gave the lacklustre performance that allowed this Roman raiding party to do so much damage.

This Parthian campaign cannot be considered a success for the Romans from a military or a political point of view, and not even a personal triumph for Severus.[142] The Romans made no territorial gains, the loss of men was heavy, and the expedition against Hatra had failed. It was Parthia that suffered greatly. Roman arms once again had violated its western capitals and the consequent destruction advanced the rapid decay which was already under-way.

Vologases survived his defeat by Severus by about ten or eleven years. For that decade, Parthian history is a blank, since the Romans write about Parthia only when there is a battle going on.[143] We hear of no effort made by Parthia at this time to recover her losses, and there were no collisions between Parthia and Rome. Vologases IV reigned until 208–209 CE, dying about two years before his great adversary, who died at York on 4 February 211 CE.

According to Dio 75.3.2, Septimius is supposed to have said that annexing northern Mesopotamia would provide a 'bulwark' for Syria (the term is *proboulos*, or outwork). It does show some sort of strategic thinking. Dio suggests other motives for Septimius – the desire for glory (75.1.1.) and perhaps the need of money (75.3.3). What he was not is defensive.

THE CAMPAIGN OF CARACALLA

Caracalla became emperor in 211, and got intelligence of a civil war going on between the two sons of Vologases V, Artabanus (V) and Vologases (VI). He seemed to revel in the weakness this would cause the Parthians.[144] Caracalla exhibited an inordinate ambition from the start and immediately set the tone for his eastern policy. He saw himself as a second Alexander and made known his desire for the glory of Eastern conquests.[145] Indeed, Fergus Millar points out that this was no superficial whim on his part but the deter-mining factor in his actions as emperor.[146]

Abgarus IX of Osrhoene began to expand his control over his neighbours. Caracalla invited the king to pay him a friendly visit and then seized him and threw him into prison. He declared its territories forfeited, and reduced them to the form of a Roman province.[147] Without its leader, Osrhoene rapidly submitted to Roman authority, and it was henceforth controlled without a king.[148]

Since this high-handed treatment succeeded with Osrhoene, Caracalla attempted to deal with Armenia in the same way, and their king fell into the same trap. When the king became em-broiled in a quarrel with his sons, they were summoned before Caracalla and eliminated. The Armenians, however, did not sub-mit quietly but flew to arms.[149] Three years afterwards, in 215 CE, Caracalla sent a Roman army under Theocritus, one of his favourites, to chastise them, but instead they inflicted a severe defeat on their assailant.[150]

One would think this dampened his ardour for an eastern campaign. Instead, he tried to pick a quarrel with Parthia as early as 214 CE. In his winter quarters in Nicomedia (Izmit), Caracalla assembled troops[151] and built two large engines, constructed so that they could be taken apart and stowed away in ships for transport to Syria.[152] Caracalla found a pretext for war in the fact that the Parthi-ans had not surrendered to him a certain Cilician cynic named An-tiochus and a Tiridates, perhaps an Armenian prince.[153] When the Parthian king Artabanus surrendered Antiochus and Tiridates to the Romans, Caracalla gave up the idea of invading Parthia for the time being. Instead, he sent Theocritus[154] with an army against the Armenians while he himself proceeded to Antioch, where he spent the winter of 215/16. Theocritus would be defeated.[155]

While this was all happening, the new Parthian king, Vologases V, was still engaged in the dispute with his brother Artabanus V.[156] He yielded the western capital to his brother Artabanus, who controlled Media and struck his coins at Ecbatana, but who was making a bid for Mesopotamia too. Caracalla claimed to have started these disputes in order to weaken Parthia.[157] By 216, Artabanus V had apparently extended his sway over Mesopotamia, but Volo-gases continued to strike coins at the Seleucia mint for some years to come.[158]

In the summer of 215 CE, having transferred his residence from

Nicomedia to Antioch, he sent ambassadors to Artabanus with gifts and a rather unusual proposition. He sent a request to Artabanus for the hand of his daughter in marriage. Perhaps this was an attempt to unite the two great powers of the world, but more likely it was simply an attempt to secure a *casus belli*.[159] According to the contemporary (but highly unreliable) historian, Herodian, Artabanus at last consented to the marriage. Caracalla proceeded to the Parthian court in great state and amid much festivity. At the meeting of the two kings in the plain before Ctesiphon, the Romans fell upon the unsuspecting Parthians and slaughtered great numbers of them, though Artabanus managed to escape. If this improbable tale is true, then Caracalla staged a very successful deception operation that got him into the Parthian capital, and into the presence of the king himself without striking a blow.[160] Whether or not the tale is true, we do know that on the way back via the Tigris route, Caracalla ravaged part of Media, sacked many of the fortresses, took the city of Arbela, and dug open the Parthian royal tombs, scattering the bones.[161]

Caracalla announced his victory to the Senate.[162] Coins with the legend *VIC[toria)] PART[hica]* were issued to commemorate the victory.[163] He passed the winter at Edessa, amusing himself with hunting and charioteering after the fatigues of his campaign.[164] The results of Caracalla's second campaign in 215–217, principally in Adiabene and Babylon, were less than spectacular. The only significant result had been achieved before the campaign even began; in 213, when King Abgarus IX of Edessa was overthrown.

Artabanus, meanwhile, retired into the mountains to gather additional forces, and returned determined to exact retribution for the treacherous massacre at Ctesiphon and the wanton impiety of desecrating the royal Parthian tombs at Arbela in Adiabene. Whether for this reason or another, he launched a vigorous counteroffensive in Mesopotamia. He had already taken the field and conducted his troops to the Roman frontier[165] when Caracalla lost his life. On 8 April 217 CE, having left Edessa with a small retinue for the purpose of visiting a famous temple of the Moon-God near Carrhae, he was surprised and murdered on the way by Julius Martialis, one of his guards, while he was relieving himself.[166] Macrinus succeeded to the throne.[167]

MACRINUS

The assassination of the emperor in 217 altered the balance between the two empires. The new Emperor Macrinus, although a Praetorian Prefect, was no soldier and felt the time was not auspicious to continue the war, so he returned the captives, laid the blame on Caracalla and requested peace. Artabanus rejected the offer and demanded that the towns and fortresses that had been destroyed be restored, that Mesopotamia once more be returned to Parthia, and that reparation be made for the injury to the royal tombs.[168] It was impossible for a Roman emperor to consent to such demands without first trying his fortunes at war, and Macrinus decided to go to battle.

Artabanus advanced toward Nisibis, where Macrinus met him. The battle was meant to terminate the long contest between Rome and Parthia and is reputed to be one of the fiercest and best-contested ever fought between the two powers. It lasted for three days.[169] The army of Artabanus was numerous and well-appointed. As with most Parthian armies, it was strong in cavalry and archers. It also had a force of cataphracts in complete armour, carrying spears or lances, who were mounted on camels.[170] The Romans were supported by light-armed troops and a body of Mauretanian cavalry.[171]

According to Dio, the battle was precipitated by a skirmish over a waterhole. Herodian says it commenced with a fierce assault of the Parthian cavalry, who charged the Romans with loud shouts and reigned arrows endlessly upon them. The cavalry and camel corps of the Parthians were particularly effective, but the Romans had the advantage in close fighting. Caltrops (spikes) scattered by the Romans hindered the movements of the Parthian mounted forces. At the end of the first day, the armies retired to their camps without any decisive result.[172]

The next day there was combat from morning until night; we have no description of this, but it presumably terminated without any clear advantage to either side. The battle was then renewed on the third day, with the difference being that the Parthians now directed all their efforts towards surrounding the enemy and thus capturing their entire force. Since they were greatly outnumbered by the Parthians, the Romans were compelled to extend their line unduly in order to meet the Parthian tactics; the weakness of the extended line seems to have given the Parthians an opportunity of throwing it into confusion, thus causing the Roman defeat.[173] The struggle lasted for three days, at the end of which the Parthians had the advantage.[174] Some have suggested this was because of the numerical superiority of the Parthians, which enabled them to extend their line in a flanking movement until the inferior Roman forces were greatly weakened.[175]

Macrinus was among the first to take flight and his hasty retreat discouraged his troops, who acknowledged themselves beaten and retired within the lines of their camp.[176] Both armies suffered severely. Herodian describes the heaps of dead as piled to such a height that the manoeuvres of the troops were impeded by them, and at last the two contending hosts could scarcely see one another. Both armies therefore desired peace. The soldiers of Macrinus, who did not have much confidence in their leader to begin with, were demoralized by ill success and showed themselves inclined to throw off the restraints of discipline. The troops of Artabanus – a militia rather than a standing force – were unaccustomed to sustained efforts, and having been in the field for some months now, had grown weary and wished to return home.

Macrinus, under these circumstances, reopened negotiations with Artabanus. He was prepared to concede something more than he had proposed originally, and he had reason to believe that the Parthian monarch, having found the Roman resistance so stubborn, would be content to insist on loss. The event justified his expectations. Artabanus relinquished his request for the cession of Mesopotamia and accepted a pecuniary compensation. Besides restoring the captives and booty carried off by Caracalla in his raid, Macrinus was able to purchase peace at the cost of 200 million sesterces (fifty million denarii?) expended in gifts to Artabanus and influential Parthians.[177] The entire affair was presented to the Senate as a Roman victory, and Macrinus was offered the title 'Parthicus' – he refused it. Coins were struck in 218 with the legend *VICT[oria]PART[hica]*.[178] What really happened was that after nearly three centuries of struggle, Rome concluded her transactions with Parthia by ignomiously purchasing peace.[179]

On 18 May 218, Elagabalus was proclaimed emperor by the Legio III Gallica at its camp at Raphana. A force marched on Antioch where it engaged a force under Macrinus on 8 June. Macrinus, deserted by most of his soldiers, was soundly defeated in the battle and fled towards Italy disguised as a courier. He was captured near Chalcedon and later executed in Cappadocia. Ironically, he sent his son Diadumenianus to seek refuge with Artabanus and the Parthians, but the young man never made it. He was captured at Zeugma and killed.[180] Thus, after two-and-a-half centuries, Roman attempts to reduce Parthia to vassalage ended in failure.

THE EASTERN CAMPAIGNS OF THE LATER EMPIRE

All available sources deny that there was any practical need for Severus's Persian campaign, while that of Caracalla is said to have been undertaken because the emperor wanted 'to acquire the Parthian kingdom for himself'.[181] Neither Severus nor Dio claims that this was a war of defence. Dio stresses that Severus had selected the wrong area for expansion, and both his attempts to subdue the stronghold of Hatra failed. The conquests were not profitable, and the new subject peoples caused trouble. Dio was not particularly prejudiced against Severus. He was no less critical of Trajan's motivations for undertaking a Parthian invasion, even though he had high regard for Trajan and approved of his Dacian war. Lucius Verus's campaign of AD 163–166 was more successful militarily, but he lost much of his army to the plague and his soldiers carried it west. All of these adventures were unprovoked, generated expensive campaigns and a great loss of Roman lives, but no territorial gain. What they proved, however, was Rome's greater willingness to make war on Mesopotamia. Whatever the wisdom of the campaigns, three expeditions in a century proved that the Romans had improved their ability to fight in the East. The Romans had taken in increased numbers of foreign auxiliaries who were familiar with eastern warfare and acclimatized to fighting in Mesopotamian terrain. These changes allowed Roman armies to advance deep into the Parthian Empire.[182]

THE FALL OF THE PARTHIAN EMPIRE

Parthia, now impoverished and without any hope of recovering the lost territories, was demoralized. The kings had to give more concessions to the nobility, and the vassal kings sometimes refused to obey. Parthia's last ruler, Artabanus V, had an initial success in putting together the crumbling state. The victories of Artabanus V were the last hurrah of the Arsacid Dynasty, which had never succeeded in expanding its territory at the expense of Rome. By the close of the second century, Parthia had been in gradual decline for several generations. The extensive Arsacid family clung to royal power, but it had suffered from civil wars and too powerful vassals. The expeditions of Severus had further weakened the dynasty, and, at the time of Caracalla's assault on Parthia in 216, his opponent Artabanus was already distracted by a war with an internal rival.

The downfall of the Parthian Empire and the rise of the Sassanids are all shrouded in that uncertainty which prevails when events in the East do not directly concern the Roman world. The Arabic sources are better on the Sassanian period than the Arsacid, but few of the Sassanian sources have survived. Archaeological evidence is also scanty.[183] All we know is that in 212 CE, there began a series of petty wars among the kings and princes of the districts about Persis, which was then independent.[184] In 220 a revolt against the authority of Parthia soon spread. Ardashir, a descendant of one Sasan, allied himself with a certain Medes, Shahrat of Adiabene, and King Domitian of Kerkh Slukh (Kirkuk). The struggle began in the springtime and in a single year the allies had overrun Mesopotamia.[185] Around 224 this 'Neo-Persian' king, Ardashir, defeated and killed Artabanus and proceeded to establish his control over what henceforth is traditionally called the Sasanian Persian Empire. The remaining Parthian forces fled to the mountains, where Artabanus's son Artavasdes continued the struggle for some years. Eventually captured, he was executed in Ctesiphon.[186] The Sansanid Dynsty never accepted the loss of Mesopotamia, and thus the history of the next two centuries was of military importance.[187]

The Parthian Empire perished after a run of almost five centuries. Its downfall can be attributed as much to internal decay as to quarrels and dissensions that gave an opening to every foreign invader or domestic rebel willing to take the initiative and grab the throne or raid for booty.[188] But certainly the constant aggression of the Romans played a part. How ironic that the Romans spent so much time attacking the Parthians, whose foreign policy was pacific and non-expansionist, only to clear the way for the third Persian Empire, ruled by the Sassanid kings.[189] It meant the birth of a new Roman enemy on the eastern frontier, more determined and more aggressive than the Parthians ever were.[190]

NOTES

1. Eutropius, *Brev.* 8.6.2; *SHA*, *Hadrian* 5.3 and 9.1. These provinces were only partially held, and even so under military control, for from one to three years at the most. Thus they should not be included on maps illustrating the greatest extent of the Roman

Empire. A comparable situation would be the inclusion of Asia Minor, Syria and Palestine on a similar map of the Parthian Empire.

2. Dio 69.2.3; *CIL*, 1, pp.377ff. and 2.4110 = *ILS*, 2931. Coins which were once thought to indicate military operations by Hadrian against the Parthians are now considered doubtful. N.C. Debevoise, *The Political History of Parthia* (New York: Greenwood Press, 1968), p.241, comments on the coins containing the legend *ADVENTIVI AUG. PARTHIAE SC* and *EXERCITUS PARTHICUS* legends are either now lost or considered possible forgeries. On the first legend see H. Mattingly and E.A. Sydenham, *Roman Imperial Coinage* (London: Spink, 1923–94), vol. 2, p.456, Parthia, note. On the second see ibid., p.462, note, and P.L. Strack, *Untersuchungen zür Römischen Reichsprägung des zweiten Jahrhunderts* (Stuttgart: W. Kohlhammer, 1931), vol. 2, 148, n.328, and 233ff., n.22. *EXERCITUS SYRIACUS*: Mattingly and Sydenham, *RIC*, vol. 2, 428, no. 690, does not relate to any Parthian war.

3. *SHA*, *Hadrian* 21.14; Debevoise, *Political*, p.241.

4. *SHA*, *Hadrian* 5.4, cited incorrectly as Parthamasiris; Dio 68.33.2; Debevoise, *Political*, p.241; A. Gutschmid, *Geschichte Irans und seiner Nachbarländer von Alexander der Grosse bis zum untergang der Arsaciden* (Tübingen: H. Laupp, 1888), p.146 and n.1. G. Rawlinson, *The Sixth Great Monarchy* (New York: Publishers Plate Renting Co., 1870), p.316 and n.2, is in error when he suggests that Armenia was given to Parthamaspates: A.D.H. Bivar, 'The Political History of Iran under the Arsacids', in *CHI*, vol.3, 1: *The Seleucid, Parthian and Sasanian Period*, ed. E. Yarshater (Cambridge: Cambridge University Press, 1983), p.93.

5. *SHA*, *Hadrian* 12.8.

6. R.H. McDowell, *Coins from Seleucia on the Tigris* (Ann Arbor, MI: University of Michigan Press, 1935), p.195; Debevoise, *Political*, p.242.

7. *SHA*, *Hadrian* 13.8; J. Dürr, *Die Reisen des Kaisers Hadrian* (Wien: C. Gerold's Sohn, 1881) pp.61ff; Gutschmid, *Geschichte Irans*, p.146; Debevoise, *Political*, p.242.

8. Dio 69.13.1ff.

9. On the Syriac sources for the invasion, see: Debevoise, *Political*, pp.242–3; Gutschmid, *Geschichte Irans*, p.146. Note that there was no coinage struck in the Seleucia mint during 134–36. See McDowell, *Coins from Seleucia*, p.195.

10. *SHA*, *Hadrian* 13.8ff; 17.12; 21.13.

11. According to the numismatic evidence, between the death of Osroes and the reign of Vologases II (128–147 CE), there was a king in Iran by the name of Mithridates IV, but there are no literary references to his activities.

12. McDowell, *Coins from Seleucia*, p.198; Debevoise, *Political*, p.244 and n.16; Rawlinson, *Sixth Great Monarchy*, p.184; Bivar, 'Political History of Iran', p.93.

13. *SHA*, *Antoninus Pius* 9.6; *SHA*, *Antoninus Pius* 8.6, on preparations for a campaign; Aelius Aristides, *Or. Sac.* 1.

14. Debevoise, *Political*, p.245; *CIL*, 9.2457 = *ILS*, 1076.

15. *SHA*, *Antoninus Pius* 9.6. On Abgarus see 'Abgar', in *RE*, no. 7, cols 94–5.

16. *SHA*, *Antoninus Pius* 9.7.

17. A. Birley, *Marcus Aurelius: A Biography* (New Haven, CT: Yale University Press, 1987), p. 61.

18. M.G. Angeli-Bertinelli, 'I Romani oltre l'Euphrate nell II secolo dC', in *ANRW*, 2, 9.1 (1976), p.23, who called it 'una grave provocazione partica'. *SHA*, *Marcus* 8.6–7; Dio 71.2.

19. See 'Sohaemus', art. in *RE*, no. 5, col. 798; Angelli-Bertinelli, 'I Romani oltre l'Euphrate', p.26.

20. Dio 71.2; 'Sedatius', art. in *RE*, no. 1, M. Sedatius Severianus, cols 1006–10; Angelli-Bertinelli, 'I Romani oltre L'Euphrate', p.26.

21. The identity of the governor's force has remained a mystery. After two decades of stability in Armenia, he can only have had the defensive garrison of Cappadocia to draw from. He may have been travelling with as little as a vexillation. See Dio 71.2.1. More than one scholar has tried to introduce the IX Hispana into the story, but this legion is never attested in north-eastern Asia Minor. See Birley, *Marcus Aurelius*, p.278, n.19, and W. Eck, 'Zum Ende der Legio IX Hispana', *Chiron*, 2 (1972), pp.459–62.

22. *SHA*, *Alex.* 27; Dio 71.2.1; Fronto, *Princ. Hist.* (Loeb Classical Library, 2, p.214). See Rawlinson, *Sixth Great Monarchy*, p.185, n.22. Various romantic stories were soon in circulation, according to Lucian *Quomodo hist.* 21 and 25, concerning his death. He was said to have fasted during a relatively lengthy siege, and a centurion named Afranius Silo was said to have delivered a lengthy funeral oration over his tomb in the high tragic

manner, and then killed himself on the spot. Birley, *Marcus Aurelius*, p.122.

23. *SHA, Marcus* 8.6; Angeli-Bertinelli, 'I Romani oltre l'Euphrate', p.26.
24. *SHA, Verus* 6: '*Syris defectionem cogitantibus.*'
25. The replacement for the fallen Severianus was Statius Priscus. Great care was taken to find the right man. See Birley, *Marcus Aurelius*, p.123; Dio 71.2.2–3; *SHA, Marcus* 9.1; *SHA, Verus* 7.1; *SHA, Avidius Cassius* 5.4–6.4; Angeli-Bertinelli, 'I Romani oltre l'Euphrate', p.27.
26. *SHA, Marcus* 8.10; *SHA, Verus* 6. On the campaign, see C. Harold Dodd, 'Chronology of the Eastern Campaigns of the Emperor Lucius Verus', *Numismatic Chronicle*, 4th series, 11 (1911), pp.209–67; A von Premerstein, 'Untersuchungen zur Geschichte des Kaisers Marcus, III' *Klio*, 13 (1913), pp.87–92; and the bibliography cited by F. Jacoby, *Die Fragmente der grieschischen Historiker*, 2D (Berlin: Weidemann, 1923), pp.628ff.
27. These were the I Minervia from Germania Inferior, the II Adiutrix, from Pannonia Inferior and the V Macedonica from Moesia Inferior. Debvoise, *Political* pp.247–8; D. Magie, *Roman Rule in Asia Minor* (Princeton, NJ: Princeton University Press, 1950), vol. 2, p.1530; Birley, *Marcus Aurelius*, p.165; Angeli-Bertinelli, 'I Romani oltre l'Euphrate', pp.26–7; A.R. Birley, *CAH2*, v. 11, p.161.
28. The III Gallica, the III Augusta, the I Adiutrix, the X Gemina and possibly the II Traiana.
29. Birley, *Marcus Aurelius*, p.123.
30. 'Avidius', art. in *RE*, no. 1, cols 2378–83; Bivar, 'Political History of Iran', p.93; *SHA, Avidius* 4.3ff. on his discipline.
31. *SHA, Avidius Cassius* 5 for descriptions of Pontius Laelianus doing formidable kit inspections. Cf. Fronto, *Princ. Hist.* (Loeb Classical Library, 2, pp.206ff.), who politely attributes the establishing of proper discipline to Verus. R.W. Davies, 'Fronto, Hadrian and the Roman Army', *Latomus*, 27 (1968), p.79; E.L. Wheeler, 'The Laxity of Syrian Legions', in D.L. Kennedy, *The Roman Army in the East* (Ann Arbor, MI: *Journal of Roman Archaeology*, Supplementary Series, 18, 1996), pp.229–76, considers the laxity of the Syrian legions as little more than a literary *topos*.
32. See the article by Ann Scott Tyson, *Washington Post*, 30 January 2007, p.A12.
33. Fronto, *Epist. ad Verum* 2.2 (Loeb Classical Library, 2, pp.116–18).
34. Fronto, *Princ. Hist.* 14 (Loeb Classical Library, 2, p. 212). On the character of Verus, compare the eulogy of Fronto and the vilification of Dio and the Augustan History. Birley, *Marcus Aurelius*, p.130. It may also be possible that Vologases interpreted the dual emperorship as a sign of weakness.
35. Dio 71.1–2; *SHA, Verus* 7.3, and *SHA, Marcus Antoninus* 8.12.
36. *SHA, Verus* 7.6.
37. Birley, *Marcus Aurelius*, p.139, on the Syrian mistress taken from Lucian, *Imagines*. *SHA, Verus* 4.4.
38. Dodd, 'Chronology of the Eastern Campaigns', p.216; Angeli-Bertinelli, 'I Romani oltre l'Euphrate', p.27.
39. Dio 71.3; *SHA, Marcus* 9; F. Cumont, *Fouilles de Doura-Europos* (Paris: Haut commissariat francaise en Syrie et au Liban, 1925), p.334 and notes, presents the evidence for Artaxata not being destroyed. Kainopolis was later called Valarshapat (*Nor Khalakh* in Armenian). Statius Priscus is not mentioned in the correspondence at the end of the year and either died or retired.
40. *SHA, Marcus* 9.1; *SHA, Verus* 7.1; Dio 71.3; Fronto, *Epist. ad Verum* 2.1; Bivar, 'Political History of Iran', p.93; Angeli-Bertinelli, 'I Romani oltre l'Euphrate', p.27.
41. *SHA, Marcus* 9.1.
42. The events of this campaign are known only from scattered references, largely geographical in character. The only thing we are certain of is that Priscus was in charge of the Armenian war and Cassius of the Mesopotamian campaign. Debvoise, *Political*, p.250.
43. *SHA, Avidius Cassius* 7; Dio 71.22–7. Rawlinson, *Sixth Great Monarchy*, p.186.
44. Angeli-Bertinelli, 'I Romani oltre l'Euphrate', p.28; *CIL*, 6.1377 = *ILS*, 1098.
45. The Parthian ruler of Edessa had been a certain Waël, son of Sahru. Debvoise, *Political*, p.246; G.F. Hill, *Coins of Arabia, Mesopotamia, and Persia* (London: British Museum, 1922), pp.xcviff. and Gutschmid, *Geschichte Irans*, pp.148ff; Dio 71.2.1; Orosius, 7.15.2; *SHA, Verus* 6.9. Procopius, *De bello Persico* 2.12.29, says the inhabitants revolted, murdered the Parthian garrison and delivered the city to the Romans. Cf. A. von Gutschmid, 'Untersuchungen über die Geschichte des Königreichs Osrhoëne', *Memoires de l'Academie Imperiale des Sciences de St Pétersbourg*, 7 ser. No.35 (1887), p.29; Hill, *Coins of Arabia*,

Mespotamia, and Persia, p.xcvii; Lucian, *Quomodo hist.* 22. Debevoise, *Political*, p.253; Birley, *Marcus Aurelius*, p.140.

46. Birley, *Marcus Aurelius*, p.140.
47. On Edessa, see Lucian, *Quomodo hist.* 22; on Dausara, see Fronto, *Epist. ad Verum* 2, 1. On Nisibis, see Lucian, *Quomodo hist.* 15; Sura is identified with Suriyyah, the ancient Sippara; *SHA, Verus* 7. Angeli-Bertinelli, 'I Romani oltre l'Euphrate', p.28.
48. Roman engineering played a large part in the campaign. See Dio 71.3, for a description of the building of the pontoon bridge.
49. Fronto, *Epist. ad Verum*, 2.1 (Loeb Classical Library, 2, p.132). There is also a Dausara near Edessa. Victories 'in Arabia' are mentioned by *SHA, Avidius Cassius* 6.5. Debevoise, *Political*, p.250.
50. Dio 71.3 on Zeugma; Fronto, *Epist. ad Verum* 2.1; Lucian, *Quomodo hist.* 29.
51. Lucian, *Quomodo hist.* 20, 24 and 28. A dedicatory inscription to Verus was found at Dura. Debevoise, *Political*, p.250. On the soldiers at Dura, see N. Pollard, 'The Roman Army as "Total Institution" in the Near East? Dura-Europos as a Case Study', in Kennedy (ed.), *Roman Army in the East*, pp.211–27; Angeli-Bertinelli, 'I Romani oltre l'Euphrate', p.28. The history of Dura as a garrison town from the 190s to its end in the 250s is well documented. For a brief summary, see F. Millar, *The Roman Near East 31BC –AD 337* (Cambridge, MA: Harvard University Press, 1993), p.131–2.
52. Birley, *Marcus Aurelius*, p.140; Dio 71.2 describes an opposed river crossing achieved by Cassius involving the construction of a bridge of boats, but this probably is not the Euphrates. *SHA, Verus* 7.1, 8.1–4; D. Magie, *Roman Rule in Asia Minor* (Princeton, NJ: Princeton University Press, 1950), vol. 1, pp.661ff; M.L. Astarita, *Avidio Cassio* (Rome: Edizioni di storia e letteratura, 1983), p.48, n.124.
53. Birley, *Marcus Aurelius*, p.140.
54. *SHA, Verus* 8.3 blames Verus but cites Asinius Quadratus, who blamed the Seleucians as the first to break the agreement. Cf. *SHA, Avidius* 1.1; Eutropius, *Brev.* 8.10. McDowell, *Coins from Seleucia*, p.234, shows that coins were again struck by November 166, and destruction in the main area excavated was relatively slight. Debevoise, *Political*, p.251; Rawlinson, *Sixth Great Monarchy*, p.187; Dodd, 'Chronology of the Eastern Campaigns', p.253.
55. *SHA, Avidius* 4.3ff. says he crucified soldiers who forcibly seized anything from provincials, and he cut the hands off deserters. Even with the plague in his midst he got his soldiers back to Italy in good order. The Romans even coined the term 'Cassian strictness'.
56. Birley, *Marcus Aurelius*, p.140.
57. Dio 71.2.3–4; Birley, *Marcus Aurelius*, p.140.
58. The superstitious soldiers believed that the disease came from a subterranean cell in the Temple of Comaean Apollo at Seleucia. The plunderers were in search of treasure, but instead were given only this fearful scourge placed there in ancient times by a spell of the Chaldeans. Smallpox has been suggested. The plague is mentioned in Chinese records, see F. Hirth, *China and the Roman Orient* (Leipzig and Munich: Georg Hirth, 1885), p.175. See also Ammianus Marcellinus, 23.6.24; Eutropius, *Brev.* 8.12; *SHA, Verus* 8.2. Debevoise, *Political*, p.252; Bivar, 'Political History of Iran', p.93, believed it was smallpox.
59. Dio 71.2.
60. Ibid., 71.2.4; Ammianus Marcellinus 23.6.23, and *SHA, Verus* 8. The plague spread west until it reached the Rhine and Gaul.
61. Eutropius, *Brev.* 8.6 exaggerates perhaps when he claims that more than half of the population and almost the entire Roman army perished. Cf. Orosius 7.15.
62. Birley, *Marcus Aurelius*, p.140.
63. Ibid., p.141.
64. *SHA, Verus* 7.1.
65. As a matter of fact, some Romans did penetrate to the East in 166. Chinese annals record that in this year ambassadors from Ngan-touen or An-toun – i.e. Marcus Antoninus, ruler of the T'a ts'in (one of the Chinese names for the Roman Empire) – brought gifts from the emperor. These were probably freelance traders from Alexandria. On this, see Millar, *Roman Near East*, p.112.
66. Birley, *Marcus Aurelius*, p.145; Dodd, 'Chronology of the Eastern Campaigns', p.259.
67. An inscription from Ostia called Lucius Verus *propagator imperium* (extender of the empire).
68. Birley, *Marcus Aurelius*, p.145.
69. Rawlinson, *Sixth Great Monarchy*, p.188; Dodd, 'Chronology of the Eastern Campaigns',

pp.2257–8; A.M. Devine, 'The Parthi, the Tyranny of Tiberius, and the Date of Q. Curtius Rufus', *Phoenix*, 33 (1979), pp.146.

70. M. Sartre, *The Middle East under Rome*, trans. C. Porter and E. Rawlings (Cambridge, MA: Harvard University Press, 2005), p.147.

71. Sartre, *Middle East under Rome*, p.147. After the victory, for example, ties with the kingdom of Edessa were strengthened. Its king, Manu VIII, issued a coin bearing an effigy of the Roman imperial family with the Greek legend *basileus Mannos philhormaios*, 'King Mannos, friend of the Romans'.

72. M.I. Rostovzteff, 'Parthia: Foreign Policy', in *CAH*, 11 (1936), p.109.

73. Dodd, 'Chronology of the Eastern Campaigns', pp.259.

74. Rawlinson, *Sixth Great Monarchy*, p.188, cf. pp.110, 167.

75. Hill, *Coins of Arabia, Mesopotamia and Persia*, pp.xc, xcvii.

76. *SHA, Avidius Cassius* 7; Dio 71.22.

77. Dio 72.22.2–3; *SHA, Marcus Aurelius* 24.6–9; *SHA, Avidius Cassius* 7.1–3; Birley, *Marcus Aurelius*, p.184.

78. *SHA, Marcus Antoninus* 22.1.

79. Ibid., 26, where they are referred to as *Persian* ambassadors.

80. The latest coins of Vologases III bear a date which corresponds to the latter part of 190 and the early part of 191 CE.

81. Herodian C. 3.1.

82. Ibid., 3.1.

83. Ibid., 3.1.2ff. and 9.1ff. Moses Chorenensis, *History of the Armenians*, translation and commentary by Robert W. Thomson (Ann Arbor, MI: Caravan Books, 2006), 2.75 states that Osroes of Armenia announced himself neutral.

84. On Hatra's position, see M. Sommer, 'Hatra: Imperiale und regionale Herrschaft an der Steppengrenze', *Klio*, 85 (2003), pp.384–98, and M. Sommer, *Hatra, Geschichte und Kultur einer Karawanenstadt im römisch-parthischen Mesopotamien* (Mainz: Zabern, 2003), pp.29–33. Rawlinson, *Sixth Great Monarchy*, p.191, believed that Hatra would not enter on the Roman side without the express permission of the Court of Ctesiphon.

85. Herodian 3.1 and 27.

86. Dio 75.8.3; Herodian 3.4.7ff.

87. Dio 75.1.1ff. (Loeb Classical Library, 9, p.194); Debevoise, *Political*, p.256; Lucian, *Quomodo historia*, 15. The reference to the plague dates the siege to about 166, if we place the fall of Seleucia in December 165. Cf. W. Weber, 'The Parthian War', in *CAH*, 11, p.347.

88. Dio 75.1ff. (Loeb Classical Library, 9, pp.194–6); Debevoise, *Political*, p. 256.

89. On Roman control in Osrhoene, see Jörg Wagner, 'Provincia Osrhoenae', in S. Mitchell (ed.), *Armies and Frontiers in Roman and Byzantine Anatolia* (Oxford: British Archaeological Reports, 1983), pp.103 –29.

90. See A.J. Graham, 'Septimius Severus and His Generals, AD 193–7', in M.R.D. Foot, *War and Society* (London: Paul Elek, 1973), p.268.

91. Herodian 3.9.2. These events should probably be placed in the first campaign (contrary to Herodian). See also *SHA, Severus* 9.9 and 18.1. Magie, *Roman Rule in Asia Minor*, pp.672–5 and 1542–5, and more recently H.J. Drijvers, *Hatra, Palmyra und Edessa*, in *ANRW*, 2, 8 (1977), pp.877ff., argued that Abgarus kept his throne despite his support for Pescennius Niger. Wagner, 'Provinciae Osrhoenae', p.106, notes that the editors of *Prosopographia Imperii Romani* prefer a different interpretation.

92. Dio 75.2.

93. T. Sextius Lateranus: 'Sextius', in *RE*, no. 27, cols 2047–9; Tib. Claudius Candidus: 'Claudius', in *RE*, no. 96, cols 2691–2; Laetus, 'Laetus', in *RE*, no. 1, col. 451.

94. P. Cornelius Anullinus: 'Cornelius', in *RE*, no. 58, cols. 1258–9; Probus, possibly the son-in-law of Severus, see *SHA, Severus* 8.1; Dio 75.3.2 (Loeb Classical Library, 9, p.198). Hatra, Adiabene, Arbelitis, Asicha near Zaitha and the Archene of Pliny, *HN* 6.128, have been suggested as possible emendations. Debevoise, *Political*, p.257.

95. Dio 75.3 says vaguely that Severus 'gave dignity' to Nisibis. The nature of the dignity is shown on the coins that give Nisibis the titles of *KOLONIA AND METROPOLIS*. See Théodore Edme Mionnet, *Description de médailles antiques, grecques et romaines* (Graz: Akademische Druck- u. Verlagsanstalt, 1972–73), vol. 5, pp.625–8. See D.L. Kennedy, 'Ti. Claudius Subatianus Aquila, "First Prefect of Mesopotamia" ', *ZPE*, 36 (1979), pp.255–62.

96. Dio 75.3.

97. Eutropius, *Brev.* 8.18; *CIL*, 8.306 and 6.954 = *ILS*, 417ff. Mattingly and Sydenham, *RIC*, 4, 97ff, nos. 55 and 62ff., probably issued in 195. The abbreviated titles 'Arabicus' and 'Adiabenicus' appear frequently. Debevoise, *Political*, p.256, n.88.

98. *SHA, Severus* 9.10; Debevoise, *Political*, pp.257, 260.

99. Graham, 'Septimius Severus and his Generals', p.268, notes that it is tempting to place the creation of the three new legions I–III Parthica to this period. Severus may have created them out of the easterners who had recently been recruited for the civil war. See n.109 to the contrary.

100. *SHA, Severus* 15.

101. Herodian 3.9.1ff.

102. Debevoise, *Political*, p.258.

103. Ibid., p.259.

104. Herodian 3.1.

105. Compare ibid. 3.27 to Dio 75.9.

106. Rawlinson gets this from reading Dio 75.9 ad fin., which he believes suggested that Vologases was ceded some part of Roman Armenia (Armenia Minor).

107. Despite the fact that three accounts of Severus's second Parthian campaign have survived, it is still extremely difficult to form a clear picture of what transpired during this war. Herodian's account is universally discounted as worthless. The *SHA* has been disfigured by a later author, and thus we must fall back on Dio's account transmitted through Xiphilinus's epitome. See Z. Rubin, 'Dio, Herodian and Severus' Second Parthian War', *Chiron*, 5 (1975), p.419.

108. *SHA, Severus* 16.

109. Dio 55.24.2. See Legio (Severus) and Legio (II Parthica) in *RE*, cols 1475–2; Debevoise, *Political*, p.259.

110. *CIL*, 8. 2975 = *ILS*, 2306; Debevoise, *Political*, p.259 and n.94.

111. On L. Fabius Cilo, see art. on Fabius in *RE*, no. 65, cols 1763–8. On Statilius Barbarus, see 'Statilius (Barbarus)', in *RE*, no. 13, cols 2187–9. On Q. Hedius Rufus Lollianus Gentiannus, see Lollianus in *RE*, no. 5, cols 1368–70. On C. Fulvius Plautianus, see 'Fulvius' in *RE*, no. 101, cols 270–8. In the cases of some of these men there is uncertainty as to whether their service was in the first campaign instead.

112. *CIL*, 8.4583, dated in the spring of 198, celebrates a victory over the Parthians.

113. Dio 75.9.

114. Rawlinson believes this is the only way of reconciling Dio 75.9, with Herodian 3.28 ad init.

115. Dio 75.9; A.R. Birley, *The African Emperor: Septimius Severus* (London: Batsford, 1988), p.129.

116. A hoard of coins dated 198/99, probably buried upon the approach of the Romans, strongly confirms the dating. See McDowell, *Coins from Seleucia*, no. 122, pp.90–1, 235. On the sacking of Ctesiphon, see Dio 76 (75.9); *SHA, Severus* 16. On the date, see M. Platnauer, *The Life and Reign of the Emperor Lucius Septimius Severus* (Oxford: Oxford University Press, 1918), p.117, n.1, on the coin evidence; J. Hasebroek, *Untersuchungen zur Geschichte des Kaisers Septimius Severus* (Heidelberg: C. Winter, 1921), pp.113ff.

117. Herodian 3.9.9 claims this, but Rawlinson finds the narrative patently absurd. Rawlinson, *Sixth Great Monarchy*, p.194.

118. *SHA, Severus* 16.

119. Dio 75.9, who implies the flight of Vologases.

120. Compare ibid. 75.9 with Herodian 3.30 and *SHA, Severus* 16.

121. *CIL*, 3.205ff; Mattingly and Sydenham, *RIC*, 4, 105, nos. 122(a)ff.

122. The cognomen *Parthicus Maximus* appears on his inscriptions and coins from 198 onward. Birley, *African Emperor*, p.130.

123. *SHA, Severus* 16.

124. Ibid., 16.

125. Dio 75.9.

126. For a description of the city, its size and architecture, see Rawlinson, *Sixth Great Monarchy*, pp.212–17. There are contradictions in the story as told by the ancient sources. According to Herodian 3.9.2–7, Severus attacked Hatra after the King of Armenia surrendered, and before marching against Ctesiphon. Dio 76.10.11, on the other hand, says that the siege of Hatra occurred after the capture of Ctesiphon.

127. There is a disagreement in the sources about this episode. Herodian seemed to believe that the entire purpose of the campaign was to take Hatra. Dio claims that Septimius attacked Hatra twice. The first attempt was in February or March 198, soon after the invading army left Ctesiphon. This attempt failed.

128. For the strategic importance of Hatra, see A. Maricq, 'Les dernières années de Hatra: l'alliance romaine', *Syria*, 34 (1957), pp.288ff; Birley, *Marcus Aurelius*, p.203; Rubin, 'Dio, Herodian and Severus' Second Parthian War', p.424; Wathiq I. al-Sahlihi, 'Military Considerations in the Defense of Hatra', *Mesopotamia*, 26 (1991), pp.187–94.

129. This date is given by the Feriale Duranum, the calendar of public days at Dura. On the documentation of the dating, see D.B. Campbell, 'What Happened at Hatra? The Problem of the Severan Siege Operations', in P. Freeman and D.L. Kennedy (eds), *The Defence of the Roman and Byzantine East: Proceedings of a Colloquium held at the University of Sheffield in April 1986*, British Institute of Archaeology at Ankara Monograph no. 8 (Oxford: British Archaeological Reports, International Series, 297, 1986), vol. 1, p.51; Sartre, *Middle East Under Rome*, p.149.

130. Dio 75.10. It is unclear whether Herodian's description is of the first or second attack. He mentions one siege only and places it before that of Ctesiphon, 3.28, 29. Dio's account goes into more detail and seems to make more sense logically. See Rubin, 'Dio, Herodian and Severus' Second Parthian War', pp.420–31.

131. One of these officers was Laetus, the man who had saved Nisibis. According to Dio, Severus was jealous of him because the soldiers declared they would only follow him and no other officer. *SHA, Severus* 15 assigns his death to a different cause and places it earlier. The complaining officer was Julius Crispus.

132. Dio 75.11.

133. Ibid., 75.12.

134. Ibid., 75.11. Cf. Ammianus Marcellinus 23.6; Sartre, *Middle East Under Rome*, p.149.

135. Dio 75.11. Numbers of heavy arrows such as the ones shot from these engines have been found at Dura Europas. Debevoise, *Political*, p.261.

136. Dio 75.12.

137. Severus was accused of not wanting the city stormed because he did not want the treasures he coveted becoming prey to the soldiers. Dio 75.12; Rawlinson, *Sixth Great Monarchy*, p.196.

138. Dio 76 (75.11–13). The campaign was commemorated in 197–198 by issues bearing the legend *VICT. PARTHICAE*: see Mattingly and Sydenham, *RIC*, 4, 105, no. 121, and 108, no. 142 (a). Numerous other coins celebrated the return of peace.

139. Dio 76 (75.10); *SHA, Severus* 15.6.

140. Ibid., 75.13. Hatra was later destroyed by Shapur in 250 CE. On its artistic contributions, see J.B. Ward-Perkins, 'The Roman West and the Parthian East', *Proceedings of the British Academy*, 51 (1965), pp.189–93.

141. Rubin, 'Dio, Herodian and Severus' Second Parthian War', pp.419–41. On the siege operations, see M.P. Speidel, '"Europeans" – Syrian Elite Troops at Dura-Europos and Hatra', in M.P. Speidel (ed.), *Roman Army Studies*, vol. 1 (Amsterdam: J.C Gieben, 1984), pp.301–9; Campbell, 'What Happened at Hatra?', pp.51–8; D.L. Kennedy, 'European Soldiers and the Severan Siege of Hatra', in Freeman and Kennedy, *Defence of the Roman and Byzantine East*, pp.397–409; Sartre, *Middle East under Rome*, p.149 and n.138.

142. Contra Rawlinson, *Sixth Great Monarchy*, p.197, who called it 'on the whole glorious for Rome'.

143. McDowell, *Coins from Seleucia*, pp.199–200; Debevoise, *Political*, p.262.

144. Dio 77.12.

145. Ibid., 77.22; Herodian 4.13; Rawlinson, *Sixth Great Monarchy*, p.200. Dio distinguishes between most of Caracalla's unprovoked campaigns, where he behaved atrociously, 77(78).12, and the wars that were 'necessary and urgent', 77(78).13.1.

146. Millar, *Roman Near East*, p.142.

147. Dio 77.12.

148. Ibid., 77.12; Herodian 4.18–20.

149. Dio 78 (77.12.1); Debevoise, *Political*, p.263.

150. Dio 77.21.

151. The legions were the I and II Adiutrix. See *IGRR*, 3.1412 = *ILS*, 8879. On the question of whether or not the legions of this inscription are the I and II Parthica, see 'Legio

(Caracalla)', in *RE*, cols 1318–19, and the articles on those legions. The II Parthica under Aelius Decius Triccianus, see *SHA, Caracalla* 6.7; the III Augusta, see *CIL*, 8.2564p; the III Italica, see *CIL*, 3.142076; the III Cyrenaica and the IV Scythica, see C. Hopkins and H.T. Rowell, 'The Praetorium', in M.I. Rostovtzeff *et al.* (eds), *Excavations at Dura-Europos: Preliminary Report of the Fifth Season of Work* (New Haven, CT: Yale University Press, 1934), pp.218 ff. There were also some German troops, see Dio 80.4.

152. Dio 78 (77.18.1). On the winter quarters in Nicomedia, see *CIL*, 6.2103b.
153. Antiochus and Tiridates were friends and had deserted to the Parthians together. Dio 78 (77.19.1ff.); Herodian 4.10ff.
154. 'Theokritos', art. in *RE*, no. 4, cols 2027–8.
155. M.I. Rostovzteff, 'Parthia: Foreign Policy', in *CAH*, 11 (1936), p.110.
156. We know of Artabanus V only from drachms; see Wroth, *Coins of Parthia*, pp.247–50, and McDowell, *Coins from Seleucia*, p.235.
157. Dio 78 (77.12.2a–3 and 13.3). Coins of Vologases issued in 214/15 and 215/16 bear a Tyche with palm, possibly a claim of victory; see McDowell, *Coins from Seleucia*, pp.94 and 199ff.
158. See McDowell, *Coins from Seleucia*, p.200; Debevoise, *Political*, p.265.
159. Dio 79 (78.1), states positively that Artabanus refused to give his daughter to the Roman monarch and that Caracalla undertook his campaign to avenge the insult. Herodian 4.11, however, says exactly the reverse. According to him, the Roman Emperor, on receiving the negative reply, sent a second embassy, and Artabanus then acceded to the request and invited him to come and get his bride. See S. Mattern, *Rome and the Enemy* (Berkeley, CA: University of California Press, 1999), p.156 on the economic benefits.
160. Herodian's account contradicts both Dio's account and that of the Augustan History. Dio 78.1 says there was no engagement at all between the Parthians and the Romans, but says there was an invasion of Adiabene and Media. *SHA, Caracalla* speaks of a battle in which Caracalla defeated the satraps of Artabanus in Babylonia.
161. A hoard of coins found at Ashur suggests that the Romans occupied the city in 216. See G. McDonald, *Coin Types, their Origin and Development: being the Rhind lectures for 1904* (Glasgow: J. Maclehose and Sons, 1905), no. 28, pp.34ff., and E. Herzfeld, 'Untersuchungen über die historische Topographie der Landschaft am Tigris kleinen Zab und Gebel Hamrin', *Memnon*, 1 (1907), pp.115–16.
162. Dio 79 (78.1ff.); *SHA, Caracalla* 6.4.
163. Mattingly and Sydenham, *RIC*, 4, 257, nos. 297(a) – 299(e). In connection with this campaign, note the dedicatory inscription to Julia Domna found at Dura Europus; see H. Rowell, 'Inscriptions grecques de Doura-Europos, 1929–30', *CR* (1930), pp.265–8.
164. Dio 78.3.
165. Debevoise, *Political*, p.266.
166. Dio 78.5. Herodian 4.24; *SHA, Caracalla* 6; Eutropius, *Brev.* 8.20; Millar, *Roman Near East*, p.144.
167. Dio 78.5.4ff; Herodian 4.13.3ff.
168. Dio 78.26.
169. Herodian 4.30.
170. Ibid., 4.28.
171. Ibid., 4.30.
172. Ibid., 4.14.3; Dio 79.26.5.
173. Herodian makes the third day's battle terminate, like those of the first two days, without decisive result, but Dio evidently regarded the Romans as defeated.
174. Herodian 4.15.4 makes the battle a draw. Dio 78.26.7ff. definitely gives the Parthians the advantage. The price of the peace seems to settle the point in their favour. The campaign is mentioned in *SHA, Macrinus* 2.2.
175. Debevoise, *Political*, p.267.
176. See the fragment of Dio restored by Fabricius, quoted by Rawlinson, *Sixth Great Monarchy*, p.632, n.37.
177. Dio 78.27.1. For mentions of Greeks who served and died in the campaigns of this period against the Parthians, see Paul Wolters, 'Ein Denkmal der Partherkriege', *Mitteilungen des Kaiserlich: Deutschen archaeologischen Instituts*, Athenische Abteilung, 28 (1903), pp.291–300; *CIG*, 1, nos. 1353 and 1495; A. von Premerstein,

'Untersuchungen zur geschichte des Kaisers Marcus, I', pp. 358–66. Cf. Dio 77.7; Herodian 4.8.3.

178. K. Regling, 'Römische aurei aud dem Funde von Karnak', in *Festschrift zu Otto Hirschfeld's 60. Geburtstage* (Berlin: Weidemann, 1903), p.297, no. 60; Debevoise, *Political*, p.267.

179. In Dio, the ignominy of the payment was disguised as presents to the Parthian king and his Lords. Dio 78.27.

180. Dio 78.39ff; SHA, *Macrinus* 10.

181. B. Isaac, *The Limits of Empire: The Roman Army in the East* (Oxford: Clarendon Press, 1992), pp.22–3. See Dio 75.5.9–12; Herodian 3.9.1; SHA, *Severus* 15.1. The two latter sources claim that the only motive was Severus's desire for glory. For the campaign of Caracalla see Dio 78.1.1; Herodian 4.10.1. Cf. Mattern, *Rome and The Enemy*, pp.33, 67, 94, 108.

182. D.L. Kennedy, 'Parthia and Rome', in Kennedy (ed.), *Roman Army in the East*, p.88.

183. Debevoise, *Political*, p.268.

184. Ardashir, son of Papak, son of Saan, expanded his territory at the expense of his neighbours, and persuaded his father to revolt against his immediate overlord. He requested that the great Parthian king Artabanus should place his son Shapur on the throne of the slain overlord. The demand was refused. Debevoise, *Political*, p.268.

185. Dio 80.3 (Loeb Classical Library, 9, p.482) seems to agree with the Syriac sources. Debevoise, *Political*, p.269; Bivar, 'Political History of Iran', p.96–7.

186. For Artavasdes's coinage see Wroth, *Coins of Parthia*, p.251, who dates it to 227/228. McDowell, *Coins from Seleucia*, p.200, assigns tentatively to Artavasdes a coin bearing the late date of 228/29, which he believes was struck at Seleucia.

187. Millar, *Roman Near East*, p.148.

188. Rawlinson, *Sixth Great Monarchy*, p.211, suggests that the Parthian soldiery lost its vigour and declined, but there really is no evidence for this.

189. Sassanids were from the province of Persis, native to the first Persian Empire, the Achaemenids.

190. B. Campbell, 'War and Diplomacy: Rome and Parthia, 31 BC – AD 235', in J. Rich and G. Shipley, *War and Society in the Roman World* (London and New York: Routledge, 1993), p.238.

10

WHAT DID THE ROMANS KNOW, AND WHEN DID THEY KNOW IT?

In order to assess what intelligence-gathering capabilities the Romans had and whether or not the intelligence they collected was adequate to their needs, we need to break down their problems into discrete categories to see whether the Romans had the bureaucratic facilities necessary for collecting and analyzing the intelligence they received on Parthia. Here are eight of the intelligence problems Rome faced:

INTELLIGENCE PROBLEM 1:
NO CENTRAL INTELLIGENCE AGENCY OR GENERAL STAFF

The lack of a standing body to assess intelligence was an important factor in the politics of the Principate.[1] It was with great difficulty that an emperor had to maintain security both along the frontiers and also at home. This required a great deal of intelligence gathering for both internal security and national defence. On the home front, the emperor was responsible for keeping the army loyal. As Caligula, Claudius and Nero discovered, the army made or destroyed emperors. On the international front, the emperor had to keep tabs on all neighbouring nations, whether ally or enemy. And although a sizeable amount of work has been done on Rome's use of spies, diplomats and military personnel connected with intelligence gathering, what always surprises a modern audience is that the emperor had to accomplish all of this without a standing diplomatic corps, a central intelligence agency, or a joint chief of staff to help him plan military strategy and gather the intelligence to implement it.[2]

Why did the Romans not have a permanent general staff, i.e. a non-political body of professional soldiers whose loyalty to the throne could be trusted?[3] Certainly among the answers must be a five-century old tradition of an emperor's magisterial command over military forces, the constitutional illusion of an emperor who was only a magistrate, and the fear that to delegate actual military power was to lose it. Without a general staff, and with little central coordination, the emperor simply assembled a pool of competent and experienced officers when the need arose, but even that had its dangers, as emperors occasionally discovered. A certain tension grew between the emperor and generals he felt were too successful. Certainly Nero believed that Corbulo had grown too important when he recalled him in the winter of 66/67 CE and had him eliminated. One of Lucius Verus's generals in the Parthian War of 162–165 CE, Avidius Cassius, attempted to seize the throne after learning the (mistaken) news that Marcus Aurelius had died. When Pertinax was murdered in 193 CE by the Praetorian Guard, the three most powerful generals made their bids for power. Even when the emperor did trust his advisors, the need to have competent military men at hand to help run the empire eventually led to the militarization of the imperial machinery as frontier challenges increased. This increase in manpower was not reflected, however, in an expansion of the field staffs that conducted the major military operations, at least not from the financial, logistical, or intelligence point of view. Successive campaigns brought new officers, but these additions were special assignments whose irregular nature argues that their function was also irregular or ad hoc.[4]

In short, the conduct of foreign affairs in the imperial period lay with the emperor and a very few people. These advisors included one or both of the praetorian prefects – commanders of the elite troops stationed in Rome,[5] plus a number of people usually called his friends (*amici*), some of whom would accompany him on a trip or campaign as 'companions' (*comites*). As a group they were sometimes called his council (*consilium principis*). The question then becomes how much intelligence did the emperor and his council have when they made major foreign policy decisions such as 'Should we go to war with Parthia?' We will never be privy to the conversations that the Roman generals had with their staffs nor will we get after-action reports. We have no view from the enemy side.[6]

INTELLIGENCE PROBLEM 2:
LACK OF ACCURATE GEOGRAPHICAL INTELLIGENCE

Around 172 BCE, Lucius Aemilius Paullus, the Roman general who fought in Macedonia, wrote:

Commanders should be counselled, chiefly by persons of
known talent; by those whose knowledge is gained from experience; by those who are present at the scene of the action
who see the country, who see the enemy, who see the advantages that occasions offer and who, like people embarked on
the same ship, are sharers of the danger. If, therefore, anyone
thinks himself qualified to give advice respecting the war
which I am to conduct, let him come with me to Macedonia.[7]

This quote suggests that a competent commander wants, as his
aides, competent soldiers who have a knowledge of the area in
which they will be operating. On the other hand, as Frederick the
Great once said: 'See that mule over there? That mule has made
every one of my campaigns and was in every battle, but in the end,
he is still a jackass.'[8] It is not enough to have just 'been there'. Experience in an area is not enough; it is how well we see deep inside
and draw an understanding out of the experience that allows us
to see the big picture and make responsible policy. A commander
needs a deep appreciation for all the dimensions of what is going
on, and then needs to use that information as the basis for making
wise decisions.[9]

What a Roman could 'know' about foreign lands was limited.
The Roman concepts of space and geography were different from
ours.[10] The Romans inhabited a world without modern surveying
techniques, adequate maps, or compasses. They had no satellites or
aerial photographs and so the 'bird's-eye view' was not available to
them. The only way they could acquire reliable information about
a place was to march through it with the army. Pliny the Elder
states quite bluntly that one could not know much about places
where the Roman army had never been.[11] What Rome knew about
Parthia, Armenia and the Caucasus was discovered through warfare.[12] It is unfortunate that none of the material acquired on campaign containing geographical information has survived. All
seventeen books of Arrian's *Parthica* have been lost.[13] Vegetius, the
fourth-century author of a military handbook, recommends that a
conscientious general should have detailed itineraries 'drawn', if
possible, ready for all regions in which a war would be fought. He
should know the intervals between places, the quality of the roads,
and know the shortcuts, the byways, the mountains and rivers.[14]
The Antonine Itinerary, a list of place names and distances along
routes through the empire dating to the third century CE, may have
originated as just such a plan for Caracalla's march to the East and

the related troop movements.[15] The Augustan History records that Severus Alexander not only followed an itinerary when he set out for the eastern front, but published it beforehand so that he could be located at any time.[16]

Modern policymakers would not dream of conducting foreign relations or planning a war, much less undertaking one, without accurately scaled maps. Roman thought processes must have been different if this type of information did not exist for them in the same way as it does for us. But even if the world beyond Rome's borders remained uncharted to a degree that rendered two-dimensional maps useless for military purposes, and even if maps were not used for those purposes, it is nevertheless true that the Romans came to the field with a general, traditional image of what they thought the world looked like.[17]

Itineraries tell us how the Romans measured space. They give only a one-dimensional view of the world – an odological measurement as distances between cities rather than a two-dimensional cartographic view. Within the empire itself, the roads were known, measured and marked with milestones.[18] For a campaign in the east a military commander with access to the Antonine Itinerary, for example, would have known the distance in miles between each stop on a particular route, and only a few points east of the Euphrates. He could have added these together to predict the length of the march between specific points, and could organize his supplies in this way. We must not overestimate either the accuracy or the availability of this information even though the Romans produced it themselves.[19] Caesar had mounted two campaigns in Gaul yet, by the time of Claudius's expedition to Britain, soldiers mutinied for fear that Britain was a myth and that they would fall off the ends of the earth.[20]

Certain kinds of geographical intelligence were not available at all, or were very problematic even with the best reconnaissance people collecting it. This is especially true about the size, shape, orientation and relative position of territories and land masses. The Romans did attempt to learn and describe such things, and also in some cases tried to correct perceived errors as new information became available. Such errors, striking to the modern historian and often noted, could be prodigious, even for places where the Romans had campaigned extensively. The Greeks were better at this sort of charting than the Romans, but even Posidonius underestimated, for example, the distance from the Caspian Sea to the Euxine Sea by half, despite his close friendship with Pompey who campaigned there.[21]

Nero's general, Corbulo, produced what Pliny described as 'places drawn' after his campaign in Armenia.[22] Information, like distances, was important to commanders who had to find food and water for their troops, fodder for the cavalry and the animals in the baggage train. While inside Roman territory, armies could be supplied by Roman roads and fed on grain collected as a tax. Once they were in enemy territory, however, they had to rely on foraging and pillaging.[23] As we saw in Chapter 6, Corbulo, on campaign in the deserts of Armenia, suffered from a lack of water and food until he reached cultivated land, and Severus's campaigns in Mesopotamia had the same difficulties with supplies even after all the other Roman armies that had passed through the region. Was there any written information about local conditions available to Severus from Trajan's campaign? We do not know.

Much of the information gathered on campaign was preserved in the form of dispatches to the Senate, together with the commentaries or memoirs of the emperor or the military commander if he produced any. The Emperor Lucius Verus had promised to send Fronto copies of dispatches written to him by generals about the tasks allocated to them. Lucius also promised to send his own letters, his harangues to the army and his communications with the enemy.[24] Fronto praised the rhetorical style of Lucius Verus's letter to the Senate in which he announced certain victories in the eastern war.[25] Fronto also planned to write a history of the Parthian War which would have been a marvellous source for us but, unfortunately, only the preface to this history survives.

Even when we have military memoirs, we should come to expect a certain amount of exaggeration in the telling of the story. There is a temptation to exaggerate the distances travelled, to convert villages into cities and to inflate the numbers of barbarians killed.[26] Trajan wrote to the Senate during his Parthian campaign that he had progressed farther than Alexander the Great, and Caracalla boasted in his letters that he had subjected the entire East.[27] Both of these claims were wildly exaggerated.

INTELLIGENCE PROBLEM 3:
LONG-DISTANCE RECONNAISSANCE, OR LACK THEREOF

A certain amount of geographical intelligence came to the Romans while on campaign, and the correspondence generated by the participants tells us what they knew. What happened, however, when the Romans invaded unknown territory? How much geographical and topographical reconnaissance was it possible for them to collect ahead of time, and how accurate and useful was it? Scouts and spies are well attested on the tactical or operational level during the course of a particular campaign.[28] One of the few surviving examples of long-term advance reconnaissance comes from the one emperor who did not lead a Parthian campaign, Augustus. Before sending his grandson Gaius on an expedition to the East in 2 BCE, Augustus had three reports prepared, according to Pliny, the first one by a certain Dionysius.[29] It is possible that part of one of these reports survives in the form of the Parthian Stations of Isidore of Charax.[30] The report, called *Stathmoi Parthikoi* in Greek, gives distances in *schoeni* – a Persian measurement – between stops across the Parthian Empire along a route from Zeugma to Alexandropolis in Arachosia. It goes into great detail for the route down the Euphrates where Isidorus provides measurements for short distances between towns, sometimes also naming their founders and whether they were fortified, and a few other items. The text becomes increasingly less informative as it progresses east. For the farthest-off regions, Isidorus offers only the name of the region, the length of the route through it, and the number of stations to be found there. Not everything listed in this report is up-to-date or accurate. His identification of Alexandropolis as the eastern border of the Parthian Empire, for example, is problematic and probably anachronistic.[31] Another source frequently cited for information on the East by authors of the imperial period is the survey conducted by Alexander the Great on his campaign. He brought with him two surveyors, or *bematistae*, Dagnetus and Baeton, who measured his march and published the results in a work called *Stations of Alexander's March,* mentioned by Pliny the Elder and later by Athenaeus. A man named Amyntas also published a *Stations of Asia*, apparently based on the same source.[32]

A second example of long-range military exploration survives from the imperial period. Nero sent scouts to the Caucasus region in preparation for a projected campaign there, but about this we are not well informed.[33] This is the only sure case after Augustus of a mission sent out to explore in advance of military action. An example of long-term military reconnaissance, but not in preparation for a campaign, is the *Periplus of the Euxine Sea*, a Greek version of a Latin dispatch from Arrian, then governor of Cappadocia, to the Emperor Hadrian.[34]

Other potential sources of information on the Parthian Empire were the merchants who plied the overland routes to India and China, though to what degree they were used or how accurate their information was is unclear. Although there is no direct evidence after Augustus that merchants were consulted for purposes of military reconnaissance, the geographical sources refer to them often.[35] More often than not, traders are cited in discussion of sea routes from the Red Sea to the Persian Gulf or to India, not the overland routes.[36]

Although the Romans portrayed the Emperor Claudius, for example, as 'victor over tribes not only unconquered before him, but in truth unknown', there were only sporadic, tenuous and dangerous exploratory missions sent out into the lands beyond the empire.[37] The rumours and reports of merchants and prisoners could flesh out this picture, but only a little. The area beyond the Euphrates remained unknown until the Romans subjected it, measured it and built roads through it. We must be careful of attributing to the Romans any geopolitical understanding that required two or three-dimensional comprehension of foreign territory. They were motivated by such psychological concepts as the pride and glory of far-flung conquest without understanding just how far 'far-flung' really was.

It seems that it is only after military intervention that we can expect detailed information about a geographical region. The critical role of the army in expanding geographical knowledge meant that the Romans perceived themselves as conquering unknown lands, and they were very proud of this.[38] Such advance reconnaissance in remote, usually hostile areas must have posed fundamental practical problems.[39] If the Romans intended to take over the world, they had to be willing to lead armies into completely unknown territory, and when reconnaissance was not done, or the intelligence was of poor quality, problems immediately arose. Thus when Aelius Gallus, the prefect of Roman Egypt, who knew little about Arabia because of poor geographical intelligence, invaded that land under orders from Augustus, his march which should have taken sixty days took six months.[40] It is not so surprising, therefore, that his republican predecessors, Crassus and Antony, should meet with disaster in Parthia when their ignorance about the region's geography left them vulnerable to treacherous guides or the victim of the terrain. This sort of situation no doubt generated Strabo's comment on the importance of geographical intelligence.[41]

Not only did what the Romans recorded about Parthia disappear, but neither do we have any of the Parthian sources used by the Romans. Strabo mentions one Apollodorus of Artemita (a Greek city east of the Tigris) who wrote a history of Parthia up to the year 87 BCE.[42] Other Parthian authorities were known to the Romans, including the source used by Trogus (if this was different from Strabo's source) and the source of Plutarch's account of Crassus's expedition. Strabo 11.9.3 claims to have described Parthian institutions in great detail, but that part of his histories is lost. The fourteen volumes of Arrian's *Parthica* have also disappeared. Even Dio does not discuss the Parthians in great detail because 'so many have written about their race and customs' (40.15.1). Pliny's account is the most detailed and he lists Corbulo as his source.[43] He describes Mesopotamia in detail, and of the kingdoms that surround it he names the major cities and the mountains. According to Pliny the Elder, the Parthian Empire measured 944 miles in width.[44] In *Historia Naturalis* 6.137, he gives information obtained from Agrippa's report, which was one of the few 'cartographic' works known from antiquity. We are told that Media, Parthia and Persia are bounded on the east by the Indus, a romantic notion which probably reflects beliefs held over from Hellenistic sources. There are other such miscalculations and anachronisms.[45] The world was a much smaller place in the minds of the Romans. Because Trajan and his advisors thought of strategy in two-dimensional geography, what looks like a vulnerable salient on a map to us was not necessarily what the Romans imagined.[46] The Roman elite's view of the world always remained a literary one, and they very often privileged older information over more modern sources.[47] For a writer like Tacitus, it was more important to record Roman views of honour and discipline than clog up the narrative with difficult place names and excessive detail. Their world view put more importance on moral and social issues than on recording geographical facts, even if the context was a military campaign. This may be one of the reasons we still do not know the location of Tigranocerta.[48]

INTELLIGENCE PROBLEM 4:
LACK OF ETHNOGRAPHIC INTELLIGENCE

As we mentioned before, military intervention could produce ethnographic, political or economic intelligence, but we have no idea what the Romans knew about the Parthians or any of the ethnic groups living within the Parthian Empire. Parthia was a diverse and multi-dimensional environment, rich in people, cultures, languages, religions, sensibilities and sensitivities.[49] Few Romans, however, got to experience that richness; fewer still immersed themselves in it. This caused a barrier to collecting ethnographic intelligence on the 'barbarians' who surrounded Rome. On the one hand, there was the practical drive to 'know the enemy' but, on the other hand, the Romans had a strong tendency to perceive outsiders in traditional and stereotypical ways. Their contempt for easterners, whom they dismissed as untrustworthy, effeminate and cowardly, acted as a blinder against discovering what the Parthians were really like.[50] The Parthian Empire was a highly organized political system with a culture much older than Rome's, and yet the Romans saw the Parthians as backwards and inferior. Any number of sources could have convinced them otherwise. Several ancient authors describe the Parthians as 'rivals of the Romans', i.e. equally large, civilized and powerful.[51] Potential sources about Parthia, as an organized political entity, were diverse. King Phraates's four sons, for example, spent decades at Rome as hostages and could have told the Romans much. Embassies back and forth seem to have been routine.[52] It is disturbing how little Roman historians knew about the enemies of the Romans or how often their information was outdated or inaccurate.[53] They had begun believing Parthians were like Cappadocians or Armenians, who rarely came to close quarters, and who had been easily beaten by Roman generals. Later they came to see Parthians as their natural enemies.[54]

The Romans saw all foreigners as inferior and they did not hesitate to say so. This attitude made it that much easier to conquer and kill the people they encountered. The Romans often used genocide as an option in their foreign policy. They had no concerns about their own legitimacy or unilateralism, as modern powers sometimes do, and the Romans were certainly not 'bringing democracy to Parthia'. It is not surprising, therefore, to encounter the words put into the mouth of Calgacus by Tacitus, that the Romans 'created a wasteland and called it peace'.[55] Getting to know the Parthians was not so important, if your goal was only to kill them. The Romans were no different from the modern world in that they perceived outsiders by means of cultural stereotypes that resisted change even in the face of available information. The demonizing of Muslims in America after 9/11 is a good example. Edward Said has written eloquently about the long tradition of western powers and their views of the Orient.[56] This was equally true of the Roman decision-making elite. Their decisions could often be based on a traditional and stereotyped view of foreign peoples, rather than on systematic intelligence about their political, social, and cultural institutions. This lack of knowledge was compounded by the problem of distance.[57]

A substantial body of ethnographic literature was produced at Rome in the imperial period, but it comes out of the same Greek tradition that invented the word 'barbarian'.[58] One of the barbarian 'types' that survives from Greek historiographical writing is the luxurious, cowardly easterner, quintessentially represented by the Persians.[59] At least one character defect was attributed to their political institutions. Herodotus and other fifth-century writers portray Persians as enslaved to a despotic tyrant, while the Greeks had the political liberty that they associated with their *poleis* and, in the case of the Athenians and their allies, democracy. Asians were more likely to be cowardly and less warlike than their European counterparts because of their political structure, but also because of the temperate climate. The Romans believed harsh weather tempered northern barbarians into good warriors. While in the hot climates of the eastern desert, the stereotype of the effete easterner persisted.[60]

In some cases, Roman information on the Parthian military was correct. Herodian knew and reported that the Parthians had no standing army – that it had to be called up when the occasion arose.[61] Other Roman ideas about Parthian military capabilities, however, had the character of legend or stereotype. For example, it was widely believed that the Parthians were invincible on their own territory but incapable of waging long campaigns outside it, and that their army was composed mainly of slaves.[62] Tacitus talks about their loose, flowing clothing that is the object of derision in Lucan 8.367–8. Both Lucan and Justin wrote that the Parthians were polygamous, as were all barbarians except the Germans.[63] Justin (41.3) writes: 'The character of the race is arrogant, seditious, untrustworthy, and shameless',[64] and Pliny (*HN* 14.144, 148) says they are all drunks.[65]

After the disastrous battle of Carrhae in 53 BCE, a new explosion of specialist literature appeared, none of which has survived. The Romans had to 'explain' how such a disaster could happen, and most of these works focused on weapons. They asserted that Crassus was defeated in part because he did not know how to counter the Parthian archers and cataphracts, the heavy-armed cavalry.[66] The Romans seem to have adapted to Parthian fighting styles and altered the composition of their own forces to some degree in response.[67] Ventidius certainly showed how, with a little planning, they could neutralize archers with slingers and, with the use of a little advance intelligence, could ambush the Parthians with no problem.

In sum, the Romans did not seem to have much intelligence on the Parthians, and they often ignored what they had. But even if their intelligence was of high quality it would not have told them much about Parthian intentions. As one writer has pointed out, even modern military intelligence does not give us a great deal of information about enemy plans.[68] Furthermore, the Roman system was self-reinforcing. Every time the Romans defeated the Parthians and took land from them, it produced 'proof' in the minds of the Romans of the inferiority of these easterners at whose expense these gains were made.[69]

INTELLIGENCE PROBLEM 5: AMATEURISH COMMANDERS

One of the major problems the Romans had during the Republic was the amateurish nature of some of their commanders. The Romans did not distinguish between a civilian administrative career and a military career. Two consuls were elected annually, and how well trained they were militarily depended on the individual interest of the candidate. Sometimes they got an experienced field commander, but at other times they might elect an individual who had had little more military experience than a tour as a legate overseas.[70] Although Livy, in Book 9, states that some Roman generals were easily the equal of Alexander, the average Roman commander was not an innovative military leader and yet could find himself commanding vast military campaigns. Crassus, for example, was not atypical of Roman generals. But like many of his type, he tended to make two major tactical mistakes. In search of a great victory and the glory that attended such a conquest, he underestimated the enemy and failed to collect the proper intelligence that would have given him a better estimate of the enemy's strength and intentions. In the case of Nero's war in Armenia there were two generals, one of each type: Corbulo, a career military man whose successes even threatened the emperor's ego, and Paetus, an arrogant, incompetent administrator who almost lost the campaign because of his foolish mistakes. Augustus had Varus, who lost three Romans legions in Germany to Arminius.

INTELLIGENCE PROBLEM 6:
SLOW COMMUNICATIONS AND MOBILIZATION

There was no difference between Rome (the capital) and field headquarters since the emperor was both the political and military leader of the state. Because of the lack of a speedy communications network, however, every emperor facing a Parthian confrontation had a serious political problem as well as a military one. Should the emperor set up headquarters more than 1,500 miles from his administrative centre at Rome in far-off Asia? This choice would allow close personal direction in field operations and on-the-spot diplomatic negotiations, plus his armies would always be at hand. The communications problem, however, would then work in reverse: Rome would be governed by a deputy, the bureaucracy would be without direct supervision, and political intrigue would have had its chance to blossom.

Targeting an enemy and collecting intelligence goes hand in hand with the ability to transmit the information to those who need it most. Much of Roman communications traffic was carried by messenger. When speed of transmission was needed in emergencies, signalling was also an option. But we know of no long-distance signalling systems in the Roman Empire.[71] Mobilizing forces was therefore predictably slow.

Mobilizing for a large campaign in the East involved a vast investment of manpower and supplies. Van Berchem has pointed out that the *Antonine Itinerary*, a route map of the empire at the time of Caracalla, is in fact a plan devised in Rome by those charged with logistical arrangements for the emperor's Parthian expedition. The whole route was traced out with estimated journeys, measured days, and provisioning stations that were prepared along the route.[72] This vast undertaking might have involved half the provinces of the empire. Supplies would have been delivered by provincials, especially through the new tax, the *annona militaris*. A major Parthian campaign would have drastic effects on the economy of the empire. For example, in Syria during Caracalla's campaign, thirty-two or more mints suddenly opened up in 214 CE and began issuing or stockpiling debased silver coins obviously intended to supply cash for the armies that were to arrive shortly. When Caracalla was murdered and Macrinus withdrew from Parthian territory, the issues from these mints declined precipitously, until nearly all closed within eighteen months. The amount of bullion to be transported, whether silver or bronze, was tremendous. No emperor should have undertaken a major campaign lightly, and no major campaign left the empire unaffected.[73]

The logistics of a campaign could involve years of preparation. As we have seen, the preparations for Corbulo's campaign stretched out over three years and involved the repair of roads in Cilicia, Bithynia, and Thrace.[74] Trajan's eastern expedition also required major road repairs, which may have begun already in 111 or 112. His planned invasion is perhaps one of the reasons for the construction of the new *via nova Traiana* through the province of Arabia to facilitate the movement of troops and supplies.[75] Paved military roads were expensive to construct or to repair and represented a significant burden on somebody, even if the government did not pay for them in cash.[76] For the most part it seems that the building or repair of roads was a *munus* (labour tax) levied on the local population. This meant that wartime preparations would place a burden on the provincials closest to the campaign, even if the army helped them. We have milestones dated from 163 to 165 recording the repair of a road in Syria, probably for Lucius Verus's Parthian campaign where the army provided the labour and the expenses were shouldered by the provincial town of Abilene.[77] The routes were probably prepublished to facilitate the collection of provisions; the Antonine Itinerary may be one of these published route marches.[78] Trajan conquered and annexed Arabia partly in order to build a fortified road through it. Besides its obvious military function in his upcoming Parthian war, this would have served to guard the transport of imported goods from the Red Sea.[79]

INTELLIGENCE PROBLEM 7:
NO SWIFT RESPONSE CAPABILITY

During the periodic crises with Parthia, the emperor was not situated for a swift or coordinated response. Some have attributed this to the Roman imperial government displaying a curious blend of the habits of a republic or a city-state on the one hand, and the requirements of a monarchy and an empire on the other. These contradictions retarded the ability of the government to meet its military obligations along the frontier and especially to undertake offensive action to secure those boundaries.[80] When the Romans faced a sophisticated rival with their own imperial resources such as Parthia, when the distance between Rome and the front was forbidding, and when the terrain did not favour Roman logistics and legionary tactics as it did in the East, then these Republican traits dramatically exposed Rome's weaknesses. In the course of two centuries and eight major campaigns, attempts to offset these problems finally brought drastic changes in Roman government. But the two-and-a-half centuries of Roman attempts to reduce Parthia to vassalage were a failure and much of the failure was due to decisions made on bad strategic and tactical intelligence.

Roman policy did not rely on swift action or even preventive action. Marcus's Parthian War and Severus Alexander's invasion of Persia were both fought after substantial preparation and not as an instant response to a crisis.[81] In the Roman system, reprisals might come at any time, even as long as a year after the attack. They usually took place in enemy territory and were not defensive wars to expel a barbarian from Roman territory. The aim was to punish, to avenge and to terrify.[82] The Romans attempted to reassert a certain state of mind in the enemy: recognition of Rome as the dominant power. Whenever a Parthian or Armenian king attempted to tip the balance, the status relationship between Rome and the barbarian had to be restored to the status quo *ante bellum*. This goal did not necessarily include annexing territory, although that was always possible.

The best-documented example of what might be involved in assembling a force for an invasion is from the reign of Nero, where Tacitus gives us a detailed account of the campaigns of Corbulo in Armenia.[83] Corbulo's original command involved two of Syria's four legions, and one-half of its auxiliaries; a third legion was transferred from Germany (Tacitus, *Annals* 13.8). In 62 he sent two legions against Tiridates, the Armenian king, plus a third transferred from Moesia, and kept the remaining three legions with him in Syria (15.6) but after Paetus's humiliating defeat he took the field himself with four legions, including one transferred from Pannonia, plus all the auxiliaries from his province (15.25–6). This reduction of the number of troops in Moesia must have affected the governor, who had his own battles to fight. In an inscription, he boasts of a military success against the Sarmatians *even though he sent a large part of his army to the expedition in Armenia*.[84] Nero's projected Caspian campaign included a new legion, the I Italica, and a military build-up in Alexandria, perhaps for a concurrent expedition to Ethiopia.[85] This laborious transfer of soldiers from place to place and from remote locations like Britain was time-consuming, expensive, and tied up available forces elsewhere.[86] When Vespasian decided to enter the contest for the throne, he was fighting the Jewish War with three legions. In preparation, he reached agreements with the kings of Armenia and Parthia, to forestall any potential invasions in case a massive withdrawal of troops from the East was required.[87] Every time Rome mounted a major campaign against Parthia, there were positive as well as negative consequences.

INTELLIGENCE PROBLEMS 8:
A SINGLE DECISION MAKER

While in the Republic decisions to go to war in the East were made by senators,[88] in the Principate this responsibility was gradually usurped by the emperor and his circle of advisors. As Fergus Millar has written: 'The active conduct of foreign relations ... rested entirely with the emperor, his advisors, and his entourage.'[89] An academic debate exists over the extent to which the Senate supervised or controlled policy and expansion.[90] Either way, foreign policy decisions were not made by trained experts in economics, political science, military theory or even strategy and tactics.[91] Foreign-policy decisions were ultimately made by emperors who were wealthy and powerful men, but experts in nothing.[92] The concept of war in the East was concretely embodied in the strategic priorities chosen by emperors.[93] How can we be sure that what the historians wrote is what the emperor thought?

As one scholar has pointed out, the class of people who made Rome's foreign policy decisions in the period under discussion in this book was largely indistinguishable from the literary types who composed the histories of the era.[94] The Roman aristocracy was educated mainly in literature and rhetoric. A division of thinking between literary types and policymakers may not be as wide as we find in modern times. Dio Cassius, for example, was a friend of three of the emperors – Severus, Caracalla and Severus Alexander – and two of these leaders fought Parthian wars. Dio himself was governor of several provinces.[95] Therefore what the historians wrote about Roman foreign policy may be, to a great extent, an accurate description of how the government made its decisions and why the Romans fought the Parthians.[96]

The ancient sources certainly recognized the personality of the emperor as a factor in his decisions. Herodian cannot imagine an aggressive, expansionist campaign being waged by anyone but the emperor. A popular general claiming his own territory would be a threat to the throne. This is what makes any scheme that attributes to the Romans a system of strategic goals stretching out over generations so inherently problematic. Whereas certain attitudes towards terror, vengeance, security and Roman prestige were persistent over generations, well-articulated, long-term strategic policies were not. The central aspect of Roman strategy was maintaining Rome's image and dominant position. The Roman army was astonishingly small for the amount of territory it had to defend. Their frontier installations and troop deployments were inadequate to the task of preventing major invasions. But this did not matter in the Roman system, as long as the enemy believed that he would suffer massive retaliation for a breach of faith, and as long as the Romans were both willing and able to enforce this principle at any cost. If the Roman army proved inadequate to the task, its image would suffer and other enemies might get the same idea about revolting.

Observers both ancient and modern question whether one president or one emperor can be responsible for starting a war. In the Roman case, the emperor's decisions were paramount.[97] Those who wish to absolve Trajan of guilt for an unnecessary war argue that the individual contribution of an emperor to foreign policy was overestimated. But if the emperor was not responsible, then who was?[98] Modern democracies can impinge somewhat on their governments; the Roman people could not. Individual rulers dictated frontier policy, not the empire's citizenry as a whole and not the Senate. There was only the emperor and his whims. It was the ambition of Romans emperors and not the collective fears of its people that led to constant interference in the politics of Armenia and Parthia. That collective fear, real or imagined, merely showed Rome's leaders where best to win the honour and glory for themselves. Military decisions on borders were often handled by governors and generals, but when it came to aggressive, expansionist campaigns during the Principate, it was the emperor's prerogative.[99]

What does this tell us, then, about the Roman decision-making elite when a crisis arose? Consider the occasion of Nero's accession, as Tacitus describes it (see Chapter 6). When disturbing news arrived from the East, was the young prince able to handle it? Relying on his advisors, he made what was perceived as a prudent decision.[100] Seneca, his advisor, is no different from Lucan or Statius, or other writers who produced historical, philosophical or ethnographic works during the Principate. The Romans could collect useful, concrete information on geography, troop locations, weapons and tactics, and itineraries – the type suitable for short-term, tactical thinking. But on a broader scale their knowledge and understanding of the world around them was insufficient, and the emperor could ignore what was collected if his intention was to go to war anyway.

There is enough evidence to suggest that the Roman emperor was able to obtain and check some intelligence about the political situation in neighbouring lands. Rome had enough allies among the Greek cities in the East to get valuable information about the number and type of troops. Whether they had the ability to know about the enemy's plans is another story. Corbulo had information that Vologases, the Parthian king, was occupied with a revolt in Hyrcania.[101] Later he received reliable news about Vologases's military build-up and planned invasion.[102] Caecina Paetus, governor of Syria, sent reports, perhaps false, to Vespasian, accusing Antiochus of Commagene of conspiracy to revolt.[103] Caracalla wrote to the Senate that a quarrel with the Parthian ruling family would weaken their state.[104] In many of these cases, we are not told how the emperor received his information. In 35 CE, Tiberius received a secret embassy from Parthia seeking a king from among the hostages in Rome, but also passing along information about the king's intent: 'he boasted, with arrogant language and threats, of the old boundaries of the Persians and Macedonians, and that he was going to invade the lands possessed by Cyrus and afterward by Alexander' (*Annals* 6.31).

Most of the time, however, we are left in the dark about how the Romans collected intelligence on their rival's social and political institutions, or their long-term military plans.

SOURCES OF INTELLIGENCE

When our sources are good, we can see how the Romans kept tabs on the enemy on a daily basis. When Cicero was Roman governor of Cilicia, he was kept informed about the anticipated Parthian invasion. He arrived at his province with no knowledge of the situation, and only after some time was he able to discover the location of his own troops. Even as his campaign progressed, doubts emerged about who exactly had invaded Syria and then later, whether the enemy had withdrawn.[105]

During the Principate, the ability to collect intelligence may have changed as the governor's office developed a larger military staff.[106] Units of *exploratores* were used to do reconnaissance in Rome's frontier provinces. Exactly what their duties were and how far they patrolled in enemy territory is uncertain.[107] Examples from Tacitus indicate how difficult it could be to obtain information, even on important military developments. In one complicated instance, King Pharasmanes of Iberia, goaded by his son, attacked and occupied Armenia, deposing its pro-Roman king, Mithridates. The Roman garrison there was under the command of an auxiliary prefect and a centurion. Pharasmanes bribed the prefect, but the centurion, taking a firmer stance, decided that 'if he could not deter Pharasmanes from the war, he would inform Ummidius Quadratus, the governor of Syria, about the situation in Armenia'.[108] This suggests that the governor would not otherwise have known. Quadratus, in fact, learned what was going on only after Mithridates was dead and his kingdom lost.[109] Later, the Emperor Nero, receiving conflicting reports about the Armenian war from his General Paetus and an embassy from King Vologases, asked the centurion who escorted the embassy, 'what was the situation in Armenia?' (*quo in statu Armenia esset*). The centurion replied that 'all the Romans had left'.[110] In another passage, Tacitus records that the critical news leading to Corbulo's Armenian expedition – that the Parthians had expelled the king of Armenia and were pillaging the country – was brought to Rome by rumours (bush telegraph).[111] Sometimes we are told that an emperor first became aware of a major invasion on receiving a message from the provincial governor, who wrote after his province had been attacked.[112] These invasions were not predicted or prevented by 'first strikes' or met at the frontier. At least one scholar has argued that in the late empire, even when such invasions were predicted, the knowledge was not enough and it could not be acted upon quickly enough to prevent an invasion.[113] Roman strategy was not based on pre-emptive attacks, but rather on punitive or retaliatory campaigns that might be waged at any time after the crisis occurred.

In all these situations, those who sought intervention from the Romans made sure they were apprised of the situation, but they also presented their case in the light most favourable to themselves. This information might easily be planted as a way to mobilize Roman intervention on a rival's behalf.

In short, the Romans had no real way of obtaining political and military information on foreign territories systematically and objectively. Merchants could be questioned, but they were unreliable. The information brought by prisoners and refugees became outdated quickly, and such people often exaggerated their own importance and the importance of the intelligence they carried in the hopes of better treatment and political asylum. Permanent legations or ambassadors to foreign lands were unknown in the ancient world. Garrisons were sometimes placed in client kingdoms, but not always.[114] Many of the leaders of allied nations had served in Rome's auxiliaries or lived in Rome as hostages or had received their education there, so they understood the Roman system.[115]

Ironically, Rome's best source of foreign intelligence was also the Achilles Heel of its intelligence programme. They relied on their allies for the intelligence that would provide them with a proper defence. The problem is that there were some people who adhered to Rome only as long as it was victorious. Many smaller groups were pawns caught between two superpowers, with no choice but to bow to whomever was the closest at the moment. The Romans believed that by relying on their allies for useful intelligence, they were keeping themselves safer and less vulnerable to attack. In some ways, the reputation Rome had gained for *fides* (faith), as an empire famous for its strong support of friends and allies, did serve its intelligence interests.[116] These very allies were expected to provide much of the foreign intelligence that Rome had neither the capacity nor the inclination to collect for itself. The Romans opted to surround themselves by a progressively-widening ring of friendly or subordinate states, who came to identify their own self-interest with sustaining and sometimes extending the Roman dominion. This strategy had been successful on the Italian peninsula in the Republic, and the Romans believed it would be the effective policy overseas in the empire. Pro-Roman regimes, especially oligarchic ones, held subjects under control. The Romans fostered cliques, and they cultivated the power-wielding aristocracies of the various tribes as sources of information and bases of support.[117] This issued in a regular flow of embassies and appeals, and with them information. The Romans, now prisoners of their own self-created reputation, were compelled to respond, sometimes, though not always, with force. The ideal of *fides Romana*, Rome's loyalty to her allies, was as characteristic of Roman propaganda as deceit was considered alien or 'un-Roman.' And while the Romans were duty-bound to provide protection, the allies in turn were expected to keep Roman officials informed of events that might threaten both parties. The problem was that when the allies became hostile to Rome, this 'distant early-warning system' simply collapsed. It is ironic that after six centuries of political and military experience, the Romans were still relying on the good will of their allies to provide the intelligence upon which their survival depended. Dependence on foreigners for intelligence proved unwise in many cases. Collecting intelligence through one's own initiative and efforts was the only viable policy.[118]

NOTES

1. This was my argument in, *Intelligence Activities in Ancient Rome: Trust in the Gods, but Verify* (London and New York: Routledge, 2005).
2. On Roman intelligence gathering, see N.J.E. Austin and B. Rankov, *Exploratio: Military and Political Intelligence in the Roman World from the Second Punic War to the Battle of Adrianople* (New York and London: Routledge, 1995), and Sheldon, *Intelligence Activities in Ancient Rome*, both with extensive bibliographies.
3. J.B. Campbell, 'Who Were the Viri Militares?' *JRS*, 65 (1975), pp.11–31; J.B. Campbell, *The Emperor and the Roman Army 31 BC–AD 235* (Oxford: Clarendon Press, 1984); F. Millar, 'Emperors, Frontiers and Foreign Relations 31 BC–AD 278', *Britannia*, 13 (1982), pp.3–16; A. Ferrill, *Roman Imperial Grand Strategy* (Lanham, MD: University Press of America, 1991), p.40; C.G. Starr, *The Roman Empire, 27 BC – AD 47: A Study in Survival* (New York: Oxford University Press, 1982). The existence in equestrian careers has been questioned by R. Saller, 'Promotion and Patronage in Equestrian Careers', *JRS*, 70 (1980), pp.44–63. E.S. Gruen, *The Hellenistic World and the Coming of Rome* (Berkeley, CA: University of California Press, 1984), vol. 1, pp.203–49, rejects the idea that there were 'Eastern experts' in the second century BCE. The sole dissenter is E.L. Wheeler, 'Methodological Limits and the Mirage of Roman Strategy', *JMH*, 57 (January 1993), part 1, pp.20–1.
4. For example, *minister bello* (assigned to Corbulo by Nero); *arbiter sequenti annonae et praefectus stationibus viarum* (under Domitian); *epimelites euthenias* (Trajan); *praefectus vehiculorum* (Verus); *cura copiarum exercitus* (Verus); *praepositus annonae expeditionis felicissimae urbicae* (Severus) which became *procurator arcae expeditionis* in 194 and *procurator annonae* in 196.
5. On the role of the praetorian prefects see F. Millar, *The Emperor in the Roman World (31 BC to AD 337)* (Ithaca, NY: Cornell University Press, 1977), pp.122–31; on the *consilium principis*, see J.A. Crook, *Consilium Principis* (Cambridge: Cambridge University Press, 1955) and Wheeler, 'Methodological Limits', part 2, pp.215–16.
6. See the comments of A. Birley, *Marcus Aurelius: A Biography* (New Haven, CT: Yale University Press, 1987), p.20.
7. Livy, *Ab urbe condita* (Cambridge, MA: Harvard University Press, 1961), vol. 13, trans. A.C. Schlesinger, p.161, 44.22 (1951).

8. Quoted in General T. Zinni, and T. Kaltz, *The Battle for Peace: A Frontline Vision of America's Power and Purpose* (New York: Palgrave/Macmillan, 2006), pp.24–5.
9. Zinni and Kaltz, *Battle for Peace*, p.25.
10. See the comments of C.R. Whittaker, 'The Eastern Frontiers', in *CAH2*, 11 (2000), p.296.
11. Pliny, *HN* 4.102.
12. On Armenia and the Caucasus see Pliny, *HN* 6.23, who writes that he had more accurate information about the interior of Asia from Corbulo's expedition. The area was also known to the Romans from the campaigns on Pompey which were recorded by the historian Theophanes who accompanied him – Strabo 11.5.1 – and from Antony's expedition, of which an account was written by his friend Dellius who was there – Strabo 11.13.3. Austin and Rankov, *Exploratio*, pp.112–15.
13. See the comments of S. Mattern, *Rome and the Enemy* (Berkeley, CA: University of California Press, 1999), p.27.
14. Vegetius 3.6. He also suggests generals have *itineraria picta*, drawings showing routes and distances, mountains and rivers. On *itineraria* in general see W. Kubitschek, 'Itinerarien', in *RE*, no. 9, cols 2308–68; O. Dilke, *Greek and Roman Maps* (Ithaca, NY: Cornell University Press, 1985), chapter 8; K. Brodersen, *Terra cognita: Studien zür römischen Raumfassung* (Hildesheim: Olms, 1995).
15. D. van Berchem, 'L'annone militaire dans l'empire romain au IIIe siècle', *Memoires de la Société Nationale des Antiquaires de France*, 24 (1937), Serie 8, tome 10, pp.166–81; Mattern, *Rome and the Enemy*, p.19; A.L.F. Rivet and C. Smith, *The Place Names of Roman Britain* (Princeton, NJ: Princeton University Press, 1979), pp.151–3, who agree with Berchem. N. Reed, 'Pattern and Purpose in the Antonine Itinerary', *AJPh*, 99 (1978), pp. 228–54, argues that the Itinerary reflects specific imperial journeys and routes for military supplies. The itinerary itself is published in O. Cuntz, *Itineraria romana*, vol. 1, *Itineraria Antonini Augusti et Burdigalense* (Leipzig: B.G. Teubner, 1929).
16. *SHA, Alex. Sev.* 45.
17. On Roman maps see Mattern, *Rome and the Enemy*, pp.41–66; Dilke, *Greek and Roman Maps*; C.R. Whittaker, *The Frontiers of the Roman Empire: A Social and Economic Study* (Baltimore, MD: Johns Hopkins University Press, 1994), pp.31–2.
18. On milestones see R. Chevallier, *Roman Roads* (Berkeley, CA: University of California Press, 1976), pp.39–47. About 4,000 milestones survive and their inscriptions are being collected in *CIL*, 17.
19. Mattern, *Rome and the Enemy*, p.39, citing the errors in Pliny on North Africa. R. Rebuffat, 'Les erreurs de Pline et la position de Baba Iulia Campestris', *Antiquités africaines*, 1 (1967), pp.31–57.
20. Dio 60.19.2.
21. Strabo 11.1.5–6. Cf. B. Isaac, *The Limits of Empire: The Roman Army in the East* (Oxford: Clarendon Press, 1992), pp.403–4. On miscalculations of Agrippa and Appian in Spain see Mattern, *Rome and the Enemy*, p.39 and n.51.
22. Pliny, *HN* 6.40; Mattern, *Rome and the Enemy*, p.28.
23. See D. Engels, *Alexander the Great and the Logistics of the Macedonian Army* (Berkeley, CA: University of California Press, 1978), on the difficulty of carrying supplies over long distances. For the Roman army see D.J. Breeze, 'The Logistics of Agricola's Final Campaign', *Talanta*, 18–19 (1987–1988), pp.19–23; and J. Roth, *The Logistics of the Roman Army in the Jewish War* (PhD dissertation, Columbia University, 1990), pp.243–67. On taxes collected in kind, see Berchem, 'L'annone militaire', pp.117–202.
24. Marcus Cornelius Fronto was a prominent Roman orator, rhetorician and grammarian who was in ancient times considered the equal of Cato, Cicero and Quintilian. This high reputation was based chiefly on his orations, all of which are lost.
25. Fronto, *Ad. Verum Imp.* 2.1 (Loeb Classical Library, 2, 129–51).
26. Mattern, *Rome and the Enemy*, p.33.
27. On Trajan, see Dio 68.29.2. On Caracalla, see Herodian 4.11.8.
28. Tacitus, *Annals* 13.5, where *exploratores* inform Corbulo about the movement of the enemy's army. Trajan's army included scouts (*proskopoi*): Dio 68.23.2. Deserters were a source of information on the enemy. See Tacitus, *Annals* 2.12, and Dio 68.14. On spying amongst the Romans in general, see Austin and Rankov, *Exploratio*, and Sheldon, *Intelligence Activities in Ancient Rome*.
29. Pliny, *HN* 6.141.

30. It has been suggested that Dionysius and Isidore are one and the same person. See Mattern, *Rome and the Enemy*, p.34.
31. Ibid., p.35. One scholar suggested that Isidorus's report is based on a survey conducted by Mithridates II around 100 CE, and that it was based on Parthian documents. This is purely conjecture. W.W. Tarn, *The Greeks in Bactria and India* (Cambridge: Cambridge University Press, 1984 [1938]), pp.54–5.
32. Pliny, *HN* 6.61, cf. 6.45; Strabo 15.1.11, 15.2.8. On these sources see L. Pearson, 'The Diary and Letters of Alexander the Great', *Historia*, 3 (1954–55), pp.440–3; P.A. Brunt (ed. and trans.), *History of Alexander and Indica by Arrian* (Cambridge, MA: Harvard University Press, 1976–83), vol. 2, pp.487–9; Engels, *Alexander the Great*, Appendix 5, table 8, on the measurements of the *Bematistae* as recorded in Strabo and Pliny versus actual distances. The measurements are very accurate. Mattern, *Rome and the Enemy*, p.35, n.37.
33. Pliny *HN* 6.181. Cf. Seneca, *Quaes. Nat.* 6.8.3, says he sent two centurions. Dio 63 (62), 8.1, scouts. See J. Kolendo, *A la recherché de l'ambre baltique: L'expedition d'un chevalier romain sous Neron* (Warsaw: Wydawnictwa Uniwersytetu Warszawskiego, 1981), chapter 3.
34. Arrian, *Periplus Ponti Euxini* (Bristol: Bristol Classical, 2003). See also Aubrey Diller, *The Tradition of the Minor Greek Geographers* (New York: American Philological Association, 1952), pp.102–17; the text is on 118–46. Arrian himself did not sail past what he describes as the limits of the Roman Empire at Sebastopolis on the eastern coast. The information he provides includes sailing distances between stops along the coast, the location of harbours, the names of cities and of kings. He also includes an estimate on the circumference of the Sea of Azov. Mattern, *Rome and the Enemy*, p.38.
35. Marinus and Tacitus both ascribe their information about Ireland to merchants, though Marinus is dismissive. Ptolemy, *Geog.* 1.11.8; Tacitus, *Agricola* 24.2. In his discussion of the amber trade, Pliny reports that a knight sent on a special expedition to procure amber in Nero's reign recorded the distance from Carnuntum in Pannonia to the Baltic Coast as 600 miles. Pliny, *HN* 37.45; Kolendo, *À la recherche de l'ambre baltique*.
36. See Strabo 2.5.12 on merchants as sources for Arabia and India. See Aelius Gallus's expedition in 15.1.4 on the limitations of their information about India. Pliny cites *mercatores* or *negotiatores* as sources for several points East: *HN* 6.101 on the sea route to India; 6.88 for a vague reference to trade with China; 6.139–40 on the town of Charax, together with King Juba and the envoys of the Arabs; 6.146 for some political history of Charax; 6.149 on the Ports of the Persian Gulf.
37. Pomponius Mela 3.49.
38. Velleius Paterculus 2.106.1 on Tiberius; Pliny, *HN* 6.160–1 on Gallus.
39. Cf. Caesar, *BG* 4.21 on the mission of Volusenus.
40. Strabo 16.4.24.
41. Ibid., 11.13.4; Mattern, *Rome and the Enemy*, p.38; Isaac, *Limits of Empire*, p.403.
42. Strabo 2.5.12 on Apollodorus and other Parthian authors known to the Romans, including Isidore of Charax. Cf. Tarn, *Greeks in Bactria and India*, pp.44–55, and Mattern, *Rome and the Enemy*, p.58.
43. Pliny, *HN* 6.23. He says that Parthia is divided into eighteen kingdoms 'around two seas, the Red Sea of the South and the Caspian Sea to the North'. Eleven of these provinces are defined as 'upper' and 'begin at the border of Armenia and the Caspian shores and extend to the Scythians' (6.112).
44. Ibid., 6.126.
45. See Mattern, *Rome and the Enemy*, pp.59–60.
46. See E. Luttwak, *The Grand Strategy of the Roman Empire* (Baltimore, MD: Johns Hopkins University Press, 1976), p.100, and Mattern's corrective in *Rome and the Enemy*, pp.61–2.
47. Mattern, *Rome and the Enemy*, p.65.
48. Ibid., p.65.
49. Moden Iraq still is. See the comments of Zinni and Kaltz, *Battle for Peace*, p.15.
50. See the comments of D.L. Kennedy, 'Parthia and Rome: Eastern Perspectives', in D.L. Kennedy (ed.), *The Roman Army in the East* (Ann Arbor, MI: *Journal of Roman Archaeology*, Supplementary Series, 18, 1996), p.67; J.V.P.D. Balsdon, *Romans and Aliens* (Chapel Hill, NC: University of North Carolina Press, 1979), pp.60–4, 66–8.
51. Manilius 4.674–5: 'and the Parthians, a sort of other world'. Strabo, *Geography* 11.9.2, describes the Parthians as having become rivals of Rome in the size of their empire. Lucan, *de Bell. Civ.* 8.290–307, Justin 41.1.1, has the Parthians dividing the world with

the Romans. See Dio 40.14.3, on the Parthians considered rivals of the Romans. For a discussion of the Greek and Latin sources on Parthia, see J. Wolski, *L'Empire des Arsacides* (Louvain, 1993), pp.12–15.

52. A document from Dura records an embassy from Parthia on its way to the emperor as though this were a routine occurrence. F. Millar, 'Government and Diplomacy in the Roman Empire during the First Three Centuries', *IHR*, 10 (1988), p.370; on this document, perhaps dating to 207, see M.L. Chaumont, 'Un document méconnu concernant l'envoi d'un ambassadeur parthe vers Septime Sévère (P. Dura 60B)', *Historia*, 36 (1987), pp.423–47.

53. Caesar's inaccuracies on the Gauls are treated in L. Rawlings, 'Caesar's Portrayal of Gauls as Warriors', in K. Welch and A. Powell (eds), *Julius Caesar as Artful Reporter: The War Commentaries as Political Instruments*. (London: Duckworth; Swansea: Classical Press of Wales, 1998), pp.171–93. As for Tacitus and the accuracy of the Germania, an overview on the subject is contained in A.A. Lund, 'Kritischer Forschungsbericht zur Germania des Tacitus', in *ANRW*, 2, 33.3, 1989–2222, esp. 2215–22 on the reliability. Tacitus's inaccuracies on the Germans are a well-known theme in modern Roman history.

54. B. Campbell, 'War and Diplomacy: Roman and Parthia, 31 BC – AD 235', in J. Rich and G. Shipley (eds.), *War and Society in the Roman World* (New York and London: Routledge, 1993), p.217.

55. Tacitus, *Agricola* 98.

56. E. Said, *Orientalism* (New York: Pantheon Books, 1978).

57. See H. Sonnabend, *Fremdenbild und Politik: Vorstellungen der Römer von Ägypten und dem Partherreich in der Späten Republik und Frühen Kaiserzeit* (Frankfurt: Lang, 1986), and Dorothy Thompsen's review in *CR*, 39, 1 (1989) pp.86–7, and Stephen Mitchell's review in *JRS*, 79 (1989), p.196.

58. A.N. Sherwin-White, *Racial Prejudice in Imperial Rome* (Cambridge: Cambridge University Press, 1967); Balsdon, *Romans and Aliens*; Mattern, *Rome and the Enemy*, p.70. On Roman ethnography, see K. Müller, *Geschichte der antiken Ethnographie und ethnologischen Theoriebildung* (Wiesbaden: Franz Steiner Verlag, 1972–80), vol. 2; Y.A. Dauge, *Le barbare: Recherches sur la conception de la barbarie et de civilisation* (Brussels: Collection Latomus, 1981), vol. 176. There are many studies on specific ethnic groups like the Germans, e.g. A. Lund, *Zum Germanenbild der Römer: Eine Einführung in die antike Ethnographie* (Heidelberg: C. Winter, 1990).

59. It was in the aftermath of the Persian Wars that Herodotus wrote his histories and began a long tradition of stereotyping the eastern 'barbarians'. See Mattern, *Rome and the Enemy*, p.73.

60. For example, Lucan, *de Bell. Civ.* 8.363–8.

61. Herodian 3.1.2.

62. On invincibility: Dio 40.15.6. Cf. Lucan, *de Bell. Civ.* 8.368–71; Justin 41.2; Tacitus *Annals*, 1.11.4. On slaves: Justin 41.2.5–6; Plutarch, *Crassus* 21.6. This is discussed in E. Gabba, 'Sulle influenza reciproche degli ordinamenti militari dei Parti e dei Romani', in *La Persia e il mondo greco-romano (Per la storia dell'escercito Romana in età imperiale* (Bologna: Patron, 1974), *Problemi Attuali di Scienza e di Cultura*, 76 (1966), pp.59–62; J. Wolski, 'Les relations de Justin et de Plutarque sur les esclaves et la population dépendente dans l'empire parthe', *Iranica Antiqua*, 18 (1983), pp.145–57; Wolski, *L'empire des Arsacides*, pp.102–4.

63. Justin 40.3.1; Lucan, *de Bell. Civ.* 8.397–401.

64. This is characteristic of easterners in Horace, *Carmina* 4.15.1, Polyaenus 7 *praef.* and Tacitus, *Annals* 12.46.1.

65. One scholar has traced the image of the lawless, meat-eating, aggressive nomad from ancient Mesopotamia to the present day: B. Shaw, ' "Eaters of flesh, drinkers of milk": The Ancient Mediterranean Ideology of the Pastoral Nomad', *Ancient Society*, 13 (1982) pp.5–31.

66. Mattern, *Rome and the Enemy*, p.66. See Justin 41.2, and Dio 40.14.4–15.6; Tacitus, *Annals* 11.10.2; Plutarch, *Crassus* 24–5 on Parthian weapons and tactics.

67. Mattern, *Rome and the Enemy*, p.67; Gabba, 'Sulle influenza reciproce degli ornamenti militari dei parti e dei romani'; and J.C. Coulston, 'Roman Parthian, and Sassanid Tactical Developments', in P. Freeman and D.L. Kennedy (eds), *The Defence of The Roman and Byzantine East: Proceedings of a Colloquium held at the University of Sheffield in April 1986*, British Institute of Archaeology at Ankara Monograph no. 8 (Oxford: British Archaeological Reports, International Series, 297, 1 & 2, 1986), pp.59–75.

68. Isaac, *Limits of Empire*, p.159.
69. B.D. Shaw, 'Rebels and Outsiders', in *CAH*, 11 (2000), chapter 12, p.374.
70. See Gruen's remarks in *Hellenistic World and the Coming of Rome*, vol. 1, p.231: 'Rome's commanders and principal officers gained their posts through election to magistracies: a matter of politics, prestige, and familial connections. Familiarity with a theater of war and knowledge of a foreign people received but slight attention and only on rare occasions.' He continues: 'The prudent general would, of course, seek the counsel of men skilled in military matters. Such skills belonged to the staff; they were not a prerequisite of the *imperator*. The lot could fall where it may upon those who had risen to the top.' Even prorogation was unusual because of the competition for military glory. Sherwin-White, *Roman Foreign Policy in the East, 168 BC to AD 1* (Norman, OK: University of Oklahoma Press, 1984), p.292, called it an 'oligarchical system of government by amateurs'.
71. All fifty-two examples are listed in Appendix One in D.J. Woolliscroft, *Roman Military Signalling* (Stroud and Charleston: Tempus Publishing, 2001), pp.159–71. See also W. Leiner, *Die Signaltechnik der Antike* (Stuttgart: W. Leiner, 1982).
72. Berchem, 'L'annone militaire', pp.117–202. D. van Berchem, 'L'itineraire Antonin et le voyage en Orient de Caracalla (214–215)', *CRAI*, 1973, pp.123–6. On mobilization against the Persians at a later date, see A.D. Lee, 'Campaign Preparations in Late Roman-Persian Warfare', in D.H. French and C.S. Lightfoot (eds), *The Eastern Frontier of the Roman Empire: Proceedings of a Colloquium held at Ankara in September 1988*, British Institute of Archaeology at Ankara Monograph no. 11 (Oxford: British Archaeological Reports, International Series, 553, 1989), pp.257–65.
73. J.P. Adams, 'Roman Imperial Army in the East', *Ancient World*, 2, 4 (1979), p.137.
74. Mattern, *Rome and the Enemy*, p.145; J.P. Adams, *The Logistics of the Roman Imperial Army* (PhD dissertation, Yale University, 1976), pp.24–9 on Corbulo and pp.11–81 on roads generally.
75. Adams, *Logistics of the Roman Imperial Army*, pp.32–4.
76. The price of building a road in Italy ranged from twenty to twenty-five sesterces per foot or somewhat more than 100,000 sesterces per mile for repair or paving of existing roads, and the cost of building new roads may have been several times that. See Mattern, *Rome and the Enemy*, p.145; T. Pékary, *Untersuchungen zu den römischen Reichsstrassen* (Bonn: R. Habelt, 1968), pp.93–6; R. Duncan-Jones, *The Economy of the Roman Empire* (Cambridge: Cambridge University Press, 1974), pp.124–5; S. Mitchell, *Anatolia* (Oxford: Clarendon Press, 1993), vol. 1, pp.126–7.
77. *CIL*, 3.199–201, cited and discussed by Isaac, *Limits of Empire*, pp.294–5. Cf. Mattern, *Rome and the Enemy*, p.145.
78. Mattern, *Rome and the Enemy*, p.146. This is also the argument of Berchem, 'L'annone militaire', pp.166–81.
79. On this aspect of Trajan's Road see S.E. Sidebotham, *Roman Economic Policy in the Erythra Thalassa, 30 BC–AD 127* (Leiden: Brill, 1986), pp.74–6. The road ran to Bostra, the legionary headquarters and capital of the new province, and the author concedes that the purpose was military. But note also Pliny, *Pan.* 29.2, on Trajan building harbours and roads to facilitate trade. Mattern, *Rome and the Enemy*, p.157.
80. Mattern, *Rome and the Enemy*, p.5.
81. See Angelli-Bertinelli, 'I Romani oltre l'Euphrate nel II secolo dC', in *ANRW*, 2, 9.1 (1976), pp.25–6, on the outbreak of the war and Verus's response, with full references.
82. The importance of terror in Roman policy is discussed briefly by Luttwak, *Grand Strategy of the Roman Empire*, pp.3–4, and Wheeler, 'Methodological Limits', part 1, pp.35–6, but Mattern, *Rome and the Enemy*, pp.116–17, was the first to bring the discussion to the fore.
83. On the forces used by Corbulo, see L.J.F. Keppie, 'Legions in the East from Augustus to Trajan', in Freeman and Kennedy (eds), *Defence of the Roman and Byzantine East*, vol. 2, pp.415–16; F. Millar, *The Roman Near East 31 BC–AD 337* (Cambridge, MA: Harvard University Press, 1993), pp.66–8.
84. *ILS*, 986.
85. The Ethiopian expedition involved vexillations from Africa and the Rhine, plus transfers of troops from Germany, Britain and Illyria, including the famous XIV Gemina which had defeated Boudicca. On Nero's projected invasion, see Pliny, *HN* 6.40 on the

transfer of troop, see Tacitus, *Histories* 1.6. Dio 63 (62) 8.1–2 states that Nero considered an Ethiopian expedition. For modern discussions of the Caucasian project, see A.B. Bosworth, 'Arrian and the Alani', *HSCP*, 81 (1977), pp.225–6; Keppie, 'Legions in the East', pp.418–19; D. Braund, 'The Causasian Frontier: Myth, exploration, and the dynamics of imperialism', in Freeman and Kennedy (eds), *Defence of the Roman and Byzantine East*, pp.31–49.

86. Keppie, 'Legions in the East', p.419.
87. Tacitus, *Histories* 2.81–2; cf. Dabrowa, 'Les rapports entre Rome et les Parthes sous Vespasian', *Syria*, 58 (1981), pp.188–9.
88. See A.M. Eckstein, *Senate and General: Individual Decision Making and Roman Foreign Relations, 264–194 BC* (Berkeley, CA: University of California Press, 1987), on foreign policy decisions in the republic. On the transition to the Principate, see R.J.A. Talbert, *The Senate of Imperial Rome* (Princeton, NJ: Princeton University Press, 1984), pp.411–25; W.V. Harris, *War and Imperialism in Republican Rome* (New York: Oxford University Press, 1979), p.107.
89. Millar, 'Government and Diplomacy', p.368.
90. Wheeler, 'Methodological Limits', part 2, p.227; A. Ferrill, 'The Grand Strategy of the Roman Empire', in P. Kennedy (ed.), *Grand Strategies in War and Peace* (New Haven, CT: Yale University Press, 1997), p.74; Eckstein, *Senate and General*, passim; Mattern, *Rome and the Enemy*, p.3 and passim.
91. On the question of whether the professional officer class (the so-called *viri militares*) were specialized in certain areas or capable of strategic planning: Wheeler, 'Methodological Limits', part 1, p.20, believed they were; Isaac, *Limits of Empire*, pp.367–87, 404–8, believed they were not. See also Campbell, 'Who Were the Viri Militares?', pp.11–31, who concludes there were no group of specialist military men with distinctive careers and special promotion; Campbell, *Emperor and the Roman Army*, pp.114, 325–47; 356–7; Millar, 'Emperors, Frontiers and Foreign Relations', pp.3–16; Ferrill, *Roman Imperial Grand Strategy*, p.40. The existence of specialization in equestrian careers has been discussed by Saller, 'Promotion and Patronage in Equestrian Careers', pp.44–63; R.P. Saller, *Personal Patronage under the Early Empire* (Cambridge: Cambridge University Press, 1982).
92. Mattern, *Rome and the Enemy*, chapter 1.
93. Millar, *Emperor in the Roman World*, pp.20, 22.
94. Mattern, *Rome and the Enemy*, pp.1–23.
95. F. Millar, *A Study of Cassius Dio* (Oxford: Clarendon Press, 1964), pp.16–27.
96. Contra Wheeler, 'Methodological Limits', part 1, p.17, where he describes the 'back to the sources' movement as 'reductionist', and part 2, p.219, on the literalist approach.
97. Mattern, *Rome and the Enemy*, pp.6–10.
98. F.A. Lepper, *Trajan's Parthian War* (London: Oxford University Press, 1948), p.106.
99. Mattern, *Rome and the Enemy*, pp.9–14; Eckstein, *Senate and General*, on the Republic.
100. Tacitus, *Annals* 13.6 on Nero's decision. His most trusted advisor is Seneca, a man who produced a substantial body of literature, much of which survives, and it is filled with images of the stereotypical ethnic barbarian. Mattern, *Rome and the Enemy*, p.79 and n.183 with references.
101. Tacitus, *Annals* 13.37
102. Ibid., 15.3.
103. Josephus, *BJ* 7.219–20.
104. Dio 77 (78).12.3.
105. Mattern, *Rome and the Enemy*, p.68; Austin and Rankov, *Exploratio*, pp.120–3.
106. I would disagree with Mattern's description of this staff as 'massive', and the word 'bureaucracy' is an anachronistic term: see *Rome and the Enemy*, p.68. The same is true of the remarks in Austin and Rankov, *Exploratio*, pp.120–3.
107. Austin and Rankov, *Exploratio*, pp.120–3; Sheldon, *Intelligence Activities in Ancient Rome*, pp.120–1, 164–70.
108. Tacitus, *Annals* 12.45.
109. Ibid., 12.45–8.
110. Ibid., 15.25.
111. Ibid., 13.6; Mattern, *Rome and the Enemy*, p.69. See A.D. Lee, *Information and Frontiers: Roman Foreign Relations in late Antiquity* (Cambridge: Cambridge University Press,

1993), pp.149–65 on 'informal channels' that transmitted intelligence.

112. Herodian 6.2.1, implying that Severus Alexander had learned of the Persian revolution only in 230, several years after it had taken place. The same is true of a revolt in Britain (3.14.1) and a revolt on the Rhine/Danube frontier (6.7.2).
113. Lee, *Information and Frontiers*, chapter 4; cf. Mattern, *Rome and the Enemy*, p.69.
114. Millar, 'Government and Diplomacy', pp.368–9; D.C. Braund, *Rome and the Friendly King: The Character of the Client Kingship* (London: Croom Helm; New York: St Martin's Press, 1984), p.94; Mattern, *Rome and the Enemy*, p.70.
115. Braund, *Rome and the Friendly King*, pp.9–21.
116. G. Brizzi, *I sistemi informativi dei Romani: Principi e realtà nell' età delle conquista oltremare (218–168 aC)*, Historia Einzelschriften no. 39 (Wiesbaden: Steiner, 1982), chapter 1.
117. Livy 23.1.2 describes them as 'families made powerful by Rome'.
118. Just such an intelligence failure happened in Britain in AD 367 during what is called 'the Great Barbarian Conspiracy'. Roman control of the province was restored only when a relief force of field army units was sent over from the continent under the command of the Count Theodosius. We are told by the fourth-century historian, Ammianus Marcellinus, 28.3–8, that Theodosius disbanded a force of locals called the *Areani* who had been used by the Romans as a scouting force. They had been paid off by the enemy, however, and betrayed the Roman army which was caught off guard. This shows, once again, the danger of using locals for intelligence gathering. This is the same problem which plagued them in Germany under Varus. Had they used Roman *exploratores*, the betrayal would not have been possible. Woolliscroft, *Roman Military Signalling*, p.80, says: 'The Areani were, then, at least a part of a regular intelligence service and they can probably be identified, if only by function, with the units of *exploratores* recorded in military inscriptions from earlier times', but this misses the point. *Exploratores* were Roman; these were foreigners.

11

THE COST OF WAR AND EMPIRE

Having seen the vague kinds of information with which the Romans worked, it is legitimate to ask whether they could have formed a grand strategy based on such limited knowledge, and used it successfully in their eastern wars. When we talk about grand strategy, we are by definition discussing policy, i.e. the capacity of a nation's leaders to bring together all the elements, both military and non-military, for the preservation and enhancement of the nation's long-term best interests, both military and non-military.[1] Strategic intelligence means the ability to know what a country's intentions and capabilities are and, if necessary, win a war against them. In looking at Rome's foreign policy toward Parthia, and seeing how often warfare played a part in their relations, one may legitimately ask what determined where and how they deployed their troops, if and when they went to war, and what the Romans hoped to accomplish by this policy with the military resources they had.[2] After all, the army of the empire was not especially large, and war on two fronts poses a dangerous problem, so getting involved in unnecessary wars was something to be avoided. As Americans ponder the wisdom of getting involved in Iraq, we might ask if the Romans ever asked themselves whether going to war in the same region was a good idea?

DEFENDING THE EMPIRE

It has been fairly well established that there is little evidence to support the traditional view that after Augustus, Rome's foreign policy was defensive and non-aggressive toward anyone, let alone Parthia.[3] Rome's behaviour against Parthia was aggressive. Several generals of the Republic planned unprovoked campaigns against the Parthians (see Chapter 1), Nero waged a major war in Armenia (see Chapter 6) and, at the end of his reign, he was planning a major offensive in the Caucasus which involved a new legion composed of Italians over six feet tall, which he called 'the phalanx of Alexander the Great'.[4] Trajan actually annexed Armenia and some (or possibly all) of Mesopotamia (see Chapter 7). Septimius Severus, the emperor responsible for the largest increase in the size of the Roman army, raised three new legions, the I, II and III Parthica, and then annexed northern Mesopotamia. Each of these wars had its contemporary critics who thought the wars were unnecessary.

Rome traditionally resolved its frontier problems by war and annexation, but the danger of concentrating troops on a single front for a war became apparent when the attempts at conquest were unsuccessful or even disastrous.[5] In the reign of Marcus Aurelius, three legions plus vexillations from others were transferred from the Rhine and Danube for Lucius Verus's eastern war of 162–166.[6] If the Augustan History is reliable on this point, trouble in the northern provinces began almost immediately. The governors of these provinces managed to put off war in their own regions while their armies were depleted to supply the eastern front.[7] In 166 or early 167, with these legions still in the East, the first invasion took place. According to Cassius Dio, 6,000 Langobardi poured over the border.[8] The plague that had broken out in the East prevented Marcus from taking any immediate military action and, probably in 170, Italy itself was invaded.

Perhaps the most graphic example of the Roman army's limitation comes under Severus Alexander. His three-pronged invasion of Parthia ended in disaster when one of the contingents was completely destroyed in battle and another was badly depleted because of the difficulty of the terrain.[9] Severus Alexander was still in Antioch planning a second campaign when news reached him of a serious invasion on the Rhine frontier, perhaps as a result of the depleted legions there, which required the army from the East.[10] After a march of 3,000 miles, he sought a diplomatic solution and offered to pay off the Germans, which caused his army to mutiny. These events illustrate an important strategic problem for the Roman army: not only was it small, but the speed of travel in antiquity was very slow.[11] Severus Alexander's march from Antioch to the Rhine probably proceeded entirely by land and would have taken over six months.[12] When journeys of this size were pre-planned, they might not be much of a problem, but when a large-scale crisis required an instant response, there could be trouble mobilizing that response when part of the army was off on campaign somewhere else. When one calculates the time it took for the emperor to receive the intelligence of the crisis (which could be great), then adds the amount of time required to transfer troops, plus the time it took to arrange supply routes, and time to locate and dispatch the proper commander, one can see why quick mobilization was impossible.[13]

Any conquest of land in the East would need to be followed up by the installation of a garrison stationed in the new territory for a substantial amount of time to prevent revolt. Only recently have scholars begun to study the Roman army as an army of occupation as opposed to a defensive force.[14] Revolts happened not only in newly conquered territories, but in provinces that were long held by the Romans. The major uprising started by Avidius Cassius in Syria is only one example, but they occurred all over the empire in spite of the myth which portrays the Principate as a peaceful period in history.[15] It took 10,000 troops just to hold a small place like Judaea, and after Hadrian's reign that number was doubled.[16] When garrisons were undersized or mismanaged, as they were in Germany, the result was a disaster like the slaughter in the Teutoburg Forest in 9 CE.[17] Even when Trajan invaded Parthia with the largest collection of Roman troops ever assembled, he could not hold what he overran. The solution to his problem was not just to bring a couple of extra legions along.[18] His problem was that there would never be enough troops to hold Parthia. The idea that expanding the empire might take more force than the Romans could safely or easily concentrate in one place may seem obvious to us, but it does not seem to have been so obvious to the Roman commanders who planned eastern campaigns. This is not to say that no other contemporary Romans got the point. In the literary sources we do encounter the idea that any further conquests would cost the Romans what they already possessed.[19]

We have a wealth of detail about the legions in Roman military records. There are the remains of rosters, duty lists, guard lists, lists of officers and soldiers in order of seniority, casualty lists, absentee lists and strength reports. Yet few exact figures have survived on the disposition of legions and troops strength.[20] Even the paper strength of a legion remains a subject of intense controversy.[21] How much Roman wars cost in manpower is not easy to calculate, nor is the question of casualties well documented in the sources.[22] Only one ancient comment on casualty figures survives, and that is a general comment by Lucian. Historians generally believe this report exaggerated casualty figures and that these figures differ from those reported in senatorial dispatches.[23] Neither type of statistic can be entirely believed. Commanders like Caesar exaggerated barbarian casualty figures in their dispatches to enhance their own reputations. Historians, too, inflated figures to capture the reader's interest or to emphasize a patriotic theme.[24] And since 'revenge' was considered a good motive for a war, exaggerating enemy casualty figures created the impression that the war was successful.

The Romans did not seem to have worried about how casualty figures played at home. Historians do not discuss the simple fact that every dead soldier probably had family back somewhere – fathers, mothers, siblings, although technically not wives and children because they could not legally marry, but there were illegitimate families. Could these people put any pressure on the government to stop a war? Probably not. Unlike an American president, the emperor did not need their vote in the next election. Too often it was the men in the field on the pointy end of the spears who paid the price for Rome's rejection of the diplomatic solution. The eminent Roman historian, Martin Goodman, captured this Roman blind spot when he wrote: 'Mass enthusiasm for war in distant countries was combined with a reluctance to admit that the human cost fell on anyone who mattered.'[25]

Of course, compared to other ancient armies, the Roman soldier enjoyed an edge in warfare through the army's ability to overcome immense logistical problems. The Romans could not only concentrate troops and import reinforcements in adequate numbers and rapidly, but they also minimized the huge losses from sickness by better managing changes in climate, food and water, and by providing above average health care, sanitation and appropriate food and clean water. We do not have specific evidence for casualties for any single Parthian war to make a comparison with modern statistics, but in every war in modern times until the Russo-Japanese War of 1905, more men died of wounds and through sickness than on the battlefield.[26] This is certainly true of the campaign under Lucius Verus. The cost in manpower was greater than we will ever know, and yet warfare remained the preferred choice.

THE COST OF WAR

Foreign conquest was expensive. The economic drain on the empire should have been an important issue in the minds of Roman decision makers.[27] We certainly have to question the 'rationality' of the economic decisions made in Roman foreign policy in the East. One scholar has speculated that the Roman aristocracy ran its empire like it ran its farms. Acting in the manner of a good paterfamilias, the emperor kept accounts that allowed him to balance income and expenses.[28] After all, the government's most important expense was the army, and it was the emperor's responsibility to balance the budget.[29] The Roman state had no tradition of deficit spending and did not borrow from the private sector.[30] If there was not enough money to pay for the army, the coinage was simply devalued. The effect this move had on inflation is highly debated.[31] The financial issue became crucial in the third century, when the need or desire to secure the loyalty of the army with money was causing the military budget to skyrocket, perhaps far beyond the state's capacity to pay for it.[32] If this situation was true in times of peace, how much more complicated did the issue become in times of war? Wars were expensive, they could exhaust the treasury, and they were a burden on the provinces.[33]

Soldiers had to be paid whether there was peace or not, but the main costs of a war were in supply and transport. These expenses fell exceptionally hard on those provinces near the theatre of operations, through which large bodies of troops had to be moved.[34] War was a strain on the regular system of supply to the army, which was complex enough to begin with.[35] Grain had to be secured at fixed prices; pack animals and cavalry horses had to be requisitioned. Starting with the reign of Augustus, provincials were required to provide carts and animals for the transport of military personnel. They also had to maintain roads. By the third century, the obligation to provide food for the troops had become institutionalized in the *annona militaris*.[36] This was probably the result of the empire being in a constant state of war in the third century. It was hard enough supplying a sedentary army stretched out along a frontier, especially a river frontier, where goods could be shipped cheaply and easily. It was quite another to provision a large concentration of troops on the move through the deserts of Parthia. The resources of a conquered people would flow to Rome through the tribute that Rome extracted from them. The annexation of a new province naturally made it liable to pay taxes. When Cappadocia was annexed and a census taken, the provincials revolted.[37] This provincial structure did not last long in the conquered territories of Parthia. Dio writes of Mesopotamia that 'it brings in very little and costs very much' (75.3.3.). The burden on the provincials can be seen in an inscription praising a local bene-factor who supported the army wintering in Ankara, and sent the one that was going to Trajan's Parthian war.[38] Numerous similar examples are attested in Greek epigraphy from the eastern campaigns of Lucius Verus, Septimius Severus, Caracalla and Severus Alexander.[39] In cases where the supplies and transports were paid for, rather than levied by requisition without payment, the expenses of war must have strained the empire's cash resources. The devaluations of the denarius under Nero and Vespasian coin-cide with peaks in the minting of Syrian tetradrachms for Corbulo's campaigns and for the Jewish and civil wars.[40] The great increase in gold output toward the end of Trajan's reign was probably the gold won in Dacia, but he spent it on his ambitious eastern campaign.

There were some economic benefits to war. Plunder, especially in the form of gold, silver and slaves, was the most obvious and well-recognized economic benefit of war – not just for the state or the generals, but apparently for the common soldier as well.[41] Corbulo, in Tacitus, *Annals* 13.39, encourages his troops with the prospect of booty, and the spoils of war formed a regular part of any triumph, although it must be said that it was not considered ethical for a general to pursue warfare only for the plunder, as Crassus was accused of doing.[42] If the war generated more expense than the booty collected, there was an economic shortfall.[43] In fact, most of Rome's lucrative wars were during the republic, not the empire.[44] Sometimes the profits from war came not from spoils but from natural resources. Mines were an important source of revenue for Rome, but Parthia never produced gold or silver in the way that Dacia and Spain did. Ctesiphon was sacked twice, and anything moveable made of precious metals was carted off, but Parthia was never occupied long enough for natural resources to be extracted.[45] The same applies to import and export taxes that were levied within the empire and its borders, and which were a substantial source of income in provinces that were occupied for longer periods, but never from Parthia.

Caracalla saw the potential of eastern wealth when he offered to marry the daughter of the Parthian king, so that 'locally grown spices of [the Parthians] and their wonderful clothes, and on the other side the metals produced by the Romans and their admirable manufac-tured goods would no longer be difficult to get'.[46] This could have been accomplished by peaceful trade. It was on the eastern trade that the Romans collected the highest taxes, a lucrative 25 per cent.[47] The Romans sometimes complained about the disgraceful drain of bullion to the east, and in part the heavy tax may have been meant to correct the trade imbalance.[48]

We can thus see that campaigns in foreign territory and the conquest of new lands were risky and difficult enterprises, and the wiser emperors had generally backed away from that option with Parthia, especially the Julio-Claudians. Augustus and his immediate successors may very well have feared a full-scale confrontation with Parthia. After all, two attempts to conquer it in the late republic had resulted in disaster, and the ghost of Crassus haunted the literature of the first and second centuries.[49] Rather than being peaceful trading partners, the Parthians were demonized as dangerous enemies. Fronto, in his *Principia Historiae*, wrote:

> Of all men only the Parthians have maintained a reputation ... as enemies of the Roman people; this is demonstrated well enough not only by the disaster of Crassus and the shameful flight of Antonius; but even under the leadership of the bravest of emperors, Trajan, a legate was killed with his army, and the retreat of the princes, withdrawing to his triumph, was by no means secure or bloodless. [Fronto, *Principia Historiae*, 2:203.][50]

Part of modern strategic thinking involves calculating the cost of a war and its affect on domestic policies. Neither Roman emperors nor historians, however, discuss the cost of the war, the revenues available, or the potential economic benefit of withdrawal. If an emperor decided to stop a campaign it would be attributed to cowardice or laziness, not a cautious economic policy.[51] The decision to withdraw from newly acquired provinces beyond the Euphrates could affect a hundred thousand lives directly, and had cultural consequences that persisted for centuries.

By recklessly attacking Parthians, all that happened was that Parthia acquired a reputation for being invincible in its own territory. This idea still persisted in the time of Cassius Dio, even though by that time Ctesiphon had been sacked three times.[52] The Parthian Empire was portrayed in Roman literature as a rival to the Roman Empire and an 'equal', which is the one thing the Roman administration never tolerated.[53] As we saw in Chapter 5, Augustus settled for a diplomatic victory over Parthia in 20 BCE by bringing back the military standards that had been lost in the disastrous expeditions of Crassus and Antony. He was wise enough not to follow Caesar's aggressive plans.[54] There were certainly covert operations going on during the reigns of Augustus and Tiberius, but these emperors were able to prevent a costly all-out war. Augustus's Parthian policy is traditionally used as the most cogent argument that he favoured a defensive foreign policy, but perhaps he knew better than to think Parthia would be a cheap victory. He would not risk the loss of face that would result from a disaster on the scale of Crassus's or Antony's.[55] Some have seen Augustus's sending out of reconnaissance teams to the East as a prelude to a full-scale invasion. These scholars believe his plans failed and thus an accord was reached with the King Phraates in 2 CE.[56] Perhaps Augustus simply realized that he could gain more by diplomacy, and that it made no sense to commit thousands of Roman lives to a campaign out of greed or simply to boost his own ego. Later, both Tiberius and Claudius wisely took actions to expressly avoid provoking a war with Parthia.[57]

It was perhaps Trajan's war that convinced the Romans that the Parthians were not as invincible as they had previously thought, but his campaign can hardly be called a success for any other reason. Campaigns into Parthia became more common after Trajan, but very little was gained for the military expenditure.[58] Ctesiphon was sacked by Lucius Verus and Septimius Severus, and Caracalla invaded Parthia twice, but not much land was annexed, and the weakening of the Parthian government just brought to power the more aggressive Persians. Later Roman emperors were criticized for their aggressive foreign policy toward Parthia. Fear of a powerful enemy may have influenced them to use diplomacy occasionally, but the peaceful route did not conform to standard Roman ideas of how to deal with their neighbours.

IRRATIONAL CHOICES

It is clear that the Romans valued conquest and domination very highly, and sometimes this caused them to make irrational decisions about expanding with the limited forces they had. Some of these campaigns, like Caracalla's, seemed irrational even to the Romans of the time. Others presumably did not. The Romans were not only motivated by the glory of conquest. The Romans considered it of the utmost importance that they maintain their image as a power that would use all the force it had at whatever cost, if it was attacked or even insulted. Susan Mattern in *Rome and the Enemy*, discusses the concept of national honour and how Roman foreign policy worked largely on the psychological, as opposed to the strictly military, level. They had a strong necessity not to appear afraid in front of barbarians. They maintained the attitude that the lack of aggressive action would undermine security by producing confidence in the enemy. They had a desire for the glory of conquest. They liked leading barbarian kings in humiliating triumphs.[59]

Modern commentators should be wary of discarding psychological needs in favour of a quest for 'scientific frontiers'. Some Roman innovations on their frontiers, like the addition of Mesopotamia, even seem counterproductive or irrational from a modern 'cartographic' perspective. They look awkward on a modern map, yet Severus claimed northern Mesopotamia was a 'bulwark for Syria'.[60] No frontier would stop the Romans if they were challenged.[61] River boundaries, for example, were honoured only as long as they served Rome's interest. Already in the time of Pompey, the Euphrates boundary (if there ever was one officially) was transgressed.[62] That the Euphrates acted as a political boundary can been seen when Augustus's grandson, Gaius, met with the king of Parthia on an island in the Euphrates, as did Tiberius's legate, Vitellius.[63] After Severus, the Tigris became the new boundary in the East.[64] Syria was the most heavily armed province in the eastern Mediterranean, and yet it never had a true network of fortifications, at least not before the end of the third century. There was also no discernible frontier line for the province of Mesopotamia in the period we are discussing, although a number of forts would appear later in the third and fourth centuries.[65]

Having large numbers of troops stationed along a frontier is no indication that Rome's intentions were defensive or offensive. When Corbulo moved troops to the Euphrates in 61 CE, it was to protect Syria from an anticipated Parthian invasion, but when Nero ordered legions to be moved 'closer to Armenia' in 54 CE, it was to prepare for a major offensive.[66] Another ambivalent example is Vespasian's reorganization of the Euphrates, which involved the annexation of two new provinces, the combination of Galatia and Cappadocia, and possibly a military presence in the Caucasus.[67] This reorganization has been interpreted by scholars as a response to a threat posed by the Alani from the northern Caucasus region, or alternatively by the Parthians, but it has also been seen as an attempt to secure strategic bases for an aggressive campaign against Armenia and Parthia.[68]

Rome's friends and allies were expected to keep their promises and maintain peace with Rome because of the terror of Roman arms. Unless the barbarians were frightened, the system would not work, and thus the peace could only be assured by the threat of Roman aggression. This mode of thinking is well attested in Roman sources. Aggression by the Romans achieves fear and compliance from the barbarians, but a weak policy results in arrogance and contempt from the enemy, thus making an invasion necessary.[69] There have been studies of the Roman use of atrocity in warfare.[70] To take just one example, there is a famous passage in Polybius when he describes the horrific sight of human and animal corpses littering New Carthage after the Romans had taken it by storm. Scipio Africanus says: 'They do this, I think, to inspire terror.'[71] Similarly, Artabanus, King of Parthia, was said to be plotting against Syria because 'he paid no penalty for Armenia'.[72] Later, another Parthian monarch requested peace because he feared Trajan, who 'proved his threats with deeds'.[73] This strategy of deterrence by terror was a Roman invention with a long history.[74]

Because of the crucial role that terror played in foreign policy, the correct response when barbarians invaded, revolted or broke treaties was at the very minimum a counter-invasion. This was supposed to result in the extraction of some formal submission to Rome and a humiliating treaty for the defeated king. Rome's responses could also include annexation and occasionally genocide.[75] When Vologases IV defeated a Roman governor in Armenia, Ctesiphon was sacked. Defence seems not the proper term to use in this situation. It was more like deterrence, or even revenge.

Of course, when all else failed, the barbarians could always be bought off. Macrinus is said to have procured peace with the Parthians for 200 million sesterces.[76] This alternative, however, often invited severe criticism. The Romans were very sensitive to the circumstances and terms of their alliances. It mattered who had asked for peace first, and what was paid to whom.[77] These status concerns could often equal or outweigh strictly military considerations. Although from a modern perspective we might argue that the Romans insisted on appointing Armenia's kings, because otherwise the Parthians might be able to station troops dangerously close to Cappadocia, in fact not a single ancient author makes that strategic argument. The Romans simply wanted their neighbours in a subservient position.[78]

To Rome, Parthia was always a special problem – sometimes a

threat and always a challenge. The deserts of Parthia held the lure of conquest and, in spite of lessons learned from the past, Roman commanders continued to lead their armies to destruction. Even when they won their battles, the cost was greater than their winnings. Roman commanders never really learned how to cope with desert conditions, where the legions lacked the essential speed and mobility. The topography of the frontier between the two empires complicated affairs since the region was either semi-arid and desert, or else dangerously mountainous as in Armenia. The Romans were never quite familiar enough with the terrain, despite repeated invasions, to succeed easily against the locals. The kingdoms of the borderlands were not valuable in and of themselves, but were important resources in the diplomatic struggle for security. Ethnographically, the needs of the Armenians themselves were generally ignored by the 'big powers', since each of them was obsessed by its own power and image. Lasting solutions were bound to fail when they did not recognize these indigenous concerns. And any lengthy stay in Parthia created logistical problems, plus the long-term problem of dealing with insurgent groups. From the point of view of strategic intelligence, Rome should have seen the impossibility of absorbing great swathes of Parthian territory. Roman intelligence never accurately portrayed the scope of the Parthian threat, which in reality was quite small.[79] The most ironic part of the story is that all Rome had to do was abandon Armenia to Parthia and there would have been no problem. The Romans could have taken whatever measures were necessary to defend their own borders and no vital interest would have been sacrificed. If there had been a strong, aggressive power on the Iranian plateau, then Armenia would have provided an avenue for attack. But Parthia was never such a power, and never could have become so without a radical transformation. Once the claim to Armenia had become historic, it could never be renounced; Roman pride would never allow it.[80]

SHOCK AND AWE, OCCUPATION AND INSURGENCIES

Never underestimate what terrorism and insurgency can do to even the largest and most powerful nation in the world. The actions of twelve men in stolen aeroplanes and some box cutters changed a nation, its foreign policy, and caused changes in a democratic society that impinge on the civil liberties of all of its citizens to this day. America's response was to wage war against not only Afghanistan but Iraq in the name of a 'war on terrorism'. We invaded Mesopotamia just like the Romans, and the war has proved no easier for us to win.

In a recent article by Robert Tomes, he suggests that the US military, not unlike the Romans, was not prepared for the kind of war it had to fight in Iraq.[81] The US used a technique called 'shock and awe', which consists of two elements: rapidity in operations and overwhelming military superiority.[82] The point is to defeat an adversary so thoroughly that you shatter their confidence and they roll over. Another term the Pentagon likes to use is 'full spectrum dominance'. Tomes points out, however, that such concepts are not well attuned to fighting a net-based counter-insurgency war, in a terrain such as Iraq, which depends upon both intelligence gathering and adaptive military organizations.[83] The US had expectations of a much quicker conclusion to the Iraq war; obviously so did the Romans.

The fact is, however, that history records few examples where occupying foreign powers fighting against counter-insurgency warfare, won decisively or even achieved their envisioned long-term results. The US Army general who suggested that 'any good soldier can handle guerrillas' vastly underestimated the task.[84] General Maxwell Taylor fell into this trap when he said 'any well-trained organization can shift the tempo to that which might be required in this type of situation'.[85] Donald Rumsfeld avoided the issue by refusing to believe there was a guerrilla war going on in Iraq.[86]

Eliot Cohen understood the situation better when he wrote: 'an intellectual comprehension of the demands of small wars does not necessarily translate into the implementation of the policies required to wage it successfully'.[87] Students of small wars and counter-insurgencies are not impressed with contemporary US military thought and its fascination with precise air strikes and the reduced need for 'boots on the ground'. The realities of counter-insurgency warfare continue to rub against mainstream US military thought and defence planning. The attractive notion of a violent but brief conflict may be as chimerical for the Americans as it was for the Romans. Once you have invaded a country, you become responsible for what happens after the victory. As one American has written: 'in post-conflict situations in which the state has collapsed, security trumps everything'.[88]

Intelligence, in these situations, is the critical enabler. Comprehensive information about the environment must be gathered and analyzed. The operational intelligence effort must remain flexible, adapting to the situation as it develops. If the Americans could not do it, how much less were the Romans able to do it, and with so many fewer men and no high-tech equipment? Some now argue that Saddam's last official orders included planning for protracted opposition to any new government and insurgency warfare against foreign troops. Could this also have been Osroes's last order? And then slowly the armed population infiltrates back, sometimes with foreign help, and picks off the invaders a few at a time. It is a tactic that has not lost its effectiveness over time.

NOTES

1. For this definition, see P. Kennedy, 'Grand Strategy in War and Peace: Toward a Broader Definition', in P. Kennedy (ed.), *Grand Strategies in War and Peace* (New Haven, CT: Yale University Press, 1997), p.5; S. Mattern, *Rome and the Enemy*, (Berkeley, CA: University of California Press, 1999), p.81. For a detailed discussion, see E.L. Wheeler, 'Methodological Limits and the Mirage of Roman Strategy', *JMH*, 57 (January 1993), part 1, pp 21–2.
2. For a simple and clear discussion of Rome's military assets, see Mattern, *Rome and the Enemy*, pp.82–8. On the Roman understanding of the psychological aspects of power and its projection, see E.L. Wheeler, 'Methodological Limits', part 2, pp.220–1.
3. Dio 54.9.1 on Augustus not thinking it was worthwhile to expand. See also 56.33.5–6 on Augustus's advice to Tiberius, and 56.41.7. The concept of 'defensive imperialism' dates back to T. Mommsen. For a summary of the arguments, see J. Linderski, 'Si vis pacem, para bellum: Concepts of Defensive Imperialism', in W.V. Harris (ed.), *The Imperialism of Mid-Republican Rome* (Rome: American Academy in Rome, 1984), pp.133–64. See also R. Werner, 'Das Problem des Imperialismus und die römische Ostpolitik im zweiten Jahrhundert v. Chri.', in *ANRW*, 1, 1 (1972), pp.501–63, which discusses Roman imperialism in the East. Mattern, *Rome and the Enemy*, p.89.
4. Suetonius, *Nero* 19.2; D. Braund, 'The Caucasian Frontier: Myth, Exploration and the Dynamics of Imperialism', in P. Freeman and D.L. Kennedy (eds), *The Defence of the Roman and Byzantine East: Proceedings of a Colloquium held at the University of Sheffield in April 1986*, British Institute of Archaeology at Ankara Monograph no. 8 (Oxford: British Archaeological Reports, International Series, 297, 1986), pp.31–49, discusses the mythological conceptions about the Caucasus region that may have fuelled Nero's ambitions. The new legion was the I Italica.
5. See numerous examples in Mattern, *Rome and the Enemy*, pp.96–7.
6. On the troops for Verus's campaign, see T.B. Mitford, 'Cappadocia and Armenia Minor: Historical setting of the *Limes*', in *ANRW*, 2, 7.2 (1980), p.1204; A.R. Birley, *Marcus Aurelius: A Biography*, rev. edn (New Haven, CT: Yale University Press, 1987), p.123.
7. *SHA, Marcus* 12.13; Mattern, *Rome and the Enemy*, p.98.
8. Dio 71.3.1a; Birley, *Marcus Aurelius*, p.249.
9. Herodian 6.5.
10. Ibid., 6.7.1–3; Mattern, *Rome and the Enemy*, p.98.
11. Mattern, *Rome and the Enemy*, p.99, who, following E. Luttwak, *The Grand Strategy of the Roman Empire* (Baltimore, MD: Johns Hopkins University Press, 1976), p.81, points out that the configuration of the empire – a hollow oblong – could hardly be less advantageous logistically.
12. M. Amit, 'Les moyens de communication et de la defense de "empire romain" ', *La Parola*

del Passato, 20 (1965), pp.216–20, calculates that the journey from Antioch to the Rhine was around 5,000 km or about 3,125 miles. It would take 200 days at fifteen miles per day. Mattern, *Rome and the Enemy*, p.99 and n.86.

13. Mattern, *Rome and the Enemy*, p.99 and n.87. On communications speeds in the empire, see R.P. Duncan-Jones, *Structure and Scale in the Roman Economy* (Cambridge: Cambridge University Press, 1990), pp.7–29.

14. See E. Le Roux and R. Étienne, *L'armée romaine et l'organization des provinces ibériques d'Auguste à l'invasion de 409*, (Paris: Centre Pierre Paris-De Boccard, 1982); and B. Isaac, *The Limits of Empire: The Roman Army in the East* (Oxford: Clarendon Press, 1992), chapters 2 and 3; Mattern, *Rome and the Enemy*, p.101.

15. On Avidius Cassius, see F. Millar, *The Roman Near East 31 BC – AD 337* (Cambridge, MA: Harvard University Press, 1993), pp.115–18; Mattern, *Rome and the Enemy*, p.101; on revolts in general, see T. Pekáry, 'Seditio: Unruhen und Revolten im römischen Reich von Augustus bis Commodus', *Ancient Society*, 18 (1987), pp.133–50, who has a chronological list of references for the period from Augustus to 161 CE. On revolt, see also Isaac, *Limits of Empire*, chapter 2; S. Dyson, 'Native Revolt Patterns in the Roman Empire', in *ANRW*, 2, 3 (1975), pp.138–75; G.W. Bowersock, 'The Mechanics of Subversion in the Roman Provinces', *Opposition et Résistances à l'empire d'Auguste à Trajan: Entretiens sur l'antiquité classique*, 33 (1987), pp.291–317.

16. Isaac, *Limits of Empire*, pp.105–7; Millar, *Roman Near East*, pp.107–8. See Mattern, *Rome and the Enemy*, pp.102–3, on the cost of holding onto Britain.

17. See R.M. Sheldon, 'Slaughter in the Forest: German Insurgency and Roman Intelligence Mistakes', *Small Wars and Insurgencies*, 12, 3 (Autumn 2001), pp.1–38.

18. H.G. Pflaum, *Les procurateurs équestres sous le Haut Empire romain* (Paris: A. Maisonneuve, 1950), pp.107–9, argues that all of Trajan's predecessors had raised new forces before annexing territory, but that while Trajan raised two legions for the Dacian War, he did not raise any for the Parthian war. He further argued that this was the reason that the new territory could not be held. As I have already argued in Chapter 7, more troops would not have worked.

19. Strabo 7.1.4; Appian, *Praef.* 7; Tacitus, *Annals* 12.32; and Tacitus, *Agricola* 14.3; Dio 68.29.1 on Trajan, and 56.33.5 on Augustus's advice to Tiberius. See Mattern, *Rome and the Enemy*, pp.104–5 for other examples of Romans speculating on how many troops it took to hold a province.

20. See, for example, R. Fink, *Roman Military Records on Papyrus* (Cleveland, OH: Press of the Case Western Reserve University, 1971). See the comments of Millar, *Roman Near East*, pp.137ff. on the Severan period.

21. Mattern, *Rome and the Enemy*, p.105.

22. On the pay of the Roman army, see Mattern, *Rome and the Enemy*, p.127; M.A. Speidel, 'Roman Army Pay Scales', *JRS*, 82 (1992), pp.87–106, and R. Alston, 'Roman Military Pay from Caesar to Diocletian', *JRS*, 84 (1994), pp. 113–23.

23. Lucian, *Quomodo hist.* 20; Mattern, *Rome and the Enemy*, p.106.

24. Mattern, *Rome and the Enemy*, p.106. See P.A. Brunt, *Italian Manpower* (London: Oxford University Press, 1971), pp.694–7 on the inaccuracy of casualty figures in the Republic.

25. M. Goodman, *Rome and Jerusalem: The Clash of Ancient Civilizations* (London and New York: Allan Lane, 2007).

26. D.L. Kennedy (ed.), *The Roman Army in the East* (Ann Arbor, MI: *Journal of Roman Archaeology*, Supplementary Series, 18, 1996), p.18.

27. Mattern, *Rome and the Enemy*, p.123, points out that the Roman elite produced no theoretical or technical treatise on any aspect of economic or fiscal activity except agriculture. On rational choices in foreign policy, see R.N. Lebow and J.G. Stein, 'Rational Deterrence Theory: I Think, Therefore I Deter', *World Politics*, 41, 2 (January 1989), pp.208–24.

28. Mattern, *Rome and the Enemy*, p.126; *SHA, Hadrian* 20.11. See the comments of Birley, *Marcus Aurelius*, p.20.

29. On the size and expense of the Roman army, see Mattern, *Rome and the Enemy*, pp.126–35.

30. Mattern, *Rome and the Enemy*, p.136; A.H.M. Jones, *The Roman Economy: Studies in Ancient Economic and Administrative History* (Totowa, NJ: Rowman and Littlefield, 1974), p.198; K. Hopkins, 'Taxes and Trade in the Roman Empire (200 BC – AD 400)', *JRS*, 70 (1980), p.122 on surplus and deficit in the imperial budget. R. Duncan-Jones, *The Economy of the Roman*

Empire (Cambridge: Cambridge University Press, 1994), chapter 1.

31. On the possible reasons for devaluing coinage, see Mattern, *Rome and the Enemy*, pp.136–40. There is almost no reference in the ancient literature on devaluation of coinage except Pliny, *HN* 33.42–6 on Nero's devaluation of the gold coinage; and Dio 77.14.3–4 on Caracalla paying off the barbarians in debased coinage. On the relation between the devaluation of coinage and inflation, see C. Nicolet, 'Pline, Paul, et la théorie de la monnaie', *Athenaeum*, n.s., 62 (1984), pp.122–9; C. Nicolet, *Rendre à César: Économie et société dans la Rome antique* (Paris: Gallimard, 1988), pp.160–2.

32. Mattern, *Rome and the Enemy*, p.140.

33. Ibid., p.142. On war's affect on the provinces, see R. MacMullen, *The Roman Government's Response to Crisis AD 235–337* (New Haven, CT: Yale University Press, 1976), p.104. A passage in Zonaras, based on Dio, praises Marcus Aurelius for not extracting money from the provinces or raising taxes for his wars.

34. K. Butcher, *Roman Syria and the Near East* (Los Angeles, CA: Getty Publications, 2003), pp.403–4; Mattern, *Rome and the Enemy*, p.143; R. MacMullen, 'The Roman Emperor's Army Costs', *Latomus*, 43 (1984), pp.571–80; MacMullen, *Roman Government's Response to Crisis*, pp.104–8 on the expenses of war. See also J.P. Adams, *The Logistics of the Roman Imperial Army* (PhD dissertation, Yale University, 1976), and J. Roth, *The Logistics of the Roman Army in the Jewish War* (Leiden: Brill, 1999); R. Ziegler, 'Civic Coins and Imperial Campaigns', in Kennedy (ed.), *Roman Army in the East*, pp.120–34 on the correlation between coin production and military campaigns..

35. Mattern, *Rome and the Enemy*, p.144. On Roman army supply, see D.J. Breeze, 'Demand and Supply on the Northern Frontier', in R. Miket and C. Burgess, *Between and Beyond the Walls: Essays on the Prehistory and History of North Britain in Honour of George Jobey* (Edinburgh: J. Donald Publishers, 1984; Atlantic Highlands, NJ: Humanities Press [distributor], 1984), pp.264–86; S. Mitchell, *Anatolia* (Oxford: Clarendon Press, 1993), vol. 1, pp.250–3. C.R. Whittaker, *The Frontiers of the Roman Empire: A Social and Economic Study* (Baltimore, MD: Johns Hopkins University Press, 1994), chapter 4, however, argues that military supplies were largely imported, sometimes over long distances, by a system of contractors and subsidies rather than purchased locally on the open market, though that system was also used.

36. Mattern, *Rome and the Enemy*, p.145; D. van Berchem, 'L'annone militaire dans l'Empire romain au IIIe siècle', *Mémoires de la Société Nationale des Antiquaires de France*, 24 (1937), Serie 8, tome 10, pp.117–202; R. Develin, 'The Army Pay Rises under Severus and Caracalla and the Question of the *annona militaris*', *Latomus*, 30 (1971), pp.687–95.

37. Tacitus, *Annals* 6.41; P.A. Brunt, 'The Revenues of Rome', in P.A. Brunt, *Roman Imperial Themes* (Oxford: Clarendon Press; New York: Oxford University Press, 1990), p.16; Mattern, *Rome and the Enemy*, p.157.

38. *IGRR*, 3.173; Mattern, *Rome and the Enemy*, p.147.

39. See M.I Rostovtzeff, *The Social and Economic History of the Roman Empire* (Oxford: Clarendon Press, 1926), chapter 8, nn. 4 and 6. S. Mitchell, 'The Balkans, Anatolia and Roman armies across Asia Minor', in S. Mitchell (ed.), *Armies and Frontiers in Roman and Byzantine Anatolia*: Proceedings of a Colloquium held at University College, Swansea, in April 1981, British Institute of Archaeology at Ankara Monograph 5 (Oxford: British Archaeological Reports, International Series, 156, 1983), pp.139–43; Mattern, *Rome and the Enemy*, p.147.

40. Mattern, *Rome and the Enemy*, p.148; R.P. Duncan-Jones, *Money and Government in the Roman Empire* (Cambridge: Cambridge University Press, 1994), p.113; D.R. Walker, *The Metrology of the Roman Silver Coinage* (Oxford: British Archaeological Reports, Supplementary Series 5, 1976), vol. 3, pp.110–12, 115–17.

41. Mattern, *Rome and the Enemy*, p.161. See Isaac, *Limits of Empire*, pp.380–2; contra Wheeler, 'Methodological Limits', part 2, p.222.

42. See Velleius Paterculus 2.46.2; Pliny, *HN* 33.134: 'nor would he be satisfied until he had usurped all the gold of the Parthians'. Seneca, *Quaes. Nat.* 5.18.10; Plutarch, *Crassus* 1.2–2.8 on his greed or *philoploutia* 'love of wealth'. See also Appian *BC* 2.18 where Crassus is motivated by lust for glory and profit. See Florus 1.46.2 on the greed of the consul Crassus, who thirsted for Parthian gold.

43. Dio 56.16.4 writes about the Pannonian revolt being expensive for just this reason. A large number of legions were maintained for it but only a little booty was taken.

44. Mattern, *Rome and the Enemy*, p.152.
45. Dio 71.2.3 on Verus's legate Cassius, and 75.9.4 on Severus. Herodian 3.9.10–11; *SHA, Severus* 16.5; see Isaac, *Limits of Empire*, pp.381–2; Mattern, *Rome and the Enemy*, p.154.
46. Herodian 4.10.4. C.R. Whittaker trans., Loeb Classical Library.
47. On the well-attested 25 per cent tax on goods crossing the border between Roman Syria and Parthia, see S.J. de Laet, *Portorium: Étude sur l'organization douanière chez les romains* (Bruges: De Tempel, 1949), pp. 335–6; Mattern, *Rome and the Enemy*, p.156; on trade through Syria, see Butcher, *Roman Syria*, pp.221–2.
48. De Laet, *Portorium*, pp.309–10, makes the argument that the tax was protectionist, to discourage the bullion drain; Mattern, *Rome and the Enemy*, p.156.
49. See D. Timpe, 'Die Bedeutung der Schlacht von Carrhae', *Museum Helveticum*, 19 (1962), pp.104–29.
50. Tacitus, *Annals* 2.2, writes 'the Parthians remember the glory of those who cut down Crassus and drove out Antony'. Official cults were established to commemorate victories over the Parthians. See R.O. Fink, 'Victoria Parthica and Kindred Victoriae', *YCS*, 8 (1942), pp.81–101. On the theology of victory, see Jean Gagé, 'La theologie de la victoire imperiale', *Revue historique*, 171 (1933), pp.1–43.
51. Herodian 4.10.3–5 on the economic benefits of cooperation. Dio 72.1.2; Mattern, *Rome and the Enemy*, p.4.
52. Dio 40.15.4; Lucan, *de Bell. Civ.* 8.368–71.
53. For Parthia in Roman literature, see M. Wissemann, *Die Parther in der augusteischen Dichtung* (Frankfurt am Main: P. Lang, 1982).
54. P.A. Brunt, 'Roman Imperial Illusions', in Brunt, *Roman Imperial Themes*, p.456.
55. E.S. Gruen, 'The Imperial Policy of Augustus', in K. Raaflaub and M. Toher (eds), *Between Republic and Empire: Interpretations of Augustus and his Principate* (Berkeley, CA: University of California Press, 1999), pp. 396–9; A. Barzanò, 'Roma e I Parti tra pace e Guerra fredda nel I secolo dell'impero', in M. Sordi (ed.), *La Pace nel Mondo Antico* (Milano: Vita e pensiero, 1985), pp.212–14; A.N. Sherwin-White, *Roman Foreign Policy in the East, 168 BC to AD 1* (Norman, OK: University of Oklahoma Press, 1984), pp.322–41, who argues about the loss of face. See also B. Campbell, 'War and Diplomacy: Rome and Parthia, 31 BC – AD 235', in J. Rich and G. Shipley (eds), *War and Society in the Roman World* (New York and London: Routledge, 1993), pp.220–8.
56. On Gaius's mission, see F.E. Romer, 'Gaius Caesar's Military Diplomacy in the East', *TAPA*, 109 (1979), pp.199–214. It included an expedition to Arabia, attested in Pliny, *HN* 6.141. On his departure, Ovid anticipates a Parthian triumph (*Ars Ama.* 1.117–228). See the conjectures of Mattern, *Rome and the Enemy*, chapter 2, about the *Parthian Stations* of Isidorus and the possibility of a full-scale invasion. Gaius's meeting with the Parthian king on an island in the Euphrates is described by Velleius Paterculus 2.101, who was an eyewitness.
57. See Chapter 5 on the evacuation of Vonones from Armenia instead of offering armed support. Tacitus, *Annals* 2.4, clearly says that if Vonones were defended by Roman forces, a war with the Parthians would have been taken up. Tacitus, *Annals* 12.49.2, and M.L. Chaumont, 'L'Armenie entre Rome et l'Iran I: De l'avènemènt d'August à l'avenèment de Dioclétian', in *ANRW*, 2, 9.1 (1976), p.81.
58. See M.G. Angeli-Bertinelli, *Roma e l'Orient: Strategia, economia, società , e cultura nelle relazioni politiche fra Roma, la Giudea, e l'Iran* (Rome: L'Erma di Bretschneider, 1979), pp.72–3 on this new phase of Roman-Parthian relations beginning with Trajan.
59. Victory over the Parthians was even personified in an official cult. See Fink, 'Victoria Parthica and Kindred Victoriae', pp.81–101.
60. Mattern, *Rome and the Enemy*, p.110; Dio 75.3.2; D. Braund, 'River Frontiers in the Environmental Psychology of the Roman World', in Kennedy (ed.), *Roman Army in the East*, pp.43–7.
61. Mattern, *Rome and the Enemy*, chapter 5, and her comments on defence, pp.109–22. See also Brunt, 'Roman Imperial Illusions', p.457.
62. On the Euphrates as a legal or political boundary, see K.H. Ziegler, *Die Beziehungen zwischen Rom und dem Partherreich* (Wiesbaden: F. Steiner, 1964), passim; E.L. Wheeler, 'Rethinking the Upper Euphrates Frontier', in V.A. Maxfield and M.J. Dobson, *Roman Frontier Studies*, 1989 edn (Exeter: University of Exeter Press, 1991), pp.506–7; Millar, *Roman Near East*, p.33, and Whittaker, *Frontiers of the Roman Empire*, pp.51–3. Philostratus, *Vita*

Apoll. 1.37, relates a fictitious but interesting story where a legate of Syria and the king of Parthia dispute control of some villages on the Euphrates.

63. On Gaius, see Velleius Paterculus 2.101. On Vitellius, see Josephus, *AJ* 18.101–2.
64. On the Tigris, see Herodian 6.2.1.
65. Butcher, *Roman Syria*, p.415; see also D.L. Kennedy and D. Riley, *Rome's Desert Frontier from the Air* (London: B.T. Batsford; Austin, TX: University of Texas Press, 1990), on all aspects of the Roman desert frontier in the East, especially p.237 for conclusions about Roman strategy on the eastern frontier. See also the comments of N. Hodgson, about there being no continuous barrier in Arabia and Syria because there was nothing to keep out except the desert and its peoples and no one had to be prevented from leaving: 'The East as Part of the Wider Imperial Frontier Policy', in, D.H. French and C.S. Lightfoot (eds), *The Eastern Frontier of the Roman Empire: Proceedings of A Colloquium held at Ankara in September 1988*, British Institute of Archaeology at Ankara Monograph no. 8 (Oxford: British Archaeological Reports, International Series, 553, 1989), p.178; M. Sartre, *The Middle East under Rome*, trans. C. Porter and E. Rawlings (Cambridge, MA: Harvard University Press, 2005), p.132. On the false notion of *limes*, see B. Isaac, 'The Meaning of "*Limes*" and "*Limitanei*" in Ancient Sources', *JRS*, 78 (1988), pp.125–47.
66. Tacitus, *Annals* 13.7.
67. On the reorganization of the provinces under Vespasian, see Butcher, *Roman Syria*, p. 43.
68. For a summary of Vespasian's innovations, see Mitford, 'Cappadocia and Armenia Minor', p.1180. On defence against the Parthians see Dabrowa, 'Les rapports entre Rome et les Parthes sous Vespasien', *Syria*, 58 (1981), pp.187–204, and 'The Frontier in Syria in the First Century AD' in Freeman and Kennedy (eds), *Defence of the Roman and Byzantine East*, pp. 93–108. This interpretation has some support from Josephus, who writes that Commagene was annexed because its king was accused of plotting with the Parthians, and Samosata, the capital of Commagene, 'lies on the Euphrates, so that it would be an easy crossing and a safe reception for the Parthians, if they intended something of this sort' (*BJ* 7.224). Suetonius also claims that it was because of frequent attacks by the barbarians that the troops were transferred to Cappadocia (Suetonius, *Vespasian*, 8.4). It was once thought that this passage supported the theory that Vespasian's primary motive was defence against the Alani, but this argument was convincingly taken apart by A.B. Bosworth, 'Vespasian's Reorganization of the North-East Frontier', *Antichthon*, 10 (1976), pp.63–78. He argues for long-range aggressive plans against Parthia. This is also the view of Isaac, *Limits of Empire*, pp.34–42. This interpretation is rejected by Campbell, 'War and Diplomacy', pp.233–4.
69. Mattern, *Rome and the Enemy*, p.119, gives a good survey of the sources.
70. On Roman atrocities, see M.M. Westington, *Atrocities in Roman Warfare to 133 BC*, (PhD Dissertation, University of Chicago, 1938).
71. Polybius, 10.15.5. W.R. Paton trans.
72. Dio 59.27.3.
73. Ibid., 68.17.2.
74. A list of examples illustrating this concept are listed by Mattern, *Rome and the Enemy*, pp.119–20, n.170.
75. When the tribes in Scotland rebelled in 210, Severus ordered his men to invade and 'kill everyone they met'. Dio 76–7, 15.1
76. Ibid., 78 (79) 27.1.
77. See Mattern, *Rome and the Enemy*, chapter 5, sec. 2.
78. Goodman, *Rome and Jerusalem*, p.71, called Rome's sovereignty over Armenia a 'political fiction'.
79. J. Wolski, *L'Empire des Arsacides* (Louvain: Peeters, 1993), pp.139–40, who points out that in the two centuries between Ventidius's victory at Gindarus and the second year of Marcus Aurelius, no Parthian was ever seen west of the Euphrates except as a hostage or a captive.
80. So argued J.G.C. Anderson, in *CAH*, 10, 9.4, p.260.
81. R.R. Tomes, 'Schlock and Blah: Counter-Insurgency Realities in a Rapid Dominance Era', *Small Wars and Insurgencies* 16, 1 (March 2005), p.40, on whether the US force was large enough, and pp.48–52 on the intelligence requirements.
82. H.K. Ullman and J.P. Wade introduced the term into defence discourse with a widely read article in a monograph, *Shock and Awe: Achieving Rapid Dominance* (Washington,

DC: National Defense University Press, 1996), and more recently H.K. Ullman and J.P. Wade, *Rapid Dominance* (London: Royal United Services Institute for Defence Studies, 1998).

83. Tomes, 'Schlock and Blah', pp.52–5. On the lack of a native-intelligence apparatus in Iraq, see G. Packer, *The Assassins' Gate* (New York: Farrar, Straus and Giroux, 1972), p.303.
84. Army Chief of Staff George Decker, cited in Tomes, 'Schlock and Blah', p.39.
85. Ibid., Tomes, p.39.
86 Quoted in Packer, *Assassins' Gate*, p.302.
87. Tomes, 'Schlock and Blah', p.39.
88. Ibid., p.43 and n.29, quoting Larry Diamond, Senior Advisor to the US-led Coalition Provisional Authority in Iraq, in *Foreign Affairs*, 83, 5 (2004), p.37.

12

CONCLUSION
BLIND INTO BABYLON

Parthia was unique among the lands bordering the Roman Empire because it was not just a group of tribal nomads, but a large kingdom with a long and distinctive tradition of civilization, coherent government, urban living and an imperial history of domination over subject peoples.[1] There was little in the Roman experience that could prepare them for dealing with such a strong adversary over a long period of time, both militarily and diplomatically. Parthian armies were able to inflict unavenged defeats on Rome and even to invade Roman territory, albeit in a very small way. On the other hand, even Tacitus could accurately identify some of the characteristics that limited Parthian military strength: dislike of distant campaigns, their inability at sieges, an incompetent commissariat, and internal dissentions.[2] Rome had to make some sort of accommodation with the power that controlled Mesopotamia and the Iranian plateau. Both sides were aggressive empires, and we are not trying to place the blame for what happened entirely on Rome.[3] We are simply saying that if one is going to pursue an aggressive foreign policy, one should at least base that policy on adequate intelligence. Too often, however, Roman leaders sought domination, trying to imitate the glory of Alexander the Great with very little hard intelligence on the enemy.[4]

What did the Romans gain by attacking Parthia? Rome could have maintained a friendly, peaceful Parthia as a buffer state to protect trade routes to China. Surely the wealth of Palmyra was a good example of what trade between the two empires could produce. Instead, Rome continued to produce glory-seeking militarists who dreamed about crossing the Euphrates and conquering the East. Sir Mortimer Wheeler believed the conflict between Rome and Parthia was 'as inevitable as it was insoluble'.[5] Perhaps he was correct in the sense that Rome would always see Parthia as a threat, and attacking it to maintain Roman honour and dignity was too much a part of the Roman mindset to resort to simple diplomacy. Could the

Romans have achieved an orderly coexistence with Parthia in any other way? Why was diplomacy not used more often?[6] What were these wars really about? Was the Roman government concerned with the defence of Roman provincials and security or were they just posturing and keeping face? What combination of factors in Roman society and government made war so attractive in the imperial period, and what factors in Roman society made settling affairs in the East by invasion and warfare from 53 BCE onwards such a frequent choice? Did they really believe that Rome could do what Alexander had done?

We may also legitimately ask whether warfare was the best way to achieve the ends Rome wanted, and if war was the chosen route, how much did Rome know about its enemy? We have argued that the Romans did not have enough of a strategic overview to realize the Parthian Empire was too large, and its strong native cultures too strong, for long-term integration into the Roman cultural and political spheres. Even with the feudal structure of the Parthian government and their constant internal squabbling, they were still resilient and strong enough to prevent their successful annexation as new Roman provinces.[7] With a large powerful imperial army, it was possible for the Romans to overrun a great deal of territory; but the problem then becomes, what does one do with it? Because if the native population decides you are going to leave, you will eventually leave.

The Romans insisted on attacking this threat on their eastern border, but scholars have questioned how big a 'threat' this really was. Roman honour motivated many a Roman–Parthian conflict. Tacitus recognized that chauvinism and emotion, which often caused such action, were more important than, and not always identical with, any rationale that can be constructed after a war. Usually a challenge to Roman 'prestige' came from Parthian intervention in a borderland or client principality, not a direct attack on Roman territory. In reality, Parthia was not a well-organized power capable of conducting sustained war or a formidable offence. They lacked the ability to organize a logistical system sophisticated enough to support sustained warfare against the Romans.[8] Parthia, in fact, could never pose a substantial threat to the Roman Empire because of its social organization, its frequent palace revolts, the quarrels among the clans, the separatist tendencies of the vassals, its lack of military infrastructure, and the absence of strong central control. Even when they were not wholly incapacitated by domestic feuds or civil strife the Parthians were hampered by the absence of a standing army and by their ignorance of the art of siege warfare.[9] And yet the Romans continued to use the threat of an eastern invasion to motivate their foreign policy. The Romans could have assumed a more tolerant attitude, and when they did use diplomacy, the policy usually bore fruit. It was diplomacy that caused Phraates IV to restore the lost standards to Augustus and, later, fearing the assassination of his sons, to send them as political hostages to Rome for their protection and to demonstrate his good will toward Rome. At least some Roman foreign policymakers realized that an entente between the two powers might benefit them both.[10]

While there is no lack of sources that stress either the profitability or the glory of victory, it is very rare to find a statement insisting on the need to defend the empire. War was not fought for the benefit of the provincials. On the contrary, it was taken for granted that provinces would suffer just because of the passage of the Roman army through it.[11] The Roman emperor's position did not depend on the goodwill of the civilians in the provinces. His position did, however, depend on being able to fight off a foreign ruler with a large army. Any military victory would strengthen his position.[12] Nero's involvement in the East was symptomatic of this mindset. The Parthians and Armenians had not been in conflict for some time, but when Vologases became king, a conflict arose. Vologases tried to impose his brother on the Armenian throne; Rome tried to stop him. The elements of this showdown are telling. The Parthians gambled that the new boy emperor would not seek a military solution. They were wrong. In spite of the fact that Roman forces on the frontier were inadequate, and corrupt Roman officials proved incompetent during the emergency, Nero preferred the military option. The fact that the emperor became jealous of his most competent general and executed the man who brought him victory shows Nero would rather risk mediocrity than be surrounded by dangerous competence.

With the exception of the territory west of the Khabur River that remained permanently in Roman hands, there was not much territorial expansion as a result of all these wars. Rome was unable to expand its eastern frontier significantly. Therefore, a strong truth lies in the myth: the faults of the Roman army exposed at Carrhae, such as its vulnerability to cavalry on open ground, were never fixed, and even recurred, as in the much later catastrophe at Adrianople against Gothic cavalry. Lucius Verus's campaign of 163–166 CE was more successful militarily than the others, but he lost much of his army to the plague, and his soldiers carried it west. In 195 CE, Septimius Severus tried twice to subdue the stronghold of Hatra and failed both times. All of these adventures were unprovoked, generated expensive campaigns and a great loss of Roman lives, but no territorial gain. Hatra remained merely an outpost that did not stay long in Roman hands.[13] One of the most striking similarities of all these campaigns is the constant lack of good intelligence. Dio explains that when Septimius Severus was campaigning in Mesopotamia he was chronically 'short of information'. And yet this was after the campaigns of so many Roman generals and emperors before him.[14]

ROMAN GRAND STRATEGY

While there is certainly evidence for strategic thinking among the Romans, it is difficult to detect any 'Grand Strategy' in the sense of an integrated effort towards a political end other than the broad imperial desire to extend their power *sine fine*. Aelius Aristides, in his speech to the Romans, correctly summed up this attitude: 'the emperor does not reign within fixed boundaries, nor does another dictate to what point your power reaches'.[15]

C.R. Whittaker was correct when he wrote: 'I do not hold so low an opinion of Roman intelligence as to suggest that they never attempted to anticipate trouble. But it is hard to find evidence of how this was translated into grand strategic military disposition.'[16] The image of the Romans as expert military strategists in the modern sense of the word is illusory, and the idea that Rome went into Parthia to rectify borders or create a 'scientific frontier' is incorrect. This is a modern concept more appropriate to the Pentagon than Rome. This position has been argued quite convincingly already by Susan Mattern, Benjamin Isaac, C.R. Whittaker and John Mann, among others.[17] To attribute Roman success to some superior insight or expertise, some science of war or administration is a trend contradicted by the ancient sources themselves that say glory and honour were a Roman commander's main motivation. Modern historians wish to see the Romans as expert strategists tracing defensible borders and buffer zones on the well-plotted topography of Europe and Asia. They believe that the Romans could evaluate, as we do, the political and military strengths and weaknesses of their enemies, collect intelligence, track enemies and allocate financial resources to meet their strategic goals. This idea is a chimera.[18] That is not to say, however, that the Romans could not calculate what each invasion of Parthia might mean in logic, cost and benefit. Even ancient authors criticized uncontrolled expansion by the Romans, and thus we too can question the wisdom of successive invasions that produced little but cost much.[19] Certainly one sees this in the case of Trajan's Parthian adventure.

There was no 'scientific frontier or preclusive border'. The Romans went as far as they could whenever they could. No river, no mountain range, desert or djebel was going to stop them any more than it could have stopped the Parthians if they had wanted to invade Roman Syria. Even Edward Luttwak himself, creator of the Roman Grand Strategy myth, had to admit that there were no permanent borders on the eastern frontier of the Roman Empire. The political boundary of the empire was irrelevant as a concept, and the military boundary was never organized as a line of defence.[20] The forces in the East were mostly used as a police force that quelled rebellions and enforced the collection of tribute.[21] That is why all the garrisons were in cities and not in the desert along some imaginary line in the sand. Luttwak wrote that the system of imperial security on the eastern front was based on three elements: first, a chain of client states; second, the buffer state of Armenia; and third, the four strong legions in Syria. Rome had all these in place when Trajan took office. How was trying to absorb the first and second, and getting a large part of the third killed, going to make Rome safer? Even Luttwak admits that the frontier Trajan inherited was much neater than the one the Julio-Claudians had to defend. Luttwak justifies Trajan's behaviour by saying the frontier was 'highly unsatisfactory' because it could not support the 'substantial forces needed to meet any high-intensity threat.' But *there were no high intensity threats*. If anything, Parthia was weaker and more divided than ever when Trajan invaded it. The Parthians had never been expansive at the expense of the Romans. Luttwak himself writes that Trajan's Parthian war was not 'a limited border-rectification offensive, nor was it usually considered to have been a purely rational enterprise entirely motivated by strategic considerations'.[22]

The truth is that Roman foreign policy was much simpler than modern strategists have portrayed it. They were not motivated by security derived from lines on a map. Roman society derived status and security from its perceived ability to inflict violence on other people. Maintaining image and achieving 'national honour' were their most important policy goals, and in this view, Roman strategy was coherent over a remarkably long period of time. In a world where the technology and intelligence necessary for our modern types of military strategy were lacking, their approach was quite effective. In the arena of international relations, Rome did not play a complex geopolitical chess game as Americans do now, but what we do share is their competition for status, with much violent demonstration of superior prowess, aggressive posturing, and terrorizing of the opponent. The value that the Romans attached to honour, which was maintained by conquest, terror, and retaliation, is the only way to explain their repeated and futile attempts at expanding their empire at the expense of Parthia, and their seemingly disproportionate investment of force, money and manpower in trying to retain territories that ultimately could not be held.

Rome gloried in the expansion of its empire because it signified the triumph of the *patria* and of Roman ideals. The Romans believed that they were superior to the people they had conquered, and that this superiority justified Roman hegemony over the entire world. The Romans had a strong necessity not to appear afraid before so-called 'barbarians', and they liked doing things like dragging foreign kings in humiliating triumphal processions. Each time the Romans failed in Parthia, a conquest there simply became more attractive to upcoming glory-seekers and fortune hunters. The cleverest Roman was Augustus, who chose to negotiate for the lost standards of Crassus rather than fight the Parthians. His policy was to consolidate an over-extended frontier with twenty-five legions at his disposal (after Varus lost three), and to develop a method of managing remote provinces efficiently. Yet even Augustus's success did not shield him from criticism for not choosing the more popular 'war option'.

WHY SHOCK AND AWE DOES NOT WORK

Rome had no grand strategy concerning how to fight the Parthians; it possessed only the single idea of dominating them. The grasping and ambitious Romans operated not by conquering and occupying the Parthians as much as by striking terror into their hearts, degrading their people to the condition of obsequious dependency, and putting them at the will and pleasure of 'the world's lords' (*Romanos rerum dominos* – Virgil, *Aeneid* 1.282). Rome saw its job as implementing, enforcing and sustaining peace, even if it meant killing everyone to accomplish it.

War, however, has dimensions beyond winning battles and counting dead enemies. The people you conquer and occupy have eventually to back your cause.[23] As the Emperor Trajan discovered, overrunning Mesopotamia was not difficult; it was what happened afterwards that caused the problems. The uprisings, the insurgencies, the assassinations and the anti-Roman reactions caused as much destruction as the battles themselves. This has been the hardest lesson the Americans have had to learn since invading Iraq. Fighting on the battlefield is only part of the story. The American-led invasion of Iraq became 'everything it was not supposed to be: a prolonged, protracted, and phenomenally expensive war'.[24]

The Romans did not have the manpower necessary to occupy Mesopotamia and put down all the insurgencies, and even the Americans, with so much more manpower, equipment and technology, are still having a difficult time of it.[25] The operational intelligence effort must remain flexible, adapting to the situation as it develops. Did he tell his men to disappear into the hills, take off their uniforms, and wait until the Romans became overconfident?

In the modern world, the whole point of having power is to increase the security and stability that becomes the foundation of peace and prosperity and allows people to improve their lives.[26] For Rome, power was used to gain glory for the empire and its emperor. The Romans thought less about negotiating peace than we do. Could Rome have developed tools other than the military force for managing a crisis in Mesopotamia? In point of fact, Rome had many weapons in its diplomatic arsenal that it could have used in place of direct warfare. Many of these techniques were used with great success by some of the early Julio-Claudians. The following paragraphs describe just a few of them.

COVERT ACTION AND CLANDESTINE OPERATIONS

The official stated Roman attitude on covert action was that they did not employ such methods, and they remained masters at presenting themselves as straightforward and opposed to anything underhanded. It was always the foreigners, such as the Armenians or Parthians, who were portrayed as untrustworthy.[27] Yet, in just this limited geographical area of the eastern border, and a limited time period of the first few emperors, we see some classic examples of covert activity.

1. *Political influence operations.* The Romans secretly influenced key governmental leaders by providing advice and counsel to senior individuals in foreign countries, whether they were pretenders to the Armenian and Parthian thrones or officials within the courts of those states.

2. The Romans developed and *assisted contacts in foreign countries*, identified future leaders and advanced the careers of those men. By keeping the Parthian heirs to the throne in Rome, they would treat them well, as befitting royalty, but also train them to the Roman way of thinking and make them sympathetic to the Roman point of view. This sympathy usually remained with these men for the rest of their lives, making them sometimes unacceptable to their own people when they were sent back to Parthia. The Romans also placed agents at the Parthian court, such as the slave girl Musa who eventually became not only queen, but a woman who guided events on the Parthian throne for decades. Perhaps it would be too much of a pun to suggest this as an example of 'seeding'.

3. The Romans *influenced political parties*, usually nationalist factions that affected the internal balance of power and political decisions in Armenia and Parthia for over 300 years. Considering how poor our sources are, the fact that we cannot turn up very much evidence for bribing factions and influence-buying among the Parthian and Armenian nobility is not unusual. We can be sure that much more went on behind the scenes, about which we know nothing. Bribery is, after all, something done in secret. Since the Parthians and Armenians did not have political parties or representative governments, there was no way to influence 'elections'. But the Romans manipulated whatever factions existed and saw to it that candidates about to be appointed to the throne would be favourable to Rome. Claudius, for example, fomented internal discord and rivalry in Parthia and established the Roman protectorate over Armenia in the classic way by reinstating a friendly client king. The Romans were constantly in touch with any leader, heir or faction that felt it could further the interests of Rome. This type of influence-buying, of course, went both ways. Parthian kings chose different sides in the Roman civil war between Pompey and Caesar. The same split occurred later between Antony and Octavian. One might call

this political 'patronage' a form of covert support. The instigation of civil unrest was used by the Parthians during the Roman civil war, and by the Romans against the Parthians always.

4. The use of *propaganda* was common in times of cold war. Although the ancient world did not have our access to mass media, they had a very acute sense of what people should know and when they should know it. News of victories was sent by constant dispatches, then 'published' in coins, inscriptions, triumphal arches and proclamations. Augustus's 'victory' over Parthia by recovering the standards was a publicity coup more than a military triumph, and the groundwork had been laid by years of secret negotiations, blackmail, kidnapping and other techniques that were never displayed on the public monuments for public consumption. The Romans realized that an announcement about the intent to use force could be just as powerful as an actual Roman army on the march. No doubt a great deal of disinformation was slipped into such announcements. As Crassus discovered, marching on Parthia without the support of Roman public opinion was a dangerous undertaking. Most commanders knew how to whip up popular support for a foreign war. Cleopatra herself became victim of a media blitz created by Augustus to blacken her name and turn the tide of public opinion in favour of a war against Antony and his 'foreign queen'.[28]

5. *Paramilitary and covert operations* have less of a place in the Roman repertoire simply because they were able to use overt force without the fear of reprisal.[29] They did, however, identify and train foreigners, namely Parthians and Armenians, who could be used in their own army. Whenever a high-ranking Parthian defected from the army he could be sure that the Romans would assign him to lead a troop of auxiliaries composed of his own countrymen and trained by the Romans.[30]
The Romans provided military advice, tactical planning and the physical protection of the leaders it placed on the thrones of foreign countries. Since the Armenian throne was so hotly contested, it was standard Roman practice to leave a detachment of 2,000 troops as a bodyguard for their appointees. The Romans would be less likely to provide training for foreign troops that would be used against them some day.

6. The Romans provided *safe havens* for every political refugee, pretender to the throne, collateral relative or high ranking traitor coming out of Armenia or Parthia. The Romans never missed

an opportunity to capitalize on personnel who could prove useful politically or militarily. What training Rome gave them is impossible to say. There were times when the troublemakers they helped caused even more trouble than the Romans bargained for, as in the case of Vonones, whom they had to deport to another part of the empire. Corrections could be made by secret delegations from the Parthians coming to Rome to negotiate a better settlement, as happened with Tiberius in 35 CE.[31]

7. *Wet Operations.* The Romans were not above killing pretenders to the throne, if necessary to affect a succession or prevent one. Caesar's son, Caesarion, and Antony's grandson, King Ptolemy of Mauretania, were dispatched with impunity. The same rules applied to foreigners. As we saw in Chapter 7, when Parthamasiris was placed on the Armenian throne without Rome's permission, Trajan marched in, arranged a meeting with him in the Roman camp and, as he was being escorted away, the leader of the Roman cavalry ordered him to reign in his horse and then killed him.[32]

8. *Using business contacts.* Merchants and traders operating between the two empires could also act as a way to nurture prosperity rather than war. Each side feared that merchants would engage in espionage under the guise of trade. Commerce was regarded by both sides as a means of receiving information as well as goods. Officially it was the policy of both Parthia and Rome to restrict the interchange of merchants and merchandise to a few places close to the frontier. Cultural contacts with each other may have been a way to foster understanding rather than hostility. Yet Roman traders did not go to Ctesiphon, and Parthian traders did not go to Antioch.[33]

For an empire with no centralized intelligence service, no State Department, and no political scientists, the Romans could still have written a book about the use of covert action.

DIPLOMACY

What Rome could not take by force, it had to negotiate by diplomacy. The Romans were capable of using diplomatic channels to solve their crises quite effectively. An outward observance of titles and tokens of respect toward each other was strictly observed unless insult and open warfare were sought. Symbols, which communicated image, were very important in such a system. The reception of embassies from very far away was perceived as an important proof of Rome's power. There was a constant exchange of embassies throughout the period we have been discussing, some of them quite secret.[34] Diplomatic intrigue was a commonplace occurrence in foreign affairs. Such techniques were used as a means of fomenting the disaffection of leading Parthian magnates and thus getting more pro-Roman candidates on the throne.[35]

There was a constant flow of embassies between Rome and its eastern allies. Kingdoms like Commagene and Cappadocia began as clients to Rome, but eventually were annexed and subjected to a Roman governor. Others, like Iberia and Bosporus, never were. Commagene was absorbed, released and reabsorbed. Tribes beyond the frontiers often owed tribute or alliance to Rome, and if they revolted they had to be reduced to submission. Osrhoene and Adiabene revolted and besieged Nisibis which provoked Severus's war of conquest.[36] Nisibis had never been formally annexed, but a Roman garrison apparently remained there after Verus's campaigns.[37] Garrisons were often placed beyond the frontier to support a Roman nominee to the throne as in Armenia.[38] There is even some evidence for a Roman presence in Iberia and Albania in the Caucasus Mountains under the Flavians.[39]

All too often, however, the Romans resorted to force even before exhausting the diplomatic option. This suggests that peace was not always the object of Rome's foreign policy. It is not the job of diplomacy to buy lasting solutions but simply to buy time and prevent more costly open warfare. For a great deal of the time there prevailed between Rome and Parthia what we would call today peaceful coexistence. But it must also be said that much of the time this policy did not seem to have worked. The pattern was constantly shifting.

Diplomacy was not an instant solution. Diplomacy, in the Roman mind, was more of a tool with which to communicate the dominance of Rome and the deference of its neighbours and allies. The Roman Empire was surrounded by a complex net of alliances and treaties. The treaties were usually sought by the neighbouring territories, and the terms were dictated by Rome. Rome extracted tribute payments, hostages, promises of alliance, sometimes the contribution of troops, the return of prisoners and deserters, and an elaborate show of obeisance to Rome. This might include accepting a king appointed by Rome, as in the case of Armenia. Pretenders were usually sent with a Roman military escort. Appian notes that the Romans 'give kings to a countless multitude of other peoples without binding any of them to their rule'.[40]

As two powerful empires whose security needs required them to deal with each other, Rome and Parthia had a number of deterrence techniques that they could use to prevent all-out war.[41]

1. *Direct Deterrence*: Deterrence to discourage attack against one's own territory. Either side might use a show of force to scare the other side into backing down.
2. *Extended Deterrence*: Deterrence to discourage attack against allies. Small-land actions in adjacent provinces, such as Armenia, might solve the problem of having Rome and Parthia fight each other. Alliances with third countries were used by both sides. The Romans used the small kingdoms bordering Parthia in their diplomatic game. Small nations trying to escape from foreign dominance by Parthia that went to Rome for help, however, often found themselves dominated by their new ally. Being Rome's ally had a price tag.
3. *General Deterrence*: This form of deterrence took the form of general political and military competition in which the possibility of war is present but neither party is actively engaging in military confrontation. Building fortifications might come under this heading. The frontier between Rome and Parthia, however, was not like some ancient Maginot line. Roman frontier defences in the first three centuries were weak, and it was not difficult for either side to rapidly capture important cities when caught in an all-out war.[42] In some places like Dara (Roman) and Nisibis (Sasanian) there were fortresses facing each other across a frontier line by the third century, but no one would try to march an army south of that line into the desert. Defences built in that desert would have been useless.

Deterrence is ultimately about intentions, and not just estimating enemy intentions, but influencing them. Before attacking another power, one must consider the utility of the attack:

1. The value of the war objectives – the expected benefits to the aggressor (booty, overcoming the status quo if it is unfair).
2. The costs – those the defender imposes by resistance (denial) and counteraction (punishment) as well as costs that are independent of defender action.

3. The probabilities of the defenders' various responses – the chances of incurring costs.
4. The possibility of achieving the war objectives given each possible response – the chances of accruing benefits.

Deterrence is a two-way proposition. While the defender is contemplating how to deter action by the attacker, the attacker is examining the benefits and costs associated with defender action.

ANCIENT DETERRENCE

Of course, what we have just described is a deterrence doctrine developed for the Cold War and nuclear deterrence. There was no atom bomb, however, threatening the Romans or Parthians. All-out war did not mean mutually-assured destruction. The biggest mistake we can make is assuming that the Romans thought like us, in modern strategic terms. The glory associated with conquest and victory was two-fold; it brought glory to successful individuals, and honour and dignity to Rome as a state. They seem to have perceived foreign relations as a competition for honour and status between Roman and barbarian peoples. By proving its superior force through war and conquest, Rome extracted deference and reverence from other nations who then remained submissive, and refrained from revolt or attack. This was the way the empire maintained its security.[43] Any sign of weakness on Rome's part, such as a show of deference to a foreign people, or failure to avenge a defeat in war or to punish a revolt with sufficient ferocity, were considered invitations to disaster. For these reasons the Romans sometimes seem to react very aggressively to apparent minor breaches of treaty, to exaggerate the threat posed by rivals, and to respond to crises with conquest or even attempted genocide, rather than with the use of diplomacy. They always insisted that their concerns were for security even when they had an obvious military superiority over the enemy. They placed a higher value on victory, conquest and humiliation of the enemy than on negotiated settlements that might leave the vanquished with some shred of dignity and perhaps prevent another war.

The rules of ancient deterrence were therefore somewhat different from modern techniques. The system was completely lopsided in Rome's favour and Rome never recognized parity with another power.[44] Among its elements were:

1. The use of subsidy payments as a popular diplomatic tool, but only if the Romans were receiving the payments. Rome never paid off the enemy to get rid of them. Cash gifts given to the enemy were acceptable when Rome was clearly in a position of superior status.[45]
2. Rome should never offer to make peace first.
3. Any withdrawal from conquered territory was unacceptable.
4. Rome reserved the right to crown kings.
5. Elaborate show of obeisance to Rome was expected, such as worshipping Roman standards or images of the emperor.
6. The enemy should give hostages as pledges of good faith.[46] The Romans never gave hostages in return during the Principate, as far as we know.
7. Rome should be in a position of judgment and authority over the enemy and should not appear to be negotiating with barbarians on equal terms.[47] Thus under Trajan, Pliny (*Pan.* 12.2–3) tells us 'enemies asked to supplicate, we grant or deny them – both from the majesty of the empire. They are grateful if they prevail, they do not dare complain when we deny them.' Under Domitian, in contrast, Rome's enemies 'would not even enter into a truce except on equal terms [*aequis condicionibus*] and would accept no laws unless they gave them' (Pliny *Pan.* 11.5).
8. Any prisoners, spoils, or other symbols of Roman military defeat, such as captured military standards, should be returned.[48]

The Romans interpreted it as rank cowardice when Macrinus came to terms with the king of Parthia after a defeat for the notorious price of 200 million sesterces. He restored a hostage – the king's mother – to Tiridates, and he returned the spoils that his predecessor, Caracalla, had captured. Dio even tells us he may have promised to restore parts of Cappadocia as well.[49]

It was important that any military defeat, breach of treaty, or revolt, which would involve a loss of face for Rome, thus inviting more of the same, should be repaid vigorously and aggressively, with invasion, conquest and the humiliation, or even attempted annihilation, of the enemy. The Romans showed extreme touchiness on such issues, so that sometimes even 'planning' or 'being about to' attack was punishable by total conquest.[50] Thus Vespasian annexed Antiochus of Commagene's territory based on the (untrue) report that he was conspiring with Parthia.[51]

Whenever there was a breakdown between Rome and Parthia it was because of the withdrawal of one or more of the deterrence factors by one or the other. It was not unusual for one or the other party to ignore the danger signals, perhaps because they had found themselves in a similar situation before but had somehow got themselves out of it. It is actually not unusual or impossible to start an accidental war.

Deterrence based on punishment was a valid policy choice for the Romans. Threatening to destroy large portions of an opponent's population, urban infrastructure and industry was perfectly acceptable. A corollary to this is deterrence based on denial, i.e. the ability to convince the enemy that he will not attain his goals by use of force. Both punishment and denial are important aspects of deterrence theory even today, when effective conventional deterrence relies on both mechanisms.[52]

Although the superiority of the Romans was ultimately a superiority in military strength, the most essential element in this system was the state of mind of the enemy. Rome's empire depended on its ability to assert and enforce an image of itself as awesome and terrifying. In this way, Rome as a state acted more like Homeric heroes or Mafia gangsters than statesmen.[53] Thus Roman diplomatic protocol was designed to impress. The general should be surrounded by a splendid and terrifying military entourage.[54] Peace was supposed to be requested by a defeated and frightened enemy, never by Rome.[55] In modern terms diplomacy implies treating great powers as equals (using round tables). In Rome, the point was to prove their own superior status, backed up by military power. Rome claimed respect based on a superiority of force. The only feelings Rome hoped to inspire in the enemy were awe and terror. If an emperor responded to a Parthian crisis with diplomacy rather than force, he would be mocked. Thus Herodian describes with contempt the first efforts of Severus Alexander to deal with the Persian monarch Ardashir. Severus Alexander had little experience with warfare and is described as loving luxury and peace. Thus his first reaction to the crisis was to send an embassy with a letter in the hopes of heading off a battle (6.2.3). Ardashir predictably ignored this overture (6.2.5). The proper procedure for the emperor would have been to reduce the enemy to a submissive state with a military defeat, then to wait for him to offer peace. Both Tacitus and Suetonius are critical of Tiberius for preferring to solve problems by diplomacy rather than by force.[56] It is thus not surprising that Augustus advertised his diplomatic success over the Parthians as a military victory. He used the slogan 'standards recaptured' on his coins and boasted that he had forced the Parthians to return the spoils and standards of three Roman armies, and to seek friendship of the Roman people as suppliants.[57] This did not impress Dio Cassius, who wrote: 'He [Augustus] received them [the standards] as if he had defeated the Parthian in some war.'[58] Even modern historians often remained unimpressed. Theodore Mommsen wrote that 'bloodless victories are often feeble and dangerous'.[59] The legate Vitellius, in the reign of Caligula, was praised because he stopped Artabanus at the Euphrates, forced him into negotiations and made him sacrifice to the images of Augustus and Gaius. Then a peace was made to the advantage of the Romans and he received the king's children as hostages. The story behind the events that Dio describes displays the sort of situation that Rome felt was a threat to its security. Artabanus had never been punished for his aggression in Armenia. Because he had not suffered any Roman retaliation, he became arrogant and attacked Syria. Both Tacitus and Dio perceived Rome's relationship with Parthia as one where a show of military weakness, usually on the issue of Armenia, led to *superbia* on the part of the enemy and ultimately to danger. Parthian *superbia* could only be controlled by inflicting terror.[60] Of course, this attitude on the part of the Romans seemed like *superbia* to the Parthians.[61] Tacitus seems consistently to represent Rome and Parthia as engaged in this sort of competition for status with each other.

It is for these reasons that discussing the Armenian questions in the Pentagon jargon of 'buffer zones' or 'springboards for attack' does not really get to the heart of the relationship between these two empires.[62] Rome and Parthia thought in terms of '*decus*' (honour or face).[63] Thus Tacitus could write that Corbulo 'considered it worthy of the greatness of the Roman people to regain what had been acquired by Lucullus and Pompey' (*Annals* 13.34), while the Parthian king wanted to avenge the dignity of the Arsacids. Both were motivated by a desire to recapture the traditional possessions of glorious ancestors.[64] In the story of Rome's conflict with Parthia, issues of honour, disgrace and deference took precedence over a search for 'scientific frontiers'.

What could have been achieved if Rome had responded to Parthia with the appropriate mix of diplomatic and military initiatives? There are outcomes of these wars that were positive, but outside the scope of this book. In between the wars we have just discussed were periods when diplomacy worked, and in these times the eastern frontier was as much a bond as a barrier. Places like Dura Europas, Hatra and Palmyra created a culture that was a mix of Greek classical roots, Parthian culture and Roman architectural techniques. This frontier culture had a character of its own and was capable of vigorous development and, at its best, of considerable creative originality.[65] With every wave of invasion came a new influx of artistic ideas. J.B. Ward-Perkins marvelled at the ability of these frontier cities to absorb and transmute these alien borrowings into something new and vital, and turn it into their own. By studying the wars alone, we tend to obscure the part played by this cultural third force within the territories on either side of the political frontiers. These territories were indeed the middlemen for the passage of goods and ideas from west to east and from east to west. But they were also something very much more than that. They were a creative centre in their own right, a melting pot and forcing-house for many of the most vital of the new ideas that were to carry the ancient world forward into the Middle Ages.[66] One can only regret that these results had to be achieved by force, rather than a peaceful exchange brought about by diplomacy and mutual respect.

For a culture that placed such immense value on the subjection of foreign peoples, there were no Parthians being dragged in triumphal processions. A succession of Armenian kings were crowned by the Roman emperor, and the Parthians figured highly in the rhetoric of imperialism, but they were only weakened, not subdued.[67] The Parthians were caught up in a Roman foreign policy that consisted of a system of national honour, insult and retribution that justified conquest and maintained security. Both the Romans and the Parthians attached a value to warfare in their concept of discipline. The Romans had a certain sophistication of tactics and organization, and they loved contrasting this to the decadence and luxury of eastern monarchs; they warned what would happen if their emperors became corrupted by money and peace. The Romans showed a deep suspicion of long peace as a source of corruption and frequently expressed the idea that a foreign war was a positive thing from this point of view. Horace looked forward to war with the Parthians because it would restore Rome   to   its   ancient military virtues.[68]

The Romans enjoyed contrasting their own superior discipline with the indiscipline of barbarian enemies. They believed that

Parthians could not endure long campaigns.[69] The ancient sources frequently criticize the perceived luxury and degeneration of the soldiers and praise emperors and commanders who restore old-fashioned discipline. Corbulo stands out in this respect. In Tacitus's tangled account of the eastern campaigns, one image that emerges clearly is that of Corbulo walking around bare-headed in the Armenian winter, encouraging his frostbitten troops. He had found them 'sluggish from long peace' but quickly rectified the situation.[70] Paetus, in contrast, fails properly to plan and organize his campaign (15.8) and grants leave to his troops liberally (15.9) – thus his disastrous loss to the Parthians. Fronto tells us that the typical soldier whom Lucius Verus found when he arrived in the east was, once again, 'reduced to idleness from long discontinuance of warfare'.[71] He writes that it is Verus who restored discipline in preparation for his Parthian war.[72]

Greed and glory were plausible, though not necessarily respectable, causes for war. Still more plausible and respectable was the motivation of revenge, and of asserting or enhancing the honour and majesty of the Roman Empire: provided, however, that it could be done without causing invasion, revolt, civil war or crippling expense. If a tribe caused too much trouble, the Romans saw no moral or ethical argument against wiping them off the face of the earth.

The Romans are also often given credit for trying to 'civilize the world', but this was not the purpose of their conquests. The purpose of the expansion was obvious. Conquest brought new wealth, more slaves, and land on which to settle veterans. By the time of Augustus, Rome was an empire in both name and function. It has been a debated point whether Augustus himself bequeathed a hope that Rome would end its expansion, but it never really gave up expansion unless forced to do so by an outside power. Some emperors were more pacific than others, but they all saw it as Rome's prerogative to add new territory to the empire, if only to keep the borders safe. The relatively slow pace of conquest under the Principate should not be explained as a result of substituting a 'defensive' strategy for the ideology of glory and conquest that prevailed in the Republic. The Romans continued at all times to value victory and conquest, as part of a system in which aggression, especially in retaliation for a perceived wrong, was crucial for maintaining honour and security. However, there were certain fiscal factors that limited the size of the army. The Romans recognized manpower constraints as a limit to the growth of the empire.

Any conquest that did not promise the immense profit perhaps did not look as attractive as the lucrative ventures of an earlier era. Isolation was never a tenable policy for Rome. No one had impenetrable borders.[73]

LESSONS TO BE LEARNED

More than one person has made a comparison between Bush's Iraq War and Trajan's Parthian campaign.[74] Danger lurks in drawing historical parallels and there are vast differences between Rome's Parthian Wars and America's Mesopotamian adventure, yet the one similarity is that both made the mistake of not planning well for the peace after the war.[75] The limits on America's military strength, manpower and sustainability have become only too obvious because of our war in Iraq. Perhaps the same limits should have become obvious to the Romans. What the two wars do seem to have in common is that they were started without the proper intelligence needed for them to have a successful outcome. The idea that a substantial body of knowledge could have improved post-war prospects in Iraq for the Americans is not far-fetched. The same is true for the Romans.[76] The ongoing financial, diplomatic and human cost of the Iraq occupation is more grievous in light of the advanced warnings the government had.[77] In the case of both the Romans and the Americans, we may legitimately ask if starting a war with one enemy produced another stronger foe. In one case the Sassanids, in the other the Shi'ites.[78]

Some of our problems, however, are not parallel. The day after the war ended, Iraq became America's problem. But the Romans did not care what happened after they left. They could destroy the political order and do much physical damage in the process without having to stay for the reconstruction. Conquered Parthians would not turn to Rome for foreign aid or care packages. Had the Romans stayed to turn the territory they overran into a Roman province, then it would have become their job to commit the time and resources necessary to accomplish genuine reconstruction and restoration of a stable society, or at least to seriously attempt it.[79] But this was never in the realm of possibility with Parthia. With the exception of Trajan, the Romans only wanted to raid Parthia and to make it weaker and dependent on Rome.

The terms the Romans used to frame their decisions about war and peace are not ours. They dealt in unscientific ethnic stereotypes and the idea that glory in war is more important than practical considerations. When an emperor or a commander decided to attack Parthia, he did not think in terms of a territory with a certain shape and extent, bounded by certain geographical features. Such intelligence would have been collected only after the conquest, if at all. To Rome, Parthia was a rich kingdom beyond the Euphrates, ruled by a king draped in luxury and decadence. Its king had humiliated Rome by defeating three Roman legions, killing its commander, and mocking him at their court. They had dared to capture Roman standards and then sent raiding parties right into Roman territory. This was no different from Saddam Hussein thumbing his nose at the United States and invading Kuwait (war number one), or refusing to give up weapons of mass destruction (war number two). It did not even matter if he actually had them. Even considering the disparity in size and power between the United States and Iraq, America invaded anyway. Was it really a strategic threat? For the Romans, as for the United States, hegemony and security depended on universal recognition of their empire's *maiestas*, its 'greatness'. Both policies depended on perceived and acknowledged military superiority, on the terror and awe of the enemy, and if this image was challenged by invasion, defeat, revolt or the bombing of the World Trade Center, both the Romans and the United States would retaliate with the maximum brutality and ferocity. These were wars of punishment and revenge. Both the Roman emperor and the American president were willing to commit military and financial resources of immense proportions, perhaps partly for personal reasons.[80] The fact that both modern superpowers and the Romans can act irrationally may teach us not only something about the forces that shaped the boundaries of one of the world's great empires, but something about ourselves as well. Both Rome and the United States can suffer from what P.A. Brunt called 'Imperial Illusions'.[81] But whereas an emperor like Trajan was able to withdraw back to his own boundaries with seemingly no permanent damage to the Roman Empire, it remains to be seen whether the Americans will be as lucky.

NOTES

1. There is not nearly enough space in this book to cover the subject of Parthia's relations with its other neighbours besides Rome. For a brief summary, see C. Lerouge, *L'image des Parthes dans le monde gréco-romain* (Stuttgart: Franz Sreiner Verlag, 2007), pp.77–81. See also the comments of B. Campbell, 'War and Diplomacy: Rome and Parthia, 31 BC – AD

235', in J. Rich and G. Shipley, *War and Society in the Roman World* (New York and London: Routledge, 1993), p.213.

2. Tacitus, *Annals* 11.10, 11. 9, 12.50, 2.2. See also Campbell, 'War and Diplomacy', p.219; D.L. Kennedy, 'Parthia and Rome', in D.L. Kennedy (ed.), *The Roman Army in the East* (Ann Arbor, MI: *Journal of Roman Archaeology*, Supplementary Series, 18, 1996), p.88.

3. There is not enough room in this book to trace the entire history of Roman–Parthian relations, nor discuss Parthian foreign policy in depth. Readers might wish to examine, however, a recent book by Ian Morris and Walter Scheidel (eds), *The Dynamics of Ancient Empires* (Oxford: Oxford University Press, 2008).

4. Lerouge, *L'image des Parthes*, pp.79–80.

5. R.E.M. Wheeler, 'The Roman Frontier in Mesopotamia', in Eric Birley (ed.), *Congress of Roman Frontier Studies, 1949* (Durham, NC: University of North Carolina Press, 1952), p.112.

6. Campbell, 'War and Diplomacy', p.229, implies it was used more frequently than I have suggested.

7. See the remarks of Campbell, 'War and Diplomacy', p.213.

8. Tacitus, *Annals* 12.50. 15.5 implies that the siege of Tigranocerta failed in 61 because the Parthians could not bring fodder to the site for their cavalry; cf. Dio 40.15.2; A. Goldsworthy, *The Roman Army at War 100 BC – AD 200* (Oxford: Clarendon Press, 1996), p.63. Parthia made insignificant changes in its armies compared to the Romans over the course of three centuries. See J.C. Coulston, 'Roman, Parthian and Sassanid Tactical Developments', in P. Freeman and D.L. Kennedy (eds), *The Defence of the Roman and Byzantine East: Proceedings of a Colloquium held at the University of Sheffield in April 1986*, British Institute of Archaeology at Ankara Monograph no. 8 (Oxford: British Archaeological Reports, International Series, 297, 1986), vol. 1, pp.59–75.

9. This is not to say that they could not field a formidable army. See the comments of Kennedy, 'Parthia and Rome', pp.84, 86–7. For a description of the Parthian army, see M. Mielczarek, *Cataphracts and Clibanarii: Studies in the Heavy Armoured Cavalry in the Ancient World* (Lodz: Oficyna Naukowa MS, 1993).

10. Herodian 4.10.4.

11. Pliny the Younger, *Ep.* 10.77.1ff.

12. B. Isaac, 'Luttwak's Grand Strategy and the Eastern Frontier of the Roman Empire', in D.H. French and C.S. Lightfoot (eds), *The Eastern Frontier of the Roman Empire: Proceedings of a Colloquium held at Ankara in September 1988*, British Institute of Archaeology at Ankara Monograph no. 11 (Oxford: British Archaeological Reports, International Series, 553, 1989), part 1, pp.232–3.

13. On the lack of a frontier in this area, see F. Millar, *The Roman Near East 31 BC –AD 337* (Cambridge, MA: Harvard University Press, 1993), p.129. Millar's work should also be consulted on the cultural effects of the Roman occupation in the Near East.

14. Dio 75.9.4. The fact that the Romans did not have a separate word for intelligence as we do speaks volumes.

15. Aelius Aristides, *ad. Rom.* in Aristides, *The Complete Works*, trans. Charles Behr (Leiden: Brill, 1981), 10.

16. C.R. Whittaker, 'Where are the Frontiers Now?' in Kennedy (ed.), *Roman Army in the East*, p.32.

17. S. Mattern, *Rome and the Enemy* (Berkeley, CA: University of California Press, 1999), pp.21–2, B. Isaac, *The Limits of Empire: The Roman Army in the East* (Oxford: Clarendon Press, 1992), pp.5–6; J. Mann, 'The Frontiers of the Principate', in *ANRW* 2, 1 (1974), pp.508–33; J. Mann, 'Power, Force and the Frontiers of the Empire', review of E. Luttwak, *The Grand Strategy of the Roman Empire*, *JRS*, 69 (1979), pp.175–83. T.B. Mitford, 'Cappadocia and Armenia Minor: Historical Setting of the *Limes*', in *ANRW* 2, 7.2 (1980), p.1196, says Trajan annexed Armenia for 'strategic reasons', but he never clarifies what the strategy was except for annexation in the name of defence. B. Isaac, 'Luttwak's Grand Strategy and the Eastern Frontier of the Roman Empire', in French and Lightfoot, *Eastern Frontier of the Roman Empire*, p.233; K. Butcher, *Roman Syria and the Near East* (Los Angeles, CA: Getty Publications, 2003), pp.405–6.

18. On grand strategy as a chimera, see Isaac, *Limits of Empire*, pp.373–4; Isaac, 'Luttwak's Grand Strategy', p.231.

19. Isaac, *Limits of Empire*, p.28.

20. Luttwak, *The Grand Strategy of the Roman Empire* (Baltimore, MD: Johns Hopkins

University Press, 1976), p.3, and yet he follows Lepper in describing the defence of a 'Chaboras–Singara line'. F.A. Lepper, *Trajan's Parthian War* (Chicago, IL: Ares, 1993), p.120, himself points out that if 115 CE was spent consolidating a line that was to become the permanent eastern frontier, none of the literary sources took note of the fact. Isaac, 'Luttwak's Grand Strategy', p.233.

21. Isaac, *Limits of Empire*, pp.1–7.
22. Luttwak, *Grand Strategy*, p.108.
23. General T. Zinni, and T. Kaltz, The *Battle for Peace: A Frontline Vision of America's Power and Purpose* (New York: Palgrave/Macmillan, 2006), p.21.
24. W. Chin, 'Examining the Application of British Counterinsurgency Doctrine by the American Army in Iraq', *Small Wars and Insurgencies* 18, 2 (1–26 March 2007), p.1; T. R. Mokaitis, *The Iraq War: Learning from the Past, Adapting to the Present and Planning for the Future* (Carlisle Barracks, PA: Strategic Studies Institute, US Army War College, February 2007), p.1, called Iraq the 'insurgency from Hell'.
25. See W. Chin, 'US Application of British Counterinsurgency Doctrine', *Small Wars and Insurgencies* 18, 1 (March 2007), p.2 on the lack of political will to maintain a commitment for decades in order to win such a war. He also comments on the absence of a post-conflict stabilization plan.
26. Zinni and Kaltz, *Battle for Peace*, p.6.
27. Tacitus, *Annals* 13.35.1. So, too, the Carthaginians, thus the concept of *Fides Punica*. Cf. G. Brizzi, *I sistemi informativi dei Romani: Principi e realtà nell' età delle conquista oltremare (218–168 AC)* (Wiesbaden: Steiner, 1982); F. Dvornik, *The Origins of Intelligence Services* (New Brunswick, NJ: Rutgers University Press, 1974); R.M. Sheldon, *Intelligence Activities in Ancient Rome: Trust in the Gods, but Verify* (New York and London: Routledge, 2005).
28. H. Volkmann, *Cleopatra: A Study in Politics and Propaganda* (New York: Elek Books, 1958); S. Walker and P. Higgs (eds), *Cleopatra of Egypt: From History to Myth* (London: British Museum Press, 2001); S. Walker and S. Ashton (eds), *Cleopatra Reassessed* (London: British Museum Press, 2003).
29. See R.M. Sheldon, 'Clandestine Operations and Covert Action: The Roman Imperative', *International Journal of Intelligence and Counterintelligence*, 10, 3 (Fall 1997), pp.299–315. On the historical connection between covert action and diplomacy, see J.D. Stempel, 'Covert Action and Diplomacy', *International Journal of Intelligence and Counterintelligence*, 20, 1 (2007), pp.122–35.
30. The I, II and III Parthica were three legions formed by Septimius Severus. *RE*, 'Legio', I Parthica, cols 1435ff; Legio II Parthica, cols 1476ff; Legio III Parthica, cols 1539ff. The first and third were organized in the East in what was then the province of Mesopotamia. The second was established at Albano, twenty miles south of Rome. I Parthica was first stationed at Nisibis near the modern town of Al Qamishi in Syria's north-east border. Although it can be assumed to have participated in the successive wars with Persia, no actual record is available. The II Parthica participated in Caracalla's Parthian campaign of 216 CE. See Chapter 8.
31. J.G.C. Anderson, 'The Eastern Frontier under Augustus', in *CAH*, 10 (1963), p.748.
32. Arrian, *Parthica* fr.39; Fronto, *Princ. Hist.* (Loeb Classical Library, vol.2, pp.212–14). Cf. Eutropius, *Brev.* 8.3. Classical scholars have tried to clear Trajan of the blame for this murder, but there are certainly enough examples of treachery on both sides.
33. See J.B. Bury, *History of the Later Roman Empire* (London and New York: Macmillan & Co., 1889), vol. 2, p.3.
34. On Roman diplomacy in a later period, see F. Millar, 'Government and Diplomacy in the Roman Empire during the First Three Centuries', *IHR*, 10, 3 (1988), pp.345–77. On diplomacy in the ancient world see E. Olshausen and H. Biller (eds), *Antike Diplomatie* (Darmstadt: Wissenschaftliche Buchgesellschaft, 1979).
35. Anderson, 'The Eastern Frontier under Augustus', p.748. On diplomatic intrigues, see A.N. Sherwin-White, *Roman Foreign Policy in the East, 168 BC to AD 1* (London: Duckworth, 1984), p.308.
36. Dio 75.1.2.
37. Isaac, *Limits of Empire*, pp.399–400.
38. See J. Crow, 'A Review of the Physical Remains of the Frontier of Cappadocia', in Freeman and Kennedy (eds), *Defence of the Roman and Byzantine East*, pp.77–91, arguing that there was no clear frontier line (that we can detect) along the Upper Euphrates before

the third or fourth centuries. Tacitus, *Annals* 12.45, attests a garrison in Armenia already under Claudius, and garrisons left there by Trajan and Verus are attested epigraphically. Mattern, *Rome and the Enemy*, p.118, n.167.

39. On the evidence for Roman garrisons in the Caucasus region, see Crow, 'A Review of the Physical Remains', p.80; Isaac, *Limits of Empire*, pp.42–5; and on garrisons in client kingdoms generally, see D. Braund, *Rome and the Friendly King: The Character of the Client Kingship* (London: Croom Helm, 1984), p.94; On Romans troops beyond the frontier, see Isaac, *Limits of Empire*, pp.398–9.
40. Appian, *Praef.* 7.
41. V.L. Bullough, 'The Roman Empire vs Persia, 363–502: A Study of Successful Deterrence', *Journal of Conflict Resolution*, 7, 1 (March 1963), p.55.
42. Bullough, 'The Roman Empire vs. Persia', p.55.
43. Isaac, 'Luttwak's Grand Strategy', p.232.
44. P.A. Brunt, 'Roman Imperial Illusions', in P.A. Brunt, *Roman Imperial Themes*, (Oxford: Clarendon Press, 1990), p.439.
45. On the problem with cash gifts, see Mattern, *Rome and the Enemy*, pp.179–80.
46. For examples, see *RGDA*, 32; J. Gagé, *RGDA*, 3rd edn (Paris, 1977), pp.142–3, who lists references; and Brunt, 'Roman Imperial Illusions', p.462 with n.61.
47. Mattern, *Rome and the Enemy*, p.181.
48. Ibid., p.181 and n.61 lists examples.
49. Dio 78.27.
50. Mattern, *Rome and the Enemy*, p.184, with reference to Dio 51.25 on the Thracians; Velleius Paterculus 2.109 on Maroboduus; Dio 67.7.1 on Domitian and the Quadi and Marcomanni; Dio 68.10.3–4 on Decebalus; P.A. Brunt, 'Laus Imperii', in P.D.A. Garnsey and C.R. Whittaker, *Imperialism in the Ancient World* (Cambridge: Cambridge University Press, 1978), pp.176, 181.
51. Josephus, *BJ* 7.7.1; Isaac, *Limits of Empire*, pp.39–40.
52. W.E. Herr, 'Operation Vigilant Warrior: Conventional Deterrence Theory, Doctrine, and Practice', Thesis, School of Advanced Airpower Studies, Air University, Maxwell Air Force Base, June 1996, p.18.
53. On Homeric heroes, see A.W.H. Adkins, *Merit and Responsibility: A Study in Greek Values* (Chicago, IL: University of Chicago Press, 1975), and H. van Wees, *Status Warriors: War, Violence and Society in Homer and History* (Amsterdam: J.C. Gieben, 1992), esp.109–25, who makes the Mafia comparison. On honour and vengeance in Roman society, see Y. Thomas, 'Se venger au Forum: Solidarité familiale et process criminal à Rome', in Raymond Verdier and Jean-Paul Poly (eds), *La Vengeance: Étude d'ethnologie, d'histoire, et de philosophie*, vol. 3: *La vengeance: Vengeance, pouvoirs, et ideologies dans quelques civilizations de l'antiquité* (Paris: Cujas, 1984), pp.65–100.
54. Onasander 10.13–14; Herodian 6.4.4–6; J.B. Campbell, 'Teach Yourself How to be a General', *JRS*, 77 (1987), p.13; Mattern, *Rome and the Enemy*, p.173.
55. This protocol remained the same for the Republic and the Empire. It is described by N.S. Rosenstein, *Imperatores Victi: Military Defeat and Aristocratic Competition in the Middle and Late Republic* (Berkeley, CA: University of California Press, 1990), pp.133–8.
56. Tacitus, *Annals* 6.32: 'holding to his decision to conduct foreign affairs through counsel and cunning, and to keep war at a distance'; Suetonius, *Tiberius* 37.4: 'hostile or suspect kings he repressed by threats and complaints rather than force'. See Dio 77.12.1–2 and 77.20.22 for similar complaints against Caracalla.
57. *RGDA*, 29. E.S. Gruen, 'The Imperial Policy of Augustus', in K. Raaflaub and M. Toher (eds), *Between Republic and Empire: Interpretations of Augustus and his Principate* (Berkeley, CA: University of California Press, 1990), pp. 397–8.
58. Dio 54.8.2.
59. T. Mommsen, *The Provinces of the Roman Empire: From Caesar to Diocletian* (New York: Barnes & Noble, 1996), vol. 2, p.38.
60. Pliny, *Pan.* 14.1 praises Trajan for doing just this. Virgil writes that it was Rome's destiny to 'spare the conquered and to subdue the arrogant' (*superbos*). Aeneid, 6.851–3.
61. Tacitus, *Agricola* 30.4. 'Romans, whose arrogance you cannot escape by obedience and self-restraint.' M. Hutton trans., Loeb Classical Library.
62. See Campbell, 'War and Diplomacy', p.220 on why it is inaccurate to call Armenia a buffer state.

63. On the difficulty of defining this term, see Mattern, *Rome and the Enemy*, pp.173–6.
64. Mattern, *Roman and the Enemy*, p.177; Tacitus, *Annals* 15.2. Cf. Dio 80.3.1–4. On the policy of the Arsacids, see J. Wolski, 'Les Achémenides et les Arsacides: Contribution à l'histoire de la formation des traditions iraniennes', *Syria*, 43 (1966), pp.65–89; J. Wolski, *L'empire des Arsacides* (Louvain: Peeters, 1993), pp.119–21; E. Dabrowa, 'Le programme de la politique parthe en Occident des derniers Arsacides', *Iranica Antiqua*, 19 (1984), pp.149–65; Isaac, *Limits of Empire*, pp.21–33.
65. J.B. Ward-Perkins, 'The Roman West and the Parthian East', *Proceedings of the British Academy*, 51 (1965), p.193.
66. Ibid., p.196.
67. On the relationship of Rome with vassal states that did not necessarily see themselves as 'vassals', see Brunt, 'Roman Imperial Illusions', pp.434–8.
68. Horace, *Odes* 3.2.1–6.
69. Justin Trogus 41.2; Tacitus *Annals* 11.10: 'The Parthians, though victors, rejected a distant campaign.' Dio 40.15.6. Also see Lucan, *de Bell. Civ.* 8.368–90. Parthians are invincible on their own territory because they have room for flight, but cannot endure hardship, have no military machines, and flee quickly.
70. Tacitus, *Annals* 13.35. Corbulo had done the same with the troops on the Rhine. He was famous for this quality. G. Walser, *Rom, das Reich, und die fremden Völker in der Geschichtsschreibung der frühen Kaiserzeit* (Baden-Baden: Verlag für Kunst und Wissenschaft, 1951), pp.42–3.
71. Fronto, *Princ. Hist.* 11 (Loeb Classical Library, v.2, p.209).
72. See Fronto's letter to Verus, Loeb Classical Library, v. 2, pp.149–51 and *Princ. Hist.* 13 (Loeb Classical Library, v.2, pp.209–10). These passages are discussed extensively by R.W. Davies, 'Fronto, Hadrian, and the Roman Army', *Latomus*, 27 (1968), pp.75–95, and E.L. Wheeler, 'The Laxity of the Syrian Legions', in Kennedy (ed.), *Roman Army in the East*, pp.229–76.
73. Zinni and Kaltz, *Battle for Peace*, p.12.
74. R.M. Sheldon, 'Trajan's Parthian Adventure: With Some Modern Caveats', in: E. O'Halpin, R. Armstrong and J. Ohlmeyer (eds), *Intelligence, Statecraft and International Power*, Historical Studies 25, papers read before the twenty-seventh Irish Conference of Historians held at Trinity College, Dublin, 2005, pp.153–74; G. Leupp, 'An Earlier Empire's War on Iraq', *Counterpunch*, 4 October 2005; M. Petrenchuk, 'US Repeating Mistakes of Roman Empire', *Rosblat News Agency*, 5 June 2004. See especially the comments of Adrian Goldsworthy, *The Fall of the West* (London: Weidenfeld & Nicholson, 2009), pp.3–4, who points out that the novels of Robert Harris on Roman themes were a way of commenting on modern America.
75. Whittaker, 'Where are the Frontiers Now?', p.31.
76. J. Fallows, *Blind into Baghdad* (New York: Vintage Books, 2006), pp.ix–xxv.
77. Ibid., p.48.
78. See ibid., 'Will Iran be Next?', pp.187–218.
79. Zinni and Kaltz, *Battle for Peace*, p.8.
80. J. King, 'Bush Calls Saddam "The Guy who Tried to Kill my Dad" ', *CNN*, 27 September 2002.
81. Brunt, 'Roman Imperial Illusions', pp.433–80.

BIBLIOGRAPHY

ANCIENT LITERARY SOURCES, INSCRIPTIONS, COINS AND REFERENCE WORKS

Ammianus Marcellinus, *The Surviving Books of the History of Ammianus Marcellinus*, trans. J.C. Rolfe, 3 vols (Cambridge, MA: Harvard University Press, 1956).

Ampelius, Lucius, *Liber Memorialis*, ed. Edwin Assmann (Stuttgart: Teubner, 1976).

Ampelius, Lucius, *Liber Memorialis (Aide-Mémoire)*, trans. Marie-Pierre Arnaud-Lindet, 2nd edn (Paris: Les Belles Lettres, 2003).

L'Année épigraphique: revue des publications épigraphiques relatives a l'antiquité romaine (Paris: Presses Universitaires de France, 1888). Issues from 1889–1961 were published as a section of *Revue archéologique*, entitled *Revue des publications épigraphiques*. From 1962 they were issued as a supplement to *Revue archéologique*.

Appian, *Appian's Roman History*, trans. Horace White, 4 vols (Cambridge MA: Harvard University Press, 1958).

Appian, *The History of Appian of Alexandria, in two parts: the first consisting of the Punick, Syrian, Parthian, Mithridatick, Illyrian, Spanish, and Hannibalick wars: the second containing five books of the civil wars of Rome* (Printed for John Amery, 1696).

Aristides, Aelius, *The Complete Works*, trans. Charles Behr (Leiden: Brill, 1981).

Arrian, *History of Alexander and Indica by Arrian*, ed. and trans. P.A. Brunt, 2 vols (Cambridge, MA: Harvard University Press, 1976–83).

Arrian, *Parthica*, original Greek and English translation in F.A. Lepper, *Trajan's Parthian War* (Chicago: Ares, 1993), pp.226–53.

Arrian, *Periplus Ponti Euxini* (Bristol: Bristol Classical, 2003). See also Aubrey Diller, *The Tradition of the Minor Greek Geographers* (New York: American Philological Assn, 1952).

Augustus, *Res Gestae Divi Augusti*, trans. Frederick W. Shipley (New York: Putnam, 1924).

Aurelius Victor, *Liber de Caesaribus of Sextus Aurelius Victor*, trans.

with introduction and commentary by H.W. Bird (Liverpool: Liverpool University Press, 1994).

Belloni, G.G., *Le Monete di Traiano: Catalogo del civico Gabinetto numismatico* (Milano: Museo Archaeologico, 1973).

Bowman, Alan K., Peter Garnsey and Dominic Rathbone, *The Cambridge Ancient History. The High Empire, A.D. 70–192* (Cambridge: Cambridge University Press, 2000, 2nd edition).

Broughton, T. Robert S., *The Magistrates of the Roman Republic*, with the collaboration of Marcia L. Patterson, 3 vols (New York: American Philological Association, 1951–52).

Bury, J.B., S.A. Cook and F.E. Adcock *et. al.*, *The Cambridge Ancient History* (New York: Macmillan, 1924–66).

Caesar, Julius, *The Civil Wars*, trans. A.G. Peskett (Cambridge, MA: Harvard University Press, 1911).

Cancik, Hubert and Helmuth Schneider (eds), *Brill's New Pauly, Encyclopaedia of the Ancient World: Antiquity*; English edition: managing editor, Christine F. Salazar; assistant editor, David E. Orton (Leiden and Boston, MA: Brill, 2002).

Cicero, *de Divinatione*, English translation by W.A. Falconer (Cambridge, MA: Harvard University Press, Loeb Classical Library, vol. 20, 1923).

Cicero, *Marcus Tullius, de Senectute, de Amicitia, de Divinatione*, trans. William Armstead Falconer (Cambridge, MA: Harvard University Press, 1959).

Cicero, *Marcus Tullius: Letters to Atticus*, trans. E.O. Windstedt, 3 vols (Cambridge, MA: Harvard University Press, 1956).

Cicero, *Marcus Tullius: Letters to His Friends*, trans. W. Glynn Williams (Cambridge, MA: Harvard University Press, 1958).

Cicero, *Marcus Tullius: Pro Rabirio Postumo*, trans. and commentary by Mary Siani-Davies (Oxford: Clarendon Press, 2001).

Cohen, Henry, *Description historique des monnaies frappés sous l'Empire romain*, 8 vols (Paris and London: Rollin et Feuardent, 1880–92).

Cook, S.A., F.E. Adcock and M.P. Charlesworth (eds), *The Cambridge Ancient History, Vol. 11.* The Imperial Peace (Cambridge: Cambridge University Press, 1936).

Corpus Inscriptionum Latinarum, consilio et aucturitate Academiae Literarum Regiae Borussicae editum, 17 vols (Berlin: Akademie der Wissenschaften, 1862–).

Dessau, Hermann (ed.), *Inscriptiones Latinae Selectae*, reprint edn, 3 vols (Chicago, IL: Ares, 1979).

Dio Cocceianus, Cassius, *Dio's Roman History*, trans. E. Cary, Loeb

Classical Library, 9 vols (Cambridge, MA: Harvard University Press, 1954).

Eutropius, *Eutropi Breviarum ab urbe condita*, ed. C. Santini (Leipzig: B.G. Teubner, 1979).

Festus Historicus, *The Breviarum of Festus*, ed. John W. Eadie (London: Athlone Press, 1967).

Florus, Lucius Annaeus, *Epitome of Roman History*, trans. E.S. Forster (Cambridge, MA: Harvard University Press, 1960).

Frontinus, Sextus Julius, *The Stratagems*, trans. Charles E. Bennett (Cambridge, MA: Harvard University Press, 1925).

Fronto, M. Cornelius, *The Correspondence of Marcus Cornelius Fronto with Marcus Aurelius Antoninus, Lucius Verus, Antoninus Pius, and various friends*, ed and trans. C.R. Haines, 2 vols (Cambridge, MA: Harvard University Press, 1962).

Groag, Edmund, *Prosopographia Imperii Romani*, 2 vols (Berlin: Walter de Gruyter & Co., 1933).

Herodian, *History of the Empire from the Time of Marcus Aurelius*, trans. C.R. Whittaker, 2 vols (Cambridge, MA: Harvard University Press, 1969).

Hill, G.F., *British Museum Department of Coins and Medals: Catalogue of the Greek Coins of Arabia, Mesopotamia and Persia* (London: British Museum, 1922).

Horace, *Horace's Satires and Epistles*, trans. Jacob Fuchs, introduced by William S. Anderson (New York: Norton, 1977).

Hornblower, Simon and Anthony Spawforth (eds), *The Oxford Classical Dictionary* (New York and London: Oxford University Press, 1996, 3rd edition).

Inscriptiones Graecae ad res Romanas pertinentes, Academiae inscriptionvm et litterarvm hvmaniorvm collectae et editae, Académie des inscriptions & belles-lettres (France) (Paris: E. Leroux, 1901).

Isidore of Charax, *Parthian Stations*, ed. Wilfred H. Schoff, reprint edn (Philadelphia, PA: Commercial Museum; Chicago, IL: Ares, 1976).

Josephus, Flavius, *Jewish Antiquites*, translated H.St.J. Thackeray, 6 vols (Cambridge, MA: Harvard University Press, 1961).

Josephus, Flavius, *The Jewish War*, trans. H.St.J. Thackeray, 2 vols (Cambridge, MA: Harvard University Press, 1956).

Julius Africanus, *Kestoi, les Cestes de Julius Africanus: Étude sur l'ensemble des fragments avec édition, traduction et commentaries* (Firenze: Sansoni Antiquariato; Paris, Librairie M. Didier, 1970).

Justinus, Marcus Junianus, *Epitoma historiarum Philippicarum Pompei*

Trogi, trans. Otto Seel (Stuttgart: B. G. Teubner, 1972).

Justinus, Marcus Junianus, *Epitome of the Philippic History of Pompeius Trogus*, books 11–12: *Alexander the Great/Justin*, trans. and appendices by J.C. Yardley; introduction and commentary by Waldemar Heckel (Oxford and New York: Clarendon Press, 1997).

Livy, *Ab urbe condita* (Cambridge, MA: Harvard University Press, 1961), vols 1–5 trans. B.O. Foster; vols 6–8 trans. F.G. Moore; vols 9–11 trans. E.T. Sage; vols 12–14 trans. A.G. Schlesinger.

Lucan, *The Civil War* (*Pharsalia*), with an English translation by J.D. Duff (Cambridge, MA: Harvard University Press, 1928).

Malalas, John, *Chronographia: The Chronicle of John Malalas*, trans. Elizabeth Jeffreys, Michael Jeffreys and Roger Scott, with Brian Croke (Melbourne: Australian Association for Byzantine Studies; Sydney: Department of Modern Greek, University of Sydney, 1986).

Mattingly, Harold and Sydenham, Edward A., *Roman Imperial Coinage*, 10 vols (London: Spink, 1923–94).

Mattingly, H. *et al. Coins of the Roman Empire in the British Museum*, 5 vols (London: Trustees of the British Museum, 1932–62).

McDonald, George, *Coin Types, their Origin and Development: being the Rhind lectures for 1904* (Glasgow: J. Maclehose & Sons, 1905).

McDowell, Robert Harbold, *Coins from Seleucia on the Tigris*, University of Michigan Studies, Humanistic Series (Ann Arbor, MI: University of Michigan Press, 1935), vol. 37.

Newell, Edward T., *Some Unpublished Coins of Eastern Dynasts*, Numismatic Notes and Monographs (New York: American Numismatic Society, 1926).

Orosius, Paulus, *Historiarum adversum paganos libri VII*, ed. C. Zangmeister (Hildesheim: Olms, 1967).

Ovid, *Fasti* (Roman Holidays), trans. Betty Rose Nagle (Bloomington, IN: University of Indiana Press, 1995).

Pauly, August Friedrich von, with Georg Wissowa, Wilhelm Kroll and Kurt Witte (eds). *Pauly's Real-Encyclopädie der classischen Altertumswissenschaft. Neue Bearbeitung unter Mitwirkung zahlreicher Fachgenossen hrsg. von Georg Wissowa* (Stuttgart: Druckenmüller Verlag, 1893–1963).

Pausanias, *Description of Greece*, trans. H.L. Jones, 8 vols (Cambridge, MA: Harvard University Press, 1954).

Philostratus, *Life of Apollonius of Tyana*, ed. and trans. Christopher P. Jones (Cambridge, MA: Harvard University Press, 2006).

Pliny the Elder, *Natural History*, 10 vols, vols. 1–4 trans. H.H. Rackham, vols. 5–8 trans. W.H.S. Jones, vol. 9 trans. H.H. Rackham, vol. 10 trans. D.E. Eichholz (Cambridge, MA: Harvard University Press, 1958–62).

Pliny the Younger, *Letters and Panygyricus*, trans. Betty Radice, 2 vols (Cambridge, MA: Harvard University Press, 1989–92).

Plutarch, *Lives*, trans. Bernadotte Perrin, 11 vols (Cambridge, MA: Harvard University Press, 1958–62).

Polyaenus, *Stratagems of War*, ed. and trans. Peter Krentz and Everett L. Wheeler (Chicago, IL Ares, 1994).

Polybius, *The Histories*, trans. W.R. Paton, Loeb Classical Library, 6 vols (Cambridge, MA: Harvard University Press, 1960).

Pomponius Mela, *Description of the World*, trans. and introduced by Frank E. Romer (Ann Arbor, MI: University of Michigan Press, 1998).

Rtveladze, Edvard Vassilevich, *The Ancient Coins of Central Asia* (Tashkent: Izd-vo lit-ry i iskusstva im. Gafura Guliama, 1987).

Scriptores Historiae Augustae (The Augustan History), trans. David Magie, 3 vols (Cambridge, MA: Cambridge University Press, 1958–60).

Sellwood, David, *An Introduction to the Coinage of Parthia* (London: Spink, 1980).

Sellwood, David, 'Parthian Gold Coins', in *Proceedings of the Eleventh International Numismatic Congress, Brussels, 8–13 September 1991* (Louvain-la-Neuve, Belgium: Association Professeur Marcel Hoc, 1993), vol. 1.

Seneca, *De tranquillitate animi*, in *Seneca, II: Moral Essays*, trans. John W. Basore (Cambridge, MA: Harvard University Press, 1932).

Smallwood, E. Mary, *Documents Illustrating the Principates of Gaius, Claudius and Nero* (London: Cambridge University Press, 1967).

Smallwood, E. Mary, *Documents Illustrating the Principates of Nerva, Trajan and Hadrian* (Cambridge: Cambridge University Press, 1966).

Stangl, Thomas, *Ciceronis Orationem Scholiastae* (G. Olms, 1964).

Statius, Silvae, *Thebaid, Achilleid*, trans. J.H. Mozley (Cambridge, MA: Harvard University Press, 1958–60).

Strabo, *The Geography of Strabo*, trans. Horace Leonard Jones, based on the unfinished version of John Robert Sitlington Sterrett (Cambridge, MA: Harvard University Press, 1982–89).

Strack, P.L., *Untersuchungen zur römischen Reichspragung des zweiten Jahrhunderts, 1: Reichsprägung zue Zeit des Trajan* (Stuttgart: W. Kohlhammer, 1931).

Suetonius, *Lives of the Caesars*, trans. J.C. Rolfe (Cambridge: Loeb Classical Library, 1960), 2 vols.

Supplementum epigraphicum graecum (Amsterdam: J.C. Gieben, Vol.1, 1923 – 51 volumes published so far).

Sutherland, C.H.V. and Carson, R.A.G., *The Roman Imperial Coinage* (London: Spink, 1984).

Tacitus, *Dialogus; Agricol; Germania* (London: W. Heinemann; New York: G.P. Putnam's Sons, 1920).

Tacitus, *The Annals*, trans. J. Jackson, 3 vols (Cambridge, MA: Harvard University Press, 1958–60).

Tacitus, *The Histories*, trans. Clifford H. Moore (Cambridge, MA: Harvard University Press, 1958–62).

Tacitus, *Agricola*, trans. M. Hutton, rev. by R.M. Ogilvie (Cambridge, MA, Harvard University Press, 2000).

Valerius Flaccus, *The Voyage of the Argo: The Argonautica of Gaius Valerius Flaccus*, trans. David R. Slavitt (Baltimore, MD: Johns Hopkins University Press, 1999).

Valerius Maximus, *Memorable Deeds and Sayings*, trans. with introduction and commentary by D. Wardle (Oxford: Clarendon Press, 1998).

Vegetius, *Epitome of Military Science*, trans. with notes and introduction by N.P. Milner, 2nd edn (Liverpool: Liverpool University Press, 1996).

Velleius Paterculus, *The Roman History*, trans. Frederick W. Shipley (Cambridge, MA: Harvard University Press, 1961).

Walker, David, *The Metrology of the Roman Silver Coinage*, 3 vols (London: British Archaeological Reports, Supplementary Series, 5, 1976).

Wroth, Warwick, *A Catalogue of Greek Coins in the British Museum: Catalogue of the Coins of Parthia* (Bologna: Arnaldo Forni, 1964).

Zonaras, Johannes, *Epitome Historiarum*, ed. L. Dinddorf, 6 vols (Leipzig: Teubner, 1868).

Zosimus, *Historia Nova* (New History), trans. with commentary by Ronald T. Ridley (Sydney: Australian Association for Byzantine Studies, 1982).

MODERN WORKS

Adams, J.P., 'Roman Imperial Army in the East', *Ancient World*, 2, 4 (1979), pp.129–37.

Adcock, F.E., *Marcus Crassus, Millionaire* (Cambridge: Heffer, 1966).

Adkins, A.W.H., *Merit and Responsibility: A Study in Greek Values*

(Chicago, IL: University of Chicago Press, 1975).

al-Aswad, Hikmet Basher, 'Water Sources at Hatra', *Mesopotamia*, 26 (1991), pp.195–211.

al-Salihi, Wathiq I., 'Military Considerations in the Defenses of Hatra', *Mesopotamia*, 26 (1991), pp.187–94.

Alexander, M.C., *Trials in the Late Roman Republic 149 BC to 50 BC* (Toronto: University of Toronto Press, 1990).

Alston, R., 'Roman Military Pay from Caesar to Diocletian', *JRS*, 84 (1994), pp.113–23.

Anderson, J.G.C., 'Cappadocia as a Roman Procuratorial Province', *CR*, 45 (1931), pp.189–90.

Anderson, J.G.C., 'The Eastern Frontier from Tiberius to Nero', in *CAH*, 10 (1934; 3rd ed. 1963), pp.743–80.

Anderson, J.G.C., 'The Eastern Frontier under Augustus', in *CAH*, 10 (1934; 3rd ed. 1963), pp.239–83.

Anderson, J.G.C., 'The Invasion of Parthia', in *CAH*, 10 (1934; 3rd ed. 1963), pp.71–4.

Angeli-Bertinelli, Maria Gabriella, 'I Romani oltre l'Euphrate nell II secolo dC', in *ANRW*, 2, 9.1 (1976), pp.3–45.

Angeli-Bertinelli, Maria Gabriella, *Roma e l'Oriente: Strategia, economia, società, e cultura nelle relazioni politiche fra Roma, la Giudea, e l'Iran* (Rome: L'Erma di Bretschneider, 1979).

Angeli-Bertinelli, Maria Gabriella, 'Traiano in oriente: La conquista dell'Armenia, della Mesopotamia e dell'Assiria', in J. González (ed.), *Trajano: Emperador de Roma, Saggi di storia antica* (Rome: L'Erma di Bretschneider, 2000), pp.25–54.

Anon., 'Phraaspa: US scientists survey big Parthian citadel where Rome's march to the east was stopped in 36 BC', *Life*, 4, 17 (25 April 1938), pp.28–9.

Applebaum, Shimon, 'Notes on the Jewish Revolt Under Trajan', *JJS*, 2, 1 (1950), pp.26-30.

Applebaum, Shimon, 'The Jewish Revolt in Cyrene in 115–117, and the Subsequent Recolonisation', *JJS*, 2, 4 (1951), pp.177–86.

Arnaud, Pascal, 'Les Guerres des Parthes et de l'Armémie dans la première moitié du premier siècle av.n.è: problèmes de chronologie et d'extensione territoriale (95 BC–70 BC)', *Mesopotamia*, 22 (1987), pp.129–45.

Arnaud, Pascal, 'Les guerres parthiques de Gabinius et de Crassus et la politique occidentale des Parthes Arsacides entre 70 et 53 av. J-C', in Edward Dabrowa, *Ancient Iran and the Mediterranean World: Proceedings of an international conference in honour of Professor Józef Wolski held at the Jagiellonian University, Cracow, in*

September 1996, Electrum Studies in Ancient History, 2, (1998), pp.13–34.

Asdourian, P., *Die politischen Beziehungen zwischen Armenien and Rom von 190 v. Chr., bis 428 n. Chr: Ein Abriss der armenischen Geschichte dieser Periode* (Freiburg, Schweiz: 1911).

Ash, Rhiannon, 'An Exemplary Conflict; Tacitus' Parthian Battle Narrative (Annals 6.34–5)', *Phoenix*, 53 (1999), pp.114–35.

Astarita, Maria Laura, *Avidio Cassio* (Rome: Edizioni di storia e letteratura, 1983).

Austin, N.J.E. and Rankov, B., *Exploratio: Military and Political Intelligence in the Roman World from the Second Punic War to the Battle of Adrianople* (London and New York: Routledge, 1995).

Badian, Ernst, 'Sulla's Cilician Command', *Athenaeum*, 37 (1959), pp.279ff., in *Studies in Greek and Roman History* (Oxford: Blackwell, 1964), pp.157–78.

Badian, Ernst, *Roman Imperialism in the Late Republic* (Ithaca, NY: Cornell University Press, 1971).

Balsdon, J.V.P.D., *Romans and Aliens* (Chapel Hill, NC: University of North Carolina Press, 1979).

Bancroft, Elizabeth, 'The Price of Toadyism and the Madness of Groupthink', *The Intelligencer: Journal of US Intelligence Studies*, 16, 2 (Fall 2008), p.5.

Barrett, A.A., 'Sohaemus, King of Emesa and Sophene', *AJPh*, 98, 2 (Summer 1977), pp.153–9.

Barzano, A., 'Roma e I Parti tra pace e Guerra fredda nel 1 secolo dell' imperio', in Marta Sordi (ed.), *La Pace nel Mondo Antico* (Milano: Vita e pensiero, 1985), pp.211–22.

Bellinger, A.R., 'The End of the Seleucids', *Transactions of the Connecticut Academy of Art and Sciences*, 38 (1949), pp.51–102.

Bengston, Hermann, *Zum Partherfeldzug des Antonius* (Munich: Verlag der Bayer Akad. der Wissenschaft, Beck, 1974).

Bennett, Julian, *Trajan: Optimus Princeps*, 2nd edn (Bloomington, IN: Indiana University Press, 2001).

Berchem, Denis van, 'L'annone militaire dans l'empire romain au IIIe siecle', *Memoires de la Société Nationale des Antiquaires de France*, Serie 8, tome 10 (1937), pp.117–202.

Berchem, Denis van, 'L'itineraire Antonin et le voyage en Orient de Caracalla (214–215)', *CRAI* (1973), pp.123–6.

Berchem, Denis van, 'La port de Séleucie de Piérie et l'infrastructure lofistique des guerres parthiques', *BJ*, 185 (1985), pp. 47–87.

Bergamini, S., 'Parthian Fortifications in Mesopotamia', *Mesopotamia*, 22 (1987), pp.195–214.

Birley, Anthony R., *Marcus Aurelius: A Biography*, rev. edn (New Haven, CT: Yale University Press, 1987).

Birley, Anthony R., *The African Emperor; Septimius Severus* (London: B.T. Batsford, 1988).

Birley, Anthony R., *Hadrian: The Restless Emperor* (London and New York: Routledge, 1998).

Birley, Anthony R., 'Hadrian to the Antonines', CAH2, vol. 11 (2000), pp.132–94.

Bivar, A.D.H., 'A Recently Discovered Compound Bow', *Seminarium Kondrakovianum*, 9 (1937), pp.1–10.

Bivar, A.D.H., 'The Political History of Iran under the Arsacids', in *CHI*: vol.3, 1: *The Seleucid, Parthian and Sasanian Period*, ed. E. Yarshater (Cambridge: Cambridge University Press, 1938), chapter 2, pp.21–99.

Bivar, A.D.H., 'Cavalry Equipment and Tactics on the Euphrates Frontier', *Dumbarton Oaks Papers*, 26 (1972), pp.271–91.

Black, J., 'The History of Parthia and Characene in the Second Century AD', *Sumer*, 43 (1984), pp.230–4.

Bosworth, A.B., 'Arrian and Rome: The Minor Works', in *ANRW*, 2, 34, 1 (1976), 'Sprache und Literatur', pp.226–75.

Bowersock, G.W., 'Syria under Vespasian', *JRS*, 63 (1973), pp.133–40.

Bowersock, G.W., 'The Mechanics of Subversion in the Roman Provinces', *Opposition et Résistances à l'empire d'Auguste à Trajan: Entretiens sur l'antiquité classique*, 33 (1987), pp.291–317.

Bowersock, G.W., *Roman Arabia* (Cambridge, MA: Harvard University Press, 1983).

Braidwood, R.J., *Mounds in the Plain of Antioch* (Chicago, IL: University of Chicago Press, 1937).

Braund, D.C., *Rome and the Friendly King: The Character of the Client Kingship* (London: Croom Helm; New York: St Martin's Press, 1984).

Braund, D., 'The Caucasian Frontier: Myth, Exploration and the Dynamics of Imperialism', in Freeman and Kennedy (eds), *Defence of the Roman and Byzantine East*, pp.31–49.

Braund, D.C., 'River Frontiers in the Environmental Psychology of the Roman World', in Kennedy (ed.), *Roman Army in the East*, pp.43–7.

Breeze, D.J., 'Demand and Supply on the Northern Frontier', in Miket and Burgess, *Between and Beyond the Walls*.

Brennan, T.C., 'Sulla's Career in the Nineties; Some Reconsiderations', *Chiron*, 22 (1992), pp.103–58.

Brigham, Robert K., *Is Iraq Another Vietnam?* (New York: Public Affairs, 2006).

Brizzi, Giovanni, *I sistemi informativi dei Romani: Principi e realtà nell' età delle conquista oltremare (218–168 aC)*, Historia Einzelschriften no. 39 (Wiesbaden: Steiner, 1982).

Brodersen, Kai, *Terra cognita: Studien zür römischen Raumfassung* (Hildesheim: Olms, 1995).

Brundage, B.C., 'Feudalism in Ancient Mesopotamia and Iran', in R. Coulborn *et al.*, *Feudalism in History* (North Haven, CT: Archon Books, 1956), pp.93–119.

Brunt, P.A., *Italian Manpower* (London: Oxford University Press, 1971).

Brunt, P.A., 'Laus imperii', in P.D.A. Garnsey and C.R. Whittaker, *Imperialism in the Ancient World* (Cambridge: Cambridge University Press, 1978), pp.159–91.

Brunt, P.A., *Roman Imperial Themes* (Oxford: Clarendon Press; New York: Oxford University Press, 1990).

Buchheim, Hans, *Die Orientpolitik des Triumvirn M. Antonius, Abh. D. Heidelberger Akad. D. Wiss. Phil.*, hist, klasse 1960, 3 (Heidelberg: Winter, 1960).

Bullough, Vern L., 'The Roman Empire vs Persia, 363–502: A Study of Successful Deterence', *Journal of Conflict Resolution*, 7, 1 (March 1963), pp.55–68.

Bury, J.B., *History of the Later Roman Empire*, 2 vols (London and New York: Macmillan & Co., 1889).

Butcher, Kevin, *Roman Syria and the Near East* (Los Angeles, CA: Getty Publications, 2003).

Cadoux, T.J., 'Marcus Crassus: A Revaluation', *G&R*, 3 (1956), pp.153–61.

Cameron, George C., *The History of Early Iran* (Chicago, IL: University of Chicago Press, 1936).

Campbell, Brian, 'War and Diplomacy: Rome and Parthia, 31 BC – AD 235', in J. Rich and G. Shipley (eds), *War and Society in the Roman World* (New York and London: Routledge, 1993, pp. 213–40.

Campbell, D.B., 'What Happened at Hatra? The Problems of the Severan Siege Operations?' in Freeman and Kennedy, *Defence of the Roman and Byzantine East*, pp.51–8.

Campbell, J.B., 'Who Were the *viri militares*?', *JRS*, 65 (1975), pp.11–31.

Campbell, J.B., *The Emperor and the Roman Army* (Oxford: Clarendon Press, 1984).

Campbell, J.B., 'Teach Yourself How to be a General', *JRS*, 77 (1987), pp.13–29.

Cancik, Hubert and Schneider, Helmuth (eds), *Brill's New Pauly, Encyclopaedia of the Ancient World: Antiquity*, English edition: managing editor, Christine F. Salazar; assistant editor, David E. Orton (Leiden; Boston, MA: Brill, 2002).

Cary, M., 'The Frontier Policy of the Roman Emperors down to AD 200, *Acta Classica*, 1, 1958, pp.131–8.

Champion, C.B., *Roman Imperialism. Readings and Sources* (Oxford: Blackwell, 2004).

Chapot, Victor, *La Frontière de l'Euphrate de Pompée a la conquete arabe* (Paris: A. Fontemoing, 1907).

Charlesworth, M.P., *Trade Routes and Commerce of the Roman Empire* (Cambridge: Cambridge University Press, 1961).

Chaumont, M.L., 'L'Armenie entre Rome et l'Iran I: De l'avenèment d'Auguste à l'avenèment de Dioclétian', in *ANRW*, II, 9.1 (1979), pp.71–194.

Chaumont, M.L., 'Armenia and Iran: The Pre-Islamic Period', *Encyclopedia Iranica* (London, 1986), vol. 2, 4, pp.417–38.

Chaumont, M.L., 'Un document méconnue concernant l'envoi d'un ambassadeur parthe vers Septime Sévère (P. Dura 60B), *Historia*, 36 (1987), pp.422–47.

Chin, Warren, 'Examining the Application of British Counterinsurgency Doctrine by the American Army in Iraq', *Small Wars and Insurgencies*, 18, 2 (1–26 March 2007), pp.1–26.

Christensen, Arthur, 'L'Iran sous les Sassanides', in *CAH*, 12 (1939), chapter 4, 'Sassanid Persia', pp.109–25.

Cizek, Eugen, *L'Époque de Trajan* (Bucharest/Paris: Les Belles Lettres, 1983).

Cobban, J.M., *Senate and the Provinces 78–49 BC* (Cambridge: Cambridge University Press, 1935).

Cohen, Henry, *Description historique des monnaies frappés sous l'Empire romaine* (Paris and London: Paris and London: Rollin et Feuardent, 1880–92).

College, M.A.R., *The Parthians* (New York: Praeger, 1967).

Coulston, J.C., 'Roman, Parthian and Sassanid Tactical Developments', in Freeman and Kennedy, *Defence of the Roman and Byzantine East*, pp.59–75.

Crook, J.A., *Consilium Principis* (Cambridge: Cambridge University Press, 1955).

Crow, J.G., 'A Review of the Physical Remains of the Frontiers of Cappadocia', in Freeman and Kennedy (eds), *Defence of the Roman and Byzantine East*, pp.77–91.

Cumont, Franz, *Voyage d'exploration archéologique dans le Pont at la Petite Arménie*, Studia Pontica, 2 (Brussells: Lamartin, 1906).

Cumont, F., 'L'Annexion du Pont Polémoniaque et de la Petite Arménie', in W.H. Buckler and W.M. Calder (eds), *Anatolian Studies presented to Sir William Mitchell Ramsay* (Manchester: Manchester University Press; London and New York: Longmans Green, 1923).

Cumont, Franz, 'Fouilles de Doura-Europos Paris: Haut commissariat française en Syrie et au Liban', *Bibliothèque archéologique et historique*, 9, 1925.

Cumont, F., 'Review of Dobrias', *Syria*, 6 (1925), p.282.

Cumont, F., 'Nouvelles inscriptions grecques de Suse', *CRAI* (1930) pp.211–20.

Cumont, F., 'Une lettre du roi Artaban III', *CRAI* (1932), pp.238–59.

Cumont, F., 'L'iniziazione di Nerone da parte di Tiridate d'Armenia', *Rivista di filologia*, 61 (1933), pp.145–54.

Cumont, F., 'The Frontier Provinces of the East', *CAH*, 11 (1963), pp.606–13.

Cuntz, Otto, *Itineraria romana* (Leipzig: B.G. Teubner, 1929).

Dabrowa, Edward, 'Les troupes auxiliaries de l'armée romaine en Syrie au 1ere siècle de notre ère', *DHA*, 5 (1979), pp.233–54.

Dabrowa, Edward., 'La garnison romaine à Douro-Europos: Influence du camp sur la vie de la ville et ses consequences', *Cahiers scientifiques de l'Université Jagellione*, Histoire 70 (1981), pp.61–75.

Dabrowa, Edward, 'Les rapports entre Rome et les Parthes sous Vespasien', *Syria*, 58 (1981), pp.187–204.

Dabrowa, Edward, 'Le programme de la politique parthe en Occident des derniers Arsacides', *Iranica Antiqua*, 19 (1984), pp.149–65.

Dabrowa, Edward, 'The Frontier in Syria in the First Century AD', in Freeman and Kennedy (eds), *Defence of the Roman and Byzantine East*, pp.93–108.

Dabrowa, Edward, 'Roman Policy in Transcaucasia from Pompey to Domitian', in French and Lightfoot (eds), *Eastern Frontier of the Roman Empire*, pp.67–75.

Dabrowa, Edward (ed.), *Ancient Iran and the Mediterranean World: Studies in Ancient History: Proceedings of an international conference in honour of Prof. Józef Wolski held at the Jagiellonian University, Cracow, in September 1996* (Cracow: Jagiellonian University Press, 1998).

Dabrowa, Edward, 'The Commanders of the Syrian Legions 1st–3rd c. AD', in Kennedy (ed.), *Roman Army in the East*, pp.277–96.

Dabrowa, Edward, *The Governors of Roman Syria from Augustus to Septimius Severus* (Bonn: Rudolf Habelt, 1998).

D'Amato, Clothilde, *Optimus Princeps. La Figura di Traiano fra storia e mito* (Rome: Ingegneria per la cultura, 1999).

Dando-Collins, Michael, *Mark Antony's Heroes: How the Third Gallica Legion Saved an Apostle and Created an Emperor* (Hoboken, NJ: John Wiley & Sons, 2007).

Danner, Mark, 'The Secret Way to War: The Downing Street Memo', *NYRB*, 52, 10 (9 June 2005), p.70.

Davies, R.W., 'Fronto, Hadrian, and the Roman Army', *Latomus*, 27 (1968), pp.75–95.

Debecq, J., 'Les Parthes et Rom', *Latomus*, 10 (1951), pp.459–69.

Debevoise, Neilson C., *The Political History of Parthia*, reprint edn (New York: Greenwood Press, 1968; originally published in Chicago by University of Chicago Press, 1938).

Dee, James H., 'Arethusa to Lycotas. Propertius 4.3', *TAPA*, 104 (1974), pp.81–96.

Degrassi, A., 'Fu Traiano a renunciare alla Mesopotamia?' *Revue de Philologie*, 64 (1936), pp.410–11.

Delbrück, Hans, *History of the Art of War, 1: Warfare in Antiquity*, trans. Walter J. Renfroe, Jr (Lincoln, NE, and London: University of Nebraska Press, 1990).

Derow, P.S., 'Polybius, Rome and the East', *Journal of Roman Studies*, 69 (1979), pp.1–15.

Devijver, H., 'Equestrian Officers in the East', in French and Lightfoot, *Eastern Frontier of the Roman Empire*, pp.77–111.

Devine, A.M., 'The Parthi, the Tyranny of Tiberius, and the Date of Q. Curtius Rufus', *Phoenix*, 33 (1979), pp.142–59.

Dilke, O., *Greek and Roman Maps* (Ithaca, NY: Cornell University Press, 1985).

Dilleman, L., *Haute Mésopotamie orientale et pays adjacents: Contribution à la géographie historique de la region du V siecle avant l'ere chretienne ai Vie siecle de cette ère* (Paris: P. Geuthner, 1962).

Dise, Jr, R.L., 'Trajan, the Antonines and the Governors' Staff', *ZPE*, 116 (1997), pp.273–83.

Dobbins, K.W., 'Mithridates II and his Successors: A Study of the Parthian Crisis', *Antichthon*, 8 (1974), pp.63–79.

Dobias, J., 'Les premiers rapports des Romains avec les Parthes et l'occupation de la Syrie', *Archiv Orientalni*, 3 (1931), pp.215–56.

Dodgeon, M.H. and Lieu, S.N.C., *The Roman Eastern Frontier and the Persian Wars AD 226–363: A Documentary History* (London and New York: Routledge, 1991).

Downey, Glanville, 'The Occupation of Syria by the Romans', *TAPA*, 82 (1951), pp.149–63.

Drijvers, H.J.W., 'Hatra Palmyra und Edessa: Die Städte der syrisch-mesopotamischen Wüste in politischer, kulturgeschichtlicher und religionsgeschichtlicher Beleuchtung', in *ANRW*, 2, 8 (1977), pp.799–906.

Drijvers, H.J.W., 'Strabo on Parthia and the Parthians', in J. Wieshofer: *Das Parthereich und Seine Zeugnisse* (Stuttgart: F. Steiner, 1998), pp.279–93.

Duncan-Jones, R.P., 'Praefectus Mesopotamiae et Osrhoene', *Classical Philology*, 64 (1969), pp.229ff.

Duncan-Jones, R.P., *Structure and Scale in the Roman Economy* (Cambridge: Cambridge University Press, 1990).

Duncan-Jones, R.P., *Money and Government in the Roman Empire* (Cambridge: Cambridge University Press, 1994).

Dürr, Julius, *Die Reisen des Kaisers Hadrian* (Wien: C. Gerold's Sohn, 1881).

Dvornik, Francis, *The Origins of Intelligence Services* (New Brunswick, NJ: Rutgers University Press, 1974).

Eadie, J.W., 'The Development of Roman Mailed Cavalry', *JRS*, 57 (1967), pp.161–73.

Eadie, J.W., 'Artifacts of Annexation: Trajan's Grand Strategy and Arabia', in J. Eadie and J. Ober, *The Craft of the Ancient Historian* (Lanham, MD: University Press of America), pp.407–23.

Earle, E.M. (ed.), *The Makers of Modern Strategy* (Princeton, NJ: Princeton University Press, 1943).

Eck, Werner, 'Trajan 98–117', in Manfred Clauss (ed.), *Die römischen Kaiser* (Munich: C.H. Beck, 1997), pp.110–24.

Eckhardt, Kurt, 'Die armenischen Feldzüge des Lukullus III', *Klio*, 10 (1910) pp.192–231.

Eckstein, Arthur M., *Senate and General: Individual Decision Making and Roman Foreign Relations, 264–194 BC* (Berkeley, CA: University of California Press, 1987).

Eilers, Wilhelm, 'Iran and Mesopotamia', in *CHI*, 3, 2, pp.481–504.

Evans, Robert F., *Soldiers of Rome* (Cabin John, MD: Seven Locks Press, 1986).

Fair, Charles, *From the Jaws of Victory* (New York: Simon and Shuster, 1971).

Fallows, J., *Blind into Baghdad* (New York: Vintage Books, 2006).

Fantham, Elaine, 'The Trials of Gabinius in 54 BC', *Historia*, 24 (1975), pp.425–33.

Fasolo, Michele, *La Via Egnatia*, 2 vols (Roma: Istituto grafico editorial romano, 2003).

Fell, Martin, *Optimus princeps? Anspruch und Wirklichkeit der imperialen Programmatik Kaiser Traians* (München: Tuduv, 1992).

Ferrill, Arther, *Roman Imperial Grand Strategy* (Lanham, MD: University Press of America, 1991).

Ferrill, Arther, 'The Grand Strategy of the Roman Empire', in Kennedy, *Grand Strategies in War and Peace*, pp.71–86.

Fiema, Zbigniew T., 'The Roman Annexation of Arabia', *The Ancient World*, 15 (1987), pp.25–35.

Fink, R.O., 'Victoria Parthica and Kindred Victoriae', *YCS*, 8 (1942), pp.81–101.

Fink, R.O., *Roman Military Records on Papyrus* (Cleveland, OH: Press of the Case Western Reserve University, 1971).

Fischer-Hansen, Tobias (ed.), *East and West Cultural Relations in the Ancient World* (Copenhagen: Museum Tusculanums Vorlag, 1988).

Frankfort, T., 'Trajan Optimus: Recherche de Chronologie', *Latomus*, 16 (1957), pp.333–4.

Freeman, Philip and Kennedy, D.L. (eds), *The Defence of the Roman and Byzantine East: Proceedings of a Colloquium held at the University of Sheffield in April 1986*, British Institute of Archaeology at Ankara Monograph no. 8, 2 vols (Oxford: British Archaeological Reports, International Series, 297, 1 & 2, 1986).

French, D.H., 'New Research of the Euphrates Frontier: Supplementary Notes 1 and 2', in S. Mitchell (ed.), *Armies and Frontiers in Roman and Byzantine Anatolia* (Oxford: British Archaological Reports, 1983), pp.71–101.

French, D.H. and Lightfoot, C.S. (eds), *The Eastern Frontier of the Roman Empire: Proceedings of a Colloquium held at Ankara in September 1988*, British Institute of Archaeology at Ankara Monograph no. 11, 2 vols (Oxford: British Archaelogical Reports, International Series, 553, 1 & 2, 1989).

Frézouls, E., 'Les fluctations de la frontière orientale et de l'empire romain', in *Colloque de Strasbourg: La géographie administrative et politique d'Alexandre à Mahomet: Actes du Colloque de Strasbourg, 14–16 Juin 1979* (Leiden: E.J. Brill, 1981), pp.177–222.

Frye, R.N., *The Heritage of Persia* (Cleveland, OH: World Publishing, 1963).

Frye, R.N., *The History of Ancient Iran*, Handbuch der Altertumswissenschaft, 3, 7 (Munich: Beck, 1984).

Fuks, A., 'The Jewish Revolt in Egypt, AD 115–117, in the Light of the Papyri', *Aegyptus*, 33 (1953), pp.153–4.

Fuks, A., 'Aspects of the Jewish Revolt in AD 115–117', *JRS*, 51 (1961), pp.98–104.

Gabba, Emilio, 'Sulle influenze reciproche degli ordinamenti militari dei Parti e dei Romani', in *La Persia e il mondo greco-romano (Per la storia dell'escercito Romana in età imperiale)* (Bologna: Patron, 1974).

Gagé, Jean, 'La theologie de la victoire imperiale', *Revue historique*, 171 (1933), pp.1–43.

Gagé, Jean, *Res gestae divi Augvsti*: ex monumentis Ancyrano et antiocheno latinis: Ancyrano et Apolloniensi graecis: texte établi et commenté par Jean Gagé *(RGDA)* (Paris: Les Belles Lettres, 1950, 2nd edn; Paris, 1977, 3rd edn).

Gagé, Jean, 'L'empereur romain et les rois: Politique et protocol', *Revue historique*, 221 (1959), pp.221–60.

Gallagher, J. and Robinson, J., 'The Imperialism of Free Trade', *Economic History Review*, 6, 1 (1953), pp.1–15.

Garnsey, P.D.A. and Whittaker, C.R., *Imperialism in the Ancient World* (Cambridge: Cambridge University Press, 1978).

Garzetti, A., 'M. Licinio Crasso', *Athenaeum*, 19 (1941), pp.1–37.

Garzetti, A., 'M. Licinio Crasso', *Athenaeum*, 20 (1942), pp.12–40.

Garzetti, A., 'M. Licinio Crasso', *Athenaeum*, 22 (1944), pp.1–61.

Gawlikowski, M., 'A Fortress in Mesopotamia: Hatra', in E. Dabrowa (ed.), *The Roman and Byzantine Army in the East* (Krakow: Uniwersytet Jagiellonskiego, 1994), pp.47–56.

Gelzer, Matthias, 'Licinius', no. 68 (Crassus), in *RE*, no. 13, 1 (1926), cols 295–331.

Gelzer, Matthias, *Pompeius* (Munich: F. Bruckmann, 1949).

Ghirshman, R., *Iran from the Earliest Times to the Islamic Conquest* (Baltimore, MD: Pelican Books, 1954).

Ghirshman, R., *Iran, Parthians and Sassanians* (London: Thames & Hudson, 1967).

Ghirshman, R., 'L'Iran et Rome aux premiere siècles de notre ère', *Syrie*, 49 (1972), pp.161–5.

Ghirshman, R., 'La 'Porte Noir' de Besançon et la prise de Ctesiphon', *Syrie*, 49 (1972) pp.215–18.

Giles, P., 'Rome and the Far East in 53 BC', *Proceedings of the Cambridge Philological Society*, 1 (1929), pp.1–4.

Gilmartin, K., 'Corbulo's Campaigns in the East: An Analysis of Tacitus' Account', *Historia*, 22 (1973), pp.583–626.

Goldsworthy, Adrian, *The Roman Army at War 100 BC – AD 200* (Oxford: Clarendon Press, 1996).

Goldsworthy, Adrian, *The Fall of the West* (London: Weidenfeld & Nicholson, 2009).

González, Julián (ed.), *Imp. Caes. Nerva Traianus Aug.* (Sevilla: Ediciones Alfar, 1993).

González, Julián, *Trajano: Emperador de Roma: Actas des Congreso Internacional* (Rome: L'Erma di Bretschneider, 2000).

Goodman, Martin, *Rome and Jerusalem: The Clash of Ancient Civilizations* (London and New York: Allan Lane, 2007).

Graham, A.J., 'Septimius Severus and his Generals, AD 193–97', in M.R.D. Foot (ed.), *War and Society: Historical Essays in Honour and Memory of J.R. Western, 1928–1971* (London: Paul Elek, 1973), pp.261–6.

Gregory, Shelagh and Kennedy, D.L. (eds), *Sir Aurel Stein's Limes Report: The Full Text of M.A. Stein's Unpublished Limes Report: His Aerial and Ground Reconnaissances in Iraq and Transjordan in 1938– 39*, 2 vols (Oxford: British Archaeological Reports, 1985).

Griffin, Miriam, 'Trajan', in *CAH2*, 11 (2000), pp.96–128.

Groag, E.D., 'Zu einer Inschrift auf Dura', *Klio*, 29 (1936), pp.232–6.

Gruen, E.S., *The Last Generation of the Roman Republic* (Berkeley, CA: University of California Press, 1974).

Gruen, E.L., 'M. Licinius Crassus: A Review Article', *AJAH*, 2 (1977), pp.117–28.

Gruen, E.S., *The Hellenistic World and the Coming of Rome* (Berkeley, CA: University of California Press, 1984).

Gruen, E.S., 'The Imperial Policy of Augustus', in K. Raaflaub and M. Toher (eds), *Between Republic and Empire: Interpretations of Augustus and his Principate* (Berkeley, CA: University of California Press, 1999), pp.395–416.

Guey, J., 'Le probleme chronologique que souleve la guerre de Trajan contres les Parthes', *CRAI* (1934), pp.72–4.

Guey, J., *Essai sur la guerre parthique de Trajan*, Bibliothèque d'Istros, no. 2 (Bucharest: Imprimerie nationale, 1937).

Günther, Adolph, *Beiträge zur Geschichte der Kriege zwischen Römern und Parthern* (Berlin: C.A. Schwetschke 1922).

Gutschmid, Alfred Freiherr von, *Untersuchungen über die Geschichte des Königreichs Osroëne*. Mémoires de l'Académie Impériale des Sciences de St Pétersbourg, VIIe serie bd. 35, no. 1 (1887).

Gutschmid, Alfred Freiherr von, *Geschichte Irans und seiner Nachbarländer von Alexander der Grosse bis zum untergang der Arsaciden* (Tübingen: H. Laupp, 1888).

Gwatkin, William Emmett, *Cappadocia as a Roman Procuratorial Province*, University of Missouri Studies, vol. 5, no. 4, 1 October 1930 (Columbia, MO: University of Missouri Press, 1930).

Haig, P.V., 'Trajan in Armenia', *Journal of the Society of Ancient Numismatics*, 1 (1969–70), pp.46–7.

Halfmann, Helmut, 'Kaiser Trajan und die Grenzen des Imperium Romanum im Osten', in Eckart Olshausen and Holger Sonnabend (eds.), *Stuttgarter Kolloquium zur historischen Geographie des Altertums*, 4, 1990 (Amsterdam: A.M. Hakkert, 1994), pp.577–88.

Hannestad, A., *Roman Art and Imperial Policy* (Aarhus: Aarhus University, 1988).

Hanslik, R.M., 'Ulpius Traianus', in *RE*, Suppl. 10 (Stuttgart, 1965), cols 1095–102.

Harris, W.V., *War and Imperialism in Republican Rome* (New York: Oxford University Press, 1979).

Harris, W.V. (ed.), *The Imperialism of Mid-Republican Rome* (Rome: American Academy in Rome, 1984).

Hasebroek, Johannes, *Untersuchungen zur Geschichte des Kaisers Septimius Severus* (Heidelberg: C. Winter, 1921).

Hasluck, F.W., 'Inscriptions from the Cyzicus District, 1906', *JHS*, 27 (1907), pp.61–7.

Hattendorf, J.B., 'Alliance, Encirclement and Attrition: British Grand Strategy in the Wars of the Spanish Succession', in Kennedy (ed.), *Grand Strategies in War and Peace*, pp.11–30.

Henderson, Bernard W., 'The Chronology of the Wars in Armenia AD 51–63', *CR*, 15 (1901), pp.159–65, 204–13, 266–74.

Henderson, Bernard W., 'Controversies in Armenian Topography, 1: The Site of Tigranocerta', *AJPh*, 28 (1903), pp.99–121.

Henderson, Bernard W., *The Life and Principate of the Emperor Nero* (London: Methuen & Co., 1903).

Henderson, Bernard W., 'Rhandeia and the River Arsanias', *Journal of Philology*, 28 (1903), pp.271–86.

Henderson, Bernard W., *Five Roman Emperors: Vespasian, Titus, Domitian, Nerva, Trajan, AD 69–117*, reprint of Cambridge 1927 edn (New York: Barnes & Noble, 1969).

Herr, W. Eric, 'Operation Vigilant Warrior: Conventional Deterrence Theory, Doctrine, and Practice', Thesis, School of Advanced Airpower Studies, Air University, Maxwell Air Force Base, June 1996.

Herzfeld, Ernst, 'Untersuchungen über die historische Topographie der Landshacft am Tigris, kleinen Zab und Gebel Hamrin', *Memnon*, 1 (1907), pp.89–143.

Herzfeld, Ernst, *The Persian Empire: Studies in the Geography and Ethnography of the Ancient Near East* (Wiesbaden: F. Steiner, 1969).

Hirschfeld, Otto, 'Dellius ou Sallustius?' in *Mélanges Boissier* (Paris: Albert Fontemoing, 1903), pp.293–95.

Hirth, Friedrich, *China and the Roman Orient* (Leipzig and Munich: Georg Hirth, 1885).

Hodgson, Nicholas, 'The East as Part of the Wider Imperial Frontier Policy', in French and Lightfoot, *Eastern Frontier of the Roman Empire*, pp.177–89.

Holleaux, Maurice, *Rome, La Grèce et les Monarchies Hellénistiques au IIIe siècle avant JC (273–205)*, reprint of 1935 edn (Paris: Boccard, 1969).

Hollis, A.S., 'Ovid A. A. I. 197–198: The Wrong Phraates?' *CR*, 20 (1970), pp.141–2.

Hopkins, C. and Rowell, H.T., 'Preliminary Report of the Fifth Season of Work', in M.I. Rostovtzeff (ed.), *Excavations at Dura-Europos* (New Haven, CT: Yale University Press, 1984), pp.218ff.

Horbury, William, 'The Beginnings of the Jewish Revolt under Trajan', in Peter Schaefer (ed.), *Geschichte – Tradition – Reflexion: Festschrift für Martin Hengel, Bd. 1, Judentum* (Tübingen: J.C.B. Mohr; Paul Siebeck, 1996), pp.283–304.

Humbert, G., 'Amicitiae', in *RE*, col. 229.

Invernizzi, A., 'Kifrin and the Euphrates Limes', in Freeman and Kennedy (eds), *Defence of the Roman and Byzantine East*, pp.383–95.

Isaac, Benjamin, 'The Meaning of "*Limes*" and "*Limitanei*" in Ancient Sources', *JRS*, 78 (1988), pp.125–47.

Isaac, Benjamin, *The Limits of Empire: The Roman Army in the East* (Oxford: Clarendon Press, 1992).

Jervis, Robert, *Perception and Misperception in International Politics* (Princeton, NJ: Princeton University Press, 1976).

Jones, A.H.M., *The Roman Economy: Studies in Ancient Economic and Administrative History*, ed. P.A. Brunt (Totowa, NJ: Rowman and Littlefield, 1974).

Junge, Peter Julius, 'Parthia: Das Partherreich in Hellenistischer Zeit', in *RE*, 18, 4 (1949), cols 1968–86.

Justi, Ferdinand, *Geschichte des alten Persiens* (Berlin: G. Grote, 1879).

Kahrstedt, U., 'La province d'Assyrie crée par Trajan: A proposal de la guerre parthique de Trajan', *Syrie*, 36 (1959), pp.254–63.

Keaveney, A., 'Deux Dates Contestée de la carriére de Sylla', *Les Etudes Classiques*, 48 (1980), pp.149–59.

Keaveney, A., 'Roman Treaties with Parthia circa 95 – circa 64 BC', *AJPh*, 102 (1981), pp.195–212.

Keaveney, A., 'The Kings and Warlords: Romano-Parthian Relations circa 64–53', *AJPh*, 103 (1982), pp.412–28.

Keaveney, A., 'Parthia and Rome', in Kennedy (ed.), *Roman Army in the East*, pp.67–90.

Keitel, Elizabeth, 'The Role of Parthia and Armenia in Tacitus' Annals 11 and 12', *AJPh*, 99 (1978), pp.462–73.

Kennedy, D.L., 'Ti. Claudius Subatianus Aquila, "First Prefect of Mesopotamia" ', *ZPE*, 36 (1979), pp. 255–62.

Kennedy, D.L., 'European Soldiers and the Severan Siege of Hatra', in Freeman and Kennedy (eds), *Defence of the Roman and Byzantine East*, pp.397–409.

Kennedy, D.L., 'The Garrisoning of Mesopotamia in the Late Antonine and Early Severan Period', *Antichthon*, 21 (1987), pp.57–66.

Kennedy, D.L., 'The Military Contribution of Syria to the Roman Imperial Army', in French and Lightfoot (eds), *Eastern Frontier of the Roman Empire*, Part 1, pp.235–46.

Kennedy, D.L., 'Zeugma, une ville antique sur l'Euphrate', *Archéologia*, 306 (1994), pp.26–35.

Kennedy, D.L., 'Parthia and Rome', in Kennedy (ed.), *Roman Army in the East*, pp.67–90.

Kennedy, D.L. (ed.), *The Roman Army in the East* (Ann Arbor, MI: *Journal of Roman Archaeology*, Supplementary Series, 18, 1996).

Kennedy, D.L. and Riley, Derrick, *Rome's Desert Frontier from the Air* (London: B.T. Batsford; Austin, TX: University of Texas Press, 1990).

Kennedy, Paul, 'Grand Strategy in War and Peace: Toward a Broader Definition', in Kennedy (ed.), *Grand Strategies in War and Peace*, pp.1–7.

Kennedy, Paul (ed.), *Grand Strategies in War and Peace* (New Haven, CT: Yale University Press, 1997).

Keppie, Lawrence, 'Legions in the East from Augustus to Trajan', in Freeman and Kennedy (eds), *Defence of the Roman and Byzantine East*, pp.411–29.

Kissinger, Henry A., *The White House Years* (Boston: Little Brown, 1979).

Kolendo, Jerzy, *A la recherché de l'ambre baltique: L'expedition d'un chevalier romain sous Neron* (Warsaw: Wydawnictwa Uniwersytetu Warszawskiego, 1981).

Kromayer, Johannes, 'Kleine Forschungen zur Geschichte des zweiten Triumvirats', *Hermes*, 31 (1896), pp.1–54.

La Berge, C. de, *Essai sur la règne de Trajan* (Paris: F. Vieweg, 1877).

Laet, Sigfried J. de, *Portorium: Étude sur l'organization douanière chez les romains* (Bruges: De Tempel, 1949).

La Motta, 'La tradizione sulla rivolta ebraica al temp di Traiano', *Aegyptus*, 32 (1952), pp.474–90.

Lang, David M., 'Iran, Armenia and Georgia', in *CHI*, ed. Y. Yarshater (Cambridge: Cambridge University Press, 1983), pp.505–36.

Laufer, B., *Chinese Clay Figures: I. Prolegomena on the History of Defensive Armor* (Chicago, IL: Field Museum Anthropological Series, 13, 2, 1914).

Lebow, Richard Ned and Stein, Janice Gross, 'Rational Deterrence Theory: I Think, Therefore I Deter', *World Politics*, 41, 2 (January 1989), pp.208–24.

Lee, A.D., *Information and Frontiers: Roman Foreign Relations in Late Antiquity* (Cambridge: Cambridge University Press, 1993).

Leiner, W., *Die Signaltechnik der Antike* (Stuttgart: W. Leiner, 1982).

Lemosse, M., 'Le couronnement de Tiridate: Remarques sur le statut des protectorat romains', in *Mélanges Gilbert Gidel* (Paris: Librarie Sirey, 1961), pp.455–68.

Lepper, F.A., *Trajan's Parthian War* (London: Oxford University Press, 1948).

Lerouge, Charlotte, *L'image des Parthes dans le monde gréco-romain* (Stuttgart: Franz Steiner Verlag, 2007).

Le Roux, E. and Etienne, R., *L'armée romaine et l'organization des provinces ibériques d'Auguste à l'invasion de 409* (Paris: Centre Pierre Paris-De Boccard, 1982).

Leupp, Gary, 'An Earlier Empire's War on Iraq', *Counterpunch*, 4 October 2005.

Liebmann-Frankfort, Thérèse, *La frontière orientale dans la politique extérieure de la République romaine: Depuis le traité d'Apamée jusqu'a la fin des conquêtes asiatiques de Pompée, 189/8–63* (Bruxelles: Palais des Académies, 1969).

Lieu, S., 'Urbanism in Hellenistic, Parthian and Roman Mesopotamia', in Freeman and Kennedy (eds), *Defence of the Roman and Byzantine East*, pp.507–8.

Lightfoot, C.S., 'Trajan's Parthian War and the Fourth Century Perspective', *JRS*, 80 (1990), pp.115–26.

Longden, R.P., 'Notes on the Parthian Campaigns of Trajan', *JRS*, 21 (1931), pp.1–35.

Longden, R.P., 'The Wars of Trajan', *CAH*, 11 (1936), pp.223–51.

Lund, A., *Zum Germanenbild der Römer: Eine Einführung in die antike Ethnographie* (Heidelberg: C. Winter, 1990).

Luttwak, Edward, *The Grand Strategy of the Roman Empire* (Baltimore, MD: Johns Hopkins University Press, 1976).

MacMullen, Ramsay, *The Roman Government's Response to Crisis AD 235–337* (New Haven, CT: Yale University Press, 1976).

Magie, David, 'The Mission of Agrippa to the Orient in 23 BC', *CP*, 3 (1908), pp.145–52.

Magie, David, 'Roman Policy in Armenia and Transcausasia and its Significance', *Annual Report of the American Historical Association*, 1 (1919), pp.295–304.

Magie, David, *Roman Rule in Asia Minor* (Princeton, NJ: Princeton University Press, 1950).

Malitz, J., 'Caesars Partherkrieg', *Historia*, 33 (1984), pp.21–59.

Mann, John, 'The Frontiers of the Principate', in *ANRW*, 2, 1 (1974), pp.508–33.

Mann, John, 'Power, Force and the Frontiers of the Empire', review of E. Luttwak, *The Grand Strategy of the Roman Empire*, *JRS*, 69 (1979), pp.175–83.

Maricq, A., 'Hatra de Sanatrouq', *Syria*, 32 (1955), pp.273–88.

Maricq, A., 'La province d'Assyrie crée par Trajan: A propos de la guerre parthique de Trajan', *Syria*, 36 (1959), pp.254–63.

Marshall, B.A., *Crassus: A Political Biography* (Amsterdam: A.M. Hakkert, 1976).

Masi, Fausto, *Traiano; il principe che porto l'Imperio romano alla Massima espansione* (Rome: International EILES, Rome, 1993).

Mattern, Susan, *Rome and the Enemy* (Berkeley, CA: University of California Press, 1999).

Matthaei, Louise E., 'On the Classification of Roman Allies', *Classical Quarterly*, 1, 2/3 (July 1907), pp.182–204.

Maxfield, Valerie A., and Dobson, M.J. (eds), *Roman Frontier Studies. Proceedings of the XV International Congress of Frontier Studies, 1989* (Exeter: University of Exeter Press, 1991).

McCormick, M., *Eternal Victory: Triumphal Rulership in Late Antiquity, Byzantium and the Early Medieval West* (Cambridge: Cambridge University Press; Paris: Éditions de la Maison des

Sciences de l'Homme, 1986).

McDermott, W.C., 'Caesar's Projected Dacian-Parthian Expedition', *Ancient Society*, 13/14 (1982/83), pp.223–31.

McGing, B.C., *The Foreign Policy of Mithridates VI Eupator, King of Pontus*, Mnemosyne, Supplement 89 (Leiden: Brill, 1986).

Merlin, A., 'Quelques remarques sur la carrière de L. Catilius Severus, légat de Syrie', in *Mélanges syriens offerts à Monsieur Rene Dussaud* (Paris: 1939), vol. 1, pp.217–26.

Meyer, Hans D., *Die Aussenpolitik des Augustus und die augusteische Dichtung*, Kölner Historische Abhandlungen, bd. 53 (Cologne: Bohlau, 1961).

Mielczarek, M., *Cataphracti and Clibanarii: Studies in the Heavy Armoured Cavalry in the Ancient World* (Lodz: Oficyna Naukowa MS, 1993).

Miket, Roger and Colin Burgess (eds), *Between and Beyond the Walls: Essays on the Prehistory of North Britain in Honour of George Jobey* (Edinburgh: John Donald Publishers Ltd, 1984).

Millar, Fergus, *A Study of Cassius Dio* (Oxford: Clarendon Press, 1964).

Millar, Fergus, Berciu, *et al.*, *The Roman Empire and Its Neighbours* (London: Weidenfeld & Nicholson, 1967).

Millar, Fergus, *The Emperor in the Roman World (31 BC to AD 337)* (Ithaca, NY: Cornell University Press, 1977).

Millar, Fergus, 'Emperors Frontiers and Foreign Relations 31 BC to AD 378', *Britannia*, 13 (1982), pp.1–23.

Millar, Fergus, 'Government and Diplomacy in the Roman Empire during the First Three Centuries', *International History Review*, 10, 3 (1988), pp.345–77.

Millar, Fergus, *The Roman Near East 31 BC–AD 337* (Cambridge, MA: Harvard University Press, 1993).

Mitchell, Stephen, 'The Balkans, Anatolia, and Roman Armies Across Asia Minor', in Mitchell (ed.), *Armies and Frontiers in Roman and Byzantine Anatolia*, pp.131–50.

Mitchell, Stephen (ed.), *Armies and Frontiers in Roman and Byzantine Anatolia: Proceedings of a Colloquium held at University College, Swansea in April 1981*, British Institute of Archaeology at Ankara Monograph no. 5 (Oxford: British Archaeological Reports, International Series, 156, 1983).

Mitchell, Stephen, *Anatolia* (Oxford: Clarendon Press, 1993).

Mitford, T.B., 'The Euphrates Frontier in Cappadocia', in *Studien zu den Militärgrenzen Roms II: Vorträge des 10 International Limes*

Kongresses in der Germania Inferior (Köln: Rheinland-Verlag; Bonn: in Kommission bei R. Habelt, 1977), pp.501–10.

Mitford, T.B. 'Cappadocia and Armenia Minor: Historical Setting of the *Limes*', in *ANRW*, 2, 7.2, 1980, pp.1169–228.

Mitford, T.B., 'The Inscriptions of Satala (Armenia Minor)', *ZPE*, 115 (1997), pp.137–67.

Mokaitis, Thomas R., *The Iraq War: Learning from the Past, Adapting to the Present and Planning for the Future* (Carlisle Barracks, PA: Strategic Studies Institute, US Army War College, February 2007).

Momigliano, Arnaldo, 'Corbulone e la politica romana verso i Parti', *Atti del II Congresso Nazionale di studi Romani*, band 1 (1939), pp.368–75.

Mommsen, Theodor, *The History of Rome*, trans. W.P. Dickson, 4 vols (New York: Scribner's, 1903).

Mommsen, Theodor, *The Provinces of the Roman Empire, From Caesar to Diocletian* (New York: Barnes & Noble, 1996).

Morley, N., 'Trajan's Engines', *G&R*, 47, 2 (2000), pp.197–210.

Morris, Ian and Scheidel, Walter (eds), *The Dynamics of Ancient Empires* (Oxford: Oxford University Press, 2008).

Morstein Kallet-Marx, R.M., *Hegemony to Empire: The Development of Roman Imperium in the East from 148 to 62 BC* (Berkeley, CA: University of California Press, 1995).

Moynihan, R., 'Geographical Mythology and Roman Imperial Ideology', in R. Winkes (ed.), *The Age of Augustus* (Providence, RI: Center for Old World Archaeology and Art, Brown University, 1986), pp.149–62.

Müller, Klaus E., *Geschichte der antiken Ethnnographie und ethnologischen Theoriebildung*, 2 vols (Wiesbaden: Franz Steiner Verlag, 1972–80).

Napp, E., *De rebus imperatore M. Aurelio Antoninio in Orientis gestis* (dissertation; Bonn: 1879).

Nedergaard, Elisabeth, 'The Four Sons of Phraates IV in Rome', in T. Fischer-Hansen (ed.), *East and West Cultural Relations*, pp.102–15.

Neusner, J., 'Parthian Political Ideology', *Iranica Antiqua*, 3, 1 (1963), pp.40–9.

Neusner, Jacob, 'The Jews East of the Euphrates and the Roman Empire', in *ANRW*, 2, 9.1 (1976), pp.46–69.

Newton, Homer Curtis, *The Epigraphical Evidence for the Reigns of Vespasian and Titus*, Cornell Studies in Classsical Philology, 16 (New York: Macmillan Co., 1901).

Nicolet, Claude, *Space, Geography and the Politics in the early Roman Empire* (Ann Arbor, MI: University of Michigan Press, 1991).

Niese, B., 'Zur Chronologie des Josephus', *Hermes*, 28 (1893), pp.209–22.

Nutton, V., 'The Beneficial Ideology', in Garnsey and Whittaker (eds), *Imperialism in the Ancient World*, pp.209–11.

Oates, David, 'The Roman Frontier in Northern Iraq', *Geographical Journal*, 122, 2 (June 1956), pp.188–99.

Oates, David, *Studies in the Ancient History of Northern Iraq* (London: Oxford University Press for the British Academy, 1968).

Oates, David and Oates, Joan, 'Ain Sinu: A Roman Frontier Post in Northern Iraq', *Iraq*, 21 (1959), pp.207–42.

Ober, J., 'Tiberius and the Political Testament of Augustus', *Historia*, 31 (1982), pp.306–28.

Olshausen, E. and Biller, H. (eds), *Antike Diplomatie* (Darmstadt: Wissenschaftliche Buchgesellschaft, 1979).

Ooteghem, Jules van, *Pompée le grand, bâtisseur d'empire* (Brussels: Académie royale de Belgique, Classe des lettres et des sciences morales et politiques. Mémoires. Collection in-8°. 2 sér., t. 49, 1954).

O'Sullivan, Firmin, *The Egnatian Way* (Harrisburg, PA: Stackpole Books, 1972).

Packer, George, *The Assassins' Gate* (New York: Farrar, Straus and Giroux, 2005).

Pani, Mario, *Potere e valori a Roma fra Augusto e Traiano* (Bari: Edipuglia, 1992).

Paratore, E., 'La Persia nella letteratura Latina', in Atti del Convegno sul tema, *La Persia e il mondo Greco-romano*, Roma 11–14 Aprile 1965, Accademia Nazionale dei Lincei 363, 1966, quaderni, 76, Anno 158, 1966, pp.505–58.

Paribeni, Roberto, *Optimus Princeps*, 2 vols, reprint of Messina, 1926–27 (New York: Arno Press, 1975).

Parker, H.M.D., *The Roman Legions* (Oxford: Clarendon Press, 1928).

Pékary, T., *Untersuchungen zu den römischen Reichstrassen* (Bonn: R. Habelt, 1968).

Petrenchuk, Maksim, 'US Repeating Mistakes of Roman Empire', *Rosblat News Agency*, 5 June 2004.

Pflaum, H.G., *Les procurateurs équestres sous le Haut Empire romain* (Paris: A. Maisonneuve, 1950).

Piganiol, André (ed.), *Les empereurs romains d'Espagne: Colloques international du CNRS, Madrid–Italica, 31 Mars – 6 Avril 1964* (Paris: CNRS, 196).

Platnauer, Maurice, *The Life and Reign of the Emperor Lucius Septimius Severus* (Oxford: Oxford University Press, 1918).

Pollard, Nigel, 'The Roman Army as "Total Institution" in the Near East? Dura-Europos as a Case Study', in Kennedy (ed.), *Roman Army in the East*, pp.211–27.

Pollard, Nigel, *Soldiers, Cities and Civilians in Roman Syria* (Ann Arbor, MI: University of Michigan Press, 2000).

Potter, D.S., 'Emperors, their Borders and their Neighbors: The Scope of Imperial Mandata', in Kennedy (ed.), *Roman Army in the East*, pp.49–68.

Premerstein, A. von, 'Untersuchungen zur geschichte des Kaisers Marcus, I', *Klio*, 11 (1911), pp.355–66.

Premerstein, A. von, 'Untersuchungen zur geschichte des Kaisers Marcus, III', *Klio*, 13 (1913), pp.70–96.

Pucci, Marina, *La rivolta ebraica al tempo Traiano, Pisa*, Biblioteca di Studi Antichi, 33 (Pisa: Giardini Editori e Stampori, 1981).

Ramsay, A.M., 'The Speed of the Imperial Post', *JRS*, 15 (1925), pp.60–74.

Rappaport, Uriel, 'The Jews Between Rome and Parthia', in French and Lightfoot (eds), *Eastern Frontier of the Roman Empire*, pp.373–81.

Raschke, M.G., 'New Studies in Roman Commerce with the East', in *ANRW*, 2, 9.2 (1978), pp.604–1378.

Rawlinson, George, *The Seven Great Oriental Monarchies of the Ancient Eastern World, or History, Geography and Antiquities of Chaldea, Assyria, Babylon, Media, Parthia, and Persia* (New York: Publishers Plate Renting Co., 1870).

Rawlinson, George, *Parthia* (London: T. Fisher Unwin, 1893).

Rawlinson, H.C., 'Memoir on the Site of Atropatenian Ecbatana', *Journal of the Royal Geographic Society*, 10 (1841), pp.113–15.

Regling, K., 'Crassus Partherkrieg', *Klio*, 7 (1907) pp.357–94, adapted from Regling, *De Belli Parthici Crassiani Fontibus* (Berlin: Diss, 1899).

Regling, K., 'Römische aurei aud dem Funde von Karnak', in *Festschrift zu Otto Hirschfeld's 60. Geburtstage* (Berlin: Weidemann, 1903).

Reinach, Théodore, 'Le mari de Salomé et les monnaies de Nicopolis d'Arménie', *Revue des études anciennes*, 16 (1914), pp.133–58.

Rey-Coquais, J.P., 'Syrie Romaine de Pompée à Dioclétian', *JRS*, 68 (1978), pp.44–73.

Rice-Holmes, T.R., *The Architect of the Roman Empire*, 2 vols (Oxford: Clarendon Press, 1928–31).

Rich, John and Shipley, G. (eds), *War and Society in the Roman World* (New York and London: Routledge, 1993).

Rich, J.W., 'Augustus's Parthian Honours, the Temple of Mars Ultor and the Arch in the Forum Romanum', *PBSR*, 66 (1998), pp.71–128.

Richmond, Ian, *Trajan's Army on Trajan's Column* (London: British School at Rome, 1982).

Rivet, A.L.F. and Smith, C., *The Place Names of Roman Britain* (Princeton, NJ: Princeton University Press, 1979).

Romer, F.E., 'A Numismatic Date for the Departure of Crassus', *TAPA*, 108 (1978), pp.187–202.

Romer, F.E., 'Gaius Caesar's Military Diplomacy in the East', *TAPA*, 109 (1979), pp.199–214.

Ross, Steven K., *Roman Edessa: Politics and Culture on the Eastern Fringes of the Roman Empire 114–242 CE* (New York: Routledge, 2001).

Rostovtzeff, M. I., 'Syria and the East', in *CAH*, 7 (1928), chapter 5, pp.155–96.

Rostovzteff, M.I., 'Parthia: Foreign Policy', in 'The Sarmatae and the Parthians', *CAH*, 11 (1936), pp.104–13.

Rostovtzeff, M.I., 'The Sarmatae and the Parthians', in *CAH*, 11 (1936), pp.91–130.

Rostovtzeff, M.I., 'Kaiser Trajan und Dura', *Klio*, 31 (1938), pp.285–92.

Rostovtzeff, M.I., *The Social and Economic History of the Roman Empire*, 2nd edn., 2 vols (Oxford: Clarendon Press, 1957).

Roth, Jonathan, *The Logistics of the Roman Army at War 264 BC–AD 235* (Leiden: Brill, 1999).

Rubin, Z., 'Dio, Herodian, and Severus' Second Parthian War', *Chiron*, 5 (1975) pp.419–41.

Said, Edward, *Orientalism* (New York: Pantheon Books, 1978).

Saller, R.P., *Personal Patronage under the Early Empire* (Cambridge: Cambridge University Press, 1982).

Saller, R.P., 'Promotion and Patronage in Equestrian Careers', *JRS*, 70 (1980), pp.44–63.

Sands, P.C., *The Client Princes of the Roman Empire under the Republic* (Cambridge: Cambridge University Press, 1908).

Sanford, E.M., 'Nero and the East', *HSCP*, 48 (1937), pp.75–103.

Sanford, E.M., 'The Career of Aulus Gabinius', *TAPA*, 70 (1939), pp.64–92.

Sartre, Maurice, *The Middle East Under Rome*, trans. Catherine Porter and Elizabeth Rawlings (Cambridge, MA: Harvard University Press, 2005).

Sasel, J. 'Trajan's Canal at the Iron Gate', *JRS*, 63 (1973), pp.80–5.

Schatzman, I., 'The Roman General's Authority over Booty', *Historia*, 21 (1972), pp.177–205.

Schieber, A.S., 'Antony in Parthia', *RAS*, 9 (1979), pp.105–24.

Schippmann, Klaus, *Grundzüge der parthischen Geschichte* (Darmstadt: Wissenschaftliche Buchgesellschaft, 1980).

Schur, Werner, *Die Orientpolitik des Kaisers Nero*, *Klio*, beiheft 15 (Leipzig: Dieterich, 1923).

Schur, Werner, 'Untersuchungen zur Geschichte der Kriege Corbulos', *Klio*, 19 (1925), pp.75–96.

Schur, Werner, 'Die orientalische Frage im römischen Reiche', *Neue Jahrbücher für Wissenschaft und Jugendbildung*, 2 (1926), pp.270–82.

Schur, Werner, 'Zur neronischen Orientpolitik', *Klio*, 20 (1926), pp.215–22.

Schur, W., 'Parthia: Das Partherreich als Grenznachbar des Römerreiches', in *RE*, 18, 4 (1949), pp.1987–2029.

Schürer, Emil, *Geschichte des jüdischen Volkes im Zeitalter Jesu Christ*, 2 vols (Leipzig: J.C. Hinnrichs, 1886–90).

Seager, Robin, *Pompey the Great; A Political Biography* (Oxford: Blackwell, 2002).

Seaver, J.E., 'Publius Ventidius – Neglected Roman Military Hero', *CJ*, 47 (1951–52), pp.275–80.

Sellwood, David, *An Introduction to the Coinage of Parthia* (London: Spink & Son, 1980).

Seyrig, H., 'Antiquités syrienne 42: Sur les ères de quelques ville de Syria', *Syria*, 27 (1950), pp.5–50.

Shabazi, S., 'Army I. Pre-Islamic Iran', in *Encyclopedia Iranica* (London and New York: Center for Iranian Studies, 1987), vol. 2, pp.489–99.

Shaw, Brent D., 'Rebels and Outsiders', in *CAH²*, 11 (2000), chapter 12, pp.361–403.

Sheldon, Rose Mary, 'The Spartacus Rebellion: A Roman Intelligence Failure?', *International Journal of Intelligence and Counterintelligence*, 6, 1 (1993), pp.69–84.

Sheldon, Rose Mary, *Intelligence Activities in Ancient Rome: Trust in the Gods, but Verify* (New York and London: Routledge, 2005).

Sheldon, R.M., 'Trajan's Parthian Adventure: With Some Modern Caveats', in Eunan O'Halpin, Robert Armstrong and Jane

Ohlmeyer (eds), *Intelligence, Statecraft and International Power*, Historical Studies 25, papers read before the Twenty-Seventh Irish Conference of Historians held at Trinity College, Dublin, 2005, pp.153–74.

Sherk, R.K., 'Roman Galatia: The Governors from 25 BC to AD 114', in *ANRW*, 2, 7.2 (1980), pp.954–1052.

Sherwin-White, A.N., *Racial Prejudice in Imperial Rome* (Cambridge: Cambridge University Press, 1967).

Sherwin-White, A.N., 'Ariobarzanes, Mithridates, and Sulla', *Classical Quarterly*, 27, 1 (1977), pp.173–83.

Sherwin-White, A.N., *Roman Foreign Policy in the East, 168 BC to AD 1* (London: Duckworth, 1984).

Sills, H.H., *Trajan's Armenian and Parthian Wars* (Cambridge: Cambridge University Press, 1897).

Simonetta, B. 'Sulla monetazione di Fraate IV e di Tiridate II di Parthia', *RIN*, 78 (1976), pp.19–34.

Simpson, A.D., 'The Departure of Crassus for Parthia', *TAPA*, 69 (1938), pp.532–41.

Sonnabend, Holger, *Fremdenbild und Politik: Vorstellungen der Römer von Ägypten und dem Partherreich in der Späten Republik und Frühen Kaiserzeit*, Europaeische Hochschulschriften Reihe, 3: Geschichte und ihre Hilfswissenschaft CCLXXXVI (Frankfurt: Lang, 1986).

Speidel, M.P., 'The Rise of Ethnic Units in the Roman Imperial Army', in *ANRW*, 2, 3 (1977), pp.202–31.

Speidel, M.P., '"Europeans" – Syrian Elite Troops at Dura-Europos and Hatra', in M.P. Speidel (ed.), *Roman Army Studies* (Amsterdam: J.C Gieben, 1984), vol. 1, pp.301–9.

Speidel, Michael, 'The Causasian Frontier: Second Century Garrisons at Apsaarus, Petra and Phasis', in *Studien zu den Militärgrenzen Roms*, 3 (13th International Limes Congress, Stuttgart, 1986), pp.657–60.

Speidel, M.P., 'Roman Army Pay Scales', *JRS*, 82 (1992), pp.87–106.

Stadter, Phillip A., *Arrian of Nicomedia* (Chapel Hill, NC: University of North Carolina Press, 1980).

Stark, Freya, *Rome on the Euphrates: The Story of the Frontier* (New York: Harcourt, Brace & World, 1967).

Starr, Chester G., *The Roman Empire, 27 BC – AD 476: A Study in Survival* (New York: Oxford University Press, 1982).

Steffen, Randy, 'The Ancient Parthian', *Western Horseman*, 20, 5 (May 1955), pp.46, 87–8.

Stein, Aurel, 'Surveys on the Roman Frontier in Iraq and Transjordan', *Geographical Journal*, 95, 6 (June 1940), pp.428–38.

Stempel, John D., 'Covert Action and Diplomacy', *International Journal of Intelligence and Counterintelligence*, 20, 1 (2007), pp.122–35.

Stout, Selatie Edgar, 'Antistius Rusticus', *CP*, 21 (1926), pp.5–20.

Sullivan, Richard D., *Near Eastern Royalty and Rome 100–30 BC* (Toronto: University of Toronto Press, 1990).

Sumner, G.V., 'The Truth about Velleius Paterculus: Prologomena', *HSCP*, 74 (1970), pp.257–97.

Sumner, G.V., 'Sulla's Career in the Nineties', *Athenaeum*, 56 (1978), pp.395–6.

Sykes, P.M., *History of Persia* (London: Macmillan, 1951).

Syme, Ronald, *Tacitus*, 2 vols (Oxford: Clarendon Press, 1958).

Syme, Ronald, 'Flavian Wars and Frontiers', *CAH*, 11 (1969), chapter 4, 2, p.140.

Syme, Ronald, 'Domitius Corbulo', *JRS*, 60 (1970), pp.37–9.

Syme, Ronald, *History in Ovid* (Oxford: Clarendon Press, 1978).

Täubler, Eugen, *Die Parthernachrichten bei Josephus*, Inaugural Dissertation Friedrich-Wilhelms Universität zu Berlin (Berlin: Ebering, 1904).

Talbert, Richard J.A., *The Senate of Imperial Rome* (Princeton, NJ: Princeton University Press, 1984).

Tarn, W.W., 'Antony's Legions', *Classical Quarterly*, 36 (1932), pp.75–81.

Tarn, W.W., *The Greeks in Bactria and India* (Cambridge: Cambridge University Press, 1984 [1938]).

Tarn, W.W., 'Parthia', in *CAH*, 9 (1963), pp.574–613.

Tarn, W.W., 'The Parthian Invasion', in *CAH*, 9 (1963), pp.47–50.

Tarn, W.W. and Charlesworth, M.P., 'The War of the East against the West', *CAH*, 9 (1963), pp.71–5.

Tarn, W.W., *Hellenistic Military and Naval Developments* (Chicago, IL: Ares Press, 1975).

Täubler, E., 'Zur geschichte der Alanen', *Klio*, 9 (1909), pp.14–28.

Taylor, J.G., 'Travels in Kurdistan with Notices of the Sources of the Eastern and Western Tigris, and Ancient Ruins in their Neighbourhood', *Journal of the Royal Geographic Society*, 35 (1865), pp.21–58.

Thomas, Y., 'Se venger au Forum: Solidarité familiale et process criminal à Rome', in *La Vengeance: Étude d'ethnologie, d'histoire, et de philosophie*, vol. 3: *La vengeance: Vengeance, pouvoirs, et ideologies dans quelques civilizations de l'antiquité* (Paris: Cujas, 1984), pp.65–100.

Timpe, D., 'Die Bedeutung der Schlacht von Carrhae', *Museum Helveticum*, 19 (1962), pp.104–29.

Timpe, D., 'Zur augusteischen Partherpolitik zwischen 30 und 20 v. Chr.', *Würzburger Jahrbücher für die Altertumswissenschaft*, n.f., 1 (1975), pp.155–69.

Tomes, Robert R., 'Schlock and Blah: Counter-Insurgency Realities in a Rapid Dominance Era', *Small Wars and Insurgencies*, 16, 1 (March 2005), pp.37–57.

Ullman, Harlan K. and Wade, J.P., *Shock and Awe: Achieving Rapid Dominance* (Washington, DC: National Defense University Press, 1996), online.

Ullman, H.K. and Wade, J.P., *Rapid Dominance* (London: Royal United Services Institute for Defence Studies, 1998).

Vervaet, Frederick Juliaan, 'Tacitus, Domitius Corbulo and Traianus' "Bellum Parthicum" ', *Antiquite Classique*, 68 (1999), pp.289–97.

Vervaet, Frederick Juliaan, 'CIL IX 3426', *Latomus*, 58, 3 (1999), pp.574–99.

Vervaet, Frederick Juliaan, 'Tacitus' Annals 15.25.3: A revision of Corbulo's imperium maius (AD 63–AD 65?)', in C. Deroux (ed.), *Studies in Latin Literature and Roman History*, 10 (Brussels: Collection Latomus, 2000), pp.260–98.

Vervaet, Frederick Juliaan, 'Domitius Corbulo and the Senatorial Opposition to the Reign of Nero', *Ancient Society*, 32 (2002), pp.135–93.

Vervaet, Frederick Juliaan, 'Domitius Corbulo and the Rise of the Flavian Dynasty', *Historia*, 52, 4 (2003), pp.436–64.

Vin, J.P.A van der, 'The Return of the Roman Ensigns from Parthia', *Bulletin Antieke Beschaving*, 56 (1981), pp.117–39.

Volkmann, H., *Cleopatra; A Study in Politics and Propaganda* (New York: Elek Books, 1958).

Waele, Ferdinand J. de, *Marcus Ulpius Traianus, Veldheer, Bouwheer, Rijksheer* (Antwerpen: Standaard Uitgeberij, 1976).

Wagner, Jörg, 'Die Römer an Euphrat und Tigris', *Antike Welt*, 16 Sonderheft, 1985.

Wagner, Jörg, 'Provincia Osrhoenae: New Archaeological finds illustrating the Military Organization under the Severan Dynasty', in Mitchell (ed.), *Armies and Frontiers in Roman and Byzantine Series Anatolia*, pp.103–29.

Walker, S. and Higgs, P. (eds), *Cleopatra of Egypt: From History to Myth* (London: British Museum Press, 2001).

Walker, S. and Ashton, S. (eds), *Cleopatra Reassessed* (London: British Museum Press, 2003).

Walser, G., *Rom, das Reich, und die fremden Völker in der Geschichtss-chreibung der frühen Kaiserzeit* (Baden-Baden: Verlag für Kunst und Wissenschaft, 1951).

Ward, Allen, *Marcus Crassus and the Late Roman Republic* (Columbia, MO: University of Missouri Press, 1977).

Ward-Perkins, J.B., 'The Roman West and the Parthian East', *Proceedings of the British Academy*, 51 (1965), pp.175–99.

Warmington, Brian Herbert, *Nero: Reality and Legend* (London: Chatto & Windus, 1969; New York: Norton, 1970).

Waters, K.H., 'Traianus Domitiani Continuator', *AJPh*, 90 (1969), pp.385–404.

Waters, K.H., 'The Reign of Trajan and its Place in Contemporary Scholarship (1960–1972)', in *ANRW*, 2, 2 (1975), pp.381–431.

Wathiq I. al-Sahlihi, 'Military Considerations in the Defense of Hatra', *Mesopotamia*, 26 (1991), pp.187–94.

Wees, Hans van, *Status Warriors: War, Violence and Society in Homer and History* (Amsterdam: J.C. Gieben, 1992).

Welch, Kathryn and Powell, Anton (eds), *Julius Caesar as Artful Reporter: The War Commentaries as Political Instruments* (London: Duckworth; Swansea: Classical Press of Wales, 1998).

Wells, Colin M., 'The Problems of Desert Frontiers: Chairman's Comments on the Session', in V.A. Maxfield and M.J. Dobson (eds), *Roman Frontier Studies. Proceedings of the XV International Congress of Frontier Studies*, 1989 (Exeter: University of Exeter Press, 1991), pp.498–504.

Werner, Robert, 'Das Problem des Imperialismus und die römische Ostpolitik im zweiten Jahrhundert v. Chr.', in *ANRW*, 1, 1 (1972), pp.501–63.

Westington, M.M., 'Atrocities in Roman Warfare to 133 BC', PhD dissertation, University of Chicago, 1938.

Wheeler, E.L., 'Rethinking the Upper Euphrates Frontier: Where was the Western Border of Armenia?', in Maxfield and Dobson (eds), *Roman Frontier Studies*, pp.498–504.

Wheeler, E.L., 'Methodological Limits and the Mirage of Roman Strategy', *JMH*, 57 (January 1993), 2 parts, pp.7–41 and 215–40.

Wheeler, E.L., 'Why the Romans Can't Defeat the Parthians: Julius Africanus and the Strategy of Magic', in W. Groenman-van Waateringe, B.L. van Beek, W.J.H. Willems, and S.L. Wynia (eds), *Roman Frontier Studies, 1995* (Oxford: Oxbow Monograph 91, 1997), pp.575–9.

Wheeler, E.L., 'The Laxity of the Syrian Legions', in Kennedy (ed.),

Roman Army in the East, pp.229–76.

Wheeler, E.L., 'The Chronology of Corbulo in Armenia', *Klio*, 79, 2 (1997), pp.383–97.

Wheeler, Mortimer, *Rome Beyond Imperial Frontiers* (London: Penguin Books, 1955).

Wheeler, R.E.M., 'The Roman Frontier in Mesopotamia', in W. Groenman-van Waateringe, B.L. van Beek, W.J.H. Willems, and S.L. Wynia (eds), *Congress of Roman Frontier Studies 1995* (Oxford: Oxbow Monograph 91, 1997), pp.112–29.

Whittaker, C.R., *The Frontiers of the Roman Empire: A Social and Economic Study* (Baltimore, MD: Johns Hopkins University Press, 1994).

Whittaker, C.R., 'Where are the Frontiers Now?' in Kennedy (ed.), *Roman Army in the East*, pp.25–41.

Whittaker, C.R., 'The Eastern Frontiers', *CAH²*, 11 (2000), pp.305–10.

Widengren, G., 'Iran der Grosse gegner Roms: Konigsgewalt Feudalismus Militarwesen', *Syria*, 49 (1972), pp.219–306.

Wieshofer, Josef, *Das Partherreich und seine Zeugnisse* (Stuttgart: F. Steiner, 1998).

Wilber, Donald Newton, *Iran: Past and Present* (Princeton, NJ: Princeton University Press, 1950).

Williams, G., *Change and Decline: Roman Literature in the Early Empire* (Berkeley, CA: University of California Press, 1978).

Williams, Richard S., 'The Role of Amicitia in the Career of A. Gabinius (COS 58)', *Phoenix*, 32, 3 (1978) pp.195–210.

Wilson, John Albert and Allen, Thomas George (eds), *Mounds in the Plain of Antioch: An Archeological Survey*, University of Chicago Oriental Institute Publications, vol. 48 (Chicago, IL: University of Chicago Press, 1937).

Winkes, R., *Clipeata Imago: Studien zu einer römische Bildnisform* (Bonn: Habelt, 1969).

Wirth, G., 'Zur Tigrisfahrt des Kaisers Traian: Vier Fragmente der Suda', *Philologus*, 107 (1963), pp.288–300.

Wissemann, Michael, *Die Parther in der augusteischen Dichtung*, Publications universitaires européennes, ser. 15: Philologie et littérature classiques, vol. 24 (Frankfurt am Main: P. Lang, 1982).

Wolski, Józef, 'Quellen zur frühen Geschichte Parthiens', *Eos*, 38 (1937), pp.492ff.

Wolski, Józef, 'The Deacy of the Iranian Empire of the Seleucids and the Chronology of the Parthian Beginnings', *Berytus*, 12 (1956/57), pp.35–52.

Wolski, Józef, 'Les Achémenides et les Arsacides: Contribution à l'histoire de la formation des traditions iraniennes', *Syria*, 43 (1966), pp.65–89.

Wolski, Józef, 'Les Parthes et la Syrie', *Acta Iranica*, 12 (1976), pp.395–417.

Wolski, Józef, 'Untersuchungen zur frühen parthischen Geschichte', *Klio*, 58 (1976), pp.439–59.

Wolski, Józef, 'Iran und Rom: Versuch einer historischen Wertung der gegenseitigen Beziehungen', in *ANRW*, 2, 9.1 (1979), pp.195–214.

Wolski, Józef, 'L'Armenie dans la politique du haut-empire parthe', *Iranica Antiqua*, 15 (1980), pp.251–67.

Wolski, Józef, *L'Empire des Arsacides* (Louvain: Peeters, 1993).

Woolliscroft, D.J., *Roman Military Signalling* (Stroud and Charleston: Tempus Publishing, 2001).

Wylie, Graham, 'How Did Trajan Succeed in Subduing Parthia Where Mark Antony Failed', *Ancient History Bulletin*, 4 (1990), pp.37–43.

Yarshater, Ehsan (ed.), *The Cambridge History of Iran* (Cambridge: Cambridge University Press, 1983), vol. 3.

Yorke, V.W., 'A Journey in the Valley of the Upper Euphrates', *Geographical Journal*, 8 (1896), pp. 317–35.

Zanker, Paul, *The Power of Images in the Age of Augustus* (Ann Arbor, MI: University of Michigan Press, 1988).

Ziegler, Karl-Heinz, *Die Beziehungen zwischen Rom und dem Partherreich* (Wiesbaden: F. Steiner, 1964).

Ziegler, R., 'Civic Coins and Imperial Campaigns', in Kennedy (ed.), *Roman Army in the East*, pp.199–134.

Ziolkowski, A., '*Urbs direpta*, or How the Romans Sacked Cities', in Rich and Shipley (eds), *War and Society in the Roman World*, pp.19–91.

Zinni, General Tony and Kaltz, Tony, *The Battle for Peace: A Frontline Vision of America's Power and Purpose* (New York: Palgrave/Macmillan, 2006).

Index